Anna Karenina and Others

Publication of this volume has been made possible, in part, through support from the **Harriman Institute, Columbia University.**

Anna Karenina and Others

Tolstoy's Labyrinth of Plots

LIZA KNAPP

THE UNIVERSITY OF WISCONSIN PRESS

The University of Wisconsin Press
1930 Monroe Street, 3rd Floor
Madison, Wisconsin 53711-2059
uwpress.wisc.edu

3 Henrietta Street, Covent Garden
London WC2E 8LU, United Kingdom
eurospanbookstore.com

Printed in the United States of America

This book may be available in a digital edition.

Library of Congress Cataloging-in-Publication Data
Names: Knapp, Liza, author.
Title: Anna Karenina and others: Tolstoy's labyrinth of plots / Liza Knapp.
Description: Madison, Wisconsin: The University of Wisconsin Press, [2016] | ©2016
    | Includes bibliographical references and index.
Identifiers: LCCN 2015038425 | ISBN 9780299307905 (cloth: alk. paper)
Subjects: LCSH: Tolstoy, Leo, graf, 1828–1910. Anna Karenina. | Tolstoy, Leo, graf,
    1828–1910—Criticism and interpretation. | Russian literature—Western influences.
    | Comparative literature—Russian and American. | Comparative literature—
    American and Russian. | Comparative literature—Russian and European.
    | Comparative literature—European and Russian.
Classification: LCC PG3365.A63 K63 2016 | DDC 891.73/3—dc23
LC record available at http://lccn.loc.gov/2015038425

ISBN 9780299307943 (pbk.: alk. paper)

For Alan, Luke, and Tom

Contents

Acknowledgments

Anna Karenina and Others has been in the making for a long time. My understanding of *Anna Karenina* as an especially glorious, troubling, complex, and unique novel has developed over the years in dialogue with teachers, colleagues, students, and friends.

I have been fortunate to spend time at Columbia and Berkeley, two institutions where literature matters. I have been surrounded by superb scholars. Their intellectual company and collegial support has meant the world to me. I am profoundly grateful for Hugh McLean's help and guidance at Berkeley. His response to early stages of this work was invaluable. It is also thanks to him that I started teaching the comparative courses in which I connected works like *The Scarlet Letter*, *Middlemarch*, and *Mrs. Dalloway* to *Anna Karenina*. My interest in how the plots of *Anna Karenina* connect dates back to graduate school days at Columbia when I was asked to write about this on my comprehensive exams. Foundational to my work on this book is what I learned about Tolstoy from Richard Gustafson and about plot from Robert Belknap. In the last decade, I have turned for wisdom and support to colleagues Cathy Popkin, Irina Reyfman, and Cathy Nepomnyashchy (her professed enmity toward Tolstoy notwithstanding).

This book builds on the body of scholarship that has made Tolstoy studies an exciting field to work in. I am grateful to a host of Tolstoy scholars who have helped me in formal and informal ways. I am indebted to Donna Orwin for her scholarship and her action on various fronts relating to Tolstoy. She and Chuck Isenberg provided very helpful editorial comments on work I submitted to *Tolstoy Studies Journal*. In working on the MLA *Approaches to Teaching "Anna Karenina,"* I learned a lot about the novel from the contributors and especially from my coeditor, Amy Mandelker. Her scholarship on *Anna Karenina* and the Victorian novel has been an important inspiration, as has Gina Kovarsky's scholarship on the moral education of the reader. And the work of Robin Feuer Miller and Robert Louis Jackson, whether on Dostoevsky or Tolstoy, has been a constant source of illumination for me. I am grateful to them too.

The superb comments from Elizabeth Cheresh Allen and Caryl Emerson, readers for the University of Wisconsin Press, helped me shape the arguments presented here. It was a privilege to have their input. I am very grateful to Gwendolyn Walker, Adam Mehring, Judith Robey, and Carla Marolt at the University of Wisconsin Press for their expert handling of the publication process. Kirsten Painter, in editing the manuscript, provided significant editorial and critical judgments; I am very lucky to have had her help. I gratefully acknowledge the financial support for this book from the Harriman Institute at Columbia University. And I express appreciation to the Schoff Fund at the University Seminars at Columbia University for help in publication. Material in this book was presented to the University Seminar: Slavic History and Culture. I am grateful to Sergey Arhangelov and the Tolstoy Museum in Moscow for permission to use the Rudakov illustration for the book jacket. Special thanks to Maria Konchatova for her help with this.

My grasp of the subject matter of this book was enriched by exchanges with students: Anne Hruska and Shanti Elliott at Berkeley and Emma Lieber, Ani Kokobobo, and Abby Rosebrock at Columbia. Teaching *Anna Karenina* has always been a special joy for me. I am grateful to all the students who have made each time around a fresh process of discovery.

Anna Karenina and Others

Introduction

Tolstoy and *Anna Karenina*'s Plots

As *Anna Karenina* moves from the messy intermingling of people in the Oblonsky house to Levin's affirmation of the "wall between the holy of holies of [his] soul and other people, even [his] wife," Tolstoy examines all manner of human relations (1:1, 1; 8:19, 817).[1] The germ of *Anna Karenina* was its adultery plot, ending with the suicide of the adulteress, but Tolstoy reached beyond the "tragedy of the bedroom" to incorporate other plots, first and foremost that of his quasi-autobiographical hero Konstantin Levin. *Anna Karenina* appears to celebrate the "family idea," which, according to his wife's testimony, Tolstoy considered to be "the main, basic idea" that holds the novel together.[2] Ultimately, however, Tolstoy was not just interested in the relations of lovers or family members. What really occupied Tolstoy's heart and mind as he wrote *Anna Karenina* were questions of faith in God and loving one's neighbor. As Tolstoy quipped in his later commentary on the gospels, the call to love your neighbor is meaningless if you do not know who your neighbor is.[3] For Tolstoy, *Anna Karenina* became a desperate inquiry into this question, a question about which there has been such radical disagreement, through the ages, across cultures, and among individuals.[4]

Anna Karenina and Others explores how Tolstoy, responding to other texts, used the content and, especially, the multiplot form of *Anna*

3

Karenina to ask how lives connect—whether loving one's neighbor can ever be done, or whether, as Anna sees it in her most desperate moment, "we are all thrown into the world only in order to hate each other" (7:30, 764). Tolstoy took a more didactic approach to these same questions when he was done with *Anna Karenina* and his only project was, as he put it, "personal, spiritual—to save [his] soul."[5] He turned away from novels and wrote works such as "What I Believe" (1881–84), "What Then Shall We Do?" (1884), "The Kingdom of God Is Within You" (1893), and "What Is Art?" (1898).[6] In these works he *tried* to resolve these questions definitively.[7] But in *Anna Karenina*, Tolstoy explores in a gloriously provisional way—one that leaves meaning open to the reader—these very questions.[8]

Beset by his own spiritual crisis, Tolstoy struggled to finish *Anna Karenina*. According to one paradigm popular in Tolstoy studies, the "crisis" at this stage marked a radical change in his life. But the emotional, spiritual, and literary desperation that were the conditions of the composition of *Anna Karenina* did not come out of nowhere. Tolstoy's letters and journals show that throughout his adult life Tolstoy reckoned with the same anxieties about brotherly love, God, and faith that overwhelmed him in the late 1870s.[9] When writing in the early stages of this quest, Tolstoy stated his conviction that eternal happiness depends on "love" and on "liv[ing] for the other," by which he meant selflessly loving one's neighbor.[10] But he felt he knew neither how to go about loving his neighbor nor who his neighbor was. In the sixties, in the early years of his marriage and family life and the heyday of his career as a writer, Tolstoy was (according to the retrospective view set forth in his *Confession*) diverted from his quest to love God and his neighbor. But this did not last. When famine devastated Samara in 1873, Tolstoy was profoundly affected. In response to what he witnessed in Samara, he wrote to Alexandrine Tolstoy, his confidante in spiritual matters, "It is shameful and painful to be a human being when one looks at their suffering."[11] He became actively involved in famine relief, raised money and consciousness, but ended up disillusioned. Still, the shame and pain he felt in the face of the suffering of others stayed with him, adding to his intensifying need to know how, in the throes of family life and writing *Anna Karenina*, he should respond to the call to love his neighbor and save his soul. The spiritual concerns that had dogged him all along and fed his fiction came to a head emphatically and artistically in *Anna Karenina*. It is true that, as has often been argued, Tolstoy "externalized" or "novelized" his own spiritual crisis in that of Levin. But more than that, he used the interplay of the plots in *Anna Karenina* to examine the interrelatedness of human lives.

Tolstoy and the Multiplot Novel

As Virginia Woolf attempted to capture the essence of the Russian point of view, she often referred to the haunting inconclusiveness of Russian fiction in general and of Tolstoy's in particular. She imagined Tolstoy still puzzling to his dying day (in 1910) over the riddles of life—starting with "Why live?"—that were posed so poignantly in his novels. In what follows, I suggest that the Tolstoyan question "Why live?" takes a special form in his multiplot novel *Anna Karenina*. "Why live?" becomes "What does my life have to do with the lives of others?" Although Tolstoy confines Anna and Levin to separate plots, the novel, through its familial, social, moral, and religious themes and through its multiplot form, makes us ponder this question: how do their lives connect?[12] This form, especially as practiced by Tolstoy in *Anna Karenina*, breeds indeterminacy. In a novel with more than one plot, we naturally still read to find out what happens to the individual characters and their plots, but that is not all that is at stake. Multiplotted novels create a special kind of desire in their readers: the desire to understand how the plots relate to each other.[13]

As William Empson observed, a double plot is easy to neglect and "does not depend on being noticed for its operation."[14] Readers and listeners have been exposed to double plots from the *Iliad* on, and they have asked, for example, whether the division of these plots is in fact healed when Priam kisses Achilles even as they know that the war will still go on. Aristotle is often credited with, or blamed for, instilling in consumers of plots the expectation of unity. And Henry James, with his notorious "horror of two stories in one," complained about "indifferent wholes" (*Middlemarch*) or "loose and baggy monsters" (*War and Peace* and other novels).[15] Whether readers have a Jamesian "horror" of double plot or a fondness for the randomness of "lifelike" "loose and baggy monsters," once readers become aware that a work includes more than one plot, they want to know what this reveals about the interrelatedness of human lives.

If Tolstoy adapted the multiplot form to express his vision of the human condition, then it is important to ask what his practice of the form tells us about the relations between Anna Karenina's life and

Levin's—or Dolly's. Is anyone Anna's neighbor? Sergei Rachinsky asked this question indirectly in an exchange with Tolstoy about *Anna Karenina*.[16] Rachinsky remarked that Tolstoy's novel lacked unity, and he wondered why Tolstoy had not linked Levin's and Anna's plots more closely. Tolstoy responded, in an oft-quoted remark, that Rachinsky was mistaken about *Anna Karenina*'s lack of structure, in that Rachinsky had failed to see that its unity depended on connections not on the level of character or plot, but beneath the surface of the action. As Tolstoy suggests, the *hidden* architectonics of his multiplot novel are essential to its meaning. But he was the first to admit that meaning in *Anna Karenina* was beset by indeterminacy and resisted being expressed directly.[17]

These hidden architectonics have cast a long shadow over scholarly responses to *Anna Karenina*. In his magisterial study of Tolstoy's work, Boris Eikhenbaum wrote that "the novel is constructed on the very open and simple parallelism of two lines. If at times between these lines links or connections are created (Kitty and Vronsky, Anna and Levin), they appear as a faint dotted line and have no significance for the plot [*fabula*]. The novel is held together not by means of events on their own but by means of the linkings of themes and images and the unity of attitude toward them."[18] A number of scholars have reverse-engineered the architectonics to find the hidden keystones to the arches and other "hidden" structures, such as the "diptych" consisting of two depictions of estate life in Part 6. These studies, which reveal glories in *Anna Karenina* overlooked by Henry James, have amplified our understanding of the artistic unity and meaning of the novel.

Scholars have celebrated *Anna Karenina* for its relative *lack* of syntagmatic links, that is, for the fact that (as he proudly declared to Rachinsky) Tolstoy had for the most part done without links "on the level of story" or "in the sphere of acquaintance." The few such links tend to be dismissed as insignificant to the story (as Eikhenbaum suggests above). Thus, for example, the only meeting between Anna and Levin, delayed until Part 7, has been recognized as an important *structural* landmark in the novel, critical to the reader's grasp of the unity, but it has often been dismissed as insignificant to the plot(s). Are actual connections and junctures as insignificant to the plot as Eikhenbaum and others maintain?[19] While we can read the plots almost completely for the "balanced contrast" (James's term for Eliot's technique in *Middlemarch*), which is often detected at work in multiplot novels, does that satisfy?

To appeal to a comparison, Tolstoy's *Anna Karenina* is fundamentally different from Faulkner's *The Wild Palms*, a novella of adultery that is interleaved chapter by chapter with another tale. Faulkner himself described this as "shuffling a deck of cards only not so haphazardly," and he explained that he "played them against each other . . . contrapuntally."[20] The reader has no choice but to read Faulkner's novel that way since the plots do not intersect at all. Nor do they even inhabit the same time/space; the reader satisfies himself with counterpoint, makes accusations of "novelistic schizophrenia," or wonders on. But *Anna Karenina* is fundamentally different because it *could* be a unified whole.

In *The Craft of Fiction* Percy Lubbock argued that there is no real interaction or even sustained or building tension between Tolstoy's plots. He writes that the story of *Anna Karenina* is "not really dramatic at all but a pictorial contrast, Anna and her affair on one side of it, Levin and his on the other. The contrast is gradually expanded and deepened through the book; but it leads to no clash between the two, no opposition, no drama."[21] Reading *Anna Karenina* for the counterpoint of its parallel plots or for what Percy Lubbock calls the "pictorial contrast" is a fruitful exercise. While Tolstoy nurtures the engrained tendency to read binarily, as he plays on the *apparent* contrasts between the two plots—or three, if one includes the Oblonskys—the novel becomes more engaging when the oppositions blur and we see that the characters are, to borrow George Eliot's phrase, "embroiled in the same medium." Tolstoy presents what appears to be a binary opposition, with Levin and Kitty as the morally righteous couple and Anna and Vronsky as their opposites (Dolly and Oblonsky occupy a middle ground) and yet he also sows the seeds of deconstruction of this and other binary oppositions. When distinctions become murky in *Anna Karenina* and conventional forms are defamiliarized, the reader must think more deeply about the connections between the plots and ask how they really fit together.[22] As Robert Belknap points out, Tolstoy "us[es] the action of this novel to force the reader into active judgment" and keep him from being "comfortable."[23] In her work on *Anna Karenina*, Gina Kovarsky has masterfully shown how Tolstoy goes about this process, in what she calls the "moral education of the reader."[24]

In *Anna Karenina*, however much he strove to establish unity through *inner* connections to the detriment of external ones (as he claimed to Rachinsky), Tolstoy still acquaints his heroes and at points intersects their stories. One of the critical debates about *Anna Karenina* regards the question of whether Anna's suicide is emplotted as the necessary wages of her sin of adultery, whether the omens that presage her death are figments of Anna's self-indulgent imagination, or whether this suicide is in fact to be seen as contingent (and an event that did not have to happen).[25] At stake, then, is the question of whether what happens to Anna was subject to the freedom that seems to be at play in other reaches of the novel. If this is the case, then, in this multiplot novel, which does give characters access to each other (unlike Faulkner's *Wild Palms*), one might ask whether the outcome could have been different, not only if Anna herself had behaved differently but if Dolly, Levin, Kitty, or others had.

Among the overarching concerns in what follows is how Tolstoy used the multiplot form to express his vision of the human condition — put in its starkest form, the question asked in *Anna Karenina* is: What does Anna Karenina's life and death have to do with Dolly's or Levin's? This question echoes those asked in the gospels, such as "who is my neighbor?" (Luke 10:29) and "what is this to you and to me?" (John: 2:4). It also relates to moral and ethical questions about the suffering of others, beyond those near and dear, that are at the heart of Tolstoy's religious concerns in *Anna Karenina*. "What did I have to do with some stranger?" ["Какое мне дело было до чужого человека?"] is the question Kitty poses to herself when her attempt at loving her neighbors in Soden goes awry. This question haunts all reaches of Tolstoy's multiplot *Anna Karenina*. And, as the novel ends, Kitty and Levin's baby Mitya demonstrates, in the "experiment" staged during his bath, that he has learned to recognize his own people, a process that, as Gina Kovarsky argued, simultaneously celebrates and reinforces Levin's "deepening understanding of the way love binds him in relatedness to other human beings" and reminds us of Anna's exclusion from the community.[26]

One of the questions posed in this multiplot novel, at times directly and at other times indirectly, is whether Anna Karenina, who is guilty — and for whom bad mother, unfaithful wife, sex fiend, drug addict, and jealous shrew all could apply — *still* evokes compassion. In *Anna Karenina*, society and individual hearts often seem to operate on the principle that compassion should be felt and acted on only when the sufferer is regarded as innocent, but Tolstoy shows a range of models of compassion that includes more spontaneous and radical forms that make no distinctions about guilt or innocence.[27] At times, Tolstoy's views of the inexorability of "the tragedy of the bedroom" or his need to promote "the family idea" seem to doom attempts at loving Anna as a neighbor or even feeling compassion for her. But thanks to the interplay of the plots, readers are given ample grounds for questioning these attitudes and possibly feeling compassion for the guilty Anna.

Even characters who have not met face to face in the plot of *Anna Karenina* are often aware of each other. (Thus, for example, Levin prejudges Anna before meeting her.) How different characters from different plotlines figure (or fail to figure) in each other's consciousnesses is an important dimension to Tolstoy's multiplot novel and amounts to a third possible type of link between plots—a link that differs from syntagmatic and paradigmatic ones. As J. Hillis Miller wrote, "The novelist's assumptions, often unstated ones, about the ways one mind can interact with other minds determine the form his novel takes."[28] What does the form of *Anna Karenina* reveal about Tolstoy's assumptions about how human minds interact? Whether Anna Karenina is anyone's sister or neighbor is a question that haunts all reaches of Tolstoy's novel and comes to a head in the finale at Pokrovskoe in which those gathered appear to wash their hands of Anna Karenina or at least be willing to forget about her.

In her reading notes on *Anna Karenina*, Virginia Woolf professed to be troubled by how Tolstoy handled his double story. Woolf wrote: "What seems to me is that the construction is a good deal hindered by the double story. It offends me that the book ends without any allusion to Anna. She's allowed to drop out; never comes into Levin or Kitty's mind again."[29] Virginia Woolf, in other words, was not necessarily asking for further connections between Anna and the other characters on the level of *external* relations. Rather, she was looking for an indication in the narrative that anyone in the finale at Pokrovskoe gave a thought to Anna. But no such thing occurs.

Anna Karenina and Other Texts

As they explore the dynamics of Tolstoy's multiplot novel, the chapters that follow treat *Anna Karenina* in relationship to other texts, with the goal of investigating how *Anna Karenina* draws on emblematic works of the Russian literary tradition, how it expands the boundaries of the novel of adultery, how it responds to the form and content of the English novel, and how it novelizes aspects of Pascal's *Pensées*. As he interwove his plots in *Anna Karenina*, Tolstoy responded to prior authors who attempted to express, through the novel, a comprehensive understanding of human life. Despite Tolstoy's social isolation, spiritual alienation, and unique approach, his novel clearly reflects his engagement with his times and with texts of all times. Tolstoy used *Anna Karenina* to address many of the same issues as other novelists, although on a grander scale. Like Gogol, he envisioned a Russian novel that would explore the human condition, reaching beyond that familiar novelistic bourne, the protagonist's acquisition of family and property. (Also recalling Gogol, who abandoned his trilogy and burned the second part of *Dead Souls*, Tolstoy all but relinquished the novel form after *Anna Karenina*.) Like Nathaniel Hawthorne, Tolstoy used a tale of adultery as the basis for an "inclusive" and poetic novel that critiqued forms of human vengeance. Like George Eliot, Tolstoy used the multiplot form to explore what our lives have to do with those of our neighbors. Like Victorian novelists, Tolstoy adapted the novel to the exploration of "matters of conscience" that had traditionally been what Karenin calls "affairs of religion," and thus Tolstoy contributed to a trend that made the novel more introspective. Tolstoy also "philosophized" in his novels (as Flaubert famously complained to Turgenev after reading *War and Peace*), but in *Anna Karenina* he focused more directly on faith (to ask, can one live without it?).

Readers of Tolstoy's novels have often remarked on how much like "life" they are, often with the implication that they lack qualities associated with "art." Gary Saul Morson has identified in Tolstoy a tendency for "internaliz[ing]" and "conceal[ing]" his "devices" and "ideas": Tolstoy does it so well that they often go unnoticed.[30] The same holds for how Tolstoy handled his sources. Thus, Tom Cain writes that "Tolstoy makes creative use of the work of other writers, 'imitating' them as classical and Renaissance artists were advised to imitate, not through plagiarism, but, in Horace's words, 'as the bees make honey,' remaking their models in the context of a new work of art."[31] In Tolstoy's works references to and even appropriations of whole scenes from other works often go undetected because they are so fully assimilated and life-like.[32] Whereas Dostoevsky leaves on the surface of his fiction more telltale signs of his creative engagement with other novelists and writers, Tolstoy transfigures the texts and submerges his borrowings in the realist texture of life. As Priscilla Meyer has demonstrated in regard to French subtexts in *Anna Karenina*, Tolstoy "tak[es] up not only their arguments but their imagery and motif systems."[33] For insight into Tolstoy's mode of reading, Meyer cites his son's observation that Tolstoy "remembered everything that he had read, and knew how to get the essence out of a book and what to discard."[34] Tolstoy was circumspect about revealing his influences.[35] Although in his youth he proudly declared himself to be a disciple of Rousseau, Sterne, Gogol, and others, in midlife he did not readily acknowledge influences and was often dismissive of fellow novelists. Yet Tolstoy read widely and deeply. Late in life, he prepared a list of works that had a strong impact on him at various stages. The list is helpful, but it is not a complete key to his sources. Tolstoy scholars have compiled "chronicles" of what he read and how he reacted to his readings in letters, diaries, and conversations. The work of Boris Eikhenbaum has been influential not only in establishing many of the texts Tolstoy appropriated but also in understanding his poetics of appropriation.

In this book, each chapter examines *Anna Karenina* in relation to one or more other works. With the exception of Virginia Woolf's *Mrs. Dalloway* (1925), discussed here as a retort to Tolstoy's incarnation of the multiplot, the other main texts, which range chronologically from the seventeenth-century *Pensées* of Blaise Pascal through nineteenth-century novelists, are all ones that Tolstoy knew well. This study plays *Anna Karenina* off of these other works in order to illuminate the features of each. (This process thus relies on something like the paradigmatic mode that Tolstoy himself often uses in his composition.) The goal is to use comparison to these texts to show how Tolstoy worked with the multiplot form. To this end, the chapters move not in chronological order, but in an order designed to tell the story of how Tolstoy worked across plots to explore the questions about human relatedness and about the meaning of life.

Chapter 1, "The Estates of Pokrovskoe and Vozdvizhenskoe: Tolstoy's Labyrinth of Linkages in *Anna Karenina*," examines the patterns that emerge from the prosaic details of the life Tolstoy depicts. These patterns draw together isolated segments of the novel, often across the different plots of *Anna Karenina*. The tension that Tolstoy felt between his yearning for faith in divine providence and in moral laws, on the one hand, and his despair at the thought that human life ("reality") could be ultimately meaningless, on the other, is palpable in the mode of realism that Tolstoy practices in *Anna Karenina*. As Tolstoy wrote in a letter to his friend the critic Nikolai Strakhov, what he wanted to express in *Anna Karenina* was embedded in "an endless labyrinth of linkages," rather than set forth directly. Tolstoy thus suggests that we should read associatively, in order to appreciate the hidden linkages. This "labyrinth" is where we find clues to understanding the elusive connections between plots, even if Tolstoy leaves interpreting this information to our judgment and imagination.

Examination of the "labyrinth" beneath the surface of Tolstoy's realist prose reveals, in addition to clues about the connections between different segments of *Anna Karenina*, a web of allusions to other texts that left their residue on Tolstoy's creative consciousness and were assimilated into his art. In this chapter, I work with allusions to Tolstoy's early master (Rousseau), to Tolstoy's forerunners in the Russian tradition (Pushkin, Gogol), to contemporary Western novels of marriage and adultery, and a Russian metaphysical poet of Tolstoy's day (Tyutchev). Tolstoy's hazy evocations of these other texts incorporate into Tolstoy's labyrinth external features (Rousseauean righteousness, Gogolian absurdity, Tyutchevian metaphysical angst, and so forth), which, in turn, are intertwined with the clusters of meaningful detail that Tolstoy considered essential to his art. The intertextual substratum in part accounts for what Boris Eikhenbaum called the "philosophical lyricism" of *Anna Karenina*, his term to describe how Tolstoy deviated from garden-variety realism or even his own *War and Peace*.[36]

With respect to the form of *Anna Karenina*, Tolstoyan details often coalesce in patterns that suggest an implicit contrast between the two major plots. For instance, Tolstoy appears to indict Vronsky for mistreating horses on his estate of Vozdvizhenskoe, as well as at the steeplechase, and seems to celebrate Levin for properly treating the horses on his estate of Pokrovskoe, not to mention for taking loving care of his milk cow when she has a calf. Yet, even as these binary oppositions become explicit, Tolstoy complicates the picture, often by including a reminder of death. At this point, Tolstoy invites us to see through to deeper truths.

In chapter 2, "*Anna Karenina* and *The Scarlet Letter*: Anna on the Scaffold of the Pillory and Levin with His Own Red Stigma," Tolstoy's and Hawthorne's novels of adultery are juxtaposed to show how each, in response to the gospel story of the woman taken in adultery (John 7:53–8:11), moves beyond the confines of the novel of adultery to give a view of the society that judges the adulteress. While *Anna Karenina* is often likened to its French predecessor *Madame Bovary*, which (like *Anna Karenina* and unlike *The Scarlet Letter*) ends in the suicide of its adulteress, the comparison with Hawthorne's novel allows us to see the organic necessity of multiple plots when the adultery novel broadens its concerns into larger questions of community. Whereas Hawthorne *literally* shows Hester with her scarlet letter on the scaffold of the pillory, judged by the goodwives and patriarchs of Puritan Boston, Tolstoy shows Anna receiving the same treatment from Petersburg society, especially at the opera, when the narrator directly likens her to someone on a pillory.

A comparison of these two works shows the inherent logic in the generation of additional plot(s) in *Anna Karenina*. Whereas Tolstoy's novel clearly has multiple plots, Hawthorne's short novel also has a divided focus in that the Hester Prynne plot threatens to become secondary (in the opinion of Henry James) to the Arthur Dimmesdale plot. Dimmesdale's tragedy ends when he is "convicted by his own conscience," following the model of the gospel story of John 8 (in which the scribes and Pharisees, once ready to discipline and punish, are convicted by their own consciences when challenged by Jesus). Despite the very different roles that Levin and Dimmesdale play in their respective novels in regard to the adulteress, these male protagonists serve a similar function in their novels—and their plots follow a similar paradigm, each culminating in a reaffirmation of faith that appears to cleanse them of the "radical individualism" associated with the adulteress. A double- or multiplot novel may thus be the logical transposition of the gospel paradigm, because it deflects attention away from the adulteress and focuses on the consciences of the community members who judge the adulteress.

In chapters 3 and 4, I discuss two aspects of Tolstoy's engagement with English culture in *Anna Karenina*. Tolstoy alerts readers to the fact that English novels are part of the world of *Anna Karenina* when Oblonsky accuses Levin of behaving like a certain "Dickensian gentleman" who "threw all the difficult questions over his right shoulder with his left hand" (1:11, 41), and when Anna pulls an English novel out of her red bag on the train to Petersburg (1:29, 99–100). From the start of Tolstoy's career as a novelist, English novels were important sources of inspiration.[37] Tolstoy's reading of *David Copperfield* was part of his apprenticeship for writing *Childhood*, while *War and Peace* owes some of its features to Tolstoy's early plans to make it an English-style novel (with the revealing title "All's Well That Ends Well"), as well as to *Vanity Fair*, the English solution in novel form to the problem of Napoleon. Although the genesis of *Anna Karenina* is complex and murky, with sources abounding in life and in art, the English novel figures prominently. Not only have scholars identified the novel in Anna's handbag when she rides home to St. Petersburg in Part 1, but they have also documented Tolstoy's creative borrowings from a number of Victorian novels and found pervasive evidence of the impact of the English novel on *Anna Karenina*.[38]

As Boris Eikhenbaum noted, *Anna Karenina* can be seen as a cross between the French novel of adultery and the English novel of family values.[39] Whereas Saltykov-Shchedrin had recently declared the genre of the family novel moribund in Russia, Tolstoy, according to Eikhenbaum, wanted to have the "last word."[40] And yet Eikhenbaum also suggests that Tolstoy in fact sought "a way out of the tradition of the love novel" and that he struggled to find a form that would move "into the wide realm of human relations."[41]

Chapter 3, "Loving Your Neighbor in *Middlemarch* and *Anna Karenina*: Varieties of Multiplot Novels," treats George Eliot's masterpiece as an English model for broadening the novel of romantic love, marriage, and family "into a wider range of human relations." George Eliot accomplished this task by opening out the plot of "Miss Brooke" into the wider world of Middlemarch. The resulting multiplot novel operates by "balanced contrast" (as Henry James observed) and counterpoint. But George Eliot also interweaves her plots to create a "home epic" that celebrates a new arête: neighborly love. Using George Eliot's *Middlemarch* as a prime example of a Victorian multiplot novel focusing on neighborly love, I show how the form Tolstoy develops—appropriate to his particular understanding of love, from sexual to familial to neighborly—differs markedly, to the point that its "hidden architectonics" limit the sphere of neighborly love, in telling contrast to *Middlemarch*. As his drafts show explicitly, Tolstoy responded in *Anna Karenina* to the approach to neighborly love represented in novels by his English contemporaries, most especially George Eliot. Although he was attracted to the literal application of the commandment love your neighbor, he critiques and undermines this English-style practice in *Anna Karenina*. He does this overtly, by revealing such love to be alien to the Russian context, as well as more powerfully beneath the surface of the novel, when he asks the questions about human relatedness that haunt his work.

"Loving Your Neighbor, Saving Your Soul: *Anna Karenina* and English Varieties of Religious Experience" (chapter 4) shows how Tolstoy reckoned with English sources as he addressed the questions about faith and loving one's neighbor that come to the fore in *Anna Karenina*. Tolstoy was fascinated by English novelists' and especially George Eliot's ability to write novels that qualified as what he would label "Christian art." In "What Is Art?" (1897), Tolstoy disparaged novels, complaining about their obsessive concern with adultery—"adultery is not only the favorite, but almost the only theme of all novels"—but at another point cited a handful of novels, which included *Adam Bede*, as exemplars of art that inspired love of God and neighbor.[42] When he first read George Eliot in

1859, Tolstoy declared her *Scenes of Clerical Life* a "Christian book" and wrote to his cousin Alexandrine Tolstoy, "Happy [or Blessed] are those who, like the English, imbibe with their milk Christian teaching, and in such a lofty, purified form as evangelical Protestantism."[43] While he recognized that this English variant of Christianity was not right for his Russian soul, he still clearly admired the fervor and conviction with which Eliot's heroes and heroines loved their neighbors.

In this chapter, I present *Anna Karenina* as Tolstoy's attempt to answer the question: "But who is my neighbor?" (When Jesus was asked this question, he responded by telling the story of the compassionate Samaritan [Luke 10:25–37].) In the finale of *Anna Karenina*, Tolstoy brings his tale to the following conclusion: after Anna commits suicide, Levin goes through his parallel struggle with suicidal desires, but after an encounter with the muzhik Fyodor, he reaffirms his faith in God and neighborly love. Levin's neighbors are those in his family circle at Pokrovskoe: neighborly love is a family affair. This seemingly definitive answer notwithstanding, this is not the last word in *Anna Karenina* since the multiplot form of the novel calls it into question.

While this conclusion that the neighbors that Levin ought to love are his near ones and dear ones appears as the natural culmination of his plot, Tolstoy arrived at this iteration of neighborly love partly in reaction to the English expression of neighborly love through acts of charity for neighbors beyond the family circle. In *Anna Karenina*, Tolstoy depicts English Evangelical Christian piety as a temptation and threat to his Russian characters. In Part 2, in Soden, Kitty comes under the influence of Mme. Stahl and Varenka, undergoes a spiritual awakening, reads the gospels for the first time, dreams of evangelical work in prisons, and attempts to act as a sister of mercy to the sick and dying of Soden. The drafts of the novel show the English pedigree of this episode: Tolstoy had originally envisioned that Kitty would be inspired by Miss Flora Sulivan, the daughter of an English preacher and a fervent believer with patently evangelical leanings, utterly devoted to acts of Christian love. From drafts to the final version (in which the Russian Varenka and the nasty "Pietist" Mme. Stahl are the agents of Kitty's short-lived spiritual awakening), Tolstoy can be seen progressively undermining what had begun as a positive expression of evangelical Christian piety. "What did I have to do with some stranger?" is the question Kitty poses to herself when her attempt at loving her neighbors in Soden goes awry. As if in order to shore up the more comfortable Orthodox piety that Kitty eventually reverts to under the influence of her father, Tolstoy shows that loving her neighbor in the English fashion is not right for his Russian Kitty.

English evangelical piety raises its ugly head again later in *Anna Karenina*'s other plot. In Part 5, we learn that Karenin has been "converted" by Countess Lydia Ivanovna to "a new explanation of the Christian doctrine that had lately spread in Petersburg." The context suggests that Tolstoy was parodying and perverting the movement associated with the English missionary Lord Radstock. (Radstock's popularity in Russia at the time provoked literary responses from both Tolstoy and Dostoevsky.) Thus, Tolstoy shows both plots of the novel threatened by alien evangelical expressions of the Christian idea. In Part 8, Tolstoy even yokes Mme. Stahl and Countess Lydia Ivanovna together as leaders of the crusade for war on behalf of the Slavic brethren suffering religious oppression under the Ottoman Empire. As Tolstoy presents it, their advocacy of military intervention on humanitarian grounds amounts to them carrying their personal perversions of the Christian idea to an international level. By undermining these English forms, in each of the two main plots and then in an overarching way at the end of *Anna Karenina*, Tolstoy sets up the importance of the revelation that Levin receives from a muzhik, who defines faith as living for God and loving one's neighbor, which to him means "not skinning another man." Levin thus reaffirms the spiritual truths that he, as the narrator puts it, "sucked in with his milk as a babe." Levin's iteration of the Christian idea comes straight from the Russian Orthodox folk. The effect is not only to reject as unchristian the notion of a Holy War for the Slavic brethren (after all, as Tolstoy was to argue later, killing your brother violates Christ's law), but also to discredit other forms, even peaceful ones, of Christian social activism and selfless neighborly love as found in the English novels that had earlier been so seminal to Tolstoy's novelistic imagination. Tolstoy ends the novel with all those near and dear to Levin safe and happy at Pokrovskoe, but this ending disturbed some readers, including Fyodor Dostoevsky and Virginia Woolf.

Chapter 5, "The Eternal Silence of Infinite Spaces: Pascal and Tolstoy's *Anna Karenina*," explores the impact on *Anna Karenina* of Blaise Pascal's *Pensées*, a work especially close to Tolstoy's heart as he struggled to finish the novel. Levin, we are told, reads various philosophers, "Plato, and Spinoza, Kant, Schelling, Hegel, and Schopenhauer," as well as the Russian religious thinker Khomyakov, but they leave him spiritually bereft. Had Levin read Pascal, Pascal might well have helped Levin find God. And this would have taken away from the impact of Levin finding this faith from the muzhik Fyodor. Tolstoy chose instead to make the influence of Pascal covert. Tolstoy novelizes the spiritual drama that can be pieced together from Pascal's fragments known as the *Pensées*, so that Levin appears as a Pascalian seeker. Thus, Levin shudders at the eternal silence of infinite spaces; he becomes obsessed with death and sees the universe as a cachot; he mistrusts language and sees the limits of reason; he occasionally goes through the motions of faith even without believing; and, above all, he suffers all the while as he seeks God, truth, and faith.

A Pascalian reading of *Anna Karenina* also illuminates the correspondences between Levin's and Anna's desperate attempts to answer life's questions and to divert themselves from death, so that even when those at Pokrovskoe appear to have forgotten Anna, Tolstoy makes the reader feel acutely the tension between the plots. We see that Anna, like Levin, faced an abyss, which, according to Pascal, only faith could fill. Above all, the Pascal-like sense of the contingency of earthly understanding shatters any sense of closure that might otherwise be felt at the end of the novel.

In chapter 6, the epilogue, "Virginia Woolf and Leo Tolstoy on Double Plot and the Misery of Our Neighbors: For Whom the Bell Tolls in *Mrs. Dalloway* and *Anna Karenina*," I follow up on Virginia Woolf's observations in her reading notebooks about how Tolstoy handled what she calls "the double story" in *Anna Karenina*. It "offend[ed]" Woolf that Anna is "allowed to drop out" at the end of the novel: nobody remembers her.[44] In her own *Mrs. Dalloway*, Woolf interweaves two plots, one about Septimus Warren Smith and the other involving Clarissa Dalloway, and leaves it to readers to wonder how the two connect. The resulting indeterminacy evokes the interplay of Tolstoy's plots in *Anna Karenina*. Indeed, Tolstoy was clearly one of the forces that spurred Virginia Woolf to make the leap to her own modernist poetics and her own "modern fiction."

Both Woolf and Tolstoy are masters of generating the reader's desire to understand how the plots fit together, which is a particular feature of double- or multiplot novels. And both shared a vision of human loneliness that, as Woolf puts it, neither "love" nor "religion" can "solve." This adds to the poignancy of the questions about human relatedness—what does another's life and death have to do with mine?—which multiplot novels so often address both on the surface and by means of the interplay (or maybe just the counterpoint) between their plots. But

Woolf diverges from Tolstoy in a profound way. Although her main heroes never meet, Woolf provides, by means of a leap of consciousness, the kind of tunnel between her divided plots that she found lacking in *Anna Karenina*. Thus, *Mrs. Dalloway*, when set alongside *Anna Karenina*, helps reveal why the latter is inconclusive in a way that accounts for its profound effect on readers, including Virginia Woolf.

1

The Estates of Pokrovskoe and Vozdvizhenskoe

Tolstoy's Labyrinth of Linkages
in Anna Karenina

Introduction to Tolstoy's Labyrinth

Tolstoy gives the illusion of writing, as Isaac Babel put it, "the way the world would write if it could write by itself." In *Anna Karenina* this quality was achieved by means of what Tolstoy called "an endless labyrinth of linkages," which he considered the "essence of [his] art." As he explained to Nikolai Strakhov in a letter written in the spring of 1876, Tolstoy used this "labyrinth" to express interrelated thoughts, and he called for readers and critics to explore these linkages instead of interpreting ideas or situations in isolation.[1] Naturally, these linkages exist within and across plotlines. That Tolstoy valued the linkages from one plot to another is made clear in Tolstoy's response to Sergei Rachinsky, who asked why Tolstoy kept his plots so separate. Tolstoy wrote that he took pride in what he called the "architectonics" of *Anna Karenina,* and specifically in the invisibility of the keystones that linked his plots together. According to Tolstoy, "the unity in the structure is created not by action and not by relationships between the characters, but by an inner continuity."[2] One labyrinth links together all plots of *Anna Karenina*.[3]

In his letter to Strakhov, Tolstoy wrote that "we need people . . . to guide readers through the endless labyrinth of linkages." Tolstoy scholars have answered this call by focusing on Tolstoy's labyrinth as they attempt to characterize his iteration of realism, that most slippery of *–isms*. Whereas Roman Jakobson noted that the "specific artistic current of the nineteenth century" known as realism (a current in which he places Tolstoy), features "unimportant" events and "unessential detail,"[4] guides to Tolstoy's labyrinth have argued that seemingly random details are essential to what Tolstoy, as he put it, "had in mind to express in [his] novel." The "interrelated thoughts" that could not be separated into discrete units and could not be "expressed separately by words" are woven into the fabric of the text. Richard Gustafson introduced the term "emblematic realism" to describe Tolstoy's mode of imbuing the (seemingly) mundane details of life with deeper significance. Gustafson notes Tolstoy's penchant for thinking allegorically both in his fiction and in other writings.[5] Amy Mandelker has described the function of detail in Tolstoy's "realism" as follows: "The random minutiae and telling details for which Tolstoy is celebrated indeed create the 'effect of the real' but also, upon close reading, interact to reiterate, at the subliminal level, the thematic of the novel. Thus Tolstoy's details sharpen the reader's focus on the texture and warp of prosaic life while acquiring the status of legitimate symbols integrated into a larger pattern."[6] Robert Belknap praises Tolstoy for his masterful use of "situation rhyme," a technique of using "analogous events time after time in the course of a novel"; as Belknap notes, a single occasion, "taken alone," "seems unimportant and unpersuasive," but subsequent tokens of the rhyme engage the reader in an interpretive process that "makes the parallel plots of the novel interact in a way that becomes a moral exercise."[7] And Vladimir Alexandrov has noted that the thematic patterning in the novel works in complex ways: expectations are created, often only to be undermined, complicated, and altered. As Gustafson, Mandelker, Belknap, Alexandrov, and others have shown, study of the seemingly random details yields clues about the meaning of the novel. But these are only clues since so much in this novel is beset by indeterminacy, with vexed questions left to the reader's judgment and imagination. In what follows, I show that scrutiny of the linkages Tolstoy creates offers keys to understanding the questions that Tolstoy left open on the surface of the novel. What does Anna have to do with Levin? And, not to forget the middle plot, how do Dolly (whom some regard as the true Tolstoyan hero) and Stiva (whom Dostoevsky, for one, regarded as the novel's villain) fit into the design of *Anna Karenina*?

Much as Tolstoy hid the architectonics of his novel, leaving the reader to decipher the interaction of the plots, so, too, did he weave his intertexts into the fabric of the narrative. As he wrote *Anna Karenina*, Tolstoy drew on residue left in his imagination by all that he had read. His allusions to other works are part of the labyrinth of linkages that Tolstoy described to Strakhov; these allusions connect the novel's labyrinth to the textual world beyond. When the presence of external text is detected in one plot of *Anna Karenina*, it often permeates the other plots as well and thus contributes to the interconnectedness that Tolstoy kept hidden but left to the reader to discern. Thus, as we reach into Tolstoy's labyrinth, we, like the ploughshare Tolstoy refers to in the famous simile of Part 8, "cut deeper and deeper" into the text, turning up more and more material.[8]

In this chapter, I will introduce Tolstoy's mode of freighting clusters of prosaic details with meaning as they appear in two particular spheres, home economics and animal husbandry. These spheres, part of the prosy, "realistic" backdrop of the novel, span across its plots. Early on, before the plots go their separate ways, configurations emerge that are further articulated later in the novel. In Part 6, in particular, Tolstoy juxtaposes and connects the two plots as he moves the action back and forth between Levin's estate of Pokrovskoe and Vronsky's estate of Vozdvizhenskoe. But even as he constructs an elaborate comparison of the two estates in Part 6, there are hints of what emerges when Anna and Levin each choose between life and death late in the novel. At these times, the residents of the estates of Pokrovskoe and Vozdvizhenskoe, for all the apparent differences in the lives they build, are bound together as co-prisoners in the labyrinth of linkages Tolstoy has created.

Spilt Coffee, Spoilt Broth, the Well-Watched Jam Pot: The Ethics of Home Economics

In the very last chapter of Part 1, Vronsky returns home from Moscow to his apartment in Petersburg to find his friend Petritsky there with the

Baroness Shilton, Petritsky's married mistress. The scene harks back to the opening chapters that show the effects of Oblonsky's adultery on his whole household. Adultery is a common denominator between these two episodes, but Tolstoy also uses mundane details, the kind Jakobson would call "unessential," to convey subliminal messages about adulterers. Chattering away in Parisian French about divorcing her husband and dividing the property, Baroness Shilton is performing the role of hostess and overseeing coffee being brewed in a new-fangled coffee pot. She tells someone else to "keep an eye on the coffee, it's boiling over—you can see I'm busy" (1:34, 113). It ultimately ends in a domestic wreck: "The coffee never got made, but splashed on every-thing and boiled over and produced precisely what was needed—that is, gave an excuse for noise and laughter, spilling on the expensive carpet and the baroness's dress" (1:34, 114). As the narrator uses free indirect discourse to ironic effect to give us not his but *their* view of what was needful in this case and, by extension, in life, he invites us to consider this mishap to be emblematic of a deeper truth about the situation and revealing about the character of those involved.

The fact that the coffee pot boils over, wasting coffee and making a mess, links this segment to the chaos in the Oblonsky household in the opening scene and, specifically, to the fact that the cook quit and one of the children was fed spoilt broth. These humdrum domestic details of spilt coffee and spoilt broth, which could easily disappear into the tissue of realia, illustrate Tolstoy's central "idea" that the effects of adultery are felt beyond the bedroom. It wreaks domestic disorder. Although this Shilton-Petritsky adultery subplot turns out to be inconsequential to the main plots, it nevertheless accrues additional meaning through the intersection of the coffee-making episode with other related episodes.

Baroness Shilton drops out of the action of *Anna Karenina*, but she, or at least the coffee she spilled, still figures (as an infinitesimal) in Tolstoy's "endless labyrinth," to be recollected in relation to other points when home economics show emblematic significance. In Part 6, the Shcher-batsky women make their jam without adding water, to the chagrin of Levin's servant Agafya, who, like her master, resents that the "Shcher-batsky element" has infiltrated Pokrovskoe (6:2, 553–54).[9] If we link the coffee-boiling and jam-boiling scenes, a Tolstoyan moral insinuates itself to suggest that adulteresses make messes, spill seeds, and spoil property, whereas faithful wives watch their jam pots closely, allow none of the fruit to spill out, and even give the sweet scum to children with their tea instead of discarding it.

The adulterous Baroness Shilton's waste of coffee is further linked to the prodigal behavior of the adulterous Oblonsky, who, by selling off Dolly's woods to the entrepreneur Ryabinin and then continuing to squander money, wastes his children's patrimony much as, Tolstoy suggests in his labyrinth, he wastes his seed in his adulterous acts (2:16–17, 166–73). Thus, segments of the novel that appear unrelated, especially when they belong to different plotlines, complement one another in Tolstoy's labyrinth through the subtle interaction of mundane details from related spheres. Yet, in articulating these linkages—that adulterers waste (coffee beans, semen, money, etc.), whereas faithful husbands and wives preserve their fruit for their family—one runs the risk of "degrading" Tolstoy's ideas.[10] The lifelike, prosaic randomness of *Anna Karenina* is clearly part of Tolstoy's deep artistic design, and Tolstoy's labyrinth of linkages is neither a neat system nor a machine. Meaning lies latent in this labyrinth; it is up to the reader's consciousness to recollect, select, and combine different segments. Thus, it is important to remember that even as clusters of meaning emerge from Tolstoy's realistic details, these figure only in a suggestive way. As will be seen below, while Tolstoy sets up modal patterns of meaning, he also draws them into question.

Tender Moments in the Cowshed; Tragic Passion at the Steeplechase

In the opening part of *Anna Karenina*, Vronsky and Levin come together briefly as they visit the Shcherbatsky home, each in the role of Kitty's suitor. (They will not meet again until the end of Part 6.) Kitty compares Vronsky and Levin, setting up an opposition between them in her mind as she prepares to receive them both. Tolstoy writes: "She felt that this evening, when the two of them would meet for the first time, must be decisive in her fate. And she endlessly considered in her mind, first each of them separately, then the two together" (1:13, 46). As Kitty contemplates each suitor on his own terms, she remembers past experiences with each and projects what would happen with each in a modal future; and then she compares them. The operations are complex and, as Tolstoy shows, when forced to select (by responding yes or no to Levin's proposal that evening) before her understanding has ripened, Kitty errs in her judgment.[11] Tolstoy provides a model here of how readers make sense of this multiplot novel: they "endlessly" "consider" each of the competing characters—and follow his plot—separately, and then at various points they draw the different heroes (and their plots) together and compare them.

As the novel moves beyond the opening scenes, after which Levin's and Vronsky's plots go their separate ways for several parts, Tolstoy uses a number of devices to cultivate in readers the tendency to compare Levin and Vronsky and see them in a paradigmatic relation. Thus, for example, the narrator notes at one point that Vronsky despises marriage and family life (1:16, 56–57) and then, as the action shifts back to Levin, mentions that he worships marriage and family life (1:27, 95). Tolstoy leaves it up to readers to note this contrast and ponder its meaning. At other points, Tolstoy plants more direct reminders of links between plotlines, such as when characters reflect back on how Levin and Vronsky were once rivals for Kitty's love.

Tolstoy uses the relations of Vronsky and Levin to horses and cows, respectively, to reveal character and to develop the contrast set up between these two bachelor heroes in Part 1. Although the episodes in question are part of the realistic backdrop of the novel, both characters' behavior in these scenes appears to be freighted with symbolic and possibly allegorical meaning.[12] Tolstoy draws on a rich network of associations at play in his cultural heritage and in other novels, among them two of *Anna Karenina*'s important precursors, Gustave Flaubert's *Madame Bovary* and George Eliot's *Middlemarch*.[13] Flaubert and Eliot use both bovine and equine motifs to convey subliminal and direct messages to the reader in ways that reveal features of their respective practices of realism. While horses and cows were a fact of the "provincial life" that was Flaubert's subject (thus, it should be within the bounds of verisimilitude when Rodolphe seduces Emma by/on a horseback ride or when her horse's bridle breaks at this climactic point; nor is there anything extraordinary about cow dung being discussed at an agricultural fair while Rodolphe speaks seductively to Emma), readers sense that Flaubert milks these realistic details for ironic effect. Further, Jonathan Culler has suggested that the proliferation of bovine elements in *Madame Bovary*, especially encoded in word play on bovine roots (puns and onomastics), signals that Flaubert was moving beyond realism to what he dubs "vealism." (As he puts it, "where we expect the real, we get more veal.")[14] And this "vealism" adds to the anxiety expressed in *Madame Bovary* about the representational quality of language, a feature all the more disturbing when one takes into account Flaubert's concern with the *mot juste*. Tolstoy creates different effects with the cows and horses that appear in *Anna Karenina*. His treatment of them brings into relief aspects of Tolstoyan realism—its nature, limits, and special characteristics—while also revealing Tolstoy's own special anxiety about what words can and cannot express.

Since Tolstoy's time, readers have noted that there is something marked in the way that Tolstoy invites the reader to consider Vronsky's racehorse Frou-Frou as a substitute for Anna, so that what happens to Frou-Frou—she is killed in the steeplechase because of how Vronsky rides her—becomes a possible allegory for what is in store for Anna. This effect is heightened by the fact that the steeplechase occurs right after Anna has informed Vronsky that she is pregnant with his child. (When Vronsky then kicks Frou-Frou in the belly, his act reverberates in Tolstoy's labyrinth of linkages.) Frou-Frou's destruction may be regarded as a prophecy (prefiguring Anna's fate) or as a cautionary tale (warning her of what, given Vronsky's character, *could* happen); or this accident may be taken as a red herring, there to fool the reader into making connections that are not really there: the reader is left to decide.

Because *Anna Karenina* is a "labyrinth of linkages," where different bits of the text are linked to others in mysterious ways, Frou-Frou's death, which is Vronsky's "own fault" (2:25, 196–200), can be juxtaposed to Levin's loving care for Pava, his prize milk cow, after she has given birth (1:26–27, 92–96).[15] After Kitty refuses his offer of marriage, Levin returns to his estate, where he appears to "sublimate" his feelings for Kitty by caring for his cow and calf.

Vronsky's death-dealing passion for Frou-Frou at the steeplechase (2:19–2:21; 2:24–25) contrasts with Levin's tender moments in the cowshed (1:26–27). In Tolstoy's "labyrinth," linkages are usually not clearly indicated on the surface. In this case, the reader is immersed in the Petersburg races but could still cradle in his or her consciousness the Pokrovskoe realm of Levin and Pava and grasp the complementarity.[16] And, as early readers noticed, much as Tolstoy presents Frou-Frou as a surrogate for Anna, he invites us to see Levin's relations with Pava as an allegory for his future relations with Kitty. Will Kitty follow in Pava's hoof prints? Is Kitty more than a milk cow? Is this the most a Tolstoyan woman can be? In Tolstoy's work, a high premium is placed on maternal breastfeeding, and a mother nursing her young is the apotheosis of womanhood. At two critical moments in the end of the novel, when Anna comes in desperation to Dolly's house just before committing suicide and when a recently suicidal Levin is contemplating the matters of life and death, Kitty is bent on one thing: giving milk to her young.

Milk for the Oblonsky Children

In Part 3, the cows that appear in the descriptions of Dolly's life with her children on their summer estate of Ergushevo are less *obviously* significant than Levin's pride and joy Pava, or than the racehorse Frou-Frou. Yet Spotty and Whiteflake, Dolly's cows, also participate in the accretion of meaning. Here again, seemingly inconsequential bits of information from the mundane spheres of home economics and animal husbandry connect one plot to other plots and, in this case, remind us that the unhappy Oblonsky family has a plot of its own, which, according to Tolstoy's masterful handling of the multiplot form, provides us with further variations on situations from the main plots. Among the numerous things that Oblonsky left undone when he attempted to prepare the estate for his family (3:7, 259–60) was to repair the fences. As a result of his neglect, cattle, including an aggressive, butting bull, were loose in the garden. Then, of the nine milk cows, for one reason or another, none was producing milk. The chaos that Dolly faces on the estate is the natural extension of the mess in the Oblonsky household in Moscow at the very opening of the novel. Within the labyrinth of *Anna Karenina*, the cows who fail to produce milk for the Oblonsky children enact *and* reiterate Tolstoy's message that adultery is a family affair that causes children to suffer. Tolstoy will use this same emblematic detail of a child in an adultery-infected home going without milk when the infant Anna Karenina goes hungry until, thanks to Karenin's intervention, it is discovered that the wet nurse is not producing the necessary milk (4:19, 420–21)—as was the case with the Oblonsky cows (3:7, 260). The Oblonsky children are also deprived of milk in the opening scenes when their mother takes to her bedroom and neglects her household duties after discovering Stiva's adultery. Many other things go wrong as well: the cook quits, the children hurt themselves on a make-believe train ride, one child is fed spoiled broth and gets sick. But when Dolly finally emerges from her bedroom, "drowning her [wifely] grief" in the "daily cares"—of motherhood—her first act is maternal. She asks: "Has the fresh milk been sent for?" (1:4, 14).[17]

When Levin visits Dolly and the children at Stiva's request, he offers to lend Dolly milk cows (3:9, 268). This is a natural thing for him to do, given his success as a dairy farmer. At the same time, his desire to provide milk for these children shows him taking (parental) responsibility for children to whom he is not related. (We have already seen him take loving pseudo-fatherly care of Pava's young, which he watches over as if it were his own.) Levin's offer to lend Dolly these milk cows prefigures his later more active "fatherly" care for Dolly and her brood once he is married to Kitty. Kitty will in fact take this as her proof that Levin is at heart a good Christian.[18] However, even as these details suggest Levin's potential for paternal love, the same details signal, on another level, his isolation from these mothers with their mystical maternal bond to their young: in a telling Tolstoyan detail, Pava moves to protect her newborn and exclude Levin as he enters the cowshed; at the end of *Anna Karenina*, for all Kitty's attempts to include Levin among Mitya's "own people" and to foster his fatherly love, Levin is doomed, by biology if nothing else, to remain an outsider at least at those points when we are told that Kitty communicates mystically with Mitya as she breastfeeds him. This exclusion from the mother/child dyad adds to his sense of cosmic loneliness but also possibly frees Levin to contemplate the Milky Way and think his own important thoughts.

In Part 3, Dolly is wary of Levin's intercession. As she rebuffs Levin's offer to loan her cows, we learn that Dolly looks askance at Levin's materialist attitude to dairy-farming, according to which the cow becomes a "machine for the production of milk." In her simpler view, all that it would take for *her* cows Spotty and Whiteflake to start producing milk properly would be for them to be fed the family's leftovers, which the cook (masc.) had been giving to the laundress's cow (3:9, 268).[19] What Dolly wants, essentially, is for what belongs to her family to stay in her family. The family would be better off that way, as it would if, instead of wasting money on a coral necklace for his current mistress, Oblonsky would save it for the winter coat that his daughter Tanya so desperately needed (4:6–7, 373). Thus, Dolly's convictions on animal husbandry (which boil down to the basic question of how to get Spotty and Whiteflake to produce enough milk to feed her children) reinforce an important Tolstoyan truth about her husband's behavior and about adultery in general.

The Estates of Pokrovskoe and Vozdvizhenskoe: Revisiting *Dead Souls*

The Tolstoyan truths suggested in the prosaic details of milk production, home economics, and horse racing in earlier parts of *Anna Karenina* are developed in Part 6 as Tolstoy depicts life on the two estates of Pokrovskoe and Vozdvizhenskoe. Here, as in the segments of Parts 2 and 3 that focus on life on the Russian country estate, Tolstoy engages in material that figured prominently in the development of the Russian novel. (If, as Tolstoy argued, Russian prose narratives deviated from Western models, did the country estate—as chronotope, as setting, as subject, and as ideal—play a determining role?)[20] *War and Peace* has been fruitfully read as the chronicle of Russia's attempt to keep Napoleon from destroying the Russian family estate.[21] When the narrative of *Anna Karenina* moves in Part 6 from one estate to another to describe, in rich detail, the material culture of estate life, Tolstoy engages the corpus of nineteenth-century novels that celebrate and/or critique life on the Russian estate. This tradition includes major realist novels such as Turgenev's *Fathers and Sons* and Goncharov's *Oblomov*, but it owes its genesis to Gogol's *Dead Souls*.[22] As he wrote *Anna Karenina*, Tolstoy, as Boris Eikhenbaum has masterfully shown, aspired to emulate features of Pushkin's (non-Gogolian) poetics.[23] At the same time, even if Tolstoy consciously took up the mantle of Pushkin and even if he did not seem to come out of the overcoat of Gogol (in the manner of Dostoevsky, according to literary lore), Tolstoy, like so many other Russian novelists, was haunted by the specter of Gogol's *Dead Souls*. Although the novels are worlds apart, key elements of *Dead Souls* appear in transfigured form in *Anna Karenina*, most notably as Tolstoy depicts life on the Russian country estate.

The narrative structure of much of *Dead Souls* depends on successive visits to country estates, which are more modest and quirky than Pokrovskoe and Vozdvizhenskoe. Gogol constructs the narrative so as to encourage the reader to make comparative judgments about the landowners, based on details of their estates and their reception of their guest. In Part 6 of *Anna Karenina*, as the action moves from one estate to another, Tolstoy uses a principle reminiscent of *Dead Souls*. He too invites comparisons. Thus, after presenting two "honeymoons" in Part 5 in a correlative way, Tolstoy shows the couples at home on their respective estates, strategically prompting direct comparison between the two realms. As if to signal this intent, Tolstoy uses an early conversation between the women at Pokrovskoe to plant the seeds of a binary opposition in the reader's mind. While watching the jam pot, the Shcherbatsky women reminisce about marriage proposals; they think back to Vronsky's courtship of Kitty (which dates from a point when the plots had not yet found their separate courses); they recall that when Vronsky jilted Kitty for Anna, "Anna was so happy" and Kitty was not; they affirm "how happily it turned out for Kitty that Anna came then." Now their states are reversed: Kitty is happy and Anna is unhappy. "How completely opposite!" Dolly concludes (6:2, 556). While it might *seem* as though the natural order has set in and Tolstoy's heroes and heroines are now getting their just deserts, Tolstoy still leaves us wondering whether fortune is not, as Herodotus suggested, a wheel that does not suffer the same family to remain happy forever. As will be seen below, Tolstoy nurtures the tension between these two possibilities, to profound effect. Even as Tolstoy appears to use his labyrinth of linkages to promote this binary opposition, with Pokrovskoe winning the stamp of approval within the order Tolstoy creates, he accesses a level of metaphysical uncertainty, so that values, distinctions, and judgments that may have seemed axiomatic on the mundane level are uncertain after all.

The core section of *Dead Souls* follows Chichikov as he travels by carriage from one estate to another in the company of his servant and a driver. As Chichikov travels between estates, Gogol's narrator intersperses with his own comments exchanges between Chichikov and his peasant interlocutors about the hosts; the transitions are also punctuated by chance meetings along the road.[24] In Part 6 of *Anna Karenina*, Tolstoy provides a variant of this model as the narrative follows Dolly from Pokrovskoe to Vozdvizhenskoe and back. (Tolstoy adds to the effect by also depicting Vasenka Veslovsky as a visitor to both places: banished from Pokrovskoe for flirting with Kitty, Veslovsky settles at Vozdvizhenskoe, where his flirtations with the mistress of the house are not only tolerated but encouraged.)[25] As Elisabeth Stenbock-Fermor observes, Tolstoy creates a "diptych," in which he sets up a close parallelism between the two estates only to highlight salient differences.[26] While Gogol presents a circuitous path and a series of estates, which makes judgments more complicated, Tolstoy presents an apparent binary opposition in the "pictorial contrast" (Percy Lubbock's term) of the two estates of Pokrovskoe and Vozdvizhenskoe.[27]

Landowners Stingy with Oats:
Out of *Dead Souls*

In Part 6 of *Anna Karenina*, Tolstoy describes Dolly's carriage rides, both to Vozdvizhenskoe and then back to Pokrovskoe. Dolly uses her time in the carriage to reflect on her life. Tolstoy reveals the depths of Dolly's consciousness and make us feel for her as, on the way to Vozdvizhenskoe, she questions the very foundation of her existence, motherhood, and even asks whether she is "any better" than Anna (6:16, 608). Although the effect is wildly different, Gogol occasionally gives us (limited) access to Chichikov's (limited) psyche as he travels between estates. Similarly, Dolly and Chichikov both interact with the peasants they ride with and encounter. Tolstoy and Gogol thus, once again, use the same topoi, although to different effect. (Tolstoy's Dolly is naturally more responsive and empathetic than Chichikov.)

On her way back from Vozdvizhenskoe to Pokrovskoe, as she settles into the carriage, Dolly exchanges opinions with Philip, Levin's driver, about life on Vronsky's estate:

> Driving out into the fields, Dolly felt pleasantly relieved, and she was about to ask the servants how they had liked it at Vronsky's when the driver, Philip, suddenly spoke himself:
>
> "Maybe they're rich, but they only gave the horses three measures of oats. They cleaned the bottom before cockcrow. What's three measures? Just a snack. Nowadays innkeepers sell oats for forty-five kopecks. At home we give visitors as much as they can eat."
>
> "A miserly master," the clerk agreed.
>
> "Well, and did you like their horses," asked Dolly.
>
> "Horses is the word. And the food's good. Found it a bit boring otherwise, Darya Alexandrovna, I don't know about you," he said, turning his handsome and kindly face to her.
>
> "I thought so, too. Well, will we get there by evening?"
>
> "Ought to." (6:24, 642)

This exchange between Dolly and Levin's servants casts Vronsky in a negative light: his character flaws reveal themselves in aspects of life on his estate, even his stables. Vronsky is also compared to Levin, and the latter emerges as the superior man in every respect that matters within the system of values that Tolstoy appears to favor in the novel, even if Dolly had started to see glimmers of the good in Vronsky, whom she "had never liked" (6:20, 622).[28]

This disparaging exchange between Levin's peasants and Dolly about Vronsky recalls the following exchange that occurs in *Dead Souls* as Chichikov leaves Nozdryov's estate. While Chichikov is upset because Nozdryov threatened him with bodily harm, Selifan (Chichikov's driver) and the horses have other grounds for indicting Nozdryov:

"What a nasty gentlemen that one was!" Selifan was thinking to himself. "Ain't never seen no gentleman like that. Whish't I could spit on 'im fer that! You don't give a man nothing to eat, that's all right, but you should oughta feed a horse, 'cause a horse do love his oats. Them's his provisionin's. What victuals is fer us, y'know, oats is fer him, them's his provisionin's."

The horses also seemed to entertain an unfavourable opinion of Nozdryov: not only were the bay and Assessor out of sorts, but even the dappled horse. Although the poorer oats always fell to his portion, and Selifan never poured them into his trough without first saying: "Here you go, you good-fer-nothing!"—still and all, it was oats and not just plain hay, and he munched them with pleasure, often thrusting his long muzzle into his comrades' troughs to find out what kind of provisionin's they had, especially when Selifan was absent from the stable. But now, just plain hay . . . that wasn't good. All were discontented. (1:5, 98–99)[29]

In both these exchanges, the passenger (Dolly; Chichikov), disgruntled with the host (Vronsky; Nozdryov), learns that others (Levin's driver and clerk; Chichikov's driver and horses) are dissatisfied because the host has been stingy with the feed for the visiting horses. The parallels between these two scenes suggest that Tolstoy's past readings of *Dead Souls* left a residue in his consciousness that was activated as he wrote *Anna Karenina*. In keeping with Tolstoy's characteristic mode of appropriating and internalizing his sources, the segment in *Anna Karenina* feels very organic to Tolstoy's narrative. Gogol's coachman Selifan and Tolstoy's coachman Philip each move from a commentary on external mundane details of estate life—both Nozdryov and Vronsky were stingy in providing oats for visiting horses—to a judgment about the landowners' souls. Tolstoy's mode of making external and even peripheral details "emblematic" (to borrow Richard Gustafson's phrase) thus appears to have antecedents in Gogol's odd poetics.[30]

The Right Attitude to Horses

Whereas Levin has what Vladimir Mayakovsky would call (in a 1918 poem of that name) "the right attitude to horses," Vronsky clearly does not—despite his passion for them.[31] The coachman Philip, showing the uncanny knack shared by both Gogol's and Tolstoy's peasants for verbalizing important truths, sets forth a moral contrast between these two landowners when he comments on the respective treatment of horses at Vozdvizhenskoe and Pokrovskoe. The negative comments about Vronsky made by Levin's driver and clerk resonate with a host of other references to horses embedded in Tolstoy's labyrinth of linkages. In addition to transforming material resurrected from *Dead Souls*, Vronsky's stinginess with Levin's horses also harks back to Vronsky's treatment of his own mare Frou-Frou. Furthermore, as discussed above, Vronsky's fatal passion for his mare Frou-Frou is opposed to Levin's protective love for his prize cow Pava, whose offspring he cherishes and protects. Within the more immediate context of this segment from Part 6, the fact that Levin takes Dolly's financial problems to heart "as if they were his own" (compounded, if not caused, by Stiva's adultery) and has charitably provided to Dolly the very horses that Vronsky mistreats, further sets the two heroes against each other (6:16, 605).

In his "diptych" of Part 6, Tolstoy uses the horse lover and womanizer Veslovsky, who, like Dolly, is shown at both Pokrovskoe and Vozdvizhenskoe, to elaborate the contrast between the two estates. Once again, the proper treatment of horses is at stake. On the hunting trip that Veslovsky takes with Oblonsky and Levin, Veslovsky extravagantly admires Levin's Don Steppe horse and fantasizes about what it would be like to gallop over the steppe on such a horse. He then expresses a desire to ride the horse back to Pokrovskoe to fetch his cigars and wallet (6:8, 577). Since Veslovsky's arrival, Levin has been torn between his duties as host and his indignation at Veslovsky's flirtatious manner with Kitty back at Pokrovskoe. Tolstoy shows Levin mentally estimating Veslovsky's weight and concluding that the hefty Veslovsky would strain the horse. Thus, Levin's refusal to let Veslovsky ride his horse can be interpreted not as Levin's possessiveness toward his own horse, but as his "right attitude to horses," which in *Anna Karenina* is indicative of moral rectitude. Levin's instinct proves to be correct, because Veslovsky later strains the horses by driving them too fast and too hard and also mires them by driving them into a swamp (6:13, 595–96; 6:9, 580).[32] Veslovsky poses a threat to the welfare of horses and, by extension, to the welfare of women. (Indeed, he and Oblonsky take advantage of local peasant women that night.) Here, too, Tolstoy relies on peasant wisdom to articulate morals: one of the muzhiks tells Veslovsky the next morning: "Don't go looking at other men's wives; you'd best get one of your own" (6:13, 596). Levin preserves both his horses and his pregnant wife from Veslovsky: he banishes Veslovsky from

Pokrovskoe for flirting with Kitty and for being generally alien to the ways of Pokrovskoe.

When Veslovsky is depicted as a member of the household at Vozdvizhenskoe during Dolly's visit (later in Part 6), differences between the two estates become more salient. At Vozdvizhenskoe, Veslovsky's flirtation with the mistress of the house is condoned and even encouraged. In another resonant detail, Veslovsky is allowed to ride Anna's horse in order "to teach him to gallop on the right leg" and Vronsky shows no concern about the strain this might cause to the animal. Although the horse is a "short, sturdy English cob" (6:17, 610), can it be expected to bear Veslovsky's weight when Levin deemed it excessive for his Don Steppe horse?[33] In this way Tolstoy continues to develop Pokrovskoe and Vozdvizhenskoe as parallel but opposing realms: whereas at Vozdvizhenskoe horses are underfed and overburdened, at Pokrovskoe they are treated humanely.

Appropriating a Gogolian topos and anticipating Mayakovsky's apotheosis of the "right attitude to horses," Tolstoy sets up a pointed contrast between the masters of the two estates. The fact that the peasant who faults Vronsky for his treatment of horses and praises Levin is named Philip (from the Greek, meaning "lover of horses") seems to grant special authority to his judgment. Peasants, especially those with meaningful Greek names, often serve as Tolstoy's bearers of truths. Philip's division of masters into two categories, those who treat horses well and those who mistreat them, is linked to a later scene in which the peasant Fyodor (from the Greek Theodoros, meaning gift of God)[34] tells Levin that there are two types of people: those who "live for the belly" and those who, like the peasant Platon, "live for the soul" and "remember God." When Levin demands that Fyodor define what it means to "remember God" and "live for the soul," Fyodor responds only by noting that there are different types of people and that Levin himself would not hurt another person. He thus affirms that Levin belongs to those who live for the soul and not for the belly (8:11, 793–94). In Tolstoy's labyrinth, those who live for soul rather than the belly also are also likely to have "the right attitude to horses."

Ladies Riding Horseback:
A Cautionary Tale from an English Novel

When Anna is seen riding her English cob at Vozdvizhenskoe, this seemingly innocent, if indulgent, activity invokes a whole network of associations. The English debate over whether it was fitting for gentle-women to ride horses figures in the novels of George Eliot and Mary Elizabeth Braddon, whose works were read at Yasnaya Polyana. On the train from Petersburg, Anna reads of how "Lady Mary rode to the hounds," and she longed "to do it herself" (1:29, 100). At that time, she is unable to act on desires inspired by her English novel.[35] But once she breaks free from her former life, Anna herself rides on horseback.

At first Dolly is taken aback at the sight of Anna on horseback. We are told that "to Darya Alexandrovna's mind, the notion of ladies on horseback was connected with the notion of light, youthful coquetry, which in her opinion did not suit a woman in Anna's position" (6:17, 610).[36] Dolly, however, arrives at Vozdvizhenskoe ready to accept the choices Anna has made. This is because Dolly has been thinking about the endless travails of motherhood, from cracked nipples to anxiety about her children's moral development. "Is it all worth it?" Dolly even asks (6:16, 607). In this mood, Dolly reconciles herself to the sight of Anna on horseback (against her better judgment, as will be seen below).

According to the linkages of Tolstoy's labyrinth, Anna's horseback-riding intimates that she engages in sex, but rejects maternity. This idea is encoded on many levels. It was a commonly held belief that riding horseback was especially dangerous to unborn fetuses, a fact that readers of George Eliot's *Middlemarch* are likely to remember. The headstrong Rosamond Lydgate ignores her physician husband's warnings, rides horseback, and miscarries their baby. Women who devote their bodies to motherhood are expected to avoid riding horses. (That Vronsky had kicked the fallen Frou-Frou in the belly on the very day Anna had announced that she was pregnant also figures into the nest of associations between horseback riding and pregnancy.) The contrast between the image of Anna on horseback at Vozdvizhenskoe and what is going on meanwhile at Pokrovskoe is telling: at Pokrovskoe, where motherhood and pregnancy are sacred, everyone, especially Levin, does everything possible to ensure the safety of the baby in Kitty's womb. In fact, Anna later that evening informs Dolly that she is practicing a form of birth control that was introduced to her by a doctor after the birth of Annie. This news shocks Dolly, who is somewhat repulsed by Anna from this point on. In her own defense, Anna boldly asks, "Why have I been given reason, if I don't use it so as not to bring unfortunate children into the world?" (6:23, 638). But, in using *reason* to justify her rejection of motherhood, Anna only damns herself further because the spiritual truths celebrated in *Anna Karenina* run counter to reason. (At the end of the novel, Levin will conclude that "reason discovered the struggle for existence and the law which demands that everyone who hinders the satisfaction of my desires should be throttled. That is the conclusion of reason. Reason could not discover love for the other, because [this love] is contrary to reason" [8:12, 797].) What Anna indicates to Dolly in words—that she will have sex but no more babies—had already been communicated subliminally, thanks to a series of intratextual and intertextual linkings, when Anna is first seen riding sidesaddle on her sturdy English cob. That life at Vozdvizhenskoe is arranged in a rational fashion to maximize comfort and pleasure reinforces the message.

Not Content to Have Ceased Breastfeeding Their Children, Women Cease Wanting to Make Them

For all her musings about escape from the pains of motherhood while she rode in the carriage on the way from Pokrovskoe, Dolly ultimately recoils from the life she finds at Vozdvizhenskoe, a realm where motherhood is denied. What has been subliminally suggested to the reader by the sight of Anna on horseback is confirmed by a series of revelations to Dolly. On her tour of the swank hospital that Vronsky is building for the local peasant population, Dolly is surprised to learn that it will have no maternity ward. Dolly also learns that Anna is a rare guest in her own daughter's nursery, leaving the maternal duties to an unsavory assembly of nannies and nurses.

Anna Karenina's abnegation of her maternal responsibilities recalls the behavior of that other fictional adulteress and horse rider, Emma Bovary, who neglects and even abuses her daughter. Through Flaubert's own system of linkages, Mère Rollet, Berthe Bovary's sinister and mercenary wet nurse, becomes an accessory to Emma's adultery. Tolstoy and Flaubert both respond to Rousseau's campaign to promote *maternal* breastfeeding and to his pronouncement that once women turn their backs on their maternal duties, especially breastfeeding, adultery and the general decay of family and society necessarily follow.[37] Egotism results: "There are no longer fathers, mothers, children, brothers, sisters. . . . Each person thinks only of himself or herself." In *Émile*, Rousseau asserts that a refusal to breastfeed is the first step in a mother's fall: "Not content to have ceased breastfeeding their children, women cease wanting to make them."[38] Tolstoy follows this same logic in presenting Anna as a mother who relegates the feeding and care of her daughter to others and reveals to Dolly that she will bear no more children, citing among her reasons her fear that physical changes brought about by pregnancy would interfere with Vronsky's attraction to her (6:23, 637–39). Anna thus separates the erotic from the reproductive. In *Anna Karenina*, as in the later "Kreutzer Sonata," Tolstoy's plots follow scenarios envisioned by Rousseau when he argued that a woman's body, once "liberated" from its reproductive functions, becomes a dangerous force, more threatening to society than any political, social, or economic forces. (Before moving for a call for total chastity in, for example, the "Postface to 'The Kreutzer Sonata,'" Tolstoy argued in "What Then Are We To Do?" that for society to be saved, women must embrace their "work" as mothers, not saying "no" after two or twenty pregnancies.)[39]

Whereas the inhabitants of Vozdvizhenskoe deny motherhood— Vronsky by failing to include a maternity ward in his hospital and Anna by neglecting her daughter and refusing to have more children— at Pokrovskoe the impending birth of the heir (whom Kitty then nurses herself, as is chronicled at key points in Parts 7 and 8 [6:16,718; 7:28, 758; 8:6, 782–3; 8:18, 814]) is the focus of everyone's attention. Thus, "with a meaningful look," Levin tells Kitty that "it is not good for you to stand" (6:1, 552); as they walk together, he tells her to "lean more on me," avoids "places where she might take a false step," and "interrupt[s] the conversation to rebuke her for making too quick a movement while stepping over a branch," confessing: "In my heart I wish for nothing except that you shouldn't stumble" (6:3, 558–60). Furthermore, when Levin lends Dolly horses for her trip to Vozdvizhenskoe, he thinks ahead to having the best horses kept back at Pokrovskoe in reserve in case the midwife needs to be sent for (6:16, 605). All this points to the inhabitants of Tolstoy's Pokrovskoe embracing the punishment—and modal salvation—that God in Genesis assigns to womankind: bearing children in pain and sorrow. As a result, Pokrovskoe appears to become not merely a safe haven for horses and mothers, where reason is not practiced, but in fact the best possible estate man can create this side of Eden.

The Exaltation of the Cross of the Savior and the Protection of the Mother of God

The names of the estates Tolstoy features in *Anna Karenina*, Pokrovskoe and Vozdvizhenskoe, have symbolic significance, both for their general etymological associations and for their evocation of Russian Orthodox Church feasts.[40] The Feast of the Pokrov, celebrated on October 1, commemorates the occasion when the Mother of God appeared to Andrew the Holy Fool and placed her *pokrov* (protective veil) over him, thereby inspiring the Orthodox to victory against their enemies. Vozdvizhenskoe evokes the Feast of the Exaltation of the Cross of the Savior (Prazdnik Vozdvizheniia Kresta Gospodnia), celebrated on September 14. This feast commemorates the occasion in the fourth century when Saint Elena (Emperor Constantine's mother) is believed to have acquired the cross on which Jesus was crucified and to have erected it for veneration. It also commemorates the occasion in 629 when Emperor Heraclius rescued the cross from the Persians (who had captured it in 614) and erected it in Hagia Sophia in Constantinople. This feast thus focuses attention on Jesus's crucifixion and martyrdom, and therefore on the symbol of the cross.[41]

In naming these two estates, Tolstoy puts into play rich etymological and cultural associations. According to Russian folkways, the time for mating cattle was the Feast of the Pokrov.[42] Thus, Pokrovskoe, with its folk associations with cattle-mating and its Orthodox associations with maternal protection, seems to express almost perfectly the ethos of this realm. The name Pokrovskoe does not necessarily draw attention to itself since it was a common name for estates, and so it can be read as an inconsequential realistic detail. (It had already figured as an estate name in Tolstoy's fiction, and Tolstoy's sister and his wife's family both owned property with this name.) But, starting in Part 6 when Tolstoy introduces Vozdvizhenskoe as Vronsky's estate, thus contrasting it to Levin's Pokrovskoe, Tolstoy activates layers of latent meaning, from martyrdom to cow-mating. The name Pokrovskoe, which the reader may have originally ignored as insignificant, suddenly becomes uncanny. The effect is one of "estrangement." Yet the significance of these names remains subtle and beneath the surface, stopping short of the "vealism" that threatens *Madame Bovary*.

In the labyrinth of linkages of *Anna Karenina*, it is fitting that Pokrovskoe evokes the Mother of God and her protective, loving, and maternal attitude toward humanity, not to mention the fecundity of the agricultural world, whereas Vozdvizhenskoe evokes the martyrdom, suffering, and tragic end of Jesus. The feast after which each estate is named offers a ritualized version of life on each estate and possibly prefigures the fate of its inhabitants. The residents of Vozdvizhenskoe will come to a tragic, martyred, end. The railroad becomes Anna's "cross," while

Vronsky departs by means of the railroad to martyr himself in the war in the Balkans. In contrast, motherly protection reigns over Pokrovskoe. Saint Andrew the Holy Fool (protected by the Mother of God) even makes an apt saintly alter ego for Levin, since he rejects Cartesian reason and defies social conventions. While each name individually fits life on the estate that bears it, the significance of the names is enhanced by their juxtaposition, which encourages the reader to recognize Tolstoy's diptych. But, especially because of how the names *suggest* (rather than dictate) possible outcomes for the plots, this double act of naming is one of the myriad of ways that Tolstoy linked together his two plots, according to his principles of keeping his architectonics hidden.

Erecting Monuments at Vozdvizhenskoe: Shades of Pushkin

"I have erected to myself [or: for myself] a monument
not made by human hand . . ."

> Alexander Pushkin

In the cultural context of *Anna Karenina*, the primary association of the estate name Vozdvizhenskoe would be with the Church holiday of the Exaltation of the Cross. But it also contains etymological associations with the root *vozdvig*, meaning "to erect," and thus evokes the image of erecting monuments other than crosses. (Since what happens in one plot finds its counterpoint in another, the phallic associations of the raising of monuments also contrasts to the maternal symbolism of the *pokrov* or protective veil.)[43] Further, in the Russian literary context, the semantic field of erecting monuments is dominated by Pushkin's poem "I have erected to myself [or: for myself] a monument not made by human hand . . ." [Я памятник себе воздвиг нерукотворный], and by extension by Horace's original "Exegi monumentum . . ." (cited directly in Pushkin's epigraph), as well as Derzhavin's earlier Russian version. In his poem, Pushkin contrasts the monument of words that he erects, as poet, with the stone monument erected to the Emperor, namely, the Alexander column in Petersburg. But he does so in a way that speaks to the human condition, especially when he affirms his hopes in the indicative future, "No, all of me will not die" [Нет, весь я не умру]. What, if anything, do we who are neither poets nor even emperors leave behind when we die and how do we live life knowing that we are bound for death?

The questions at stake in Pushkin's poem haunt Vronsky in Part 6 of *Anna Karenina* when we see him settle at his family estate of Vozdvizhenskoe and endeavor to erect monuments lest he die without leaving a trace or, to put it in Pushkin's locution, so that, no, all of him will not die. As Vronsky reveals to Dolly, he desperately wants a legitimate heir so that his name and legacy will live on; Dolly acknowledges that Vronsky's desire to legitimize his relations with Anna may be seen as "egoism," but "it's such legitimate and noble egoism!" (6:23, 636). Anna, however, thwarts him by refusing the divorce from Karenin that would allow her to marry Vronsky and by her decision (of which Vronsky is unaware) not to bear any more children. Lacking a little Vronsky—a fleshly memorial to himself—Vronsky must content himself with his role as landowner, and so he erects a monument to himself in the form of the hospital. Anna herself recognizes this: "Yes, it is a monument [памятник] that he will leave behind here," says Anna, "turning to Dolly with the same sly, knowing smile as when she had spoken of the hospital earlier" (6:20, 622).

Immortalizing the Family Name
at Pokrovskoe and Vozdvizhenskoe:
Shades of Gogol

At Pokrovskoe, in contrast, Levin will have his fleshly monument, his heir Dmitry Konstantinovich Levin. (Even before the baby is born, Levin is certain he will have a son.) One of the central questions hanging over what is left of *Anna Karenina* is whether this will satisfy Levin, so that he can carry on with life and affirm, like Pushkin's "I," that "No, all of me will not die" [Нет, весь я не умру].[44] In *Dead Souls*, Gogol provided Tolstoy with another model of a hero who asks himself, in the face of death, what he will leave behind. Chichikov certainly lacks the gravitas of Pushkin's "I" in his "*Exegi monumentum*" poem. (And it may even be hard to think of Chichikov as a "real" person who partakes of the human condition.) But Gogol's Chichikov still gives voice in his own way to the same angst that besets Pushkin's "I" and Tolstoy's heroes. As Chichikov presents it, his scheme to acquire an estate and a fortune (by speculating in dead souls) will enable him to "immortalize the family [name] of Chichikov" [увековечить фамилию Чичиковых] (2:1, 315) and populate the world with little Chichikovs. As Part 1 of *Dead Souls* reaches its climax, Gogol depicts (the still childless) Chichikov as focused on his own mortality, which hits him most poignantly when he catches a cold: "As it so happened, he had caught a slight cold at that time and had an abscessed tooth and a mild inflammation of the throat, in the distribution of which the climate of many of our provincial capitals is extremely generous. Lest his life should, God forbid, somehow be cut short without heirs, he determined that it was better to keep to this room for three days or so" (1:10, 239).[45] While Chichikov's response to the common cold appears ridiculous, it is still a memento mori. Meanwhile, the public prosecutor in the town has been so affected by Chichikov's doings that "on arriving home, he fell to thinking and thinking, and suddenly, for no rhyme or reason, as they say, he up and died." The narrator then comments: "What the deceased was asking, why he had died or why he had lived, God alone knows" (1:10, 238). Readers of Tolstoy's works will recognize in this the Gogolian equivalent of the existential questions that plague Tolstoy's heroes when they realize that they are living in the Valley of the Shadow of Death.

While Tolstoy's Vronsky and Gogol's Chichikov are worlds apart, we might still see in Vronsky's desire to leave memorials to himself, which Dolly supports as a "legitimate and noble" form of egoism, something analogous to Chichikov's concern with dying without leaving a trace. This concern, in fact, surfaces as Chichikov escapes from near-death at the hands of Nozdryov, in the very segment of *Dead Souls* that Tolstoy reprises when Levin's driver, Philip, complains of Vronsky's stinginess with the oats. Chichikov expresses his anxiety lest he vanish "like a bubble on the water, with no trace at all, leaving no descendants, bequeathing neither property nor an honest name to my future children!" As the narrator confirms, "Our hero was very concerned about his descendants" (1:5, 98).

Vronsky is not the only hero of *Anna Karenina* to share Chichikov's fear of dying without leaving a trace. Would it be a travesty to suggest that Levin's dreams and aspirations are also not so very unlike those of Chichikov?[46] Early on in the novel, after his first proposal to Kitty Shcherbatsky fails, we are told that Levin wanted to perpetuate his ancestors' way of life, which was to him "the ideal of all perfection" that "he dreamed of renewing with his wife, with his family" (1:27, 95). And we are told that his dream is not of some beloved woman as much as it is of family life on his ancestral estate: "He first pictured the family to himself and only then the woman who would give him that family" (1:27, 95). To be sure, Tolstoy stresses the purity of Levin's feelings about marriage and family life, especially in contrast to those of Vronsky, whose lack of respect for them is identified early in the novel. Still, like Gogol's Chichikov but in his own Tolstoyan way, Levin is obsessed with "immortalizing his family name." With a corrective for the differences between Gogol's style and Tolstoy's, we might see Levin's dreams of Kitty as analogous to Chichikov's dreams of the "young, fresh, fair-complexioned little woman" (2:1, 315) who would provide him with little Chichikovs. For both Chichikov and Levin (at least at certain points), a wife is the means to achieve an end: patriarchal life on an estate.[47]

Carriage Collisions, Tragedies at Train Stations, and the Power of Romantic Love

Even if Levin and Vronsky both can be said to resemble Chichikov in that they seek to immerse themselves in patriarchal life on a Russian estate out of fear of dying without leaving a trace, Tolstoy's heroes differ from Chichikov in one crucial way: they are capable of romantic love and sexual desire for a woman. Chichikov is not. The desire that drives Chichikov—and Gogol's narrative—does not seem to be erotic. The presence of sexual desire in Tolstoy's heroes results in the love plots (an adultery plot for Vronsky and a conjugal love plot for Levin) that animate *Anna Karenina* and make it an entirely different kind of novel from *Dead Souls*, even if both novels are haunted by the same *ultimate* concerns, in the face of which even love proves impotent.

From the start—and in accordance with his plan for *Dead Souls* beyond Part 1—Gogol limits Chichikov as a human being and suggests that he is incapable of love (1:5, 100).[48] Thus, when in the midst of Chichikov's anxious reverie about dying without leaving descendants, his carriage collides with that of the governor's daughter, with her egg-like face and Madonna-like qualities, Chichikov, instead of falling in love, thinks in terms of her dowry and social status, which make her a worthy candidate for peopling his future estate with little Chichikovs ("Why, if this girl, let's suppose, were given a tidy little sum of two hundred thousand or so by way of a dowry, she could turn out to be a very, very tasty little morsel" [1:5, 103]). What would be a fated encounter for a romantically fit hero fails to do much for Chichikov.[49] The narrator speculates about what might have happened had someone else encountered this maiden: "If on this occasion some twenty-year-old youth had happened to be there instead of Chichikov, whether a hussar, or a student, or merely someone who had just embarked on the course of his life, then Lord! What would not have awakened, not have begun to stir, not have begun to speak within him!" (1:5, 102). But as Gogol presents it, romantic love for this pure maiden will not resurrect the dead soul of Chichikov.

Tolstoy's more virile heroes behave very differently in chance encounters with Anna and Kitty that might be seen as *Anna Karenina*'s answers to Chichikov's (fruitless) encounter with the governor's daughter in *Dead Souls*. In *Dead Souls* the encounter occurs just as Chichikov flees from Nozdryov's estate: while Selifan is musing about Nozdryov's stinginess with the oats and Chichikov focuses on the fact that he might have died without leaving a trace, their carriage collides with that of the governor's daughter, threatening the childless Chichikov's life once again. For Tolstoy's Vronsky, passionate love dawns when he has his chance encounter with Anna Karenina, at the site of a train accident that has killed a man (1:28, 64–65). And Levin catches sight of Kitty, with her egg-like face, passing by in a carriage, after he has spent the night on a haystack mooning about marrying a peasant and giving up Pokrovskoe, which would mean abandoning his dreams of immortalizing his family name and renewing the ideal life of his parents. No collision with Kitty's carriage occurs, but this fleeting encounter is enough to make him realize that the loves *her* and only her (3:12; 277–78). (That he needs her pedigree for the perpetuation of the Levin name may also play a role.)[50]

For Tolstoy's heroes, then, an encounter with a maiden riding by in a carriage or with a sexually vibrant, mature woman at the site of a railway accident engenders love plots and results in descendants (a bastard daughter for Vronsky; a legitimate male heir for Levin). For better or for worse, Vronsky and Levin escape the fate of childless Chichikov, who is left to nurse his cold. Tolstoy thus reprises and revises the scene from *Dead Souls*. In what he wrote after *Anna Karenina*, Tolstoy would draw into question romantic love and family happiness even in Levin's pure variant. And anxiety about the salvific potential of marriage and family life may be detected in *Anna Karenina* (despite Tolstoy's wife's report that the "family idea" unites and rules the novel): as will be seen below, at certain points and with increasing intensity from Part 6 on, intimations are to be found of the Gogolian stance in *Dead Souls* according to which faith in God is the only salvation for dead souls. Earthly estates do not matter; nor does the perpetuation of the family name. Readers of *Anna Karenina*, then, are left to consider how sex, love, and family relations (the stuff of most novels, if not of Gogol's), signify.

Erecting the Gogolian Ladder of Human Perfectibility in *Anna Karenina*

Surely we are not meant to read *Anna Karenina* as we read *Dead Souls*. And yet dim specters of *Dead Souls* in Tolstoy's labyrinth suggest other, more Gogolesque, models of making sense of Tolstoy's plots. On the one hand, the opposition between Pokrovskoe's family happiness and Vozdvizhenskoe's life in sin prompts a reading of the novel that celebrates Pokrovskoe and condemns Vozdvizhenskoe. On the ladder of Tolstoyan values, Levin and Kitty's way of life appears to be higher than Anna and Vronsky's. Tolstoy's elaborate anatomization of their estates—from how they feed the horses in their barns to what happens in their bedrooms—encourages this kind of comparative judgment. On the other hand, Tolstoy undermines this mode of reading to leave us questioning the whole enterprise. If only fitfully, Tolstoy calls all earthly pursuits into doubt, so that at certain points readers of *Anna Karenina* may feel they have landed in *Dead Souls* where the narrator, in the midst of his estate-by-estate exposé of local landowners (which similarly prompts readers to seek patterns of meaning and make value judgments based on the details), pauses to comment on the ephemerality of human life and to make us question the earthly judgments we make: "Whether Korobochka, or Manilova, whether household life or non-household life—let us pass them by! That is not what is cause for wonder in this world: in an instant joy can turn into sadness, if only you linger too long before it, and then God only knows what will pop into your head. Perhaps you will even begin to think: enough now, does Korobochka really stand so far down on the endless ladder of human perfectibility? Is the chasm really so great that separates her from her sister, who is shut up inaccessibly behind the walls of an aristocratic house . . .?" (1:3, 63).[51] In *Anna Karenina*, too, as we linger over the details of estate life, we might experience this same anxious dissonance. Are the differences between Pokrovskoe and Vozdvizhenskoe really so great?

This is not to deny Anna's or Vronsky's guilt, but rather to suggest that, even as Tolstoy appears to rank his characters according to a system of values that monitors everything from stinginess with oats in the barn to adultery on the couch, Tolstoy constructs his narrative so that, in the spirit of *Dead Souls*, "God only knows what will pop into your head." Perhaps the reader will even begin to think: enough now, does Anna Karenina really stand so far down on the endless ladder of human perfectibility? Is the chasm really so great that separates her from her sister Kitty? Who are we to judge? Can we really say who is higher on

Jacob's ladder? In the face of death, the systems of reward and justice that are used to hierarchize life seem to collapse by Tolstoyan design, much as they do in *Dead Souls*.[52] In *Anna Karenina*, as in *Dead Souls*, when we run across a memento mori, or some other reminder of the vanity of earthly endeavors, including erecting monuments for the public welfare and perhaps even perpetuating our family name by peopling the world with our legitimate descendants, the narrators will suddenly remind us of an abyss that perhaps only faith will fill. Tolstoy's narrative, like Gogol's, sometimes only hints at this abyss and then wends its way in another direction, as if piling on words to distract us from it.

The Veil Thrown Over the Abyss

Life at Levin's Pokrovskoe *seems* to take place under the protective veil of the Mother of God: a legitimate heir is conceived; the horses are properly fed; the jam pot does not boil over; womanizers and horse-abusers are banished. But is Pokrovskoe protected from all evil and chaos? After Anna Karenina's suicide—which can be interpreted variously: as a contingent suicide that could have been averted; as a fatality presaged in omens and predetermined by masterplots; as a cruel attempt to punish Vronsky; or as an act of self-punishment—the master of Pokrovskoe finds himself on the brink of suicide, as a result of intense metaphysical questioning, of the sort Gogol ultimately had in mind for readers of *Dead Souls* and of the sort that Tyutchev encoded in his verse. At this point, the "protective veil" (покров) evoked by the name of Levin's estate begins to recall the "veil" of Tyutchev's poetry, thrown over a threatening abyss, rather than the Mother of God's protection.

In Tyutchev's poem "Day and Night," day appears as a veil [покров] cast in divine mercy over the primal chaos or "nameless abyss" of night. Come night, the grace-bestowing fabric of the veil is ripped off, leaving humankind face to face with the abyss. Similarly, another of Tyutchev's metaphysical lyrics, "Holy night ascended to the sky," presents day as a veil that is thrown over the primal abyss:[53]

Святая ночь на небосклон взошла,
И день отрадный, день любезный,
Как золотой покров, она свила,
Покров, накинутый над бездной.

И, как виденье, внешний мир ушел . . .
И человек, как сирота бездомный,
Стоит теперь и немощен и гол,
Лицом к лицу пред пропастию темной.

На самого себя покинут он—
Упразднен ум, и мысль осиротела—
В душе своей, как в бездне, погружен,
И нет извне опоры, ни предела . . .
И чудится давно минувшим сном
Ему теперь всё светлое, живое . . .
И в чуждом, неразгаданном ночном
Он узнает наследье родовое.

$$(1848\text{-}1850)^{54}$$

As he is left to face the primal chaos when the protective veil of day is pulled away, Tyutchev's man resembles Levin in the final part of *Anna Karenina*. The "orphaned" Levin hides his gun and rope lest he, to borrow Tyutchev's imagery, plunge into the abyss. At this point, the daylight realm of Pokrovskoe, the estate that Levin attempts to set in order with such loving care, provides no veil to protect him from the chaos.

Tolstoy's fondness for Tyutchev's poetry has been well documented.[55] Dmitry Merezhkovsky has suggested correspondences between Tolstoy's and Tyutchev's understandings of nature.[56] In particular, Merezhkovsky notes that for Tolstoy, as for Tyutchev, the "protective veil" of daylight sometimes lifts to reveal the underlying abyss. (As illustration, Merezhkovsky quotes the first four lines of "Holy Night," the poem quoted above) When the protective veil has been lifted, Tyutchev sees something uplifting in the abyss beneath (as the last four lines of the poem suggest), whereas Tolstoy, according to Merezhkovsky, sees "only a bottomless, black, terrifying hole."[57]

In Tyutchev's "Silentium!," the poet declares words spoken out loud to be a lie and asserts the general inexpressibility of what is most sacred to the soul. Tolstoy presents kindred views in *Anna Karenina*.[58] When, at the very end of the novel, Levin finally comes to a truth that will allow him to continue to live and when he determines that these meaningful thoughts are "inexpressible in words" and for "him alone" (8:19, 817-18), he seems to take to heart Tyutchev's advice in "Silentium!": "Be silent, hide yourself and conceal."[59] Levin applies this Tyutchevian oath of silence and secrecy even to his wife, with whom, during the second proposal, he communicated by means of a wordless "mystical intercourse" (4:11, 389-90; 4:13, 397-98). Consequently, the novel ends with Levin affirming a variant of the very notion Anna comes to before her death, that, whatever their relations with God, human beings live in verbal isolation from one another. Verbal intercourse has its limits in human life.

Insofar as Tyutchev's poetry provides a poetic expression of the truth about language and life that Tolstoy encodes in *Anna Karenina*, the message of "Silentium!" interweaves with that of Tyutchev's poems about the protective veil. In Tolstoy's *Anna Karenina*, human discourse is, ultimately, a facet of the protective veil thrown over the abyss of night. During the "protected" hours of daylight, Tyutchev's man feels like a "resident" (to borrow Richard Gustafson's term) who has the illusion of being able to express himself in words. But in those dark hours of the soul, when this man faces the abyss of night, language—a "protective veil, thrown over the abyss" [покров, накинутый над бездной], a veil that may console or at least distract in daytime—ceases to provide comfort or be adequate to the task of narrating what he feels.

In Part 6, the impending birth of a new Levin distracts the residents of Pokrovskoe from this abyss. But earlier, when Konstantin Levin's dying brother Nikolai visited Pokrovskoe and brought him face to face with death, the protective veil of the life Konstantin Levin was attempting to create for himself at Pokrovskoe had been lifted. He was faced with the nameless abyss. At this point language failed the two brothers: they tacitly recognized that no golden, honey-mouthed veil of words they could weave would ever protect them from death or veil the abyss. They also found themselves under the command to remain silent, at least in regard to what was weighing on their souls: what they would have said, had they spoken what they really felt, would have been on Konstantin's part, "You will die, you will die, you will die!" and on his dying brother's part, "I know I shall die, but I am afraid, afraid, afraid" (3:32, 349). Instead, they speak about other things.

Levin, in the spirit of Tyutchev's lyrical "I," understands that dissimulation—saying what you do not really mean and keeping silent about the chaos and death—is necessary in order to maintain a grip on the cosmos and continue with life in the social world. Tolstoy's narrator explains: "But it was impossible to live that way, and therefore Konstantin tried to do what he had tried to do all his life without succeeding, and what, in his observation, many could do so well, and without which it was impossible to live: he tried to say what he did not think, and kept feeling that it came out false, that his brother noticed it and was annoyed by it" (3:32, 349–50). Levin's experience here confirms the truth that those who attempt to voice directly what is in their souls or those who fail to weave a protective veil of words to cover up the abyss of death (and sex) will find it impossible to live; instead they might merge with the abyss, as nearly happens to Levin at various points.[60] (By contrast, those, like Stiva Oblonsky, who use small talk and engaging language to distract themselves and others from the fear of death, survive and even flourish in the social world.)

In Part 6, at Vozdvizhenskoe, Anna and Vronsky have ceased to use language as a means of real communication.[61] While the dinner table conversation is witty and cultured, spoken words prove meaningless in the face of the ultimate questions that concern them. Attempts to use language to communicate, like attempts to erect an ordered cosmos at Vozdvizhenskoe, are simply a "veil thrown over the abyss." Late in the evening of Dolly's visit to Vozdvizhenskoe, Anna and Dolly have a private chat. They broach subjects they had been avoiding in the course of the activity-filled day. (Furthermore, Vronsky had commissioned Dolly to try to convince Anna to seek a divorce so that they could marry and have legitimate children.) Anna's revelations about not having more children alienate Dolly to the point where "she suddenly felt she had become so distant from Anna that there were questions between them which they would never agree on and of which it was better not to speak" (6:23, 639). Dolly "[pities] Anna with all her soul while talking with her" (6:24, 641) and defends Anna and Vronsky from criticism once she is back at Pokrovskoe, but their relations have changed irrevocably (as will be discussed in chapter 3). When Anna enters her own bedroom after her talk with Dolly and after taking morphine, Vronsky attempts to learn the results of this conversation with Dolly by studying Anna's face rather than by using words. When, wanting to know whether Dolly convinced Anna about the divorce, he "looks questioningly into [her] eyes," "she, understanding that look differently, smiled at him" (6:24; 641). Whereas Vronsky's unspoken question relates to his desires to legitimize his life and, ultimately, seek a form of protection from the finality of death, Anna takes his question to relate simply to sex, which, aside from morphine, is the only diversion she has from the abyss she faces at night. Vronsky and Anna, once able to communicate wordlessly, by glance or touch, have now lost that. Silence, meaningful at certain points, has become an abyss of lies and deceit.

Much as the Pushkinian associations of "erecting monuments" at Vronsky's Vozdvizhenskoe also have resonance for those gathered at Levin's Pokrovskoe, so, too, do the residents of Vozdvizhenskoe fear the Tyutchevian chaos of night when "the veil thrown over the abyss" is ripped off. Come night, they are, like Tyutchev's lyrical "I," orphaned and homeless, buried in their own souls as in an abyss. The further we go into Tolstoy's labyrinth of intertextual and intratextual linkages, the more complex the diptych of Pokrovskoe and Vozdvizhenskoe in Part 6 becomes. The residents of both estates struggle in the face of the abyss of death and sex. Language is no consolation.[62] The attempts made by residents of Vozdvizhenskoe and Pokrovskoe to erect monuments before being merged with the abyss or to throw a veil over the abyss become parallel endeavors. Though life at Pokrovskoe seems to be a solution (horses and cows are treated properly, mothers breastfeed their own young and refrain from adultery), this cannot alter the fact that the same abyss threatens both estates and each man or woman in Tolstoy's world faces this abyss alone.

Anna Karenina's Red Bag and the Cross of the Savior

In narrating Anna Karenina's suicide, Tolstoy focuses attention on the red bag Anna carries with her, in a detail that Roman Jakobson fixed on as proof of his theories about the metonymicity of realist prose.[63] When Anna finally manages to rid herself of the red bag (thus ending her Jakobsonian contiguity with it), it becomes clear that this handbag was not just a metonym, or, in Roman Jakobson's view, an inessential realistic detail, but a Tolstoyan metaphor for Anna's sexual/reproductive organs with rich associations in Tolstoy's labyrinth.

The true function of Anna's handbag was suggested by Osip Mandelshtam when he referred to the bag of the French-speaking Russian peasant in Anna and Vronsky's shared dream as a lady's bag [дамская сумочка].[64] In using this term, Mandelshtam was not subject to a Freudian slip but a Tolstoyan linkage: Mandelshtam conflates the red bag Anna carries with her on her trips and the bag the iron-beating French-speaking peasant carries in Anna's recurrent dream.[65] The peasant in Anna's dream is rummaging around in a sack (мешок) and muttering in French, "il faut battre le fer, le broyer, le pétrir" [you must beat the iron, pound it, knead it]; in her dream, her husband's servant interprets this to mean she will die in childbirth (5:3, 361). Tolstoy uses the same Russian word to refer to Anna's handbag when she carries it on the train back from Moscow to Petersburg and extracts a book and knife from it (1:29, 99–100): "[little] red bag" [красный мешочек]. In his analysis of this passage, Richard Gustafson refers to the red bag as "the container of [Anna's] desires" out of which Anna takes "her pillow, the novel with its fantasy scenarios, and the knife that cuts in two." Gustafson then relates this red bag to the peasant's bag in Anna's dream, calling the peasant's bag "the bag of her pleasures."[66] Whereas all of the associations of this red bag still hold, by analogy, Tolstoy indicts Anna for eventually making her other red bag (her sexual/reproductive chambers) into the "container of her desires" and "the bag of her pleasures" rather than into a protective womb. In Part 6, at Vozdvizhenskoe, Anna reveals to Dolly—in an ellipsis that leaves unspoken the truth that is so horrifying to Dolly—that Anna is taking measures so that she will have no more children (6:23; 637). Anna's abuse of her anatomy is, via the Tolstoyan labyrinth, linked to Vronsky's abuse of horses, as was discussed above. It is also opposed to the maternal use to which the Shcherbatsky sisters put their own "red bags" and breasts. And Tolstoy glories in providing yet another "realistic"—but richly symbolic—detail in the form of the cracked nipples, the mere recollection of which causes Dolly to shudder (6:16, 607).[67]

If one reads *Anna Karenina* as a precursor to Tolstoy's later writings, fictional and non-fictional, which (referring explicitly or implicitly to Matthew 5:27–29 and Matthew 19:10–12) proscribe chastity or, as second best, a marriage where all sex is devoted to the procreation of child after child, the significance of Anna's struggle with her red bag becomes clear. In Matthew 5:27–29, in the Sermon on the Mount, Jesus declares: "You have heard that it was said, 'You shall not commit adultery.' But I say to you that every one who looks at a woman lustfully has already committed adultery with her in his heart. If your right eye causes you to sin, pluck it out and throw it away; it is better that you lose one of your members than that your whole body be thrown into hell." In Matthew 19:10–12, following a discussion of divorce, Jesus answers queries about whether it may be better not to marry at all by noting: "Not all men can receive this precept, but only those to whom it is given." Jesus then goes on to explain that "there are eunuchs who have been so from birth, and there are eunuchs who have been made eunuchs by men, and there are eunuchs who have made themselves eunuchs for the sake of the kingdom of heaven." Anna has been troubled throughout the novel by her sexuality, represented metonymically and metaphorically by her red bag. As she reveals to Dolly at Vozdvizhenskoe, she attempted to make this red bag into a bag of pleasures—and nothing more. But, in her final moments at the train station, when she crosses herself and then successfully rids herself of her red handbag, with all its metaphorical associations—Anna symbolically becomes the eunuch that, throughout her recent life, she had such trouble being. She "plucks out and throws away" that part of her that was, Tolstoy suggests, the cause of her troubles.[68]

Tolstoy links the description of Anna's suicide with her (and Vronsky's) dream about the peasant with the sack and the iron, which Kornei interpreted to mean that Anna would die in childbirth. When Anna nearly dies from puerperal fever after the birth of her daughter, thus nearly fulfilling Kornei's prophecy in her dream, Anna, Karenin, and Vronsky undergo an intense spiritual crisis. Karenin joyously and spontaneously fulfills the "Christian law of forgiveness" that he had consciously sought to obey all his life (4:17, 413). Vronsky realizes that "he had never loved her before then." If previously he felt only a waxing and waning passion, now "during her illness, he had come to know her soul" and experienced a new form of love (4:18, 415).[69] The new (Christian? Platonic?) love in Karenin, Vronsky, and Anna is brought about because, at this point, eros is eradicated from their lives. Anna's "red bag," once a bag of erotic pleasures, has now become a bag of pain; this kind of martyrdom yields a purer form of love. But is it real? Can it last?

According to Tolstoyan linkages, it seems that only when eros is brought to naught, as when a woman's red bag is infected, heavy with child, or in the throes of labor, can Christian forgiveness and/or Platonic love of the soul be felt between a man and a woman—or two men and a woman. This is true also for the residents of Pokrovskoe. In Part 6, we are told "alone with [Kitty] now, when the thought of her pregnancy never left him for a moment," Levin "experienced what was for him a new and joyful delight, completely free of sensuality, in the closeness of a loved woman. In her voice, in her look, there was a softness and seriousness such as occurs in people who are constantly focused on one beloved task" (6:3, 558). At Vozdvizhenskoe, we will find that relations are ruined between Anna and Vronsky because her red bag is devoted to pleasure. In contrast, back at Pokrovskoe, Levin appreciates what he perceives as a higher form of love for Kitty when her pregnancy rids him of sexual design. (As is made explicit in "The Kreutzer Sonata," it was a commonly held view in Tolstoy's milieu that sexual intercourse during pregnancy and breastfeeding was a threat to the baby and to the mother.) When Kitty is in labor in Part 7, Levin's love reaches new heights of purity. By timing Kitty's labor so that it occurs the morning after Levin's (sole) meeting with Anna Karenina, Tolstoy draws on the labyrinth of linkages to reinforce the notion that a woman like Anna whose "red bag" is not devoted to bearing children will pollute men with her sexuality—on Levin's return home, Kitty is convinced that "that vile woman" bewitched her husband—whereas a woman in labor inspires pure love. Indeed, once labor begins, "however little unnaturalness and conventionality there was in Kitty's character generally, Levin was still struck by what was uncovered to him now, when all the veils were suddenly taken away and the very core of her soul shone in her eyes" (7:13, 708). In Part 8, Pokrovskoe continues to be an eros-free zone—in which Kitty is shown beatifically breastfeeding baby Mitya on two occasions (8:7, 783–85; 8:18, 814–15). Whether it is Anna or Kitty, for all the distance that separates them on the Tolstoyan ladder of moral perfection, their red bags threaten men who will only be able to perceive and love their souls when the atmosphere is free of sensuality.

When Anna throws away her red bag of pleasures before dying, she symbolically returns to the state she experienced when she was nearly killed by an infection in her womb at her lovechild's birth. In his description of Anna's last moments, Tolstoy links Anna's ability to rid herself, finally, of her little red handbag, to her act of making the sign of the cross over herself, which brings back memories from her maidenhood and childhood (7:29, 768). Whereas previously she had looked at the daytime cosmos and seen only semiotic chaos, now, as she faces the abyss of death, she finds meaning in the sign of the cross (the meaning of which she had questioned at various points in the inner monologue before her death). By crossing herself and throwing away her red bag, she returns, if only at death, to her virginal state, before she carried the bag and traveled by train.

The red handbag and the sign of the cross, if read as metaphorical details, link the final moments of Anna's life back to both Pokrovskoe and Vozdvizhenskoe as metaphorical estates. In the labyrinth of linkages, Anna at her death appeals both to the cross (the symbol of Vozdvizhenskoe) and to the protective veil of the Mother of God (the symbol of Pokrovskoe). By crossing herself and throwing away her red bag, Anna takes on the cross of a martyr; perhaps she also becomes pure like the Virgin Mother of God. Perhaps Anna Karenina will find ultimate heavenly protection under her veil. God only knows. By this point, Tolstoy has introduced into his labyrinth of "realistic" detail enough of the spirit of Gogolian uncertainty that each reader must decide whether this is just a figure of speech or gospel truth.

Readers sometimes feel that the life that goes on at Pokrovskoe "without any allusion to Anna" is built on the corpse of Anna Karenina (much as the railroad in Nekrasov's poem is built on the corpses of those who died constructing it).[70] Since *Anna Karenina* is a double story, readers may wonder why those assembled there do not even seem to remember Anna, even if what matters at Pokrovskoe most is that Levin has survived his dark hour of the soul. The clean living and family love that prevail there show the potential of life on a Russian family estate. But even as Kitty breastfeeds baby Mitya, putting Rousseauean prescriptions into practice, the double story exerts tension by means of Tolstoy's labyrinth of linkages, which connects Kitty and Levin to Anna although they do not recollect her. Anna's plot is still inextricably linked with Levin's—and her death with his near death.

Tolstoy and His Labyrinth of Linkages

Throughout *Anna Karenina*, Tolstoy uses his labyrinth of linkages to suggest patterns of meaning, which often depend on the binary opposition of two elements. He develops the most elaborate opposition of this kind in the diptych in Part 6, which is used to contrast life on the estates of Pokrovskoe and Vozdvizhenskoe and to depict the plots as parallel yet opposite. Even as he privileges the former in whatever evaluative hierarchy emerges, Tolstoy makes the distinctions he establishes murky in ways that hinder judgment and put the reader in a questioning frame of mind.

When Tolstoy wrote to Strakhov that in writing *Anna Karenina* he was guided by the need "to gather together interrelated thoughts in order to express [himself]" and that separating one thought from another to express it by words degraded it, he was struggling between his yearning for faith in divine providence and his despair at the thought that human life ("reality") could be ultimately meaningless. In *Anna Karenina* Tolstoy expresses *his* view that what human beings do in this real world—at every moment—matters and has significance, but only when we take into account the abyss of death, an abyss that only faith can fill. (See chapter 5 for further discussion on this point.) This tension shows up in the poetics of Tolstoy's double-storied *Anna Karenina*, making it qualitatively different from Tolstoy's other works. One manifestation of this difference is the novel's elaborate network of symbolism and allusion, in which the "real" prosaic world interacts with its metaphorical realm, together forming an endless labyrinth *in which the plots are intertwined*.

2

Anna Karenina and
The Scarlet Letter

Anna on the Scaffold of the Pillory and Levin with His Own Red Stigma

Anna Karenina's American Cousin: The Scarlet Letter

The Scarlet Letter (1850), Nathaniel Hawthorne's New World novel of adultery, stands apart from the corpus of nineteenth-century Old World novels of adultery that followed it. Its adulteress, Hester Prynne, dies of natural causes. *The Scarlet Letter* thus deviates from the morphology of the adultery tales of Emma Bovary and Anna Karenina, with its sequence of fall, degeneration, and suicide.[1] Hawthorne's heroine did in fact contemplate infanticide and suicide ("At times, a fearful doubt strove to possess her soul, whether it were not better to send Pearl at once to heaven, and go herself to such futurity as Eternal Justice should provide" [13, 145]), but she lives on in devotion to her daughter, Pearl, and to others in the community on whose outskirts she lives. "Self-ordained as a Sister of Mercy," she shows a "wellspring of human tenderness" as she nurses the sick, feeds the hungry, and comforts the dying, for she was "ever quick to acknowledge her sister-hood with the race of man" (13, 141).[2] At the death of Roger Chillings-worth, Hester's husband, Pearl becomes "the richest heiress of her day, in the New World" (24, 225). Hester leaves with Pearl for the Old World, where Pearl appears to find happiness as a wife and mother. Eventually, Hester returns alone to Boston and "resume[s],—of her own free will" wearing the scarlet letter. She lives out the remainder of her life sadly and selflessly, comforting others, "women, more espe-cially," in their wretchedness and sorrow, and "assur[ing] them, too, of her firm belief, that, at some brighter period, when the world should have grown ripe for it, in Heaven's own time, a new truth would be revealed, in order to establish the whole relation between man and woman on a surer ground of mutual happiness" (24, 227). Hawthorne leaves it up to readers to decide whether "the scarlet letter had done its office" of reforming the adulteress (13, 145). But, as Sacvan Bercovitch has argued, Hawthorne's heroine embodies a "radical individualism" even as the scarlet letter burns on her breast.[3] By contrast, in Tolstoy's novel of adultery, the wages of "radical individualism" is death under a train.[4]

In *Tolstoy in the Seventies*, Boris Eikhenbaum demonstrates that Tolstoy was occupied with the polemics about what to do with an adulterous wife as set forth by Alexandre Dumas fils, in his works of theater and fiction and, especially, in the pamphlet "The Man-Woman" (1872), which, in its notorious last words of "Tue-la!" ("Kill her!"), granted cuckolds the right to kill intractable wives.[5] That Tolstoy wrote *Anna Karenina* in reaction to *French* treatment of adultery has become axiomatic in discussion of the novel, and *Anna Karenina* is often com-pared to Gustave Flaubert's *Madame Bovary* (1856).[6]

The connection between *Anna Karenina* and *The Scarlet Letter* is remote. *The Scarlet Letter* is not on the list of works that Tolstoy acknowl-edged as important to his development as a writer. In fact, Tolstoy documented a strong dislike of *The Scarlet Letter* early on, when *The Contemporary* published it in Russian translation in 1856.[7] As was the case with his response to Dostoevsky, Tolstoy could be caustic about, and dismissive of, other novelists but still take their work to heart. (Tolstoy also wrote disparagingly about *Madame Bovary*.) If, as Osip Mandelshtam and others have suggested, Anna is Emma's French sister, then at the very least Hester is her American cousin.[8] In what follows, my concern is not with Hawthorne's influence on Tolstoy, although *The Scarlet Letter* should be acknowledged among the many sources figuring in the depths of Tolstoy's creative consciousness. Rather, *The Scarlet Letter* will be examined alongside *Anna Karenina* in order to illuminate the conditions under which male heroes enter the tales of adulteresses and threaten to divide the plots.[9]

When *The Scarlet Letter,* which Hawthorne called a "romance," was published in 1850, one reviewer observed that it read like "a prose poem." Writing a century later, in an essay called "Hawthorne as Poet," Q. D. Leavis identifies the poetic quality of *The Scarlet Letter* as a distinctive feature that it shares with Tolstoy's *Anna Karenina.* She argues that "the just comparison with *The Scarlet Letter*" is *Anna Karenina,* which "in theme and technique it seems to [her] astonishingly to resemble." What accounts for the poetic quality of these novels? Leavis observes that *The Scarlet Letter* "has a richer life than any other of Hawthorne's works because it is the most inclusive." According to Leavis, in composing *The Scarlet Letter,* Hawthorne "swept" material from his earlier works "into a finely organized whole, so that every portion is concentrated with meanings and associations and cross-references. Only something in the nature of a poetic *procédé* and technique could have coped with such an undertaking."[10] Thus, readers of *The Scarlet Letter* must read for these paradigmatic links and not just for the adultery plot.

Leavis's argument about *The Scarlet Letter* works for *Anna Karenina* as well. Tolstoy's "endless labyrinth of linkages" makes *Anna Karenina,* in its own way, into a prose poem, even if not as tightly organized as *The Scarlet Letter.* And Tolstoy, like Hawthorne, made his novel of adultery "inclusive." As Leavis noted, Tolstoy wanted to give a full picture of life, as if to say, "This is the society that condemned Anna!" But Leavis also remarked that "in *Anna* Tolstoy managed to find room for all his interests, experiences, and problems."[11] While this may be just another way of accusing *Anna Karenina* of being a "loose and baggy monster," Leavis's suggestions about how and why *Anna Karenina* became so inclusive is a key to understanding how it works as a novel of adultery and why the plot is double or triple.

What happens to the tale of the adulteress when the author includes, as Leavis puts it, "all *his* interests, experiences, and problems [my emphasis, LK]"? In Tolstoy's case, this includes debates about materialism, peasant-landowner relations, and the war in the Balkans. Is this merely realistic backdrop, or does it connect in some way to the kernel of Tolstoy's adultery plot? One strategy Tolstoy used to fit all this into *Anna Karenina* was to add Levin's story to Anna's. As Peter Garrett observed in relation to (Victorian) multiplot novels, when plots are multiplied, attention is divided.[12] However, a woman with a scarlet letter attracts attention; by extension, a plot designated by a scarlet letter exerts a pull on other plots in the novel. Anna's scarlet letter casts a shadow on all reaches of the novel. Thus, even as Tolstoy enriches the picture of human life by including other plots, all the plots contribute, if only indirectly, to the drama of the judgment of the adulteress. In this respect, its dynamic is similar to that of *The Scarlet Letter,* a novel in which a covert double plot can be detected (despite its economy of form, which contrasts with the expansive and overtly multiplot *Anna Karenina*).

The Woman Taken in Adultery
Brought Before Hawthorne and Tolstoy

We find significant affinities between *The Scarlet Letter* and *Anna Karenina* because Tolstoy and Hawthorne, more obsessively than most authors of adultery novels, responded specifically to the gospel pericope of the woman taken in adultery (John 8:1–11).[13] According to this gospel story, a woman taken in adultery—"in the very act"—is led by the scribes and the Pharisees into the temple and set before Jesus, with the challenge: "Now Moses in the law commanded us, that such should be stoned: but what sayest thou?" Jesus, pretending not to hear them, stoops down and writes or draws with his finger in the sand. When they persist, he rises to the challenge and tells them, "He that is without sin among you, let him first cast a stone at her." And, in a remarkable plot development, the scribes and Pharisees, "being convicted by their own conscience, beginning at the eldest, even unto the last, file out" without casting stones. They leave Jesus to tell the adulteress to go, and sin no more.[14]

   This story captivated the imagination of Christian culture to become inordinately popular, as Tolstoy pointed out in his revision of the Gospels.[15] And, as David Parker has argued, its hold on the moral imagination of nineteenth-century European novelists was great: not only do many novels engage with its ethical message, but they also often reenact its drama.[16] If novels of adultery show a high degree of reflexivity, giving them the feel of twice-told tales and inspiring readers like Mandelshtam to regard their heroines as sisters, the seminal importance of the passage in John 8 is partly responsible. In *Adultery and the Novel: Contract and Transgression*, Tony Tanner suggests that engagement with this gospel pericope is a marker of adultery novels by Rousseau, Goethe, and Flaubert.[17] According to Tanner, classic novels of adultery are marked by a tension between the two modes of "confronting adultery": condemnation according to the law, on the one hand, and compassion, on the other, which in John 8, includes the call to look within one's own conscience. Tanner observes that Jesus "dissolves [the] group identity" of the scribes and Pharisees, "thrust[ing]" them and the adulteress "back into their interiority" (where they are "convicted by their own conscience").[18] Thus, the central arena of dramatic action shifts into the individual consciences of the scribes and Pharisees, of the adulteress—and by extension, of Jesus's audience. The gospel story, with its shift of focus from an act of adultery to the interiority of different individuals including members of the community, thus provides the kernel of multiplot adultery tales.

Both Hawthorne and Tolstoy scatter a series of references to this gospel story on the surface of their novels. In *The Scarlet Letter*, for example, when the Puritan children, whose favorite pastimes mimic their elders' vengeful behaviors to include "playing at . . . scourging Quakers; or taking scalps from Indians," would gather around Hester Prynne's daughter to torment her, Pearl would "snatch up stones to fling at them" (6, 84). As she arms herself with stones, Pearl reverses the gospel scenario and challenges its ethos; Hawthorne thus signals how far the little band of Puritans (Pearl included) has deviated from the ethos of the gospel. In *Anna Karenina*, casual allusions to (not) casting stones in characters' speech and the narrator's comments likewise recall and estrange the gospel precedent.[19]

These references to throwing stones are symptomatic of Hawthorne's and Tolstoy's deeper engagement with both the message and the form of the source text in the Gospel of John. Both novelists play on the tension between the two modes of response to the adulteress: persecution and compassion. As they depict goodwives, society women, servants, cuckolded husbands, magistrates, ministers, opera-goers, and others all judging the adulteress, the novelists draw the very process of condemning the adulteress into question and possibly hint that vengeance is God's alone. And, ultimately, both novelists issue a "what sayest thou?" to the reader, thus giving the reader the last word.

"The Persecuting Spirit" and "Writers of Story-Books"

In Hawthorne's novel, Hester's scarlet letter embodies the play between the letter of the law, which spells death for the adulteress, and the mercy of the magistrates, who sentence Hester not to death but to wear the scarlet letter on the scaffold of the pillory and beyond.[20] Hester's judges regard this punishment as merciful because it can conceivably "do its office" and lead her to repentance. Yet this punishment, especially at first, cruelly deprives her of "intercourse with society" and "human sympathy" and leaves her to wonder if life is worth living.[21]

In "The Custom House," which is "introductory to *The Scarlet Letter*,"[22] Hawthorne vexes the question of vengeance in ways that prime the reader for the contradictions to follow in the novel proper. In "The Custom House," a first-person narrator, whom the reader is encouraged to identify with Nathaniel Hawthorne, reveals the tension in his own heart as he approaches his subject, Hester Prynne and the scarlet letter. The narrator describes how, while working in the Custom House, he came across the scarlet letter itself ("a certain affair of fine red cloth," with golden embroidery, "wrought . . . with wonderful skill of needlework"), together with a manuscript about its creator ("The Custom House," 32). When he reveals that he held this letter to his own breast, but then felt a sensation of "burning heat," this "Hawthorne" presents himself as someone ready to identify and sympathize with the adulteress, to wear her letter, if only for a moment. But this "Hawthorne" also confesses to having had Puritan forefathers who participated in the persecution and punishment—unto death—of deviant women, not adulteresses but witches and Quakers. He even begs God for mercy for the sins of his fathers.[23] "Hawthorne" then wryly notes that these same forefathers might have persecuted him for being a "writer of storybooks," which is no better than being "a fiddler." Thus, "Hawthorne" by analogy once again identifies himself with deviant women persecuted by Puritan fathers and, hence, with Hester Prynne. And yet, after presenting himself as someone who is prone to sympathy for deviant women, capable even of identifying with them (suggesting, in anticipation of Flaubert, that "Hester Prynne, c'est moi!"), and ashamed of his forefathers' persecuting ways, "Hawthorne" declares that "strong traits of their [his forefathers'] nature have intertwined themselves with mine." He thus signals that he has also possibly "inherited the persecuting spirit," which could surface in his retelling of the tale of the scarlet letter.

Thus, "The Custom-House" prepares a reader for the tension between persecution and compassion that is vital to the rest of the novel, as it will be to *Anna Karenina* and others of the genre. Darrel Abel describes the interplay between condemnation and compassion as follows: "In fact, Hawthorne does feel moral compassion for Hester, but her role in the story is to demonstrate that persons who engage our moral compassion may nevertheless merit moral censure."[24] Hawthorne's narrator seems to bear in mind that we are all sinners. His sympathy may be an imitation of Christ or, perhaps, the occupational hazard of being a "writer of story-books," especially a story-book that presents to us the interior world of others. (And we will see that Hester Prynne takes great liberties in her thinking.) But the author keeps the plot in check to ensure that the adulteress's lot is miserable and that *The Scarlet Letter* remains "a tale of human frailty and sorrow."

At the threshold of his own narrative, Tolstoy takes measures analogous to Hawthorne's in "The Custom House," to introduce a similar tension between persecution and compassion. Tolstoy accomplishes the task deftly through his epigraph ("Vengeance is mine; I will repay"), which, with its history of mystifying readers, is gloriously polysemous. When we take into account the implications of Jesus's reference to God's words, as recorded by Paul in Romans (12:19), what sounds like an ominous declaration of retribution also reminds us that, while God may well have vengeance in store for (unrepentant) sinners, people should be compassionate and not take it upon themselves to punish sinners ("Dearly beloved, avenge not yourselves, but rather give place unto wrath: for it is written, Vengeance is mine; I will repay, saith the Lord" [Romans 12:19]).[25] The message of the epigraph, understood in this way, is close to the message of the gospel pericope of the woman taken in adultery as Tolstoy set it forth in his commentary on the Gospels, where he noted that *only* whosoever is without sin (i.e., God alone) has a right to punish and all sinners should focus on their own conscience.[26] And yet, as Tolstoy is reported to have explained late in life, the epigraph still means that the evil that you do catches up to you.[27] Thus, Anna's death under the train suggests this meaning, but Tolstoy undermines this message in that only Vronsky's mother declares that Anna deserved this end. As for Tolstoy's narrator, he often (but not consistently) shows and encourages compassion for Anna, thus providing *Anna Karenina* with its version of the tension that Tanner identified as vital to the classic novel of adultery.

Anna at the Opera:
Hester on the Scaffold of the Pillory

Whereas the most profound affinities between *The Scarlet Letter* and *Anna Karenina* lie in the hidden architectonics of their poetic structures,

Tolstoy at one significant point signals the kinship of Anna Karenina to Hester Prynne. This occurs when the narrator announces that Anna "was experiencing the feelings of a person on display at the pillory" (5:33, 547). This image recalls Hester Prynne, with the scarlet letter on her breast, set forth on the pillory of the scaffold in the opening of *The Scarlet Letter*. Tolstoy conjures up the pillory late in Part 5 of *Anna Karenina*, when Anna goes to the opera in St. Petersburg. Although this setting is far removed from Hester's seventeenth-century Puritan world, the chronotope of the opera is familiar to the adultery novel: Flaubert regales readers of *Madame Bovary* with an elaborate description of Emma and Charles at the opera in Rouen for a performance of *Lucia di Lammermoor* (end of Part 2). Emma's trip to the opera feeds the adultery plot, by fanning her desire for dramatic excitement (according to the syndrome that bears the Bovary name) and by bringing her back into contact with Léon, who becomes her second lover the next day.[28] Tolstoy, however, places Anna Karenina in a setting associated with Emma Bovary only to emphasize that Anna's experience is like that of a more distant adulteress, Hester Prynne.

When Anna and Vronsky return to Petersburg after their Italian journey, society becomes, as Vronsky puts it later, "hell" for Anna. Vronsky, however, does not suffer the same abuse; society plays what is described as a cat and mouse game with Anna and Vronsky so that the arms that let Vronsky through bar Anna's path. Throughout this segment of the novel, Tolstoy makes it clear that the society that condemns Anna is not without sin, and he enhances the effect by including allusions to the gospel pericope.[29] The narrator announces in Part 2 that Anna's community was "already preparing the lumps of mud they would fling at her when the time came" (2:18, 174). Clearly, in Part 6, the time has come.

Anna undertakes this trip to the opera, thus courting scandal, in the aftermath of her heartbreaking visit with Seryozha on his birthday. Anna steals into her former house after she has been forbidden access to her son by Karenin's "comforter," Countess Lydia Ivanovna. Her letter of refusal to Anna is full of gospel rhetoric—appeals to Christian charity, claims not to want to put Seryozha in the position of judging his mother, and prayers for God's mercy for Anna—but it clearly aims to punish the adulteress and "wound her to the depths of her soul" (5:25, 519–20): the message of John 8:1–11 is lost on Lydia. Having refused to believe Countess Lydia Ivanovna's announcements of her death, Seryozha is overjoyed to see his mother; in fact, repeating his favorite phrase, Seryozha declares that he "knew" his mother would come. Anna's maternal love is so transcendent that it moves all of the servants from nanny to tutor; when Kornei, Karenin's valet—the only servant to object to Anna's presence—censures Kapitonych for having let her in, Kapitonych replies that for ten years he had seen nothing but kindness (милость) from her and then reminds Kornei of his own sins ("You mind yourself, robbing the master and stealing raccoon coats!") in a folksy invocation of Jesus's message to the scribes and Pharisees. Before parting, Anna tells Seryozha to love his father, that he is better than she is, that she is guilty before him, and that when Seryozha grows up he will judge (5:30, 537). Seryozha's response is to declare nobody better than his mother and to sob in anguish. Tolstoy thus alludes to the gospel theme of the judgment of the adulteress even before Anna appears at the opera.

Anna's rash decision to attend the opera appalls Vronsky, whose point of view is reflected by the narrator throughout much of the scene. (That Vronsky is unaware of Anna's heartbreak earlier that day exacerbates the sense of distance between them and makes Anna's actions all the more bewildering to him.) As Vronsky feared, Anna's very presence at the opera causes a scandal. When Vronsky's mother later informs Vronsky with malicious pleasure, "[Anna] *fait la sensation. On oublie la Patti* [the diva] *pour elle*," her remarks make graphic the need these Petersburg opera-goers feel to punish the adulteress by making a spectacle of her.

Anna suffers a particular insult from her neighbor in the next box. Mme. Kartasova becomes incensed when her own husband speaks in a friendly way to Anna, their former acquaintance, instead of shunning her. Vronsky, as a latecomer, does not witness the scene:

> Vronsky did not understand precisely what had taken place between the Kartasovs and Anna, but he realized that it had been humiliating for Anna. He realized it both from what he had seen and, most of all from Anna's look. He knew she had gathered her last forces in order to maintain the role she had taken upon herself. And in this role of ostensible calm she succeeded fully. People who did not know her and her circle, and who had not heard all the expressions of commiseration, indignation and astonishment from women that she should allow herself to appear in society and appear so conspicuously in her lace attire and in all her beauty, admired the calm and beauty of this woman and did not suspect

that she was experiencing the feelings of someone set forth at the
pillory [она испытывала чувства человека, выставляемого у
позорного столба]. (5:33, 547)

The narrator's observation that Anna, humiliated at the opera, experienced the feelings of someone set forth "at the pillory" recalls the weird
similes that Tolstoy incorporates elsewhere in the novel at critical
moments. For example, in Part 2, the narrator informs us that Anna and
Vronsky's first sexual act was like a murder, in an act of verbal violence,
which not only punctuates the event, but also alarms the reader (2:11,
149–50). The narrator then extends the simile, outdoing Homer and
moving into an allegorical mode as he describes the murderer cutting
up the body to dispose of it. This murder simile is part of the web of symbolism that Tolstoy—in a manner that recalls Hawthorne—embedded
in the narrative, with occasional cross-linkings to the real action and the
psychic worlds of the characters.[30] In these instances (the murder simile
in Part 2 and the reference to the pillory in Part 5), the histrionic imagery
cannot be ascribed to the consciousness of a given character in a manifestation of free indirect style; the narrator is operating on his own. The
narrator thus becomes responsible for adding to the sense of doom and
fatalism often ascribed to Anna, who is sometimes blamed for believing
in omens, being fatalistic, and not taking responsibility for her actions.[31]
Although not technically a simile, the assertion that Anna experiences
the feelings of a person pilloried connects Anna's shame to something
outside of her reality.[32] In a novel of adultery, this invocation of the "feelings of a person set forth at the pillory" conjures up the opening scene
of *The Scarlet Letter* and likens Anna's experience to Hester's, as the
latter stood at the scaffold of the pillory, wearing the scarlet letter on her
breast.[33]

    While a judgment scene in which the community condemns the
adulteress is *a scène à faire* in the novel of adultery, Tolstoy turns this
scene into a startling homage to the opening of *The Scarlet Letter*. Hawthorne presents an official judgment scene, with an iron-and-wood
pillory on a scaffold, when Hester is brought from the prison, with
Pearl in her arms, and appears before the crowd that has assembled to
behold "the spectacle of guilt and shame in a fellow-creature." By contrast, the Petersburg society crowd that judges Anna has gathered for a
different kind of spectacle, the opera, but is ready to "forget Patti for
[Anna Karenina]" as they turn from the fiction on stage to participate in
real-life drama.

Hawthorne's Hester is to stand before the crowd on the scaffold of the pillory wearing the scarlet letter, in accordance with the sentence meted out to her by the Puritan patriarchs. The goal of the punishment is to label her as an adulteress and thereby set her apart from the community. But Hester continues to express her individualist spirit, both in her demeanor and in the artistic license she took in embroidering the scarlet letter:

> With a burning blush, and yet a haughty smile, and a glance that would not be abashed, [she] looked around at her townspeople and neighbors. On the breast of her gown, in fine red cloth, surrounded with an elaborate embroidery and fantastic flourishes of gold thread, appeared the letter A. It was so artistically done, and with so much fertility and gorgeous luxuriance of fancy, that it had all the effect of a last and fitting decoration to the apparel which she wore. (2, 50)

The matrons take Hester's artistry as proof that the "brazen hussy" mocks the authority of the godly magistrates; they declare it would be "well" "if we stripped Madam Hester's rich gown off her dainty shoulders" (2, 51).

In describing Anna's humiliation at the opera, the narrator notes that the crowd reacts similarly to the fact that the adulteress dares to appear "so conspicuously in her lace attire and in all her beauty" (5:33, 547). In the previous chapter, the narrator had already drawn attention to her choice of dress ("a light-coloured gown of silk and velvet with a low-cut neck that had been made for her in Paris") and to her lace adornment ("costly white lace on her head, which framed her face and showed off her striking beauty to a particular advantage") (5:32, 542). The context suggests that Vronsky foresees that Anna's luxurious and eye-catching attire will intensify the crowd's need to humiliate her.

Tolstoy's and Hawthorne's narrators both comment on observers' perceptions about the adulteress's dazzling beauty, while drawing attention to the fact that these observers have only limited understanding of what the adulteress is actually feeling. Of the response to Hester, Hawthorne writes: "Those who had before known her, and had expected to behold her dimmed and obscured by a disastrous cloud, were astonished, and even startled, to perceive how her beauty shone out, and made a halo of the misfortune and ignominy in which she was enveloped. It may be true, that, to a sensitive observer, there was something exquisitely painful in it." Hawthorne thus suggests that *even* those who knew Hester would just see her beauty and not penetrate to the depths of her feelings to feel her pain, unless they were "sensitive observers" (2, 50–51). Tolstoy makes a different point but similarly draws attention to distinctions between what observers who know her and observers who do not grasp about the inner torment of the beautiful adulteress: "People who did not know her and her circle . . . admired the calm and beauty of this woman and did not suspect that she was experiencing the feelings of a person set forth on the scaffold of the pillory" (5:33, 547). Only the most sensitive observers sense the depths of the adulteresses' pain; others simply marvel at their beauty.

The Feelings of a Person Set Forth at the Pillory: Phantasmagoric Forms

When the narrator asserts that Anna was "experiencing the feelings of a person set forth at the pillory," he reminds us of Anna's interiority during her humiliation. But he does not elaborate, leaving the details of those feelings to the reader's imagination, and possibly to the reader's recollection of *The Scarlet Letter*. In "The Market-Place" Hawthorne reveals the particulars of his heroine's emotions as she stands before the crowd on the pillory. To convey Hester's anguish, the narrator first appeals to a simile: "Haughty as her demeanor was, she perchance underwent an agony from every footstep of those that thronged to see her, as if her heart had been flung into the street for them all to spurn and trample on." The narrator goes on to note that "the unhappy culprit sustained herself as best a woman might, under the heavy weight of a thousand unrelenting eyes, all fastened upon her," even though she felt "as if she must needs shriek out with the full power of her lungs, and cast herself from the scaffold down upon the ground, or else go mad at once." We are told that while she stood on the scaffold of the pillory, Hester's "mind, and especially her memory, was preternaturally active."[34] Thus, Hester's way of "sustain[ing] herself as best a woman might" is to turn inward, to retreat from the world around her (which shows her so little compassion) into her own interiority (2, 53–54).

As he draws attention to Hester's heightened, disheveled, eerily penetrating state of mind, Hawthorne's narrator offers a precursor of the first-person stream of consciousness that Tolstoy composes for Anna in the hours before her death. Anna's mind (like Hester's on the scaffold) will be "preternaturally active" as she rides, first by carriage and then by train, before casting herself under a train.[35] While she is on the scaffold, Hester's mind, "seeking to relieve itself, by the exhibition of these phantasmagoric forms, from the cruel weight and hardness of reality," conjures up scenes of her past back in England. Thus, "passages of infancy and school-days, sports, childish quarrels, and the little domestic traits of her maiden years" "came swarming back upon her, intermingled with recollections of whatever was gravest in her subsequent life; one picture precisely as vivid as another; as if all were of similar importance, or all alike a play" (2, 54). In her final inner monologue in Part 7, Anna similarly seeks meaning in a phantasmagoria of signs. Like Hester, Anna will recollect random but significant scenes of her childhood and maiden years, in her desperate attempt to understand what has become of her life. Thus, for example, Anna remembers riding to the Trinity Monastery by carriage and asks, "Would I have believed then that I could come to such humiliation?" (7:28, 757). For both heroines, these rare glimpses into the past poignantly remind us that they are severed from their former innocent selves. While there seems to be no return to the past, nor real escape from the scarlet letter—as Hawthorne describes Hester's present: "Yes, these were her realities—all else had vanished!"—the heroines' consciousness still remains beyond the control of those who condemn them. This suggests that their souls still stand ajar and open to Heaven.

Disciplining the Adulteress: Puritan Goodwives, Petersburg Opera-Goers, and Other Self-Constituted Judges

In the opera scene in Part 5, Tolstoy's narrator, not specifying the nature of Anna's thoughts and feelings beyond the comment that they were the feelings of someone at the pillory, focuses on the behavior of Anna's "circle" as it takes vengeance into its own hands. Tolstoy's mean-spirited opera-goers, more interested in being scandalized by Anna Karenina than in listening to the diva Patti, recall the crowd of Puritan settlers gathered at the Prison Door, as for a spectacle, to condemn and punish the adulteress at the beginning of *The Scarlet Letter*. In these scenes of judgment (which also recall the judgment of the adulteress in the gospel of John), Hawthorne and Tolstoy present the adulteress in relation to a community that feels the need to stand in judgment over her. In turn, as

Richard Brodhead observes (in relation to Hawthorne's version), these judgment scenes put us in the vicarious role of judge and present us with the spectrum of the spectators' different responses, "by which to frame our own response" to the adulteress.[36]

The Scarlet Letter sets the scene at the prison door and market-place before Hester emerges to be put on display on the scaffold of the pillory. The first speech recorded in the novel belongs to a group of matrons in the assembled throng: "'Goodwives,' said a hard-featured dame of fifty, 'I'll tell ye a piece of my mind. It would be greatly for the public behoof, if we women, being of mature age and church-members in good repute, should have the handling of such malefactresses as this Hester Prynne. What think ye, gossips?" Her fellow "goodwives" and "gossips" are convinced that the "godly magistrates," who passed judgment and determined the punishment, had been bewitched by Hester, with the result being too much mercy (2, 48).[37] Hester's neighbors demand more vengeance. They conclude even before Hester emerges, unabashed, with the letter so luxuriantly embroidered, that the punishment was too lenient. One suggests that "at the very least, they should have put the brand of a hot iron on Hester Prynne's forehead." Another of these goodwives, "the ugliest as well as the most pitiless of these self-constituted judges," wants no punishment short of death: "This woman has brought shame upon us all, and ought to die. Is there not law for it? Truly there is, both in the Scripture and the statute-book." Hawthorne sets up an implicit contrast between these vindictive "self-constituted" judges and those selected for the office, the magistrates. But in the process Hawthorne causes us to wonder about the whole system of human justice: does it really have divine sanction? Why not leave it up to God?[38]

In *The Scarlet Letter* the woman singled out as the "most pitiless" of the "self-constituted judges" reasons that law and order—and family values—depend on making an example of the adulteress. "Then let the magistrates . . . thank themselves if their own wives and daughters go astray." Tolstoy shows the same social dynamic at work in *Anna Karenina*. In Part 5, a few chapters before the opera scene, Vronsky's sister-in-law offers a similar rationale to Vronsky for why she will shun Anna: "I have growing daughters and must live in society for my husband's sake" (5:28, 529). This same husband has a mistress of his own, which the reader knows, whether his wife does yet or not. Although Tolstoy's society lady and Hawthorne's Puritan goodwives make different excuses for not showing compassion to a sinner, they all do so in the name of family values, which the novels give the reader good reason to question.

The responses of the women of Russian high society to Anna Karenina in this scene and at other points are not so different at heart from those that Hawthorne depicts: much as the Puritan goodwives suspect Hester of having bewitched the magistrates, wives wonder whether Anna is bewitching their husbands, from Mme. Kartasova at the opera to Kitty, who later in the novel is convinced that this "vile woman" has "bewitched" her husband (7:11, 703).

Hawthorne, however, presents a feminine voice among the crowd that is compassionate to Hester. It comes not from a middle-aged matron, but from "a young wife, holding a child by the hand," who says that "the pang of it always will be in her heart" and who bids them "Peace, neighbors, peace! . . . Do not let her hear you! Not a stitch in that embroidered letter, but she has felt it in her heart" (2, 49; 2, 51). Not only does she show compassion for Hester, but she also focuses on the inner world of conscience, as she bids her neighbors to consider what Hester feels in her heart. In keeping with his characteristic economy in regard to peripheral characters, Hawthorne tells us nothing more about this young mother, nor does he construct a subplot for her. But he uses her effectively to indicate an alternative to the matrons' cries for vengeance. Although Hester Prynne remains a lonely figure, tempted at times by suicide (13, 145), cut off from most forms of human intercourse except for her bonds to her daughter, she lives on. And, in the epilogue-like last chapter, Hawthorne notes the comfort Hester gives to other women in need, suggesting that some of the daughters of the good-wives who condemned her now turn to her for compassion, thus indicating within the community over time a possible change.

In contrast to Hawthorne, Tolstoy provides no real female fellowship for Anna. After being shamed by Mme. Kartasova and the other "self-constituted [female] judges" at the opera, Anna Karenina retreats from society and suffers in her isolation.[39] In an early draft of the novel, Tolstoy had Kitty resolve to try to rehabilitate Anna in society (only to learn that she had killed herself) (20:379), but he discarded this idea. In the final version, Anna is cut off from the companionship of women, except Dolly. In Part 6, when Anna and Vronsky settle at Vozdvizhenskoe after leaving Petersburg, Dolly braves a visit in an act of sisterly compassion. As she rides there, liberated from her maternal cares, Dolly's mind is subject to its own somewhat phantasmagoric stream of consciousness—it is "preternaturally active," much as Hester's was on the scaffold and as Anna's will be on her last carriage ride. As Dolly thinks about Anna, she examines her own conscience, asking herself whether in Anna's place she might have done the same, even musing about an affair of her own and picking Turovtsyn as her modal lover. She refuses to condemn Anna because "God has put into our souls [the desire to live]" (6:16, 608). Dolly thus seems to embrace the moral of the gospel paradigm about judging the adulteress. However, Dolly has trouble sustaining her compassion for Anna. She becomes alienated from her while still at Vozdvizhenskoe, although on her return to Pokrovskoe she "would not let anyone say a word against [Anna and Vronsky]" (6:24, 642). When Anna, just before her suicide, visits Dolly and finds Kitty there, Kitty does battle between "animosity toward this vile woman" and "the desire to be lenient to her." Eventually Kitty conquers her nasty feelings and looks into Anna's eyes with compassion; later, when left alone with her sister, Kitty professes her pity for Anna (7:28, 759–60). In this scene, Tolstoy thus shows in Kitty the tension between two opposing responses to the adulteress.

Whether the Shcherbatsky sisters might have done more for Anna in her last hour is a question that haunts the end of *Anna Karenina*. (For discussion, see chapter 3.) Anna sought Dolly's comfort, but as she leaves, Anna is bitter and merciless toward others (and herself). As Tolstoy shows Anna beyond the pale in her final hours, he exaggerates and makes perverse a quality also seen in Hester Prynne. Ostracized and condemned, the adulteresses become preternaturally aware that their persecutors are themselves not without sin.[40] Hester's scarlet A gives her a "new sense"—so that as she circulates among "her neighbors and townspeople," she is well aware that "if the truth were to be shown, a scarlet letter would blaze forth on many a bosom besides" her own. She develops "a sympathetic knowledge of the hidden sin in others' hearts," which is "awful and loathsome"; "the red infamy upon her breast would give a sympathetic throb, as she passed near a venerable minister or magistrate, the model of piety and justice"; or she would feel a "mystic sisterhood" with a matron or young maiden (5, 78). Hawthorne also observes that Hester looks "from [an] estranged point of view at human institutions, and whatever priests or legislators had established; criticizing all with hardly more reverence than the Indian would feel for the clerical band, the judicial robe, the pillory, the gallows, the fireside, or the church." This "estranged point of view" has "set her free" (18, 174). The "estranged point of view" of Hawthorne's free-thinking New World adulteress, which is like that of the "Indian," anticipates Tolstoy's practice of *ostranenie* [defamiliarization], which readers remarked on even before Shklovsky assigned it a name.[41]

Tolstoy makes it amply clear that "if the truth were to be shown" in the world he creates, scarlet letters would blaze forth on many bosoms beyond Anna's: the society that shames and shuns Anna is depraved and, for all its Christian rhetoric, does not live according to the spirit of Christ's teaching in 8:1–11. Anna becomes uncannily aware of the sins of others early on: starting with the anger she (correctly) notices in the "Christian" Countess Lydia (1:32, 108), who later becomes one of Anna's more stern and vicious judges, and culminating in Anna's assertions in her inner monologue at her death that "we all hate each other" and "we all want something sweet, tasty. If not candy, then dirty ice cream. And Kitty's the same: if not Vronsky, then Levin" (7:29, 760). Whereas Hawthorne makes us feel that Hester's judgments about her neighbors' hidden sin are on target, Tolstoy shows Anna's judgments become more and more vicious. And he provides us with more access to the inner worlds of those Anna judges. As with Hester, Anna's position as adulteress estranges her from human institutions and makes her prone to free-thinking. But, in contrast to Hester, Anna is never "set free" by her estranged point of view. On the contrary, it becomes a hell from which Tolstoy offers her little hope of escape.

Convicted by His Own Conscience, Sharing the Scarlet Letter, and Dividing the Plot

In "The Custom House," Nathaniel Hawthorne (or the narrator) announces that *The Scarlet Letter* will be "Hester Prynne's story" and prepares the reader for the revelation of the mysteries of her life and of the scarlet letter. He describes holding it up to his own breast, only to let it "fall upon the floor," so intense was the sensation of its "burning heat." Although he goes on to tell the story of this "singular woman," as promised, much of the narrative tension and dramatic interest depends on what goes on in the conscience of Arthur Dimmesdale, the charismatic young minister who, unbeknownst to the community who worships him, was Hester's lover and is Pearl's father. (The cuckolded husband, Roger Chillingsworth, also plays a significant role.) As the narrative describes Hester's life with the scarlet letter on her breast and Pearl by her side, it includes interactions between them and Dimmesdale, which are tantalizing for the reader who suspects, then knows, what is really being said between them, whereas the community does not. (One critic calls Dimmesdale "a master of doublespeak.")[42]

Hawthorne builds suspense through the expectation that truth will out. At length, several years into the action of the novel, right after his triumphant Election Day sermon, Dimmesdale stands with Hester and Pearl on the scaffold, confesses paternity, reveals a scarlet letter "imprinted in the flesh" of his breast, which he declares to be "no more than the type of what has seared his inmost heart," only to die in Hester's arms, praising God's name and surrendering to his will. At last, Dimmesdale has been "convicted by his own conscience" (John 8:9).

At this point Hawthorne makes masculine guilt the dramatic focal point of his novel. In doing so, Hawthorne brings it in line with the gospel pericope. As Larry J. Kreitzer points out, Dimmesdale corresponds to the figure who has mysteriously disappeared from the gospel story: if the woman was "taken in adultery—in the very act," then what happened to the man with whom she was doing the act?[43] But, at the same time, Dimmesdale, as a member of the religious establishment responsible for the judgment of the adulteress, also occupies the position of the scribes and Pharisees. In the gospel story, the scribes' and Pharisees' recognition of their own sin constitutes the real dramatic denouement of the story.[44] Hawthorne's novel thus simultaneously answers the gospel mystery of the hidden partner and graphically dramatizes the conviction of one of the Pharisees by his own conscience. This even makes us wonder whether the woman taken in adultery was ever as central to the gospel story as expected. Was it ever really her plot?

Critics from Henry James through Darrel Abel have argued that Arthur Dimmesdale is the real tragic hero of *The Scarlet Letter*. James declares that "the story indeed is in a secondary degree that of Hester Prynne" and that she is "an accessory figure" after the first scene; Abel considers Dimmesdale's to be "the main tragic problem" and argues that the plot consists of the struggle for his soul.[45] But what about Hester Prynne? Nina Baym rebuts these arguments, reminding us that Hester is announced as the subject in "The Custom House" and that she appears throughout the novel whereas Dimmesdale's appearances are limited. Baym asserts that "if a single protagonist is to be chosen, the identity of Hester as protagonist is established as the true center of the novel." But she concedes: "At the most, one could make an argument for a divided focus in the romance between Hester and Dimmesdale."[46] For all its apparent unity, *The Scarlet Letter* splits its focus. The story of the adulteress Hester Prynne threatens to become the agony of the male hero, Arthur Dimmesdale. *The Scarlet Letter* is a double plot.

The overtly multiplot *Anna Karenina* has been subject to similar questions. Critics often divide the novel between Anna and Levin, with the Oblonskys also getting some share. Explanations abound for why Tolstoy ended up with a double story. Victorian multiplot novels by authors he openly admired (Dickens, Eliot) provided models for this form. Eikhenbaum has argued that Tolstoy was inspired by English family novels, and wanted to move beyond the strict confines of romantic love plots associated with the French novel. *Anna Karenina*'s multiplot form could also have developed out of Tolstoy's need (as Leavis puts it) to "to find room for all his interests, experiences, and problems." Levin's quasi-autobiographical status makes him a good vehicle for this. But evidence within *Anna Karenina* suggests that *part* of Tolstoy's rationale for the divided focus (the inclusion of the Levin plot) was intrinsic to the adultery plot as he understood it. Like Hawthorne, Tolstoy felt the need to divert the focus from the adulteress and incorporate a tragic struggle for the soul of a masculine hero.

Obviously, Dimmesdale's and Levin's respective roles in the adultery plots are very different. Dimmesdale is integral to the adultery plot as Hester's lover and Pearl's father. Yet Dimmesdale actually remains curiously withdrawn from Hester, even when he briefly unites with her in the forest and contemplates escape, and even when he dies in her arms. Dimmesdale denies Hester and Pearl even as he acknowledges them, because his ultimate concern is not for them, but for his own soul. What matters to him is his own "triumphant ignominy before the people!" (23, 222)—the public confession, which he believes essential to his salvation. Although the narrator asserts that Pearl's reunion with her father was critical to her development ("as her tears fell upon her father's cheek, they were the pledge that she would grow up amid joy and sorrow, nor for ever do battle with the world, but be a woman in it"), the long-anticipated revelation of Dimmesdale as her father does not heal the alienation between the two plots. What matters to Dimmesdale is his relationship with God and the community.

In the final epilogue-like chapter, the narrator also mystifies Dimmesdale's revelation of that red stigma on his own breast by reporting different versions of events circulated by spectators, then announcing: "The reader may choose among these theories."[47] The narrator even adds that "certain persons" denied that Dimmesdale admitted to his adultery with Hester or paternity of Pearl: "Neither, by their report, had his dying words acknowledged, nor even remotely implied, any,

the slightest, connection, on his part, with the guilt for which Hester
Prynne had so long worn the scarlet letter." Rather, "according to these
highly respectable witnesses," Dimmesdale "by yielding up his breath
in the arms of a fallen woman . . . had made the manner of his death a
parable, in order to impress on his admirers the mighty and mournful
lesson, that, in the view of Infinite Purity, we are sinners all alike" (24,
224). Thus, Dimmesdale's friends attempt to whitewash him of the taint
of Hester's scarlet letter by presenting his final act as a (histrionic) expression of the Christian doctrine of shared sin: nobody is without it. For
the record, the narrator believes that Dimmesdale was Pearl's father
and that these "highly respectable" friends of Dimmesdale are prevari-
cating. Yet their argument, even if fabricated to veil the truth, is an
attempt to reimagine their community as less vindictive. The masterplot
of the pericope is still in operation: Dimmesdale, according to his friends,
was *not* Hester's partner in adultery, but he was acting out—in tragic
mode—the part of scribe and Pharisee, as he is convicted by his own
conscience and acknowledges that nobody is without sin.

In *Anna Karenina*, Levin and Anna, despite their family connections
(through Dolly and Stiva), are not even acquainted until Part 7, when
they meet for the first and only time. In his letter to Sergei Rachinsky,
Tolstoy defended his design, explaining that the unity of his novel did
not depend on acquaintance between the characters or on events in
the plot.[48] Tolstoy leaves us to wend our way through the novel, fueled
by the desire to solve the mystery of the connection (or lack thereof)
between Anna and Levin. The suspense in *Anna Karenina*, like that in
The Scarlet Letter, arises from the tension of the divided plot. Does
Levin's plot have "the slightest connection with the guilt" of Anna? If
in *The Scarlet Letter* the "tragic problem" emerges from Dimmesdale's
recognition of his connection to Hester, then in *Anna Karenina* does the
"tragic problem" come from Levin acknowledging his connection to
Anna Karenina, if only by admitting that "we are all sinners alike" and
that in this respect he is her brother?

Readers thus seek the links between the two plots in Levin's conscience, if not in his actions. *Anna Karenina* does not treat its readers to a
grand revelation of Levin's "own red stigma" on the order of Dimmesdale's confession.[49] Yet the novel intimates that Levin may feel a connection to Anna, and not simply because of a possible erotic attraction
(although that is not irrelevant). What readers may seek is for Levin to
acknowledge his human connection to Anna: does Levin feel that
Anna's death diminishes him? The "tragic problem" Tolstoy poses in his

multiplot *Anna Karenina* is about what Anna's misery and death have to do with the rest of mankind, starting with Levin.

As if to invite readers to connect Levin to the adultery plot, Tolstoy punctuates Levin's romantic and religious quest with his struggle between, on the one hand, a righteous, even judgmental, attitude toward adulterers and fallen women and, on the other, his awareness of his own sexual sins. Early in the conversation between Oblonsky and Levin over dinner and wine that recalls Plato's "Symposium," Levin, trying to screw up his courage to propose to Kitty, confesses to Stiva his horror at the thought of his own impurity in the face of Kitty's purity. Oblonsky immediately tries to dismiss Levin's sexual sins, on the grounds of there not being many of them. Oblonsky's own are legion, but the irony is that he lacks a sense of sexual guilt. Levin, however, says that his only consolation is "that I should be forgiven not according to my deserts but out of loving-kindness, as in the prayer that I have always loved. That is the only way she can forgive" (1:10, 39). At this point, Levin puts Kitty, his modal bride, in the position of God granting him absolution, which is troubling. That the prayer Levin loves in fact contains echoes of Psalm 50/51, David's prayer for mercy after his adultery with Bathsheba (which led to her husband's slaughter), adds to the meaningfulness of this detail in the context of Levin's conversation with Oblonsky (about forgiving sexual sins). For the present, all Levin is concerned with is *his* sin and *Kitty's* forgiveness. Will he move to true David-like humility before God?

But then Levin, appealing to Plato, divides love into two mutually exclusive kinds: pure and dirty. He labels women associated with the latter vermin and dismisses them as beneath contempt. Oblonsky protests against Levin's categorical judgments and tries to get him to see individual cases. "Just then Levin remembered his own sins and the inner struggle he had gone through." Levin "added unexpectedly: 'However, it's possible you're right. Very possible . . . But I don't know, I really don't know'" (1:10, 42). Here, as David Parker has argued, Tolstoy gestures at the gospel pericope as he shows Levin being, like the scribes and Pharisees, convicted by his own conscience, so that he refrains from further censure of Oblonsky and other sexual sinners.[50] Levin even seems to make a concerted effort to internalize the dictum of "go and sin no more" when, in his misery over the failed proposal to Kitty, he vows "never again to allow himself to be carried away by a vile passion" (1:26; 92). Later in the novel, finally engaged to Kitty, Levin attempts to lay his guilty conscience to rest by staging a form of confession as he has Kitty read his diary. The act of baring his heart (with its scarlet stigmata), even though done in private to Kitty, may not be as overtly histrionic as Dimmesdale's more public revelations, but it shows his Dimmesdale-like concern with his own righteousness.

When, at last Levin meets Anna in the flesh, he finds himself responding compassionately to her, wondering about her interior life, in marked contrast to his past harsh judgments about Anna (7:10, 700–701). (For discussion of this scene, see chapter 3.) At this point, Levin overcomes his tendency to judge others for their sexual sins, a fact that the narrator signals by drawing attention to the switch in Levin's attitude to Anna (7:10, 701). He no longer treats Anna as a token of a type (women with scarlet letters), but as an individual. Yet what begins as a novelization of the message of the gospel pericope takes another turn. In the mode of Hawthorne, the narrator gives us different versions of what really occurred (as with Dimmesdale's revelation of his red stigma) and leaves "the reader [to] choose among these theories." In the aftermath of this scene, with Kitty again in the role of confessor, Levin concludes that whatever feelings of pity and fear he (seems to have) felt in response to Anna were misguided, and that he was guilty of what Jesus calls "adultery of the heart." Kitty, sounding like one of Hawthorne's goodwives, says: "You've fallen in love with that vile woman. She's bewitched you" (7:11, 703). Levin acquiesces to Kitty's version of the events. But, as with the scribes and Pharisees in the gospel story, we are left to wonder, what next? Levin eventually suffers his own crisis, which twins him with Anna, yet Tolstoy includes no Hawthorne-style solidarity with "the fallen woman"—not even any indication that Levin recollects her in the depths of his consciousness.

Hush, Hester, Hush!
Convicted by His Own Conscience

To the bewilderment of many readers, including Virginia Woolf, the final section of *Anna Karenina* focuses on Levin's "religious feelings" to the *apparent* exclusion of Anna Karenina. Woolf writes: "All the stress finally upon his religious feelings—as if they predominated momentarily, as they wd [would] in real life; but this is unsatisfactory in a work of art where the other feelings have been around for so long." Woolf also observes that Tolstoy seems to have been "hindered by the double story."[51] Like Hawthorne, Tolstoy splits the focus of his adultery novel so that the agony of the masculine hero, as he is convicted by his own conscience and "remembers God," brings the action to a climax. The male hero's plot in each novel ends as he reaffirms God's law. Where does this leave the adulteress? Has she become, in the words of Henry James, "an accessory figure"? In *Anna Karenina*, Anna is dead by the time Levin resolves his religious crisis, whereas Hester lives on after the religious agony and ecstasy that come right before Dimmesdale's death. Yet in both novels the reader is left to ask how the resolution of the hero's religious crisis, treated as a matter of life and death, relates to the heroine's fate.

The *Scarlet Letter* is known for the anxiety it generates about interpreting signs and texts, from the letter A, to the Scriptures, the Laws and the Statutes, the Logos, not to mention "awful hieroglyphics, on the cope of heaven." While the narrative invites freedom of interpretation, Hawthorne also reminds us of the corollary: as John Irwin observes, "the shattering of all absolutes because of the loss of objective knowledge."[52] Of particular concern are questions of how the law is interpreted by "a people amongst whom religion and law were almost identical" (2, 47). Figuring in the background and often cropping up in the body of *The Scarlet Letter*, as well as more directly in the introductory "Custom House," is the Puritan patriarchs' struggle to discipline Quakers, Antinomians, and others who offered their own interpretations of the Word and the Law. At stake is a New World version of the challenge to Jesus and his response in the gospel tale of adultery: the scribes and the Pharisees appeal to the rule of law as interpreted by the patriarchs, saying, "Now Moses in the law commanded us, that such should be stoned." To their challenge, "What sayest thou?," Jesus finds a way of upholding the law while at the same time calling for the scribes and Pharisees to find their own interpretation of the law in their individual conscience and, on that basis, cast the first stone or not.

The Scarlet Letter is haunted by the presence of Ann Hutchinson, "foundress of a religious sect" (13, 144), an Antinomian expelled from Massachusetts for refusing to accept the Puritan patriarchs' interpretation of the Scriptures as authoritative and definitive. Hutchinson believed that the Holy Spirit might dictate to an individual conscience (even a feminine one) behavior that defies the patriarchal exegesis of the Word. Hawthorne's fascination with Ann Hutchinson, documented in an early sketch, is manifest in Hawthorne's own "labyrinth of linkages" in *The Scarlet Letter*. Most significantly, at what the narrator calls the "threshold" of his narrative, he pauses to draw our attention to a rosebush. The narrator tells us that it may be a native plant that "merely survived out of the stern old wilderness"; but then he adds that there is "fair authority for believing that it had sprung up under the footsteps of the sainted Ann Hutchinson, as she entered the prison-door." (In typical fashion, Hawthorne's narrator leaves interpretation open by refusing to provide one authoritative version of the genesis of this rosebush.) The narrator then "pluck[s] one of its flowers" and "present[s] it to the reader" (1, 46). In doing so, the narrator hands the reader the power and the freedom to interpret signs for himself, according to his individual conscience, in imitation of Ann Hutchinson (or Hester Prynne). It is also possible that if the reader is clutching this rose from Ann Hutchinson's rosebush, he or she may be less likely to cast the stones.

As Michael J. Colacurcio has shown, Hawthorne suggests that Hester Prynne is walking in Ann Hutchinson's footsteps as she experiences her own personal form of antinomianism in which "the world's law [is] no law to her mind" (13, 143) or when she tries to confirm with Dimmesdale that what they did had "a consecration of its own" (17, 170).[53] The narrator writes that Hester was prone to "a freedom of speculation, then common enough on the other side of the Atlantic, but which our forefathers, had they known of it, would have held to be a deadlier crime than that stigmatized by the scarlet letter" (13, 143). From the start, when Hester took up her needle to embroider the letter dictated to her by the powers that be, she interpreted the sign by her own inner light, which was beyond their control. Thereafter, Hawthorne seems to take particular interest in showing that interpretations of its meaning were similarly unfettered: some members of the community come to believe that the "A" on Hester's breast stood for angel.

While the Hester plot of *The Scarlet Letter* introduces us to an inner freedom, the Dimmesdale plot toes the Puritan patriarchal line. This becomes clear in his confession, which Henry James and others have identified as the tragic denouement of the whole novel. After his triumphant Election Day sermon, Dimmesdale, finally convicted by his own conscience, mounts the scaffold, confesses his sin, and reveals "his own red stigma," presenting it as proof to the people of "God's judgment on a sinner" (23, 221). In his farewell to Hester, spoken from the scaffold, the dying Dimmesdale, even as he relies on Hester's strength, reminds her (and the crowd witnessing this scene) of God's law, thus intimating that while he did give way to temptation years ago, and while he had been *tempted* more recently by Hester's antinomian attitudes (when she urged flight to Europe), he was now fully submitting to the rule of

God's law as traditionally understood. And when Hester asks, "Shall we not meet again? Shall we not spend our immortal life together?," suggesting that "surely, surely, we have ransomed one another, with all this woe," Dimmesdale's response is:

> "Hush, Hester, hush! . . . The law we broke!—the sin here so awfully revealed!—let these alone be in thy thoughts! I fear! I fear! It may be that, when we forgot our God,—when we violated our reverence each for the other's soul,—it was thenceforth vain to hope that we could meet hereafter, in an everlasting and pure union." (23, 222)

As he hushes Hester, Dimmesdale reveals that his concern is the salvation of his own soul. Dimmesdale believes that without this repentant confession and "this triumphant ignominy before the people" he would be lost forever. As he dies, he surrenders himself to God's will, saying "Praised be his name! His will be done! Farewell!" In this respect, he plays the role of penitent prodigal son, surrendering to his father's mercy. The fact that this follows his Election Day speech, in which, drawing on his subject ("the relation between the Deity and the communities of mankind, with a special reference to the New England which they were here planting in the wilderness"), he, prophet-like, "foretell[s] a high and glorious destiny for the newly gathered people of God," further aligns the dying Dimmesdale with Puritan patriarchal values, among them the triumphalist notion that the Puritans are God's chosen people.[54] He is a penitent prodigal son.

Convicted by His Own Conscience:
The Prodigal Son Plot in the Novel of Adultery

The resolution of Levin's religious crisis, different as it is from that of the Puritan Dimmesdale, fulfills many of the same functions in *Anna Karenina*'s structure: Levin's crisis, like Dimmesdale's, diverts attention from the adulteress. Anna, as Woolf put it, "is allowed to drop out." Levin is certainly not burdened with a hidden sin, as is Dimmesdale. (Levin even appears to have purged himself of the sexual guilt that tormented him earlier in the novel.) Still, both novels of adultery focus on a masculine hero who is desperate for a clean conscience.

Dimmesdale and Levin each seek signs of approval from God. Dimmesdale, while tormented by his conscience, travels around Boston (much as Levin travels around Pokrovskoe), taking possibly random phenomena as personal messages from God. For example, Dimmesdale interprets a meteor, which looks like an A, as a sign from heaven directed to him individually. The narrator, willing to accept the Puritan tendency to believe that "the destiny of nations should be revealed, in these awful hieroglyphics, on the cope of heaven," is skeptical about Dimmesdale's assumption that the meteor is a personal message to him in particular: "But what shall we say, when an individual [Dimmesdale] discovers a revelation, addressed to himself alone, on the same vast sheet of record! In such a case, it could only be the symptom of a highly disordered mental state, when a man, rendered morbidly self-contemplative by long, intense, and secret pain, had extended his egotism over the whole expanse of nature, until the firmament itself should appear no more than a fitting page for his soul's history and fate" (12, 136). Hawthorne's narrator thus views Dimmesdale's penchant for seeking signs as a symptom of his egotistical obsession with his own sin and salvation.

Tolstoy's Levin similarly looks to natural phenomena in the sky (clouds, stars, etc.) for signs from God. Then, at the bitter end of the novel, Levin once again contemplates the sky. He takes the stars that reappear following flashes of lightning "in the same places, as if thrown by some unerring hand" as confirmation of God's active presence in the universe and then acknowledges that "the laws of goodness" that he had just embraced, after a long struggle with his own conscience, had in fact been revealed by God. Furthermore, Levin reasons, "by acknowledging [these laws of goodness] I do not so much unite myself as I am united, whether I will or no, with others in one community of believers which is called the Church" (8:19, 815). In this gesture of surrender to the community of the Church, Levin appears to overcome his willful egotism. Presumably, he will no longer seek "revelation, addressed to himself alone" on the cope of heaven. Levin, who has up until now been nonconformist, may chafe under the constraints of membership in this "community of believers." After all, Levin shares some of Hester's nonconformist and outsider tendencies, as well as her wariness about institutions. But *Anna Karenina* ends abruptly with Levin's return to the fold.

Both Levin's and Dimmesdale's plots thus follow the familiar Christian morphology of the prodigal son. While Dimmesdale and Levin initially feel lost in a realm of hieroglyphics, which they struggle to decipher, they come to see the Logos writ clear.[55] Levin's revelation (from the muzhik Fyodor) is about the need to "remember God" and "to "live for the soul" (8:11, 794) while Dimmesdale bemoans that he and Hester "forgot our God" and "violated our reverence each for the other's soul" (24, 216). Levin embraces the law of loving one's neighbor, whereas Dimmesdale is more concerned with having broken one of God's laws. But both men reaffirm God's law and surrender to God's will.

Levin, now viewing himself as united "with others in one community of believers which is called the Church," is, however, still bothered by one question—namely, whether God would have revealed himself only to Christians, excluding from salvation those of other faiths. By contrast, Dimmesdale unabashedly declares, in his Election Day sermon, the glorious destiny of the Puritans in their own New Jerusalem. Tolstoy's Levin has no interest in this kind of triumphalism (although it does show up at the end of *Anna Karenina* in Koznyshev's vision of united Slavic brethren spreading the Slavic idea throughout the world). In his different frame of reference, Levin embraces and celebrates an alternative (Russian) mix of politics and Christian theology. Thus, as Levin reminds those who, gathered at Pokrovskoe, debate whether Russians should fight in the Balkans, the Russian folk express their Christian spirit by abnegating political power, surrendering it to the Varangians (once upon a time) and to the tsar (in the present). They are content to let the tsar decide matters of destiny and declarations of war. As the beekeeper says of the tsar, "He sees better" [Ему виднее] (8:15, 807). The Russian idea set forth here is the opposite of what Hawthorne presents as the Puritan view of religion and law being identical.

Levin argues against a special connection to his "co-religionists," the Serbs, which would justify war against the Turks. However, in his desire to belong to the community of the Christian faithful, Levin consciously decides to stop worrying about what had hitherto been an obstacle to faith, namely, the fate of righteous non-Christians. (Levin could not understand how they could be "deprived of the highest good, without which life has no meaning" [8:19, 815].) When Levin decides that he does not "have the right or possibility of resolving the question of other believers and their attitude to the Deity," he concludes that his earthly, rational judgment is nothing in comparison to the wisdom of God the Father. In the final line of the novel, which emphasizes that his life is "no longer meaningless as before," and now has "the unquestionable meaning of goodness, which it is in [his] power to put into it," Levin re-embraces the faith of his fathers, although on his own terms and by his own free will (8:19, 815–17). Thus, both heroes end their plots yielded to God, Dimmesdale in his histrionic mode and Levin more modestly.

At the ends of their novels, Hawthorne and Tolstoy also suggest the penitence of the adulteress, but only in cursory terms, so that the women's plots lack the male heroes' more complete returns to the bosom of God. Just before dying, after the inner monologue in which she, not unlike Levin, seeks meaning in life, Anna Karenina begs God for forgiveness. But Anna drops out here. Vronsky's mother is granted the final and only eulogy, which is full of animosity, and suggests that "she ended as such a woman should have ended," while Koznyshev reminds her that "it is not for us to judge" (8:4, 778). Koznyshev's words return us to the epigraph in which we are reminded that vengeance is the Lord's. The corollary is that the Lord may have mercy. In *The Scarlet Letter*, we learn briefly from the epilogue-like final chapter that "penitence" was in store for Hester Prynne in the long years before her death, even if she continued to show freedom of spirit in affirming to those she comforts that she believes that "a new truth would be revealed, in order to establish the whole relation between man and woman on a surer ground of mutual happiness" (24, 227).

As *The Scarlet Letter* ends, Hester and Dimmesdale share a tombstone with one enigmatic epitaph, although their graves are kept apart, "with a space between, as if the dust of the two sleepers had no right to mingle" (24, 228). Thus, Hawthorne brings Arthur Dimmesdale and Hester Prynne—and their plots—together at the end, only to remind us of what separates them. In *Anna Karenina*, Tolstoy leaves the (hidden, analogical) relations of Anna and Levin murky and he plays on the reader's desire for the mysterious relationship between the two plots to be revealed. (That there is a kind of novelistic counterpoint in action is clear enough already.) But, just as Hawthorne creates mystification at the end, challenging "the curious investigator" "to perplex himself with the purport" of the engraving on the shared tombstone (24, 228), Tolstoy leaves it up to the reader "to perplex himself with the purport" of his double plots and their interrelation.

As Q. D. Leavis observes, Tolstoy and Hawthorne both made their novels of adultery "inclusive." The blueprint for this expansion of novelistic boundaries is to be found in the gospel pericope of the woman taken in adultery, which focuses on the members of the community judging the adulteress and looking at their own conscience. In both *Anna Karenina* and *The Scarlet Letter*, the novelists show the community's response, but also develop a masculine plot that divides the novel's focus. This is less pronounced in *The Scarlet Letter*, but perhaps more disturbing because of the actual connection between Hester Prynne and Arthur Dimmesdale. In *Anna Karenina*, where Levin's plot is largely independent of Anna's, the reader must ultimately do what the narrator of *The Scarlet Letter* asks of his reader—that is, choose for himself among various possibilities. In this case, the choice is how to relate the two (or three) plots, or how much tension to see between them. To be sure, the reader can read the plots as related in the manner of counterpoint, and leave it at that.[56] Or the reader can assume that the adultery theme exerts a pull on the novel as a whole, so that even when Levin's plot apparently has nothing to do with Anna's, it is still to be read in relation to it. Anna's misery and death diminish the life of those who gather at Pokrovskoe, whether they acknowledge it or not. One profound effect of Tolstoy's multiplot is to prime the reader for the multiple choice that is a key to Hawthorne's poetics and ethics. Even when it seems that the adulteress has "dropped out," the novel never loses sight of the questions of conscience, community, compassion, and judgment that the tale of adultery raises. And in this respect, the scarlet letter in *Anna Karenina* does its office.

3

Loving Your Neighbor
in *Middlemarch* and
Anna Karenina

Varieties of Multiplot Novels

Anna Karenina and the English Novel of Neighborly Love

Anna Karenina has been hailed as the Russian response to Flaubert's classic French novel of adultery, *Madame Bovary: Moeurs de province* (1856–57).[1] But *Anna Karenina* also responds to the English novel. Russian formalist Boris Eikhenbaum notes that *Anna Karenina* "initially appears to have been created according to European forms": it seems to be what results when the "tradition of the English family novel is crossed with that of the French adultery novel." Eikhenbaum goes on to explain, however, that what Tolstoy really sought was to break away from these traditional forms and subjects and out "into a wider sphere of human relations."[2] On these grounds, the English forerunner for *Anna Karenina* is George Eliot's *Middlemarch: A Study of Provincial Life* (1872). In this multiplot study of *English* provincial mores, George Eliot provides a riposte to *Madame Bovary* and the tradition of the French novel of adultery.[3] But she also challenges the conventions of the

English novel of courtship and family life. What she was really after in *Middlemarch*, according to J. Hillis Miller, was "a total picture": to do this, her strategy was to "cast a wide net" and "aim at inclusiveness."[4] She thus adapted the multiplot form to capture (English-style) the "wider sphere of human relations" that beckoned to Tolstoy as he wrote *Anna Karenina*.

In embracing this "wider sphere of human relations," *Middlemarch* retains features that Tolstoy and other Russian readers associated with the English novel. *Middlemarch* still celebrates family values. And it includes its share of courtship plots and it also builds on that other staple of the English novel, the inheritance plot, which likewise depends on selection and exclusion. But George Eliot makes *Middlemarch* more than the tale of how Dorothea Brooke got (re)married, achieved family happiness, and produced an heir to the Brooke patrimony. As George Eliot weaves together several plotlines, she programmatically encourages the reader to value human relations beyond courtship, marriage, and family life. In this way *Middlemarch* provided Tolstoy with an English form, if not to follow, then to depart from.[5]

Tolstoy openly admired the work of George Eliot and listed her among the writers who had a strong impact on him as he wrote *Anna Karenina*.[6] Her *Adam Bede* was one of the handful of novels singled out in *What Is Art?* as good art because they promote love of neighbor and love of God (30:150); adultery, Tolstoy complained, seemed to be the "only" and "favorite" theme of other novels (30:88). When the young Tolstoy first read *Scenes of Clerical Life* in 1859, he announced that it was "a moral and religious book." Writing about it to Alexandrine Tolstoy, Tolstoy declared: "Happy [or Blessed] are those who, like the English imbibe with their milk Christian teaching, and in such a lofty, purified form as evangelical Protestantism."[7] It is clear from the context that the Russian Orthodoxy Tolstoy imbibed with his milk left him spiritually hungry. But he understood that George Eliot's pure English forms would neither suit his Russian reality nor satisfy his needs.[8] Still, for the rest of Tolstoy's career, George Eliot figured in his (often very critical) mind as a master of the art of representing English moral and religious experience in novelistic form.

In *Middlemarch* George Eliot treats openly the questions that haunt *Anna Karenina*: Who is my neighbor and how should I love him—or her? In critical moves that affect the construction and meaning of her novel, George Eliot sets forth her multiplotted *Middlemarch* as a new literary form—a "home epic"—grounded in a new heroism based on acts of neighborly love (Finale, 832).[9] While *Anna Karenina* is more obviously a novel of adultery and family love, and whereas Tolstoy declared that the "family idea" provided this novel's artistic coherence, it is vexed with questions about loving one's neighbor.[10]

In *Anna Karenina*, Tolstoy adapts the multiplot form in a way that is very different from George Eliot: neighborly love is channeled and controlled rather than "dispersed" as in *Middlemarch*. Formal differences between the two novels—especially in how their various narrative lines combine—reflect Tolstoy's and Eliot's different conceptions within their novels of the question "who is my neighbor?" In *Anna Karenina*, Anna and Levin, the two characters who emerge as the heroes of the two main plots of the novel, are kept apart throughout most of the novel.[11] When chided by his friend Sergei Rachinsky for failing to draw together his two main plots, Tolstoy responded that he was proud of the "architectonics" of *Anna Karenina* and that he purposely concealed the keystones of its arches. He dismissed the idea of linking together his plots on the level of plot (фабула) or through the "relations (acquaintance) of characters" [на отношениях (знакомстве) лиц].[12] As Joan Grossman has observed, this letter makes overt what Tolstoy does differently from George Eliot: whereas Eliot's method in *Middlemarch* was to use "the principles of analogy and convergence," Tolstoy relied on the former to the virtual exclusion of the latter.[13]

The *hidden* architectonics of *Anna Karenina* has often been taken as a sign of artistic sophistication and proof that Henry James and his disciple Percy Lubbock were wrong to dismiss Tolstoy's novels as baggy monsters lacking in artistic meaning and devoid of literary craftsmanship. Tolstoy's decision to "hide" the plot connections puts the burden on the reader to identify paradigmatic links. Indeed, according to Tolstoy, meaning in *Anna Karenina* is embedded in a "labyrinth of linkages": it is the reader's task to discern and interpret these linkages.[14] Yet the reader is still left with the morphology of Tolstoy's multiplot novel. Why the dark labyrinth? Why not allow convergences of plot and interaction of characters?

When we examine *Anna Karenina* in the light of *Middlemarch* with an eye to differences in how they treat neighborly love, not only does the hidden architectonics of Tolstoy's novel become more apparent, but so, too, do the abysses. Whereas George Eliot creates a realm in which souls cry out to each other simply because they are "embroiled" in the same "fitfully-illuminated" medium of life (30, 290), Tolstoy leaves us wondering whether any human being hears Anna's cry.

George Eliot and the Multiplot Form of Victorian Fiction: The Blessed Influence of One True Loving Human Soul on Another

Middlemarch is often regarded as George Eliot's masterpiece, one of the great Victorian novels, and a sterling example of the multiplot form.[15] While the form of the multiplot novel exhibits wide variation, it lends itself naturally to questions of human relatedness, not merely among kin and lovers. According to Gillian Beer, *Middlemarch* encourages readers to think about different kinds of relations between disparate and separate characters by "set[ing]" them "alongside" and thus "revealing further and further affinities of event and of feeling between characters who have no personal relationship to each other."[16] Although narrative lines will sometimes intertwine to produce links between plots and characters, the multiplot form has a special affinity for highlighting paradigmatic connections. In many multiplot novels the narrator explicitly draws attention to the interrelatedness of the lives of those George Eliot calls "unintroduced strangers." And some of the heroes themselves ask what their lives have to do with those of their neighbors, both familiar and unintroduced.[17] Particular narrators and characters do this to varying degrees, but the general effect is enough to prompt J. Hillis Miller to regard a heightened "awareness of self *in relation to others*" as vital to the form of Victorian fiction (including the multiplot novels). As Miller argues, these novels "aim at inclusiveness."[18]

The rise of this particularly *inclusive* form has been tied to the specific conditions of Victorian England: scientific, religious, and political factors heightened the importance of relatedness. Scientific developments went hand in hand with anxieties about the role of God in the universe and of religious faith in daily life.[19] Darwin played a central role, even if his "discoveries" were the natural extension of ideas that were already in the air—and of plots that were already in print. In *Darwin's Plots: Evolutionary Narrative in Darwin, George Eliot and Nineteenth-Century Fiction,* Beer draws attention to the cross-fertilization between Darwin and his contemporary Victorian novelists, including George Eliot.[20] Like Darwin, nineteenth-century novelists celebrated forms of diversity while revealing new manifestations of relatedness. In *Darwin and the Novelists,* George Levine observes that while "novels are not science," "both incorporate the fundamental notions of the real that dominate the culture"; furthermore, Darwinian science acted on the *form* of the Victorian novel, as well as on "the patterns it exploits and develops, the relationships it allows." Victorian novels invite the reader to see that "all living things are related in intricate and often subtle patterns of inheritance, cousinship, mutual dependence." In Levine's words, "the Victorian multiplot novel is a fictional manifestation of the attitudes implicit in the metaphor of entanglement in Darwin."[21] But this metaphor has been subject to a variety of interpretations.

Tolstoy believed that Darwin's thought merely rationalized and validated the struggle for survival and made life godless and meaningless. (As Hugh McLean has demonstrated, Tolstoy was to remain an inveterate Darwin-basher until his dying day.[22]) By contrast, George Eliot found in Darwin's plots and metaphors scientific corroboration of her belief that altruism and brotherhood would increase as humankind evolved. Sally Shuttleworth explains that George Eliot shared the view of her companion George Lewes that "sexuality in the highly evolved being is transmuted into altruism."[23] Whereas Tolstoy is known for his despair at the apparently invincible power over human life of what he is reported (by Maxim Gorky) to have called "the tragedy of the bedroom," George Eliot did not take such a bleak view. Her apparent optimism is achieved, in the view of some of her readers (such as Barbara Hardy), at the expense of "sexual truth," by downplaying sex. Eliot's and Tolstoy's different takes on Darwin—and sex—correspond to telling differences in how the two novelists adapted the multiplot form.

Franco Moretti has argued that the classical nineteenth-century Bildungsroman as it appeared in England "narrates 'how the French Revolution could have been avoided.'"[24] According to Moretti, these English novels depict reform, social concessions, and the overcoming of class prejudice, as if to model alternatives to violent political action and radical social upheaval. George Eliot's decision to make the Bildungsroman of Dorothea Brooke into a multiplot novel has profound consequences, especially since Dorothea herself, not to mention the narrator, wants to know how her life interacts with those of her neighbors: she is interested in social change for "the good of all" (2, 17) "here—now—in England" (3, 29). English (as well as Russian) *multiplot* novels that intimate that the entangled bank they depict does not have to be consumed by violent struggle, but *could* be ruled by neighborly love, are therefore, like the classical Bildungsroman, also engaged in this narration "of how the French Revolution could have been avoided." These novels suggest a variety of alternatives, from reconciliation to the status quo, to the spread of reform and mutual aid, to the growth of love in imitation of Christ.

In constructing her multi-plotted *Middlemarch* George Eliot responds to the hopes and fears of her Victorian age. She depicts human life in Middlemarch as a tangled skein, but in her novelistic universe one person can have a profound effect on another. In "Janet's Repentance," the early work that first attracted Tolstoy to her fiction, George Eliot celebrated the "[b]lessed influence of one true loving human soul on another" and made it the motive force of her plot (19, 364).[25] In the novels that followed, even though competition, abuse, indifference, and selfishness are still the way of the world she represents, Eliot *envisions* this "blessed influence" in a variety of contexts, within marriage and family and outside of it, among neighbors. As George Eliot developed as a novelist, her fascination with "the influence of one . . . soul on another" not only continued to provide dramatic interest, but also accounted for convergences of the multiple plots that she drew together in single novels. Eliot tends to diffuse the sexual tension and egotistic drive that traditionally animate plots, as she moves beyond the courtship plot and family saga. Accordingly, the events that determine the course of her novels include not just kisses between brides and grooms and between family members, but kisses between neighbors, or what she calls "sacramental kisses—kisses that seal a new closer bond between helper and helped" ("Janet's Repentance," 15, 347).

The ethos of neighborliness, with its rich possibility of lateral connections, is the *ideal* held forth in *Middlemarch*. In George Eliot's world the positive heroes are not those who act like Napoleon or have a memorial, but rather those who are merciful and love their neighbors, such as Caleb Garth. And in a *Middlemarch* miracle, even Rosamond Vincy, who normally thinks only of herself (and often is the butt of the narrator's mild but nipping irony), can herself respond with loving-kindness when she surrenders to the blessed influence of another loving soul. Neighborly love in *Middlemarch* may not fill the theological void that J. Hillis Miller regards as vital to the genesis of Victorian novels; nor does it eradicate injustice or eliminate the need for reform; nor does it make the tangled bank of Middlemarch into a loving community.[26] All too often in Middlemarch, as elsewhere, neighbors are nasty and mean-spirited, and neighborly love ends up dispersed among hindrances or, at best, diffused. From some perspectives, Dorothea's life is a failure. Still, this capacity for fellow feeling is the holy of holies in George Eliot's multiplot novel.

The comparative discussion of *Middlemarch* and *Anna Karenina* that follows focuses on three concerns. First, Eliot's and Tolstoy's respective modes of linking together multiple plots—converging and overt in Eliot, separate and hidden in Tolstoy. Second, the contrasting treatment of the pairs of heroes in the two novels—Dorothea and Lydgate in *Middlemarch*, Anna and Levin in *Anna Karenina*. And third, the different conceptions of human relatedness, revealed in parallel scenes of feminine friendship and sisterly love that are pivotal in the denouements of each novel.

Architectonics in the Open:
The Convergence of Neighbors' Lots in *Middlemarch*

Whereas Tolstoy keeps the architectonics of *Anna Karenina* hidden, George Eliot lays bare the structure of her novel and draws attention to her practice of the multiplot form. In doing so, she illuminates the interconnectedness of human lives. In regard to double plot in drama, William Empson observed that "it does not depend on being noticed for its operation."[27] George Eliot ensures, however, that her readers will notice the different plots and will engage in the special way of reading that a double-plotted or multiplot novel requires: the reader seeks not only to know how each plot comes out but also to understand how the plots relate to each other.[28] As Peter Garrett explains, the different sense-making strategies that a multiplot novel demands—"the centripetal impulse that organizes narrative around the development of a protagonist and the impulse that elaborates an inclusive pattern of simultaneous relationships"—pull the reader in different directions and create "fundamental tensions" that "prevent [these novels] from resolving into any single stable order or meaning." In reading for the multiplot, desire is often conflicted.[29]

As George Levine observes, *Middlemarch*, "like almost all multiplot novels . . . though yet more intensely, requires that every particular narrative be read in the light of others. . . . The highest morality in this narrative lies in the quest, at whatever cost, to make one's individual life both internally coherent and coherent with the community in which it moves. Ethics and epistemology are one in dealing with the questions of how to understand the ultimate entanglement of all things, and how to respond to that entanglement, how to act without hurting others (even, and particularly, those whom one doesn't know) or compromising oneself."[30] In *Middlemarch*, the ethics and epistemology described above cannot be separated from the (multiplot) form George Eliot uses.

The narrator of *Middlemarch* is a virtuoso of the multiplot form and uses various means—modulating the point of view, shifting into free indirect discourse, and lacing irony with compassion—in order to show that everyone in the novel (and in life) has an "equivalent center of self," that everyone has a "point of view" deserving of consideration and compassion, and that everyone is also "in the same embroiled medium" (21, 211; 29, 278; 30, 290). Furthermore, the narrator of *Middlemarch* often intrudes to comment on the lessons of the multiplot form.[31] The "Prelude" and the "Finale" offer the same in concentrated format. The reader is expected to move beyond Aristotelian poetics, traditional conceptions of heroism and virtue, and even certain forms of novel-reading. But George Eliot's narrator is there to *train* readers so that they adapt to reading *Middlemarch*.

Readers of *Middlemarch* are eased into its multiplot form. The novel starts out in a conventional mode by tracking the *Bildung* and courtship plot of a single protagonist, Miss Brooke, the eponymous heroine of Book 1. Miss Brooke becomes Mrs. Casaubon before *Middlemarch* shows its true colors as a multiplot novel. However, from the start there are intimations that a heroine like Dorothea would chafe under the constraints of a courtship novel, that feminine variant of the Bildungs-roman. The narrator affirms her marriageability ("And how should Dorothea not marry?—a girl so handsome and with such prospects?"), but also reminds us of features that would mitigate against selection of her as a mate. Dorothea's impulse to love her neighbor is too intense. Who, asks the narrator, wants a wife who might kneel "suddenly down on a brick floor by the side of a sick labourer and [pray] fervidly as if she thought herself living in the time of the Apostles" or a wife who "might awaken you some fine morning with a new scheme for the application of her income which would interfere with political economy and the keeping of saddle-horses?" (1, 9). A heroine so prone to outbursts of neighborly love may disqualify herself from traditional courtship plots, but, as George Eliot shows, she is a natural for a multiplot novel. And, given her ardor for loving her neighbor, it is likely to be one in which plotlines tangle.

In his study of the genesis of *Middlemarch*, Jerome Beaty explains that George Eliot had started, but abandoned, a work called "Middle-march," featuring Lydgate, the Vincys, and others. She then began to write "Miss Brooke" and, part way in, decided to join the two works together into one multiplot novel.[32] Since the novel in its final form still begins with ten chapters of "Miss Brooke" before the plot opens up to include material from "Middlemarch," readers experience a shift from single-plotted to multiplot form.[33] Even the Prelude leads the reader to expect the story of one later-day Theresa, not two or more.[34]

The overt "bridge" (to use Beaty's term) from "Miss Brooke" into the wider world of *Middlemarch* occurs when a dinner party before Dorothea's wedding gathers Middlemarchers beyond the characters of "Miss Brooke": it "was large and rather more miscellaneous as to the male portion" (10, 88).[35] Included is Tertius Lydgate, the new doctor in town. The narrator draws attention to the multiplot structure at this critical juncture by recording the mutual disinterest in each other of Lydgate and Dorothea at this first meeting. "But any one watching keenly the stealthy convergence of human lots, sees a slow preparation of effects from one life on another, which tells like a calculated irony on the indifference or the frozen stare with which we look at our unintroduced neighbour. Destiny stands by sarcastic with our *dramatis personae* folded in her hand" (11, 95). The narrator thus prompts the reader to wonder whether the lots of Dorothea and Lydgate will converge in the future.[36] Repeated mentions of Lydgate's sexual disinterest in Dorothea ("evidently Miss Brooke was not Mr. Lydgate's style of woman" [10, 93]) and his sexual preference for Rosamond Vincy (he has been "fascinated by a woman strikingly different from Miss Brooke" [11, 95]), aside from indicating the "spots of commonness" (15, 150) that are his flaw, call to mind the general assumption—among Middlemarchers and perhaps among readers schooled on other novels—that any convergence of the lots of Lydgate and Dorothea would take the form of a love plot. But the "Destiny" that rules *Middlemarch* proves these assumptions wrong. The feelings between Dorothea and Lydgate end up being neighborly rather than sexual.

As "Miss Brooke" opens into the multiplot world of *Middlemarch*, the reader must shift attention away from Dorothea's pursuit of happiness to focus on other plots that—as the narrator reminds us—have equal claim and interest. (And if readers are moved by desire, then the object of this desire is no longer just to find out what happens to Dorothea or, for that matter, Lydgate, but to learn how lives in Middlemarch relate to each other.) Moving us from the single-plot "Miss Brooke" to the polyfocal world of *Middlemarch* proper, the narrator is attentive to the reader, offering directives and providing epistemological models and metaphors to help us discern the meaning that emerges as the different plots are considered side by side.[37] The narrator prods us to rid ourselves of conventional old reading habits. Thus, the narrator asks "but

why always Dorothea?" and thrusts us into the interiority of a less attractive character, reminding us that his soul is spiritually ahungered, too,
and has equal claim to attention (29, 278).[38] Regardless of how readers
respond to them, these narrative intercessions draw attention to the
poetics, ethics, and form of the multiplot structure. And habits die hard
for narrators, too: as critics and readers have noted, the narrator of
Middlemarch at times falls back on old-school narrative practices and
attitudes.

Points at which different plotlines converge in *Middlemarch* often
become key events, even when there is no significant interaction between
the characters of the separate plotlines (as when Lydgate ignores
Dorothea, who is not "his style of woman"). The narrative capitalizes
on these convergences because they are graphic reminders of George
Eliot's vision of a modal neighborhood or entangled bank—where
there is a range of possible behaviors, from engaging in mutual aid to
going about their lives red in tooth and claw. When plots converge, the
characters themselves have the opportunity to respond (or not) to the
call for neighborly love and to "amplify" understanding by fuller awareness of the experience of those "beyond [their] personal lot."[39] The
narrator also comments on the multiplot dynamics as if to encourage
the reader to pay attention to its meaning. While the reader could set
about attempting to discern the connections between the plots without
prompts, George Eliot's chosen method is to *train* the reader for the
empathetic understanding at the heart of her art.

George Eliot provides a formal hinge between her plots in the Featherstone funeral scene (34, 323–30). The cast from "Miss Brooke" gathers
at Casaubon's house, perched above the churchyard, to watch Peter
Featherstone's extended family (Garths, Vincys, and others) gather for
his funeral. That the characters of the two main plotlines do not interact
reminds us that they inhabit different social spheres within Middlemarch. Thus, the interactions between members of these different
spheres that occur later in the novel—often thanks to Dorothea's interest
in her neighbors—are special events.

In one of the intrusions that offer lessons not only in life but in how
to read a multiplot novel, the narrator comments:

> But for her visitors Dorothea too might have been shut up in the
> library, and would not have witnessed this scene of old Feather-
> stone's funeral, which, aloof as it seemed to be from the tenor of her
> life, always afterwards came back to her at the touch of certain

sensitive points in memory, just as the vision of St. Peter's at Rome was inwoven with moods of despondency. Scenes which make vital changes in our neighbours' lot are but the background of our own, yet, like a particular aspect of the fields and trees, they become associated for us with the epochs of our own history, and make a part of that unity which lies in the selection of our keenest consciousness. (34, 326)

The narrator affirms that the mere contiguity of our neighbors' lives with our own, whether or not we have anything to do with them, still affects us—and all the more so if we, like Dorothea, are responsive to our neighbors' lots. On another level, this observation about the effect of this scene on Dorothea reminds the reader that he or she should make lateral associations between the current plot and other plots in the background.

The Featherstone funeral, an event of vital interest to his relatives but not to Dorothea, still marks an epoch in her spiritual development and in her relation to her neighbors. Whereas Mrs. Cadwallader, proud of her high birth and known for her turn of tongue, has come to observe the spectacle because she "like[s] to see collections of strange animals such as there would be at this funeral" (34, 325), Dorothea intuits a similarity between her own loveless state and that of her neighbors at the funeral, which leads her to conclude that it is so piteous to live and die and "leave no love behind" (34, 328). As Harry Shaw explains, "Dorothea senses and we soon recognize that the scene of the funeral resonates with her own feeling of entrapment in the stillborn world of Mr. Casaubon. The funeral provides an ideal expressive metaphor for Dorothea."[40] Thus, Dorothea herself, as she intuits similarities between her life and those of others, makes the paradigmatic association that a reader of a multiplot novel makes in order to appreciate hidden (unarticulated) links between plots. As Dorothea declares to her sister, "'I am fond of knowing something about the people I live among. . . . It seems to me we know nothing of our neighbours, unless they are cottagers. One is constantly wondering what sort of lives other people lead, and how they take things'" (34, 326). George Eliot positions Dorothea, with her yearnings for intersubjectivity, as someone who seeks out the kind of insight into her neighbors' lives and psyches that the narrator spoon-feeds to readers of *Middlemarch*.

Dorothea does not, however, content herself with *wondering* about her neighbors' inner lives. The Featherstone funeral marks a turning point in her life. As Shaw explains, Dorothea henceforth connects to her neighbors and their plots not simply through "metaphorical" associations, intuited and grasped in her interiority, but also through actual "metonymical" connections that develop as she converges her lot with those of neighbors. In fact, as Shaw notes, one of the glories of *Middlemarch* may be the way it collapses the distinction between these two.[41]

The Hidden Architectonics of *Anna Karenina*: "Everyone Has Enough to Bear in His Own Grief"

The multiplot form in *Anna Karenina* reflects a model of community and insights into the human condition that differ from those in *Middlemarch*.[42] As it opens, *Anna Karenina* is multiplot and polyfocal. And yet the title *Anna Karenina* suggests a single-plot novel.[43] Indeed, the germ of the novel was a single adultery plot. Levin—or Neradov, as he was known when he first appeared in the drafts—was not there from the very start. Levin and Kitty's plot seems to oppose and complement the adultery plot, but Tolstoy also includes the plot centering on the Oblonskys. It occupies the middle ground, provides linkages across plots, and mitigates against the tendency to read the other two plots for contrast: all three plots have, in the words of John Bayley, "a disquieting amount in common."[44]

As the novel begins, "All is mixed up" in the Oblonsky household. And the narrator provides no Eliot-style prompts about how to read or sort out the characters. However, before the end of Part 1, Tolstoy has segregated the plot of Anna and her two Alekseis from the (late-blooming) plot of Levin and Kitty. The impulse toward separate plots contrasts with *Middlemarch*, where the plots, initially distinct, intersect more freely and possibly even eventually fuse or coalesce, as some critics argue.[45]

George Eliot uses a single place, the fictional town of Middlemarch, as the organizing focus in her multiplot novel; she gestures at inclusiveness by providing a "sample" of the population.[46] Tolstoy joins plots according to a different principle: family ties.[47] Viktor Shklovsky observes that linking opposed groups through kinship is standard practice for Tolstoy as it is for most novelists.[48] Since family connections provide the framework, the focus in *Anna Karenina* is not—as it is in *Middlemarch*—on how random "changes in our neighbors' lot" provide the background for our own or on "the stealthy convergence of human lots" as the lives of unintroduced neighbors come together. The ties that Tolstoy features—by blood, by marriage, by membership in the hereditary nobility, or by passion—often dictate behavior, within the parameters of the relation in question. For the most part, the characters operate in the same constrained social world and encounter each other as if randomly in train compartments, at the English club, at elections, and so forth. But, by and large, these chance encounters are significant for how they figure in *Anna Karenina*'s love plots, rather than for their potential for forging (more unpredictable?) relations of neighborly love of the Middlemarch variety. (One exception to the Tolstoyan rule might be what happens to Kitty in Soden in Part 2. As will be discussed in chapter 4, the plot possibilities opened up here, which have an English pedigree, are quickly shut down.)

The action of *Anna Karenina* roves from place to place, but, with the exception of two European episodes, mostly fixes in the two capital cities and on the country estates of Pokrovskoe, Ergushevo, and Vozdvizhenskoe. These Tolstoy places close enough to each other to allow visits back and forth, as well as Dolly's request that Levin bring over his mother's sidesaddle for Kitty. While the relative proximity of these estates possibly keeps the coincidence of Levin spotting Kitty as she passes in her carriage (just as he was musing about marrying a peasant) from seeming like a cheap novelistic trick, the reader still feels Tolstoyan Destiny is at work.

Tolstoy embeds the love stories—the courtship and the adultery plots—in the larger context of family relations. While relations between parents and children figure prominently, Tolstoy also has a keen, often anxious, interest in showing his heroes and heroines as brothers and sisters.[49] Thus, as the novel opens, Anna comes from Moscow to Petersburg, leaving husband and, for the first time, child behind, on a mission of sisterly love to reconcile her brother, Stiva, and his wife, Dolly; Vronsky is amusing himself in Moscow, but his mother has told Anna tales of how he wanted to surrender his portion of his patrimony to his brother (who has married the dowerless daughter of a Decembrist); Konstantin Levin comes to Moscow drawn by his sexual desire to make Kitty his mate and the mother of his children, but in the proximity of his brothers in Moscow he must face the responsibilities of brotherly love, to Koznyshev, who irks him, and to Nikolai Levin, who is in desperate need. As *Anna Karenina* unfolds, Tolstoy presents all of the major characters as brothers and sisters and relies to a surprising degree on these interactions for the tissue of his narrative.

For all the concern with sexual love and caring for one's young within *Anna Karenina*, "Am I my brother's keeper?" is a question that resonates in this multiplot novel. It is what holds its multiple strands together. In Tolstoy's world, family love and marital fidelity sometimes seem to be the ideals: if one focuses on them, the community will function. Attempts to dedicate oneself overtly to the common weal often yield nothing. And yet, at the same time, *Anna Karenina* is vexed by an anxiety about whether there are others beyond the family circle who should be loved like brothers and sisters. If so, then the boundary blurs between sibling love and neighborly love.

The dinner party at the Oblonskys' in Part 5 has been recognized as an important structural landmark, a possible hidden "keystone" to the "arch" that holds the novel together.[50] The role of this scene in *Anna Karenina* is analogous to that of the Featherstone funeral scene in *Middlemarch*. Both scenes are roughly midway through the novel and set up the action for the second half. Both scenes draw together characters from different plotlines as they mark what Eliot's narrator calls "epochs" in the individual histories of major characters. The gathering hosted by Stiva and Dolly Oblonsky confirms their intermediary role. Without their active involvement in the lives of their respective siblings[-in-law], there would be even fewer *surface* connections between Anna's plot and Levin's plot.[51] Aleksei Karenin's presence at the Oblonsky party marks a rare point of intersection between the Levin plot and the plot of Anna and her two Alekseis (Vronsky and Karenin).

As Tolstoy's narrator records the conversation in realistic detail, he intimates that whatever is said is immaterial in comparison to the "mystic communication" of Kitty and Levin that culminates in their agreement to marry. But Tolstoy does not simply use the conversation to create an aura of verisimilitude: it is also freighted with layers of significance in Tolstoy's "endless labyrinth of linkages." Thus, for example, when Oblonsky brings together Karenin and Levin, whom he assumes are strangers but who had ended up in the same train compartment on their way to Moscow (Levin boarded the train fresh from a bear hunt), their very separate plots momentarily connect. Oblonsky sees to it that Levin and Karenin make small talk. On the surface, nothing significant happens. (It is an instance of the syntagmatic links that Tolstoy dismissed as unimportant in his letter to Rachinsky.) In fact, the exchange between Karenin and Levin seems to exist simply to interrupt and temporarily retard the "mystic communication" between Kitty and Levin that will culminate in a marriage proposal. Just as the momentum builds in the Levin/Kitty courtship plot, Tolstoy crosses the plots by having Oblonsky interrupt them to introduce Karenin to Levin, who is probably the person in the room least interested in meeting this very important person. Tolstoy is not merely introducing one more hindrance (of a banal and thus comedic nature) to delay the fruition of the courtship plot. He also reminds us, at this key juncture, that we are reading a multiplot novel. Whereas George Eliot would rely on her narrator to remind us overtly of other plots and that the world of *Middlemarch* is one, Tolstoy more subliminally prompts the reader to read for the multiplot. Just when the reader may want to surrender, vicariously, to the pure desire of the Levin and Kitty plot, Tolstoy reminds us subtly but hauntingly of how this relates to Anna's plot and to the world at large.

The seemingly inconsequential verbal exchange between Levin and Karenin is pregnant with meaning and rife with linkages to other parts of the novel. On the surface, it serves to contrast the relative positions of Levin and Karenin, but reminders of the larger context act on the reader who, unlike the characters, bears all in his or her consciousness. In the midst of general conversation about how to russify Poland and right after Koznyshev's bon mot about how he and his brother Konstantin Levin, both childless, have failed to do their part for the patriotic cause of "breeding as many [Russian] children as possible," Oblonsky suddenly turns to Levin to exclaim on his muscles, causing Levin to smile and flex his arm so that "under Stepan Arkadyich's fingers a steely bump rose like a round cheese under the thin cloth of the frock coat" (5:9, 384). At this point, Tolstoy's narrator gets carried away in his own variation of the tendency to strain the boundaries of realism in Flaubert's narration, observed by Jonathan Culler and others. When this happens in *Anna Karenina*, it often signals that the overwrought narrative moment is richly connected in the Tolstoyan web of allusions. Oblonsky's comments on Levin's virility hint that Levin has something to contribute to the future of Russia (and the end of Poland) in the terms of the general discussion, but they also shore up Levin's self-confidence. Indeed, as Koznyshev then listens to his brother Levin, he notices that Levin has the aura of a conquering hero. By the end of the dinner party, he will be just that.

Karenin responds to Oblonsky's comment on Levin's muscles by saying, "I suppose it takes great strength to hunt a bear" (4:9, 384). Karenin makes a simple metonymical shift from Oblonsky's reference to the muscles to a comment on what can be done with those muscles. Karenin thus sets it up so that Kitty can chime in, saying "And you've killed a bear, I'm told." She says this while "trying in vain to spear a disobedient, slippery mushroom with her fork and shaking the lace through which her arm showed white," in a detail that goes beyond the call of realism to complement with perfect symmetry the recent description of Levin's arm. But, in addition, this detail recalls the sight that Levin witnessed of a young peasant, her bosom heaving under her blouse, skillfully spearing hay with a pitchfork and, in the process, arousing pure sexual desire in her husband (3:11, 274). At that point, Levin himself had nursed fantasies of marrying a peasant lass and living a pure life, but then in the next chapter he caught sight of Kitty Shcherbatsky, "holding the ribbons of her white bonnet," as she rode by on her way to visit her sister. Levin realizes that he loves "*her*" and now feels disgust at the idea of marrying a peasant (3:12, 278). Through this subtle echo, we are reminded that Levin's destiny is, after all, to marry lacy-sleeved Princess Kitty Shcherbatsky, who struggles to spear a mushroom with her silver folk, rather than some pitchfork-wielding peasant. And even as Levin joyously embraces his destiny and duty, the situational rhyme conjures up Levin's fantasy of escape into another life of pure peasant toil. In the labyrinth of *Anna Karenina*, Tolstoy leaves it to the reader to make associations and thus bear in mind what is absent.[52] Obviously, the effect is subtle, and what it means is open to the reader's interpretation. In this case, any reminder of peasant life, a source of such anxiety for Levin throughout the novel, may cast a slight shadow over the happy occasion.

Of Kitty's comment about the bear (prompted by Karenin's), we are told that it sent Levin into ecstasy: "It seemed there was nothing extraordinary in what she said, yet for him, what meaning inexpressible in words, there was in every sound, in every movement of her lips, eyes, arm, as she said it! Here was a plea for forgiveness, and trust in him, and a caress, a tender, timid caress, and a promise, and hope, and love for him, in which he could not but believe and which choked him with happiness" (5:9, 384). The narrator denies the denotative significance of what Kitty has said to Levin (about killing a bear). But for the reader, the reference to bears will signify because bears have already figured in Tolstoy's labyrinth of linkages, as well as in a web of literary, folk-symbolic, and mythic intertexts external to the novel.[53] In these collective systems of knowledge, bears are associated with sexual selection, marriage, fertility, and childbirth, while in Greek mythology the bear is sacred to Artemis. Thus, it is very apt for this betrothal to take place under the sign of the bear.

Tolstoy does not leave it at that. This casual reference to bears also activates the tension between the two plots. On the most tangible level, this happens because the Russian masculine pastime of bear-hunting figures in both plots. Thus, the bear Levin has killed is connected, through one of the hidden links that Tolstoy relies on to grant unity to *Anna Karenina*, to Vronsky's bear hunt with the visiting English dignitary, featured in the most recent episode in the Anna/Vronsky plot. That both heroes hunt bears, in their separate plots, prompts further contemplation of parallels and differences between the plots.

Furthermore, Vronsky's actual bear hunt haunted Vronsky and Anna's shared nightmare about the peasant poking an iron stick in a bag (4:2, 355–56; 4:3, 362). In Vronsky's version, the peasant is the beater from his recent bear hunt. That Vronsky and Anna have variants of the exact same nightmare is uncanny. In Anna's extended variant of the dream, Karenin's servant interprets the first segment—about the peasant poking the iron stick in a bag as he mutters in French—as a harbinger of death in childbirth: a prophecy that the reader soon learns has all but come true as Anna lies mortally ill from puerperal fever after having given birth to Vronsky's love child. (Upon his return to his "lonely" hotel room that evening, Karenin will read a telegram from Anna summoning him to her bedside.) Meanwhile, back at the Oblonsky dinner party, Levin's success at the bear hunt augurs his future marriage with Kitty and their eventual fertility. While Anna and Vronsky incur the wrath of Artemis, goddess of childbirth, Levin and Kitty appear to have her stamp of approval. This is Tolstoy's fabled hidden architecture at its most glorious, and most disturbing. The effect seems to escalate when Tolstoy brings into play the dream worlds of his characters and when he draws on bodies of collective knowledge external to the novel. The point of reference outside the novel appears to confirm the meaningfulness of the patterns that emerge from seemingly random details across the different plots, but just what all this means is uncertain. The reader is left to interpret these patterns, as they apply both to a given plot and across plots in what turns out to be an unstable process.

Tolstoy constructs the scene so that what is a "vital change" in the lives of Levin and Kitty (resolving their courtship plot) is set against the background of the lives of Anna, Vronsky, and Karenin *but only in the reader's mind*—Kitty and Levin are oblivious. And the narrator does not prompt the reader to make the connection. Tolstoy thus continues to make use of a particular form of multiplot irony, according to which the reader has access to knowledge about other plots that the characters are ignorant of. Is Tolstoy's reader expected to yoke the two realities into what Eliot's narrator calls "that unity which lies in the selection of our keenest consciousness"?[54] Whereas the narrator of *Middlemarch* offers metacommentary on how to read her multiplot novel as she tracks Dorothea's attempts to connect to other people's lives, Tolstoy's reader is left at the entrance of his labyrinth and expected to weave and then follow his or her own Ariadne's thread. Tolstoy, as he defiantly declared to Rachinsky, keeps his architectonics hidden by design.[55]

As the conversation at the dinner party turns to the woman question, a topic of common interest, the reader is likely even without Eliot-style promptings to think laterally, to consider how the discussion relates to the different plots. The narrator signals that the characters' responses are conditioned by their own personal concerns, as when he informs us that Oblonsky's defense of a woman's right to work—"what is a girl to do who has no family?"—was inspired by his interest in his current mistress, a ballerina (4:10, 389). When Dolly expresses exasperation, the narrator suggests that Dolly "probably" was also thinking of her husband's mistress. Meanwhile, Levin understands Kitty's fear of being left an old maid (4:13, 397), as in the midst of this general conversation he and Kitty engage in their own "mystic communication" (4:11, 390). It is typical of *Anna Karenina* that sexual desire or familiarity is needed to bring about this kind of awareness of another person's inner world, whether in its pure form, as here with Kitty and Levin, in its macabre form, as in the shared dream of Anna and Vronsky, or in its banal version, as when Dolly knows Stiva had his mistress in mind. In other contexts, Tolstoy's heroes and heroines do not often wonder about their neighbors' inner lives (as Dorothea does). They tend to be focused on themselves or to regard the consciousness of another as an inaccessible abyss.

Alone among those present, Dolly's consciousness encompasses her own concerns and those of others. Thus, she not only delights in her sister's transcendent joy in Levin, but also recalls the plight of Anna, far away in Petersburg. Dolly takes Karenin aside to entreat him not to divorce Anna and leave her as "nobody's wife" (4:12, 394).[56] As if to create a bond, Dolly reminds him that the two of them, different as they are, share the lot of being married to unfaithful Oblonskys. Dolly's comments thus lay bare the situational parallels between their respective plots. Dolly has forgiven. Should not Karenin, as a Christian, do the same? Karenin, however, rejects or at least deflects Dolly's sisterly comfort and advice—and by implication the whole ethos of neighborly love—declaring in parting, "Every one has enough to bear in his own grief" (as translated by Constance Garnett) ["У каждого своего горя достаточно!"] (4:12, 395).[57]

In *Middlemarch* the narrator and some of the characters believe that human consciousnesses can connect, that we should embrace the stealthy convergence of human lots, that we are not all alone on this earth with our grief, that neighborly love is an ideal to strive for—and may even be possible on earth (in Middlemarch, "here—now—in England," as Dorothea believed). In contrast, Tolstoy's vision of the human condition and of the possibility of neighborly love is murkier. The notion that "everyone has enough to bear in his own grief" is Karenin's personal opinion. And yet Tolstoy often reminds us that this is true, so that this becomes an anxious leitmotif of *Anna Karenina* as a whole. In Tolstoy's novel, it is marked when one person comes to the aid of another, as when, for example, Dolly comes to inquire about Kitty's health after Kitty is jilted by Vronsky. The narrator notes, explicitly, that Dolly came despite the fact that "she had many griefs and cares of her own," which included a nursing infant and a sick child (2:2, 120). And, when her mother asks Dolly how her family is ["Что, как твои?"], Dolly's initial response is to say, "Ah, maman, you have enough grief of your own" (thus, acknowledging Kitty's plight) before going on to tell her that she fears that her daughter Lili has scarlet fever. Even though Dolly and her mother nominally distinguish each other's pain, they come together in mutual aid. But in *Anna Karenina* this kind of love does not appear to extend beyond blood. Instead the message is that the only hope of mutual aid is from blood relations. The novel thus leaves us to wonder until the bitter end whether "Everyone has enough to bear in his own grief" is not just Karenin's personal motto, but a universal truth.

The Embroiled Medium of *Middlemarch*: Lydgate and Dorothea

Henry James famously quipped that in *Middlemarch* the novelist created a firmament with two suns, Dorothea and Lydgate, "each with its own independent solar system."[58] Out of the many characters who all, according to the ethic promoted by the narrator of *Middlemarch*, have equal claim to heroic status, Lydgate is often singled out by critics as the hero who pairs with and counters Dorothea. Among the parallels in their plots is that, having begun with "high ideals," they are frustrated by unhappy marriages. Jerome Beaty has suggested that the modal parallels between them may have encouraged George Eliot to combine "Miss Brooke" with "Middlemarch" to create a multiplot novel.[59] The connections between Dorothea and Lydgate provide for many readers, Henry James foremost among them, the semblance of unity that, according to some theories and some tastes, a novel, even a multiplot one, needs.

The relations between them also provide an eloquent expression of George Eliot's vision of the human condition and of her conception of the multiplot novel. After their initial "indifference or frozen stare," Dorothea and Lydgate come into contact with each other when the doctor Lydgate cares for the sick Casaubon. After Lydgate reveals that her husband is dying, Dorothea appeals to him, asking him what she should do:

> He was bowing and quitting her, when an impulse which if she had been alone would have turned into a prayer, made her say with a sob in her voice—"Oh, you are a wise man, are you not? You know all about life and death. Advise me. Think what I can do. He has been labouring all his life and looking forward. He minds about nothing else. And I mind about nothing else—"
>
> For years after Lydgate remembered the impression produced on him by this involuntary appeal—this cry from soul to soul, without other consciousness than their moving with kindred natures in the same embroiled medium, the same troublous fitfully-illuminated life. But what could he say now except that he should see Mr Casaubon again tomorrow? (30, 280)

The naïve Dorothea still assumes that educated men like Casaubon with his book learning and Lydgate with his stethoscope have special access to truth. Although Lydgate does not really have answers beyond his promise to return, the fact that Dorothea appeals to him takes on significance in *Middlemarch*. The narrator affirms that something profound, mysterious, and transcendent takes place between them as they enter into a loving communion in the face of death. And we are told that this moment will live on in Lydgate's memory. This "cry from soul to soul" between Dorothea and Lydgate with their "kindred natures" is an important landmark in this multiplot novel. George Eliot shows that the "influence of one true loving human soul on another" can be profound even if its effects remain hidden with no tangible results in the here and now. Eliot's narrator thus affirms that souls can and do cry out to each other simply because they are embroiled in the same medium. Although this medium is only "fitfully illuminated," and not basked in divine light, their cries to each other can be heard. In this respect, it is very different from the universe of Tolstoy's *Anna Karenina*, which resembles, in the sense it often gives that man dies alone, that of Pascal.[60]

Evidence later in *Middlemarch* confirms the seminal importance of this act of neighborly love between Dorothea and Lydgate. Dorothea engages in a "Quixotic" quest to help Lydgate when he is humiliated before the town (76, 763). (Lydgate appears to be guilty of having abetted Bulstrode in acts that possibly led to the death of Raffles and of then having been bought off by Bulstrode, who lent him money, so that he would keep silent.) But Dorothea believes Lydgate to be innocent and wants to restore him in Middlemarch. She explains: "What do we live for, if it is not to make life less difficult to each other? I cannot be indifferent to the troubles of a man who advised me in *my* trouble, and attended me in my illness" (72, 734). At this point, Dorothea declares that "people glorify all sorts of bravery except the bravery they might show on behalf of their nearest neighbours" (72, 735). Here, as in other key spots, Dorothea gives direct voice to tenets that are dear to the narrator. Dorothea's declaration thus offers a key to the narrator's periodic announcements, concentrated in the Prelude and Finale, of a new genre with new poetics: if *Middlemarch*, a tale of many neighbors, is a "home epic" (as the narrator suggests), then its heroism, its arête, is to be found in acts of neighborly love.[61]

In the short run, we learn that the earlier exchange with Dorothea (that "cry from soul to soul") had left an impression on Lydgate, as it had on her. As the crisis with his wife, Rosamond, escalates ("Between him and her indeed there was that total missing of each other's mental track" [58, 587]), Lydgate recalls this moment with Dorothea. As he is casting aspersions on womankind, he is suddenly overtaken by "wondering impressions from the behaviour of another woman—from Dorothea's looks and tones of emotion about her husband when Lydgate began to attend him—from her passionate cry to be taught what would best comfort that man for whose sake it seemed as if she must quell every impulse in her except the yearnings of faithfulness and compassion" (58, 592). In his reverie, Lydgate repeats to himself, verbatim, what Dorothea had said earlier (nearly three hundred pages ago): "Think what I can do!" (30, 289–90; 58, 592). Later that evening, his heart softened, Lydgate speaks "kindly" to his wife, saying that they must "think together" about their troubles and that she must help him. At this point, Rosamond asks, "What can *I* do, Tertius?" The narrator comments, "That little speech of four words, like so many others in all languages, is capable by varied vocal inflexions of expressing all states of mind from helpless dimness to exhaustive argumentative perception, from the completest self-devoting fellowship to the most neutral aloofness. Rosamond's thin utterance threw into the words: 'What can *I* do' as much neutrality as they could hold. They fell like a mortal chill on Lydgate's roused tenderness" (58, 594). Although Tertius Lydgate clearly yearned for a more Dorothea-like response from his wife, his comparisons of Rosamond and Dorothea still do not appear to have become tinged with sexual desire for Dorothea.

Dorothea helps Lydgate in different ways, by rehabilitating him with townspeople, by offering to support his hospital with her superfluous income, and by agreeing to visit Rosamond to renew Rosamond's faith in Lydgate and to convince her that it would be possible for them to continue life in Middlemarch. As he and Dorothea part after she has promised to visit Rosamond, Lydgate marvels at Dorothea's kindness, thinking to himself: "This young creature has a heart large enough for the Virgin Mary. She seems to have what I never saw in any woman before—a fountain of friendship towards men—a man can make a friend of her" (76, 768–69). Lydgate thus affirms Dorothea's heroic potential within the parameters of the "home epic" (which does not depend on tragic or histrionic sacrifice). His admiration for Dorothea, however, remains chaste: he marvels at her capacity for Mary-like non-sexual love for men. He still wonders "if she could have any other sort of passion for a man" beyond the "heroic hallucination" that Casaubon "must have raised . . . in her" and, specifically, whether Ladislaw might be a love interest (76, 769), but sexual desire (even suppressed or sublimated) does not drive their relations.

As Dorothea pursues her mission to rehabilitate Lydgate, George Eliot insistently brings Dorothea and Lydgate into passionate, but platonic, relations. Readers of novels have been schooled to expect erotic desire to come into play, but George Eliot defies novelistic convention. Much as, according to Virginia Woolf, the novelist Mary Carmichael enriches the genre of the novel when she introduces the new topic of friendship between two women, so too does George Eliot when she describes the non-sexual friendship between a woman and a man

(Dorothea and Lydgate). Like Woolf's Mary Carmichael, George Eliot "light[s] a torch in that vast chamber where nobody has yet been."[62] Of course, it is possible to attribute the chaste relations of Dorothea and Lydgate to a deficiency in how George Eliot handles sexuality. Indeed, in the criticism on *Middlemarch*, one of the questions asked is whether "domestic realism is . . . up to the task of representing sexuality."[63]

Yet Eliot's novel of neighborly love defies the expectation that relations between a man and a woman must necessarily be either sexual or familial. Experts from Lydgate himself within the novel to contemporary critics have intimated that Dorothea Casaubon's effusions of compassion should be attributed to what Lydgate calls "the strain and conflict of self-repression" (popularly associated with hysteria) and thus to her unhappy sex life during and after her marriage to Casaubon (50, 492). Yet *Middlemarch* is the particular masterpiece it is largely because George Eliot envisions scenes of neighborly love rather than dwelling on "the tragedy of the bedroom." By the same token, if, as Barbara Hardy argues, *Anna Karenina* contains greater sexual truth than *Middlemarch*, then does Tolstoyan "sexual truth" in *Anna Karenina* end up subverting the ethic of neighborly love? This is not to say that Tolstoy's heroes do not harbor love for their neighbors in their hearts, but do they act on it?[64]

Zones of Liability to Pain in *Anna Karenina*: Anna and Levin

What Henry James wrote of *Middlemarch*, that "it is an illustration of the generous scale of the author's picture and of the conscious power of her imagination that she has given us a hero and heroine of broadly distinct interests—erected, as it were, two suns in her firmament, each with its own independent solar system," is true of *Anna Karenina*, too.[65] If Dorothea and Lydgate are the two suns of *Middlemarch*, then Levin and Anna occupy the analogous roles in *Anna Karenina*. But, whereas in *Middlemarch* George Eliot presents her firmament as an "embroiled medium" in which Dorothea appeals to Lydgate with a "cry from soul to soul, without other consciousness than their moving with kindred natures in . . . the same troublous fitfully-illuminated life," Tolstoy's firmament is very different. George Eliot delights in bringing her heroine and her hero into each other's proximity—so that their lots converge—but Tolstoy keeps Anna and Levin apart.

In her discussion of the architecture of *Anna Karenina*, Joan Delaney Grossman notes Tolstoy's use of "parallel" stories with their respective "risings and fallings" "carefully orchestrated for contrast and comparison." In this respect, as Grossman explains, Tolstoy structures his multiplot novel differently from George Eliot: "Of the principles of analogy and convergence favored by his great English contemporary George Eliot, only the former seems to bear on Tolstoy's method. Nothing in *Anna Karenina* demands that the fates of characters unknown to one another at the start must inexorably touch and influence each other before the novel is over. There seems no reason intrinsic to the stories of Anna and Levin why they must ever meet."[66] All this is true. Yet, readers might still wonder about Tolstoy's design. Why does Tolstoyan destiny stand by so long with these two "unintroduced strangers" "folded in her hand"?[67]

Since the readers of multiplot novels yearn to understand how the plots fit together, they are likely to anticipate the one meeting of Anna and Levin. Tolstoy enhances this expectation by orchestrating a meeting between Kitty and Vronsky, billed in retrospect as "an event that was very important for them both" (7:1, 672). Kitty and Vronsky had not met since he jilted her for Anna in Part 1. Their meeting happens by chance early in Part 7 when Kitty and her father call on Marya Borisovna, Kitty's godmother, and find Vronsky there. Even if she blushes brightly when she first sees him, Kitty recovers her composure and ends up, like her father, "very pleased" with how she handles the meeting. Once home, she discloses all to Levin, presenting it as a triumph over her past sexual feelings and a badge of honor as a faithful wife. Since Tolstoy's architectonics depends so heavily on symmetry and opposition, the reader may even expect for the meeting between Kitty and Vronsky to be balanced by one between the other pair.

Levin's visit to Anna occurs at the end of the long day that Levin spends out and about in Moscow, seeing Katavasov at the University, visiting the Lvovs, hearing the fantasia "King Lear on the Steppe," calling on Countess Bohl, attending a meeting of the South-Eastern Committee, and dining at the club. After being civil to Vronsky at the club, Levin agrees to go with Oblonsky to visit Anna. "What would Kitty say?" Levin wonders during the carriage ride: he "began to reflect on his actions, asking himself if he was doing the right thing by going to Anna" (7:9, 694). Oblonsky, as if reading Levin's mind ("as if guessing his doubts"), "dispersed them." He tells Levin that Lvov "has called on [Anna] and keeps dropping in." Lvov, the third Shcherbatsky brother-in-law (married to Nathalie), is a believer, an upright husband, and, in Levin's opinion, a model father, yet Lvov seems to have no qualms about visiting Anna. Is it simply because he is more cosmopolitan than Levin? Or, is it because he, following Christ's example, is not afraid of keeping company with sinners and publicans?

Even as they continue their ride, Levin responds in a judgmental way when Oblonsky describes the difficulties of Anna's situation. Levin suggests that her daughter should be enough to occupy her. Moreover, he is dismissive of the children's book she is writing and even of the care she is taking of Vronsky's English horse trainer's wife and children, effectively widowed and orphaned because he has "drunk himself up completely, delirium tremens." Oblonsky counters Levin's snide suggestion that it is "some sort of philanthropy" by assuring him that Anna's acts are "heartfelt" rather than patronizing. As Oblonsky notes, Levin prejudges Anna because he simply regards every woman as "a mere female, *une couveuse*" (7:9, 695). As Levin sees it, a woman has no business caring for others who are in need; her focus should be first and foremost on the survival of her own offspring. Much as Dolly recoiled from Anna when she learned at Vozdvizhenskoe that she would have no more children, Levin condemns Anna before they meet.[68]

When Levin arrives at Anna's, he first beholds not the living Anna, but rather her portrait by the artist Mikhailov, a work of art that mysteriously reveals her inner self. As Joan Grossman has argued, this is critical to his transformation because the painting reveals Anna in a very intimate way.[69] Vronsky had marveled at Mikhailov's genius for penetrating to "that sweetest expression of her soul" that even he who knew her and loved her had not yet noticed (5:13, 477). A work of art reveals Anna's soul in a way that does not happen in the ordinary life of Tolstoy's novel,[70] where consciousnesses remain relatively impenetrable to each other even among those who love and think they know each other. Although the novel provides the reader excellent access to the characters' consciousnesses, that is because the nearly omniscient or "telepathic" *narrator* is a master at revealing the workings of his characters' minds and hearts, from Laska the dog to Anna Karenina herself.[71]

At the same time, the narrator continually reminds us that intersubjectivity between the characters themselves is limited and troubled. (This might be a key to Tolstoy's *realism*.) Of Karenin, for example, we are told that "to put himself in thought and feeling into another being was a mental act [душевное действие] alien to [him]. He regarded this mental act as harmful and dangerous fantasizing." For him, Anna's inner world "was that bottomless deep into which it was frightening to look." Karenin justifies his stand by saying to himself, "Questions about her feelings, about what has been or might be going on in her soul, are not my business; they are the business of her conscience and belong to religion." The narrator adds that Karenin felt "relieved at the awareness that he had found the legitimate category to which the arisen circumstance belonged" (2:8, 144).[72]

That Karenin would declare Anna's inner life none of his business and in the domain of religion is not surprising. But do others in *Anna Karenina* see into one another's consciousness? Vladimir Alexandrov has noted "the rarity of deep communion" between Tolstoy's characters; they are lonely "in some fundamental level of emotional and mental life."[73] Tolstoy's narrator celebrates the telepathic powers of Levin and Kitty in their coded exchange at the second proposal scene when they engage in their "mystic communication." Yet, during their wedding ceremony, when Levin is ecstatically moved by the profundity of the words of the liturgy "that correspond to what one feels at this moment!," he looks at Kitty and wonders, "does she feel the same as I do?" He "conclude[s] that she understood it as he did." The narrator immediately intervenes to point out that Levin was wrong about what Kitty was thinking and feeling: "But that was not so; she had almost no understanding of the words of the service and did not even listen" (5:4, 452–53).[74] Levin's lack of access to Kitty's inner world at this blessed moment of union sends a message to the reader about the human condition, reminding us that we have only very limited understanding of the innermost thoughts of other human beings, no matter how much we love them. (Is part of Levin's problem that he assumes that the other thinks or feels the same way he does?) By comparison, in *Middlemarch*, George Eliot places more of a premium on intersubjectivity between characters (as an ideal to strive for), even if they, too, know little of each other's inner worlds. George Eliot treats as a valuable exercise the "mental act" of "put[ting] [one]self in thought and feeling into another being," the very act that Karenin avoids out of principle or simply from lack of empathy and that Tolstoy's narrator tends to dismiss once he indicates that a character's understanding was incorrect.[75]

When he finally meets Anna Karenina, Levin wants to know her inner world; in other words, he wants the kind of access available to Tolstoy's narrator but not generally to his fictional characters (with the exception of a true artist like Mikhailov): "As he followed the interesting conversation, Levin admired her all the while—her beauty, her intelligence, her education, and with that her simplicity and deep feeling. He listened, talked, and all the while thought about her, about her inner life, trying to guess her feelings. And he who had formerly judged her so severely, now, by some strange train of thought, justified her and at the same time pitied her, and feared that Vronsky did not fully understand her" (7:10, 701). Levin's prejudice and censure appear to have given way to pity and compassion. As Oblonsky notes wryly when Levin expresses his sympathy on the way out, "Well, so don't go judging beforehand" (7:11, 701).

Has a profound change occurred in Levin? As Grossman observes, "he is for once able to go out of himself in unrestrained sympathy."[76] That he was trying to understand Anna marks a change from the Levin who had earlier declared all fallen women vermin (1:11, 41–42), even stating that looking at individual cases (as Tolstoy the novelist was certainly doing in *Anna Karenina*) was not worthwhile. What will come of Levin's new interest in the interior world of others? Has Levin gone too far into the abyss that Karenin avoided, when Karenin declared Anna's inner world none of his own business?[77] Or, on the other hand, does "religion" teach us not to judge, but rather to have compassion, because, as the epigraph declares, vengeance is God's?

Whereas the "cry from soul to soul" between Dorothea and Lydgate brings comfort, has a lasting effect, and results in Dorothea's helping Lydgate and Rosamond in their time of trouble, Tolstoy treats the analogous moment between Levin and Anna very differently.[78] Tolstoy's embroiled medium is much more troubled: although he brings Levin and Anna together, the meeting has no further overt consequences in the storylines. The softening of Levin's heart in Anna's presence still possibly leaves its mark. It could come back to haunt him later and contribute to his crisis. In a draft, Levin's crisis in Part 8 was precipitated by his response to beholding the corpse of Anna Karenina at the train station. (By Tolstoyan coincidence, he was to be in the vicinity.) In this discarded version, the sight of Anna dead made him so conscious of the mystery of death that he could not go on living without coming to terms with the thoughts that torment him (20:562). In the novel as Tolstoy published it, however, there are no indications that Levin even remembers Anna at the time when he wrestles with the meaning of life and is close to suicide himself. Certainly, within Tolstoy's murky labyrinth of linkages, the reader can see that Anna and Levin are kindred natures, with his suicidal impulses mysteriously linked to hers.[79] (This is one of the links that Tolstoy kept hidden.) On the surface of the novel, however, Anna is hereafter out of range of his fellow-feeling.

In the letter that prompted Tolstoy to declare his pride in *Anna Karenina*'s hidden architectonics, Sergei Rachinsky singled out the meeting of Levin and Anna as "one of the best episodes of the novel." Rachinsky wrote that this meeting had given Tolstoy "a chance to bind all the threads of the story" and thus "provide an integrated finale." But Rachinsky acknowledged that Tolstoy must have had his reasons for not following up on the meeting between Anna and Levin: "But you didn't want to—God be with you."[80] In his oft-cited response, Tolstoy explained that the unity of the construction depended on neither plot nor the interactions of characters from different plotlines. Tolstoy then urged Rachinsky to pay more careful attention, assuming that Rachinsky had missed the artistic subtlety of *Anna Karenina*. In his response, Rachinsky maintained that he was "not denying that there was an *inner* link between the two parallel plots that make up [Tolstoy's] novel."[81] Rachinsky, in other words, appreciated the inner or "hidden" structure and unity (all the implicit paradigmatic connections), but Tolstoy's handling of syntagmatic relations disturbed him. He objected to how Tolstoy channels and limits human interaction. In effect, Rachinsky was asking: Why can't *Anna Karenina* be more like *Middlemarch*?

Rachinsky's original complaint suggests that he felt that Tolstoy, after bringing Anna and Levin together in a scene with great potential, missed an opportunity to link the plotlines. In *The Architecture of Anna Karenina*, Elisabeth Stenbock-Fermor concludes that Rachinsky thought that the seduction that Anna had envisioned should run its course.[82] What she assumes is logical, given the conventions of the novel and especially given Tolstoy's preoccupation with sex. But is this what Rachinsky envisioned? When Rachinsky asked for further connection between Anna and Levin, I think he could have been wondering why the compassionate connection between them did not take some other more unexpected turn, in the spirit of George Eliot. Could a bond have developed between Levin and Anna analogous to that between Dorothea and Lydgate? But, perhaps, short of a sexual relationship between Anna and Levin, Tolstoy simply could not imagine any further interaction between the two of them or their two plots.[83] This may be Rachinsky's real point. Whereas George Eliot could novelize the "blessed influence of one living human soul on another!," Tolstoy may have found this material right for an English fairy tale, but not for Russian reality, nor for his fiction.

Tolstoy forestalls possibilities for further connection between Anna and Levin by suggesting that the compassion between Anna and Levin was wrong to start with. When Levin returns home, Tolstoy provides us with Kitty's perspective on what has just taken place. Kitty is convinced that, although Anna is to be pitied, that "vile woman" has bewitched her husband (7:11, 703). The narrator reports: "It took Levin a long time to calm his wife down. When he finally succeeded, it was only by confessing that the feeling of pity, along with the wine, had thrown him off guard and made him yield to Anna's cunning influence, and that he was going to avoid her" (7:11, 703). Does Levin's "confession" mean that Kitty's view is right or the only one possible?[84]

If Kitty is right, then the Tolstoyan message is here, as elsewhere in the novel, that neighborly love between a man and a woman is impossible without sex rearing its ugly head (unless the woman is what Tolstoy's narrator calls a "sterile flower"). What might otherwise be dismissed as Kitty's jealous imagination seems to be corroborated when the narrator later observes that Anna had "unconsciously the whole evening done her utmost to arouse in Levin a feeling of love— as of late she had fallen into doing with all young men" (7:12, 704). Barbara Hardy praises *Anna Karenina* for its greater "sexual truth," suggesting that *Middlemarch* is deficient in this respect.[85] Indeed, it may seem as though George Eliot's vision of sexuality as a force that can be contained makes it possible in *Middlemarch* for Dorothea and Lydgate to cry out to each other soul to soul and for neighborly love to be an *ideal* that may even be possible "here—now—in England." Conversely, does Tolstoy's sex-ridden view of the human condition, coupled with his insistence on the "family idea," foreclose the possibility of Levin's compassion amounting to anything?

But does the fact that Anna was guilty of trying to arouse sexual feeling in Levin necessarily mean that nobody should have compassion for her? Theorists of compassion from Aristotle to Martha Nussbaum maintain that perceived innocence is a precondition for compassion.[86] But where does this put the Christian ethics that Tolstoy engages in the novel and encodes in the epigraph (Vengeance is God's), in the Orthodox aphorism that Koznyshev quotes to Vronsky's mother, "it is not for us to judge" (8:7, 774), and in the gospel admonitions about casting stones?[87]

Even if Levin and Anna are "kindred natures embroiled in the same medium," the message seems to be that Levin should not allow his compassion for Anna to interfere with his familial responsibilities.

Levin hereafter surrenders to this Tolstoyan imperative. As he arrives back home, Levin finds letters waiting for him, including one about farm issues back at Pokrovskoe and another from his sister, reproving him for having neglected a matter he had promised to take care of. These letters remind him that since he has been in the city, he has been neglecting his real duties, passing the time listening to program music ("King Lear in the Steppe"), eating and drinking at the English Club, and attempting to penetrate Anna's inner world. As Joan Grossman aptly observes, his time in Moscow is characterized by "dissipation of both energies and money," as well as a "general distortion of the pattern of [his] life."[88] The guilt he feels about having neglected his sister's business reminds him that his first duties are to his blood sister; he is not Anna's keeper. Anna may be a kindred spirit—and she may be in dire need of brotherly love—but Levin must focus on his real family. The message is subtle but insistent. According to the way of the world, both in Middlemarch and in Moscow, family comes first and people protect their own interests. While George Eliot celebrates the diffusive heroism of Dorothea and Caleb Garth, Tolstoy emphasizes not diffusion but preservation—at least on the level of plot. (Even as Levin's story-line distances him from Anna and ties him to his family, with Tolstoy and/or his narrator apparently sanctioning this as the right solution, the poetics of the double plot casts shadows over this process.)

When on the morning after Levin—from Kitty's point of view—was carried away by inappropriate feelings for Anna that need to be exterminated from his heart, Kitty goes into labor and gives birth to their child, further reminding Levin of the restrictions on his love. He experiences fatherhood as "the consciousness of a new sphere of liability to pain" (Constance Garnett's translation of сознание новой области уязвимости) (7:16, 719). As he beholds his son, he experiences "a new tormenting fear" and "compassion" (жалость) (7:16, 719), the same emotions that he felt the night before for Anna Karenina (7:10, 701). The implicit message is that his "sphere of liability to pain" does not include Anna (except in a theoretical way). From now on, his son claims Levin's love and attention, and Levin's duty will be to provide for his son and preserve patrimony. And any love and resources left over should go to his biological sister (whose affairs he has been neglecting), his former nurse, or to his sister-in-law Dolly. (Anna, had she lived, would have been out in the cold.) Whereas *Middlemarch* was a realm where neighbors loved more freely, love in *Anna Karenina* is circumscribed.

The Tangled Bank, Struggle for Survival or Mutual Aid:
Rosamond and Dorothea Embrace "As If They Have Been
in a Shipwreck"

As the novel continues, Tolstoy twins Anna and Levin beneath the
surface, revealing aspects of kinship when Levin undergoes a crisis that
sets him asking, in his pastoral setting, the same desperate questions
that torment Anna on the city streets and at the railroad track. But in
the surface world of the plot of *Anna Karenina* mutual aid appears to be
possible only between close family members.[89] Or, in what may be seen
as a corollary to this, as Anne Hruska has argued, the Tolstoyan family
thrives by excluding others.[90]

Questions about the possibility of mutual aid beyond the immediate family circle come into sharp focus as we examine another pair of
analogous scenes from *Anna Karenina* and *Middlemarch*, each of which
epitomizes the dominant ethos of its novel. Toward the end of *Middlemarch*, Dorothea Casaubon visits Rosamond in the hope of offering her
aid. On her arrival, Dorothea finds Will Ladislaw with Rosamond and
concludes that relations between Will and Rosamond are amorous;
horrified and hurt, Dorothea leaves, aborting her mission of sisterly
love. After a night spent wrestling with her feelings, Dorothea (who
loves Ladislaw herself) conquers her sexual jealousy and tries to think
of others. "Clutch[ing her] own pain," and embracing the "involuntary,
palpitating life" around her, a life of relatedness to other people in all
its messiness, she sets off to complete her mission of sisterly love toward
Rosamond (80, 788). Dorothea's initial actions are marked by "convenient condescension," as Sharon Marcus observes. After all, Dorothea
intends to "save" Rosamond.[91] But then the narrator heralds an important change: "But it is given to us sometimes even in our everyday life
to witness the saving influence of a noble nature, the divine efficacy of
rescue that may lie in a self-subduing act of fellowship. If Dorothea,
after her night's anguish, had not taken that walk to Rosamond—why,
she perhaps would have been a woman who gained a higher character
for discretion, but it would certainly not have been as well for those
three who were on one hearth in Lydgate's house at half-past seven that
evening" (82, 803). These two women, for all their differences, embrace,
"clasp[ing] each other as if they had been in a shipwreck," and confiding
in each other that marriage is like murder (81, 797).

In an act of fellow feeling that, as the narrator keeps reminding us, is
a rare thing for the likes of Rosamond Vincy, she kisses Dorothea and

then reveals to her a truth that will make Dorothea's eventual union with Will Ladislaw possible.[92] Thus, this outburst of sisterly love proves to be critical to the unraveling of Dorothea's love plot.[93] George Eliot signals the "erosion" of differences between Dorothea and Rosamond as they come together in their common misery and confess their sorrows to each other.[94] The novel has invited us to think of these two women as opposites; they belong to different spheres of Middlemarch society and different plotlines of the novel. Perhaps the plots of the novel coalesce here in this kiss, which, as Sharon Marcus points out, is a fine example of an Eliot-style "earnest sacramental kiss," like the one that was pivotal in the early "Janet's Repentance."[95]

After this meeting, Rosamond reverts to her former ways—George Eliot does not make this a tale of Rosamond's repentance. But the embrace between the two women still has lasting impact, all the more so because, as Marcus argues, *Middlemarch* is a novel "so concerned with charting every possible filament of community."[96] In the Finale, we are told that even when Lydgate would hold Dorothea up as a paragon, while calling Rosamond, his own wife, "his basil plant" because basil plants "flourished wonderfully on a murdered man's brains," Rosamond "never uttered a word in depreciation of Dorothea, keeping in religious remembrance the generosity which had come to her aid in the sharpest crisis of her life" (Finale, 835). This is a tribute to Dorothea, certainly, but it also shows Rosamond's own potential.

The mysterious effusion of sisterly love between these two women in their shared misery over marriage is one of the triumphs of this novel, muted and bittersweet, in keeping with the mode of the "home epic." Here George Eliot adopts Homeric similes—as when she compares Dorothea and Rosamond in their passionate embrace to survivors of a shipwreck and then in the next paragraph describes Rosamond as "urged by a mysterious necessity to free herself from something that oppressed her as if it were blood-guiltiness" (81, 797–98)—and also introduces the Homeric thematics of shipwreck and blood guilt. Even if the plot of her home epic does not feature shipwreck or bloodguilt (beyond that associated with the death of Raffles), its action is *like* that of traditional epic in its emotional intensity and human meaning. When Rosamond kisses Dorothea, the pathos is not as epic as when Priam kisses Achilles in that grand act toward the end of the *Iliad*, which binds them together in fellow feeling and causes Achilles to give way and commiserate with Priam. War resumes, but what has happened between Achilles and Priam shows Achilles becoming a true hero and changes the feel of the epic for the reader. (And, as Robert Rabel has argued, this scene converges the storylines of this double-storied epic.)[97] Although the encounter between Dorothea and Rosamond is less grand, George Eliot's mission is to readjust the sensibility of readers and to teach us to see the tragic in the everyday. Rosamond's kiss, epic within *Middlemarch*, is part of George Eliot's redefinition of heroism in her "home epic," as she replaces old notions of valor and desire with new values based on diffusive forms of love. She also encodes a message not unlike that of the *Iliad*: in Middlemarch, as in Troy, the possibility of mutual aid, sealed by a sacramental kiss, gives hope for humankind even if it is an isolated event and even if the bitter reality of struggle and competition prevails.

The fact that "on the level of plot [фабула] and in terms of the relations (acquaintance) of characters" (as Tolstoy wrote to Rachinsky) George Eliot shows that mutual aid is possible—but not the norm—adds to the texture of *Middlemarch*, even if, as many argue, it is in its own way a bleak novel despite or because of the promise associated with the reforms heralded in the novel. The neighborly ethos that permeates this multiplot novel depends on Rosamond's kiss, as it depends on the cry from soul to soul between Dorothea and Lydgate. George Eliot believed not only that the sexual instinct could be subdued, but also that altruistic impulses could become part of the fabric of social life. As she revised George Lewes's *Problems of Life and Mind* after his death, George Eliot inserted references to the possibility of "submerg[ing] egoistic desire" to create "an habitual outrush of the emotional force in sympathetic channels." As Sally Shuttleworth noted, George Eliot may well have been making this revision with her Dorothea in mind.[98] And how Dorothea behaves with Rosamond shows sympathy taking over when egoistic desire is submerged.[99]

The Tangled Bank, Struggle for Survival or Mutual Aid: The Shcherbatsky Sisters Confer about Breastfeeding; Anna Commits Suicide

In *Anna Karenina*, at the point when Anna seeks comfort from Dolly in what end up being her last hours, Tolstoy composed what could have been a narrative equivalent to this sisterly embrace of Dorothea and Rosamond in their mutual desperation.[100] Why do Anna and Dolly not confide in each other and clasp each other as if they had been in a shipwreck? That they do not lays bare an important feature of Tolstoy's *Anna Karenina*, in which human beings, especially those who lack blood ties or sexual relations, very seldom confess to each other their sorrows or comfort each other. In the last segment of Part 7, after trying to distract herself with her daughter, Anna, desperate, follows the suggestion of her maid Annushka and goes to Dolly for help. This visit harks back to Anna's mission of sisterly love at the opening of the novel, when she came to help Dolly and Stiva in their time of need; Dolly is now in a position to reciprocate, as she also was when she visited Anna at Vozdvizhenskoe in Part 6, in what started off as an act of solidarity with Anna but ended up, in the words of David Herman, marking her "flight from sisterly love."[101]

Anna's inner monologue reveals that she goes to Dolly with an open heart, ready to surrender to Dolly's counsel: "She loves me, and I'll do what she says." Anna even registers that Dolly "doesn't like Vronsky." Anna thus knows that Dolly will advise her to renounce Vronsky and, presumably, to return to Karenin and Seryozha. Anna also admits that she is guilty and deserves to suffer: "No, I'll go to Dolly, and say straight out to her, I'm unhappy, I deserve this, I'm to blame, but still I'm unhappy, help me" (7:28, 757). The question that haunts this novel is not about whether Anna is to blame but whether anyone can or will help Anna in her misery. Anna seems to hold hope that Dolly will have compassion on her, guilty though she is, and help her out of sisterly fellow-feeling.

When she arrives at Dolly's, Anna, alas, does not find her alone. Her arrival interrupts a consultation between Kitty and Dolly about the breastfeeding of baby Mitya. (Kitty, too, has come to Dolly for help.) Kitty wrestles between her own feelings of "animosity towards this bad woman and the wish to be lenient with her" (7:28, 759). Kitty conquers her sexual pride, comes out to greet Anna, seeing her for the first time since the ball in Part 1. Kitty looks with compassion into Anna's eyes as Anna leaves, before remarking to her sister, once Anna is gone, on how pretty Anna looked in spite of everything and how piteous she seemed. Anna, however, is overwhelmed by enmity, bitterness, and jealousy toward Kitty.

On the surface, the meeting of these three women seems to reinforce the opposition between Kitty who chooses compassion and Anna who chooses enmity; between Kitty the good mother focused on nursing her young and Anna the bad mother who has abandoned Seryozha and ignores Annie, and so forth. And yet in Anna's inner monologue as she rides on (having abandoned all hope of help from Dolly or anyone), Anna suggests that Kitty, who, Anna presumes, regards herself as superior to Anna, is really no different: "We *all* want something sweet and tasty. If not candy, then dirty ice cream. And Kitty's the same: if not Vronsky, then Levin. And she envies me. And hates me. We all hate each other. I Kitty, Kitty me. That's the truth" (7:29, 760). Anna surely judges Kitty too harshly: she fails to see Kitty's compassion; Kitty is not full of hatred. (Like others in *Anna Karenina*, Anna tends to project onto others what she herself feels.) And yet, when Anna ends up throwing herself under a train after leaving Dolly's house, is it only because she is so consumed by hatred and jealousy?

Has Dolly let her down? Certainly the idea of death, along with the desire to punish Vronsky, had entered Anna's mind before her visit to Dolly, but she had rejected it then, feeling her love for Vronsky and her desire to live. Throughout what is left of her life, until the last minute, she is torn between life and death. One might argue that there was no way she could escape the death sentence of Dumas fils or that contained in the dream of the peasant, a dream that had returned to haunt her that morning.[102] But what if this suicide does not belong to the category of inevitable suicides? What if it were a contingent suicide? Anna makes one final attempt to escape, to live, by going to Dolly's in search of love and comfort. As Amy Mandelker has written, "Ultimately, when Anna most needs her, Dolly lets her down."[103]

The narrator does not reveal Dolly's thoughts and feelings during Anna's visit.[104] Anna's arrival is reported as follows: "Between the sisters, at the time when Anna arrived, was being held a consultation about breastfeeding. Dolly went out alone to meet the guest who had at that minute interrupted their conversation" (7:28, 759). The use of the word "sisters" makes the main point that Anna is an outsider who interrupts the Shcherbatsky sisters as they occupy themselves with the survival of the Shcherbatsky species. And, right after Anna leaves, as he records what Kitty says to Dolly about Anna, the narrator qualifies the verbum dicendi with an adverbial gerund stating the condition under which she speaks—"left alone with her sister"—to remind us that Anna is outside of the fold of their sisterly love (7:28, 760). Throughout the scene, Dolly seems awkward in her response to Anna; the context suggests that Kitty's presence inhibits her. Dolly's first words to Anna are: "So you haven't gone away yet? I wanted to come and see you myself" (7:28, 758). Dolly then mentions the letter that has just come from Stiva from Petersburg where he was trying to secure the divorce.

But Dolly indirectly acknowledges that she has not done what she wanted to or could have done for Anna.

Whatever excuses Dolly has for having neglected Anna, her reception of Anna is not what Anna had hoped for. Dolly at one point looks "with curiosity" at Anna, and the narrator notes: "She had never seen her in such a strange, irritated state" (7:28, 759). After Anna's departure, when Kitty says that Anna was "just as attractive and pretty as ever, but with something terribly piteous," Dolly responds: "No, today there was something unusual [or peculiar] about her." Dolly briefly explains: "When I was seeing her off in the front hall, I thought she was going to cry" (7:28, 760).

Unlike the reader, Dolly has not been privy to Anna's inner thoughts or nightmares, so Dolly has no way of knowing the depths of Anna's desperation. Nor does she know that Anna came to her specifically for help. However, Dolly clearly knows that Anna was not her usual self and was near tears. Yet, even when they have a moment alone together in the hall, Dolly does not try to comfort Anna or find out what is wrong. Although Anna might be beyond help at this point, Dolly is probably the one person we might expect to have a heart large enough to love, comfort, and help the desperate Anna in her time of need. But she does not.

Insofar as the desire that motivates the reader in *Anna Karenina* is a desire not only to know the outcome of this plot or that but also to understand the connections between these plots, this meeting, like that of Levin and Anna earlier in Part 7, promises answers. Protagonists from all three plots come together. Yet again, as with Levin's meeting with Anna, the message *on the level of plot* seems to be that Anna's plot is separate, that Anna is on her own and nobody's sister or neighbor.[105] Why does Dolly, who has been regarded by some as the heroine of Tolstoy's "home epic," in a moment that reminds us how far we are from the world of George Eliot's English "home epic," let Anna down?[106] Has Dolly reverted to Karenin's motto of "Everyone has enough to bear in his own grief"? As Tolstoy orchestrates this scene, the Shcherbatsky sisters *feel* compassion for Anna, but their focus, ultimately, is on themselves.

As she leaves Dolly's, Anna sees the world around her as filled with enmity. She rejects Christian love as humbug and declares: "We all hate each other . . . Yashvin says, 'He wants to strip me of my shirt, and I him of his.' Yes, that's the truth!" (7:29, 760–61). Here Anna recalls Vronsky's friend Yashvin's declaration that he felt no pity for the man who had lost so much to him at the gambling table. What Anna sees as the truth at this point is not the truth, as she herself seems to grasp fitfully now and finally only later just before her death as she crosses herself and begs God for forgiveness. Now, as she leaves Dolly, she sees the world in terms of the struggle for survival that Darwin's theories seemed to confirm or dictate (at least to Tolstoy). As Anna puts it, "Yes, it was what Yashvin said: the struggle for survival and hatred—the only thing that connects people" (7:30, 762).

Anna is wrong when she meanly declares to herself that Dolly would have been pleased at her misery. But, at the same time, no one, not even Dolly, really tries to give Anna the help she needs. In the drafts of the novel, Tolstoy had Anna comment directly on Dolly's failure to help and comfort her. As evidence that "we are all cast into the world," forsaken, "only out for ourselves," "pretending that we have faith, that we love, that we make sacrifices, whereas we love nothing but ourselves and our passions and never sacrifice anything for anyone else," Anna sarcastically asks herself "what kind of friendship" she should have expected from Dolly with her "five children" and "an unfortunate passion for a husband who is throttling her" (20:533; 20:547). There would be nothing left in Dolly's heart for Anna.[107] Anna is extreme in her bitterness, but on the level of plot and relations it is hard to deny the truth of what she says. Tolstoy's model is thus a closed system of limited resources: patrimony, grain, milk, kitchen scraps, and perhaps even loving kindness all are in short supply—what is given to one is taken away from another, according to the principle articulated by Levin to Oblonsky when he sells woods to Ryabinin: his children would have "the means to live and be educated" whereas Oblonsky's would not (2:17, 171). Tolstoy's world operates as a tight economy: Dolly, for example, is aware that Kitty and Levin, generous to her and her children now, will not be able to afford to be as generous once their own family grows (6:16, 607). In accordance with the image of the ploughshare (8:20, 790), Levin's sphere of interest has grown since his marriage, but in the context of *Anna Karenina* interests and love still need to be rooted in the self and family rather than dispersed or diffused. What Karenin said to Dolly at times starts to seem like an axiom *on the level of plot* in *Anna Karenina*: everyone has enough to bear in his own grief.

In one of the inner links of the novel of which Tolstoy was so proud, Levin comes to the conclusion in Part 8 that "loving your neighbor" is the answer; without this commandment, imbibed with one's milk, people would "skin" and "throttle" their neighbors, and the struggle for survival would be the way of the world (8:11,794; 8:12, 797). Levin thus responds fairly directly to Anna's vision of human beings cast into the world to hate and struggle, according to Yashvin's maxim of "he wants to strip me of my shirt and I him of his." (For further discussion of this point, see chapter 4.) Whereas in George Eliot's world, Darwin's plots could have a happy ending as more evolved beings aided each other instead of throttling and skinning each other, Levin and Anna, like Tolstoy, interpret Darwin differently, seeing a hateful and violent struggle for survival as Darwin's only plot. (As the Russian Darwinist K. A. Timiriazev wrote in 1878 after the publication of the finale of *Anna Karenina*, it is clear that Levin never actually read Darwin; had Levin done so, he would have discovered that "as applied to humans the struggle for existence signifies not hatred and extermination but, on the contrary, love and protection.")[108] In *Anna Karenina*, only by faith in God would human beings learn to love their neighbors and cease to be, like nature, red in tooth and claw.

If Levin is, in the end, reassured that he has been living in accordance with God's commandment to love one's neighbor, imbibed with his milk, then the evidence of his neighborliness and Christian spirit, as Kitty affirms to herself as she breastfeeds baby Mitya (before Levin himself is even aware he is obeying Christ's law), is his generosity toward Dolly and her brood when he suggests that Kitty give her share of the Shcherbatsky family property to Dolly, as well as his decency to their peasants who trust and rely on him (8:7, 785). Thus, when the novel ends with Levin's revelation about loving one's neighbor, it is clear that Levin's love will trickle down or radiate outward in a controlled way, to family first, then to peasants.[109] As will be discussed in the next chapter, Anna Karenina appears to be out of the range of Levin's neighborly love. In *Anna Karenina*, on the surface of the plot, Tolstoy thus relies on the "family idea" to keep the sexual instinct under control, to ensure the preservation of the Levin species, to secure the transmission of patrimony, and to guard against the kind of diffusion and dispersal of neighborly love that George Eliot celebrates in *Middlemarch*.[110]

As *Anna Karenina* draws to its close, Levin appears to complete the quest "to make one's own individual life both internally coherent and coherent with the community in which it moves," which George Levine sees as the "highest morality" in *Middlemarch*.[111] But Tolstoy leaves the reader to wonder whether Anna Karenina is part of this community. Tolstoy adapted the multiplot form to depict his Russian environment and to reflect his own unique understanding of the relations of human beings with each other and with God. He provides us with two (or three) plots and invites the reader to feast on the lateral relations between them. Readers may intuit about Anna and Levin what George Eliot's narrator announces about Dorothea and Lydgate, that they are "moving with kindred natures in the same embroiled medium, the same troublous fitfully-illuminated life" (30, 290). But, as he explained to Rachinsky, Tolstoy avoided unity on the level of plot or story [фабула] or through the "relations (acquaintance) of characters" [на отношениях (знакомстве) лиц]. This feature of his novelistic form, however, cannot be understood in isolation from the understanding of human relations that is embodied in *Anna Karenina*. Tolstoy keeps Anna and Levin apart, on the level of "unintroduced strangers" throughout most of the novel. Yet, when their lots converge with a "cry from soul to soul," Tolstoy suggests that whatever compassion Levin might feel for Anna is inappropriate. Furthermore, even Dolly does not come to her aid. At this point, the reader may well feel that Tolstoy's realism in *Anna Karenina* makes George Eliot's epic of neighborly love feel like an English fairy tale. (After all, Tolstoy's specialty was "the tragedy of the bedroom" and incarnating "the family idea.")

When Rachinsky wondered why Tolstoy essentially cuts Anna off from others when she is most desperate for comfort, Rachinsky was asking why *Anna Karenina* was not more like *Middlemarch*. After translating not only Charles Darwin but also George Lewes, Rachinsky may well have developed affinities for English forms and been more open to George Eliot's English variation on the multiplot novel, which allowed neighbors to love more freely, even on the surface of plot.[112] Perhaps Rachinsky had been taken in also by the Eliot/Lewes belief that sexual and family instinct could be subdued so that sympathetic impulses could become part of the fabric of life.

Tolstoy himself, however, remained true to his initial response on reading George Eliot—namely, that she was able to fictionalize a pure incarnation of the Christian idea, but that her forms were not right for him. Thus, when Anna dies, nobody but God hears her cry. Compassion possibly reigns in the hidden architectonics of *Anna Karenina* and possibly in the reader's consciousness, thanks to Tolstoy's narrative techniques. His use of the multiplot does not inhibit that. As will be discussed in subsequent chapters, Anna's cry still reverberates throughout the rest of Tolstoy's double or triple story so that the reader is left, at novel's end, to come to his or her own understanding of what Anna's lot has to do with Levin's—and with Dolly's. And so the form and ethic of Tolstoy's multiplot *Anna Karenina* vary from *Middlemarch* in subtle but significant ways even as both novels celebrate what Dorothea calls "widening the skirts of light" by "desiring what is perfectly good, even when we don't quite know what it is and cannot do what we would" (39, 392).

4

Loving Your Neighbor, Saving Your Soul

Anna Karenina and English Varieties of Religious Experience

But Who Is My Neighbor?

As *Anna Karenina* draws to a close, Anna is dead, but Levin survives. On the last day of the action, inspired by the words of a muzhik about remembering God, living for the soul, and not harming others, Levin suddenly resolves the questions about life that had left him suicidal. Levin thanks God for granting him faith and embraces the law of loving one's neighbor rather than throttling him, declaring that these truths had been with him all along. But who is Levin's neighbor?[1] This question comes to the fore as Levin and family members gather at Pokrovskoe. The answer set forth is that Levin's neighbors (or "near ones" [ближние], according to the term used in Russian and Slavonic for neighbor in the biblical context) are those who are literally near and dear to him at Pokrovskoe.[2] Whatever neighborly love reigns at Pokrovskoe in Part 8 does not appear to extend to Anna Karenina. As Virginia

Woolf observed, Anna is "allowed to drop out": nobody at Pokrovskoe bears her in mind.[3]

In the July–August 1877 *Diary of a Writer* Dostoevsky took Tolstoy to task because Levin's love for his near ones did not extend afield from Pokrovskoe.[4] When war in the Balkans is debated in Part 8 of *Anna Karenina*, Koznyshev argues, advocating military intervention inspired by humanitarian principles, that Russian volunteers should come to the defense of their Slavic brethren and co-religionists and out of Christian feeling provide "brotherly aid" to the Serbs and wage war against the Turks. Levin objects that killing and revenge violate Christ's law and, furthermore, that war is "such a beastly, cruel, and terrible thing that no man, to say nothing of a Christian, can personally take upon himself the responsibility for starting a war" (8:15, 805). But Levin does not let his case rest there: he goes on to deny feeling any love for his Slavic brethren and co-religionists. This is what prompted Dostoevsky to ask of Tolstoy, how near does the neighbor have to be for compassion to register?

Dostoevsky sarcastically grants that we feel nothing for suffering babes on Mars, but he wants to know why Levin feels nothing for innocent children suffering in the Balkans. Dostoevsky asks how Levin, who so loved his own baby Mitya (and delights when he takes a bath), was not ready to extend his compassion to other children beyond his family circle, the Serbian victims of Turkish atrocities, which Dostoevsky describes with Ivan-Karamazov-like relish. Dostoevsky's stance was clear. As he pushed for military intervention on behalf of these "neighbors," Dostoevsky's compassion for the Serbs was bolstered by a mix of factors (ethnic solidarity, Orthodox triumphalism, and Russian imperialism). And Dostoevsky appears to identify the neighbor one should love as a member of one's sect (Orthodox Christians), rather than as all human beings (following a universalist approach), or as those with whom one shares a face-to-face encounter, which makes them a neighbor regardless of ethnic, social, religious difference.[5] But, if we move beyond Dostoevsky's topical concern to the larger concerns of Tolstoy's multiplot novel, the question about neighborly love still holds. Who is Levin's neighbor?

In Luke 10:25–37, when asked what must be done in order to inherit eternal life, Jesus confirms what is written in the Law; namely, that you must love God with all your heart and your neighbor as yourself. His interlocutor counters with a tough question: "But who is my neighbor?"

As Tolstoy observes in his commentary on this passage in his later revision of the Four Gospels, the words "love your neighbor" are meaningless if we do not know who our neighbor is.[6] How do we know? As Tolstoy observes, "you cannot love everyone." What is to be done? Tolstoy warns that "ratiocination about who my neighbor is is a trap that lures away from the truth and, in order not to fall into it, one must not reason, but act."[7] Tolstoy reminds us that Jesus avoids this trap. In lieu of an answer, Jesus tells a parable about a man robbed, beaten, and left half-dead on the road from Jerusalem to Jericho. A priest goes by, followed by a Levite, but neither helps the man; next to pass by is a Samaritan, who stops and cares for the man. Jesus then asks his interlocutor: Who was a true neighbor to the man left half dead? Jesus thus puts the burden of interpretation on his interlocutor and, by extension, on us. Tolstoy will do much the same in *Anna Karenina*.

Tolstoy's own *Anna Karenina* is an attempt in (double or triple) story form to address the vexed question: "But who is my neighbor?"[8] The problematics of loving one's neighbor appear in many contexts, across plots. For example, Anna will ask, on arriving by train on her mission to help her brother's family in its distress, whether nothing can be done for the widow and children of the man who died on the tracks. The question "who is my neighbor," which arises time and again in different reaches of the novel, becomes especially vexed when Levin, Kitty, Karenin, and others seek meaning in life, faith in God, or both. The novel invites us to consider various definitions as Tolstoy's heroes, at different points, take compassion on others, turn their backs on them, or fall into the trap that Tolstoy would warn about in his commentary on the gospels—doing no more than ratiocinating about neighborly love. Tolstoy presents a variety of different possible answers, from acts that recall the Samaritan's compassion for a stranger to Levin's final illumination about loving one's neighbor and God that seems to imply that if he loves those at Pokrovskoe, God will take care of the rest.

Anna Karenina reflects Tolstoy's own often desperate concern with loving his neighbor. Even as he retreated into family life at Yasnaya Polyana, Tolstoy struggled with the question of how his world related to the world beyond his own estate. There were many facets to this question. Like many of his contemporaries, he was concerned with questions of distributive justice that came to the fore urgently in the wake of the emancipation of the serfs. Nor could he ignore the misery of others, especially when he witnessed it face to face. For example, in 1873, when famine hit Samara, where Tolstoy had recently bought land, he wrote to his cousin Alexandrine Tolstoy that it was "painful and humiliating to be a human being" in the face of this suffering.[9] He could not sit idly by. In addition to trying to help locally, he collected information and rallied support by using his position to wage a campaign through the press and other connections. But he was chagrined when famine relief became embroiled in the politics of charity. Whereas it should all be simple, so that "if you want to give, you give, if you don't, you walk on by," "no, it turns out, that if you give, you thereby demonstrate that you are someone's enemy, that you wish to offend someone or to win someone over."[10] The "simplicity" that Tolstoy so valued was lost.[11]

As Tolstoy wrote *Anna Karenina* in the period following this famine, he was tormented by his own need for faith. He understood that neighborly love was a correlate of love of God, but he needed to understand how the two intertwine. And he was desperate to know whether faith, once he found it, would mean a radical break with life as he and his family knew it. What form would loving his neighbor take? These concerns were not new to Tolstoy's spiritual life. Back in 1859, in what Tolstoy called a "profession de foi," he explained to Alexandrine Tolstoy that he had come to believe in immortality and that "one must live for others in order to be eternally happy." Tolstoy acknowledged that what he had come to on his own was very close to "the Christian religion." (In fact, Tolstoy arrived at his own formulation of the "double commandment" that Jesus gives before telling the parable of the Good Samaritan.) Still, the young Tolstoy suffered because he did not know how to live according to these principles, for his heart was silent and "doing good *on purpose* is shameful."[12] Tolstoy carried on, through his eventual marriage and family life, only to return to these questions more desperately as he wrote *Anna Karenina*. Over the years, especially later when he wrote didactic treatises rather than novels, Tolstoy may have fallen into the trap of ratiocination that he himself warned against. But in *Anna Karenina* Tolstoy avoided ratiocination. By having his fictional characters "act" or "do" by trial and error and in (double or triple) story form, he explored a spectrum of answers to the vexed question "who is my neighbor?"

Apostles of English Evangelical Christianity on Russian Soil: Lord Radstock in Petersburg and Bobrinsky at Yasnaya Polyana

As Tolstoy wrote *Anna Karenina*, incursions of evangelical Christianity of English origin and a concomitant upsurge in Christian social work nearly caused what Nikolai Leskov called "a high society schism."[13] Expressions of the Christian idea that the young Tolstoy had found so striking in George Eliot's English fiction—he had declared blessed the English who imbibe with their milk this pure, evangelical Protestant form of Christian teaching—now made their way into Tolstoy's Russian reality and into his Russian fiction, and were sullied in the process.[14]

The ministry of the English evangelical missionary Lord Radstock (as Granville Waldegrave, Baron Radstock was known), who was in Russia 1873–74, 1875–76, and 1878, was an important impetus for this "schism," although forms of non-Orthodox evangelical piety in Russia predated his arrival, transcended his ministry, and were associated with movements beyond what came to be known as Radstockism or Pashkovism (after Vasily Alexandrovich Pashkov, one of the Russian leaders of the movement). Radstock was known for bringing about quick conversions, preaching faith in Christ in drawing rooms, handing out Bibles in the streets of Petersburg, and inspiring his Russian followers to charitable social work.[15] Pashkovites eventually took their ministry beyond high society to the peasants. At this point, the movement came to be regarded as a threat by government authorities, who barred Radstock from Russia, attempted to limit activities of Pashkov and other Russian followers, and eventually exiled Russian leaders of the movement. The Radstock movement was also criticized in the press, in exposés, in profiles, and in fiction. Responses included Prince Meshchersky's nasty attack in a novel called *Lord Apostle in Petersburg High Society* (1875), Dostoevsky's profile in *Diary of a Writer* (March 1876), in which he describes Radstock's preaching as lackluster but acknowledges the ardor of his followers' faith and notes the good deeds they set about doing, and Leskov's masterful *Schism in High Society* (first published serially starting in 1876 and then as a monograph in 1877). Hugh McLean explains that Leskov's *Schism*, which appears to be "a pro-Orthodox attack on a Protestant heresy," ends up being critical of the state of Russian Orthodoxy. That this evangelical movement associated with the English Lord Radstock was able to win hearts and inspire action speaks to the spiritual hunger—or disillusionment—among educated Russians of the time. As Leskov reported, many were dissatisfied with how the official Russian Orthodox Church embodied and communicated its message.[16] Orthodox Russians were tempted by Radstockism/Pashkovism because they found the Orthodox Church to be, in the words of Leskov, "formalistic and lifeless."[17] In 1880, as Konstantin Pobedonostsev, the Procurator of the Holy Synod, proposed strategies to the tsar for containing the threat of the Radstock-Pashkov movement, he wrote that "in order to gratify the religious want which drew people to Mr. Pashkov's meetings, it is necessary to call similar meetings and have prayers in the spirit of the Orthodox Church, with the assistance of the ablest and most zealous priests."[18] With his suggestions to the tsar that the Russian Orthodox Church would benefit from imitating features of the very dissent movement it sought to suppress, Pobedonostsev acknowledged that the Church was not answering the religious needs of its people.

The rise of Radstockism/Pashkovism motivated defenders of Russian Orthodoxy to intensify efforts to reform the Russian Orthodox Church and revitalize Orthodox practice. As part of this process, they advanced Russian expressions of the Christian idea through various means, such as celebrating Russian monks, elders, and wanderers, promoting monasteries as a vibrant focus of religious life, countering or supplementing the dissemination of Bibles by evangelicals with the publication of the writings of Church Fathers and works of Orthodox piety, intensifying efforts to bring folk piety to the attention of high society, reminding the faithful of Orthodox commitment to active love of neighbor by recalling, for example, St. Yuliana of Lazarevo, known for feeding the hungry, and by championing charismatic and kenotic figures, such as St. Tikhon of Zadonsk (1724–82, canonized in 1861), who, in the words of Georgy Florovsky, rivaled John Chrysostom in his message of "love of neighbor, social justice, and mercy."[19] Malcolm Jones has argued that the incursion of Radstockism in the late 1870s made Dostoevsky's mission to "validate and express the truths of Orthodoxy" all the more urgent.[20] As Dostoevsky explained to readers of *Diary of a Writer*, the success of Lord Radstock in Russia—Dostoevsky admitted that he "works miracles over human hearts, people flock to hear him, many are deeply moved"—resulted from the detachment of the educated and upper classes from the soil and the people: they had lost touch with true Orthodoxy.[21] Dostoevsky's piece on Lord Radstock followed one month after "Muzhik Marei," a work in which Dostoevsky offers his credo in story form about the bond he himself shared with the Russian people, a bond sealed by the sign of the cross made over him as a child by a Russian muzhik. As Dostoevsky saw it, this was the way to social justice. Dostoevsky continued his mission of acquainting Russian readers with the faith of the Russian people (and countering Radstockism and other forms of deviation) by providing compelling models of Russian piety in *The Brothers Karamazov*, his final masterpiece. Edmund

Heier has suggested that the rising Radstock movement could have contributed to Dostoevsky's plan to make the wandering pilgrim Makar Dolgoruky so important in the denouement of *The Adolescent*, which appeared in 1875.[22]

Radstock was known—and scorned—for preaching justification by faith alone. (This was contrary to Orthodox doctrine as set forth, for example, in the catechism of Filaret, which states that a life of good works is inseparable from faith, citing, in support, James 2:20: "Faith without works is dead." As will be seen below, even Stiva Oblonsky remembers this line from the catechism.)[23] And yet Radstock, Pashkov, and other members of the movement actually devoted themselves to good works in addition to evangelizing; theirs was a very active form of loving their neighbor in Christ's name. Radstockists were famous for their ministry to prisoners and for helping the poor, the hungry, and the homeless.[24] The movement established soup kitchens, laundries, and homeless shelters in Petersburg;[25] in the provinces Radstockist landowners set up schools and erected hospitals for local peasants. Detractors, however, mocked Radstockists not only for their doctrine of "faith alone" but also for the way in which some went about their good works. Thus, Leskov writes dismissively of the charitable activity of what he calls the "lady evangelists":

> The blessed of this type, mainly ladies, find their way into poor families. . . . They go into hospitals, prisons, common lodging houses, and have recently even begun to enter camps. To be honest, in the majority of cases this more closely resembles a pastime than real Christian action: the material help brought to the poor by these women preachers is utterly negligible, and their attempts to repair the damage done to these people's live are even less substantial. Unfortunately this does not embarrass them in any way. Their entire concern consists of instilling into unhappy people that God so loved them, that He gave them His Son, and if they love Him, then they are justified and saved. The lady evangelists expect that, hearing this, the poor people will feel ever so much better and more cheerful, and when they do not succeed (and they nearly always fail), they become angry like spoilt children, as if to say, "We have piped unto you, and ye have not danced" (Luke 7:32). They complain of the coarse Russian character which causes people to frown when they, these anxious ladies, want everyone to smile.[26]

While Leskov articulates the standard critique of this kind of charity work, he also reminds his readers that the efforts of non-Radstockist Russian philanthropy, such as charity benefits and balls, were often just as ineffective and ridiculous. He notes that these efforts have "long been the target of satire," possibly alluding to Dostoevsky's parody in *Demons* of the "literary quadrille" (a benefit for poor governesses). As Leskov's response suggests, the charity work of the Radstockists stirred up the question that was all important to Tolstoy: how should members of high society respond to the plight of the Russian people? Do they know what is right for the people? Do they know how to go about helping them? Tolstoy addresses these questions in *Anna Karenina* and devoted much of the rest of his life to trying to determine what is to be done in response to these questions. He, too, was leery of philanthropy, Christian and otherwise, and he was scathing in his exposés of do-gooders. The Radstockists could easily be dismissed as insincere or benighted (and Tolstoy attempted to do that in *Anna Karenina*). But, at the same time, they commanded Tolstoy's attention because many of them, like Tolstoy, actively sought to love their neighbor and God with their whole heart.

Tolstoy incorporates Radstockism into *Anna Karenina* as part of the contemporary Russian life in which he set his action. But, as Georgy Florovsky argues, Radstockism was also part of the background and historical context for Tolstoy's own religious crisis.[27] Radstock's followers, who included some of Tolstoy's old friends and acquaintances, regarded Tolstoy if not as a kindred spirit, then as someone who shared some of their concerns.[28] Tolstoy certainly was loath to follow others—what he ultimately arrived at was Tolstoyism, not Radstockism/Pashkovism.[29] The form of Christian faith Tolstoy fashioned (after he began to distance himself from the tradition, creed, and liturgy of the Orthodox Church, all of which he had tried to embrace for a period that began as he was finishing *Anna Karenina*) would be anchored, like that of the Radstockists/Pashkovites, in his personal reading of the Bible. But Tolstoy's Jesus was very different from the Christ the Savior of the evangelicals; St. Paul's theology was of little use.[30]

Aleksei Pavlovich Bobrinsky, an acquaintance from Sevastopol days, a fellow landowner in the Tula region, and now an important figure in the Radstock movement, visited Tolstoy at Yasnaya Polyana in February 1876.[31] At this time, Tolstoy was midstream in *Anna Karenina* and suffering from his own spiritual crisis. The two men spoke about faith at length and heatedly (according to one of Tolstoy's daughters, who remembered them sitting on a bench and arguing). Tolstoy wrote to Alexandrine Tolstoy about the ardor of Bobrinsky's faith with awe and admiration. As Tolstoy explained, Bobrinsky did not try to convince or convert him, he just told him what faith was like for him. Tolstoy commented that you could not arrive at this kind of faith by means of the intellect—it took a miracle, and he confessed to hoping for one of his own.[32] His response to Bobrinsky's evangelical, Radstock-inspired faith in 1876 reads like a reprise of his 1859 response to the "lofty, purified form" of "Christian teaching" that, after reading George Eliot, he associated with English evangelical Protestants. Tolstoy was fascinated by this English-style evangelicalism, but in his gut he knew it was not for him.

At the bitter end of *Anna Karenina*, Tolstoy's Levin would, as Dostoevsky wryly put it, "get faith in God from a muzhik" back at Pokrovskoe—no influence of English evangelicals there. But, as part of the process of preparing the ground for Levin's illumination and of setting (and attempting to justify) the boundaries of neighborly love in *Anna Karenina*, Tolstoy contended with English iterations of Christian teaching. The evidence in the drafts and in his letters suggests that Tolstoy found this process of discrediting English-style evangelicalism to be a necessary step as he himself struggled with his own doubt and longing for faith. Tolstoy introduced English elements into the world of *Anna Karenina*, rehearsed and discarded scenarios from English novels, and even lampooned English evangelicalism. The drafts of the novel reveal, more explicitly than the final version, how intensely engaged Tolstoy was with this English material, from Radstock to the host of English novels that Tolstoy read not just for their treatment of family life but also for their expression of Christian ideas.[33] As Tolstoy moved from draft to final version, he tended to shed or cover up the more direct and serious indications that he was assimilating—and rejecting—the English material. But this material still figures beneath the surface, making its presence felt especially at those points when Tolstoy addresses the question of "who is my neighbor?"

Tolstoy's most pointed exploration of the problematics of loving your neighbor is based on an explicitly English model and involves Kitty's religious awakening, which inspires her to acts of Christian charity among the sick and dying in the German spa of Soden (Part 2). At the same time Levin, at Pokrovskoe, explores the call to love his neighbor in a different realm, using rhetoric about economic disparity, social injustice, and self-interest as he pursues what Tolstoy in the drafts refers to as Levin's "Russian idea"—namely, his schemes for the "amelioration of the life of the peasants."[34] Tolstoy's concern with what he regarded as English modes of loving your neighbor resurfaces toward the end of the novel (written when Tolstoy's interest in Radstockism was especially strong), both in the depiction of Karenin in Parts 6 and 7 after his "conversion" by Countess Lydia Ivanovna "from a lazy and indifferent believer into an ardent and firm adherent of that new explanation of Christian doctrine that had lately spread in Petersburg" (5:22, 511), and in the debate over the war in Serbia in Part 8. In these segments, Tolstoy works through questions of faith and neighborly love that are keys to understanding the novel as a multiplotted whole and to addressing the question at the heart of this novel: "But who is my neighbor?" What does Anna's plot have to do with Levin's?

An English Preacher's Daughter in the Drafts of Anna Karenina: Princess Kitty Shcherbatsky's New Life in Soden

After refusing Levin's proposal and being jilted by Vronsky in Part 1 of *Anna Karenina*, Kitty Shcherbatsky falls ill and is brought by her parents to the spa of Soden to recover. There Kitty discovers a "new life." The old life it replaced now seems bereft of meaning. Under the influence of new acquaintances, Varenka and her guardian, an invalid named Mme. Stahl, Kitty starts reading the gospels, playing the role of sister of mercy in the family of a very ill compatriot, and even dreaming of visiting prisoners as Aline, the niece of Mme. Stahl, does. In general, Kitty seems to take to heart Jesus's message in Matthew 25:31–46, when he conflates feeding the hungry, comforting the sick, clothing the naked, and visiting those in prison with loving him. Kitty undergoes what even her mother, who is leery about what is happening to her daughter, recognizes as "some kind of serious spiritual upheaval" (2:33, 225). The episode concludes with Kitty's father arriving in Soden to reassert paternal authority over his daughter. He discredits the piety of Mme. Stahl by revealing to Kitty that she is faking her affliction.[35] Once this is accomplished, Kitty heads home to her Russian reality and to her destiny, which, as hinted all along, will be to marry Levin and produce heirs. Eccentric to *Anna Karenina* in many ways, this episode in Soden takes Kitty out of her native milieu and, briefly, opens up new possibilities of plot.

In Part 1 of *Anna Karenina*, the focus had been primarily on sexual love—from Oblonsky's justification of stealing "sweet rolls," Levin's pure desire to make Kitty his wife and the mother of his children, Kitty's delight at Vronsky's attention, to the dangerous passion that develops between Anna and Vronsky. Brotherly and sisterly love, literally understood, also came into play in subsidiary way. Levin had been drawn from Pokrovskoe to Moscow by romantic desire for Kitty, but, while there he was reminded of his duty to be his brother Nikolai's keeper. (Levin put off seeing him until after his failed mission with Kitty.) Anna, leaving her son for the first time, had come to Moscow on a mission of sisterly love, to help her brother's family through their crisis. Significant (in the labyrinth of linkages of the novel) was one act of neighborly love, in the form of Vronsky's charity to the widow of the man killed under the train.[36] Although his behavior could recall that of the Samaritan of the parable, in the context of the nascent Anna-Vronsky plot it becomes suspect because Anna wonders guiltily whether Vronsky acted not out of simple compassion but in the hope of pleasing her.[37]

In Part 2 of *Anna Karenina*, Tolstoy polarizes the two plots. As Vronsky and Anna's adulterous passion develops and is consummated in Petersburg (a year into the action of the novel), Levin and Kitty both appear to have been rid of sexual desire and, in separate but parallel activity, they pursue other forms of love that are neither romantic nor strictly familial. Levin, living chastely, devotes himself to animal husbandry, farming, and bettering the lot of his neighboring peasants. His retreat from traditional patriarchal expectations about how a man of his class should behave subverts the status quo, as does Kitty's new life in Soden.[38] Kitty finds in her new friend Varenka and in her "way of life" "a model for what she now sought so tormentingly: interest in life, virtues in life, outside the social relations of a girl with men, which Kitty found repulsive, picturing them now as a disgraceful exhibition of wares awaiting their buyers" (2:30, 215–16). Thus, in Part 2, Tolstoy seems to channel all the erotic energy of the novel into the Anna/Vronsky plot, while Levin and Kitty explore new plot possibilities for (non-erotic and non-familial) neighborly love.

Tolstoy thus thrusts Kitty, a creature of the Russian courtship plot, into a new world of feminine friendship,[39] evangelical piety, and neighborly love beyond the family circle, all of which is familiar to the Victorian novel, but not the Russian one. The drafts show the English pedigree of this episode. Varenka, the model and inspiration for Kitty's ill-fated attempts at loving her neighbor, initially appeared in drafts not as a

Russian changeling, brought up by the nasty Mme. Stahl, but as Miss Flora Sulivan, a twenty-eight-year-old English woman, "the daughter of a reverend" [дочь пастора] (20:271). Flora Sulivan reveals to Kitty "a whole new world, a whole new sphere of action" (20:271), which Kitty embraces with all her heart. Flora Sulivan lives a life of self-forgetfulness as she cares for and comforts the sick in Soden and practices forms of active neighborly love to strangers that Tolstoy associated with the English.[40] In one of his revealing onomastic plays, Tolstoy also relates his Flora Sulivan to Florence Nightingale.[41] The surname Tolstoy uses, a variant or misspelling of the familiar British surname Sullivan, is an inexact but resounding homonym for the Russian word for nightingale, соловей.[42] As Amy Mandelker has argued, Varenka can be seen as a Florence Nightingale figure.[43] Her predecessor in the drafts, Miss Flora Sulivan, appears to have figured directly as such in the mind of Tolstoy.

As a new model for womanhood in the nineteenth century, Florence Nightingale presented an alternative to both the courtship plot and the nunnery. As Frances Power Cobbe wrote shortly after the Crimean War: "The hospital in Scutari was the cradle of a new life for the women of England" because "Miss Nightingale's band and their sister nurses" broke down prejudices and changed conceptions of the "public function of women."[44] Especially since she continued to work in nursing and reform after her return from the war, Florence Nightingale became the emblem of a new form of heroism, with a far-reaching effect on English culture.[45] In their own very different milieu, the Russian nurses who served during the Crimean War provided a new model for women's philanthropy and activism, as had the Decembrists' wives before them. While serving at the siege of Sevastopol, the young Tolstoy had seen Russian sisters of mercy at work; in his Sevastopol tales, these sisters of mercy appear only briefly but emerge as true heroes of compassion.[46] However, these same sisters of mercy were objects of romantic desire both in Tolstoy's diary (April 11, 1855), in which he muses about falling in love with one of them, and in his Sevastopol tales, in which the young Kozeltsov fantasizes about a pretty, young sister of mercy shortly before his death. This is relevant to what happens to Kitty when her attempt to imitate Varenka—and, by extension, Florence Nightingale and Russian sisters of mercy—ends up arousing illicit romantic feelings. This incident in which sex raises its ugly head during Kitty's foray into nursing the sick of Soden serves as further proof that Tolstoyan women should not have professions or even do "women's work" in strangers' households. (Thus, Dolly speaks up when this question is debated at the

Oblonsky dinner party in Part 5 to suggest that a woman who does not marry can still always find work in the household of a family member.) In Tolstoy's fictional world, the threat of sex is too great to risk letting Russian angels out of the house, even to perform acts of Christian love.[47]

Princess Kitty Shcherbatsky is attracted to Miss Flora Sulivan's English ways and, especially, to how her faith inspires her actions. "[E]verything [in her life] was firm, clear, lofty, and not subject to doubt" (20:230). Whereas Kitty had hitherto lived "an animal life," in Flora's life "there was no place for instincts, everything was subjugated to Christian law" (20:230).[48] In the drafts, Tolstoy sketches the background of Miss Flora Sulivan as follows:

> She grew up in the large family of a moral, strict minister, received an excellent education, taught her younger brothers and sisters, and while still a child had fallen in love with the son of a Gentleman Farmer [Tolstoy transliterates the English phrase into Cyrillic] already eighteen years ago. She had started to love him when she was ten and to him *pledged her troth* [phrase in English (and roman alphabet) in original]. But they were both poor, so she waited. He worked in London as a lawyer, and it was decided that he would marry when he had 800 pounds revenue. Meanwhile, she did not live a life of waiting for future happiness, but rather lived her own full life, fulfilling her Christian duty with all her heart and all her soul. She lived at her father's and tended to the poor and schools of the parish with Lady Herbert. She did not, however, tend to them for the sake of propriety, as they do in England; she gave her whole self to the endeavor. She visited the cottages, schooled the children, reconciled spouses, pleaded with drunks, and comforted the sick, the old, those afflicted by misfortune. Even all this activity was not enough for her, for she was very energetic; she also took part in a society for aid to criminals. All this work ruined her health, but she could not abandon her post and was working to that point when the Lord would call her either to Himself or to the duties of wife and mother. But she was far from being a pedant. She was an avid reader, had opinions on everything, was skilled at, and enjoyed, drawing flowers, and was accomplished at sewing, housekeeping, and conducting conversation in a drawing room. (20:230–31)

Like the English novel Anna reads on the train (as "tracked" by Cruise and others),[49] this portrait is a composite drawn from Tolstoy's imagination and his reading of English novels. The genetic material of Miss Flora Sulivan has been provided by the heroines of Charles Dickens, Anthony Trollope, Charlotte Yonge, George Eliot, and others.[50] In concocting Miss Flora Sulivan, Tolstoy seems almost to lapse into parody as he enumerates her charitable works, endows her with all the graces and skills that befit a lady, and reassures us that she is not a pedant. But Tolstoy asserts that, unlike the rest of her compatriots who perform acts of charity "for the sake of propriety," Miss Flora Sulivan devotes herself fully to what she does and fulfills her "Christian duty" (the commandment to love her neighbor) with all her heart and all her soul. Tolstoy's objects of ridicule are those other English people who simply go through the motions of pious charity, "as the English do." In Miss Flora Sulivan, Tolstoy creates an ideal incarnation of English womanhood and pure English evangelicalism.

Miss Flora Sulivan does not seem destined to make it to the altar, even though she had "pledged her troth" to her childhood sweetheart, according to what is identified in *Anna Karenina* by Kitty's mother as the English custom of "giving the girl complete freedom" (1:12, 44–45). But what has become of her groom? Has he been distracted in London from the goal of marrying her? Although she once imagined family happiness, it now looks as though Flora will spend what is left of her life as a maiden, selflessly devoted to her Christian duty. Tolstoy thus outlines a pattern, according to which those who devote themselves to loving their neighbors do not marry and have families of their own.

The Victorian novels Tolstoy read suggested this paradigm but also upset it in significant ways in the "happily ever after" of their epilogues. In George Eliot's *Adam Bede* (an important English prototype of *Anna Karenina* and one of the few novels that Tolstoy deemed good art in *What Is Art?*), Dinah Morris devotes her life to acts of sisterly love, preaches the gospels in the fields, and ministers to the poor and sick. When Hetty Sorrel is condemned to death for infanticide, Dinah shows herself to be her "sister to the last," comforting Hetty in her cell and bringing her to penitence. (As Adam Bede observes, "the Methodists are great folks for going into the prisons" [41, 470].[51]) Dinah Morris seems destined to remain unmarried, for, as she puts it when she refuses Seth Bede's offer of marriage, "God has called me to be minister to others, not to have any joys or sorrows of my own" (3, 79). And, later, when Adam Bede proposes, she turns him down, out of fear she would "forget the Divine Presence and seek no love but [Adam's]" and that she would "forget to rejoice and weep with others" (52, 552). Yet, in the epilogue, we find her married to Adam Bede and the mother of his

children.[52] Bede family happiness does not mean that Dinah's Method-
ism will wear off with marriage (as had been predicted by Lisbeth Bede,
mother of Seth and Adam) (51, 544). As Adam tells Dinah, seductively
and persuasively, when he proposes the second time, Dinah will still
actively love and help her neighbors even after marriage: "I don't believe
your loving me could shut up your heart, it's only adding to what
you've been before . . . for it seems to me it's the same with love and
happiness as with sorrow—the more we know of it the better we can
feel what other people's lives are or might be, and so we shall only be
more tender to 'em, and wishful to help 'em." And, as Dinah affirms, "it
is the Divine Will," her soul "is so knit with [his]" that without him she
will not have the "fullness of strength to bear and do our heavenly
Father's will" (54, 576). Thus, in the English novelistic realm of George
Eliot, Dinah Bede has it all: she is a wife and mother but remains perfectly devoted to her Christian duty to her neighbors.[53]

In introducing Miss Dorothea Brooke in *Middlemarch*, George Eliot
once again entertains the notion that heroines with fervent faith in God
and a passion for acts of neighborly love may not always be seen as
desirable brides—Middlemarch grooms might be wary of a wife "who
knelt suddenly on a brick floor by the side of a sick labourer and prayed
fervidly as if she thought herself living in the time of the Apostles" or a
wife who "might awaken you some fine morning with a new scheme
for the application of her income which would interfere with political
economy and the keeping of saddle-horses" (1, 9). But, at the same time,
the community assumes that marriage will prevail (especially in Dorothea's case, given her dowry and good looks) and that it will temper
religious fervor. Dorothea Brooke teaches in a village nursery, draws
plans for better housing for the cottagers, then marries Casaubon. Once
widowed, she returns to practice an active, beneficent form of neighborly
love, even if she sometimes wonders how best to go about it. However,
once she is Ladislaw's wife and a mother, Dorothea's "beneficent activity" consists of "wifely help" to Will, "an ardent public man" devoted
to reform. As the narrator reports, "many who knew her, thought it a
pity that so substantive and rare a creature should have been absorbed
into the life of another and be known in a certain circle as a wife and
mother" (only to leave it unclear whether these people simply objected
to her marriage to Ladislaw in the first place) (Finale, 836). The cases of
Dorothea Brooke and Dinah Morris both show that in George Eliot's
world a woman's life can include both fervent Christian devotion to
love of neighbor *and* happy marriage. By contrast, in *Anna Karenina*

Christian devotion to love of neighbor is *only* for the "sterile flowers"
like Varenka.[54]

Miss Flora Sulivan as Levin's Brother's Keeper:
A Christian Woman's Duty

Flora Sulivan, the original agent of Kitty's conversion in Soden, embodies the Christian teaching in its "pure" English Evangelical Protestant
form that first impressed Tolstoy in his reading of "Janet's Repentance"
in 1859. In this novella, Eliot offers the following description of Evangelicalism and its effect on its devotees:

> Nevertheless, Evangelicalism had brought into palpable existence
> and operation in Milby society that idea of duty, that recognition of
> something to be lived for beyond the mere satisfaction of self, which
> is to the moral life what the addition of a great central ganglion is
> to animal life. No man can begin to mould himself on a faith or an
> idea without rising to a higher order of experience: a principle of
> subordination, of self-mastery, has been introduced into his nature,
> he is no longer a mere bundle of impressions, desires, and impulses.
> Whatever might be the weaknesses of the ladies who pruned the
> luxuriance of their lace and ribbons, cut out garments for the poor,
> distributed tracts, quoted Scripture, and defined the true Gospel,
> they had learned this—that there was divine work to be done in
> life, a rule of goodness higher than the opinion of their neighbours,
> and if the notion of a heaven in reserve for themselves was a little
> too prominent, yet the theory of fitness for that heaven consisted in
> purity of heart, in Christ-like compassion, in the subduing of selfish
> desires. They might give the name of piety to much that was only
> puritanic egoism, they might call many things sin that were not sin,
> but they had at least the feeling that sin was to be avoided and
> resisted. (321)

Since this is the most concentrated description of Evangelicalism in
"Janet's Repentance," it is likely to have inspired Tolstoy's outburst in
1859 about how blessed were those English who imbibed Christianity
in its pure and lofty Evangelical form.[55] He seems to have recalled this
passage as he envisioned Miss Flora Sulivan's effect on Kitty. Tolstoy's
narrator in the drafts thus comments that Flora, referred to as "the

English woman," did not act on instinct, in contrast to Kitty, who had lived hitherto "an animal life" according to "instinct." With her moral awakening, under Flora's influence, Kitty acquires that equivalent of the "central ganglion" that George Eliot refers to. Faith for Flora is not just a matter of instinct or doing what comes naturally: she acts according to a law, not one created by people, but a law given and revealed by God (20:230). Miss Flora Sulivan also has a clear sense of "the divine work to be done" on this earth; she knows who her neighbor is. She appears to follows the exhortation of John Wesley to Christian women: "Whenever you have opportunity, do all the good you can, particularly to your poor, sick neighbor."[56] And Flora does so in a spirit of self-forgetfulness and "Christ-like compassion" like that attributed to Evangelicals by Eliot above.

As Flora cares for the gravely ill in Soden, Kitty admires her from afar (as she will do with Varenka, once Varenka replaces Flora in the drafts and novel). By chance, among the seriously ill Russians at Soden is Konstantin Levin's brother Nikolai, in the company of Masha, a former prostitute.[57] The Shcherbatskys avoid them: Kitty's mother is contemptuous of them because of their disreputable pasts and lack of social graces; Kitty finds Nikolai Levin's presence unpleasant because it reminds her of what happened between her and his brother. In one of many mentions of Kitty's sexual attractiveness, which, in Tolstoy's conception, dooms her from the start to fail as a sister of mercy, Kitty senses that Nikolai finds her attractive. She also feels sorry for him because he is so ill. Miss Sulivan not only feels for Nikolai Levin, she tries to help him. At one point, when Miss Sulivan needs an interpreter as she tends to Nikolai, she approaches Kitty and asks her to find out if he has any kin. (Little does Miss Sulivan know that, by Tolstoyan coincidence, his nearest of kin is the man who had proposed to Kitty.) Flora's question about Nikolai Levin's family cuts to the heart of a central concern in *Anna Karenina*: the expectation that families will care for their own, especially in sickness and at death. When families fail, those in need are forced to depend on the charity of others, such as Flora Sulivan. That Kitty *might* have been his sister-in-law adds to the tangle. From the very start of *Anna Karenina*, Tolstoy haunts the action, and Konstantin Levin himself, with the question of whether he is his brother's keeper. Konstantin Levin had vowed to himself that "he would never again allow himself to forget him, would watch over him and never let him out of his sight, so as to be ready to help" when things got worse (1:26, 92–93). Although Levin gave money to his brother for this trip to Soden, at this point in the action he is tending to his own affairs in Pokrovskoe. (When an un-expected visitor arrives at Pokrovskoe, Levin thinks it might be his brother and finds the thought "frightening and unpleasant" because he himself was in a "happy spring mood." Levin immediately feels ashamed and is then ready to embrace him with tender joy, only to find the visitor is Stiva Oblonsky, who, after all, is more pleasant company [2:14, 159].) Meanwhile, the question that Flora Sulivan poses (in the drafts for Part 2) about whether Nikolai has any kin is a disturbing reminder that Levin is not by his brother's side and that the selfless Flora Sulivan is caring for this gravely ill man, who is not her kin, nor even her compa-triot. Tolstoy's Flora Sulivan thus embodies the English-style "evangeli-cal protestant" and "purified" Christian idea, according to which having faith means doing all the good that she could in the spirit of the good Samaritan and taking compassion on a stranger.

When Kitty admires Flora for what she has done for Nikolai Levin, Flora humbly dismisses the praise, telling Kitty that she had simply "fulfilled the duty of any Christian woman" (20:229). Kitty then reveals that she is disappointed in herself for not fulfilling *her* duty as a Christian and worries that she may be incapable of such acts of neighborly love in the spirit of Christ. Miss Sulivan replies that Kitty's very concern that she is not fulfilling her Christian duty shows that she at least under-stands the call to help others. As Kitty struggles to fulfill Miss Sulivan's definition of "the duty of every Christian woman," Tolstoy raises doubts about whether in fact Miss Sulivan's definition suits his Russian Kitty.

Miss Sulivan Reads the Gospels to Levin's Brother: Is the Message of the Savior One in All Languages?

As this segment of the draft continues, Miss Sulivan stays by Nikolai Levin's side after he has an attack and reads to him from the gospels in French. When she next sees Nikolai at the spa, Miss Sulivan offers to read to him from the gospels again. Kitty's father, who "didn't like" Miss Sulivan, mocks this evangelical moment with an anecdote at her expense: the Englishwoman Miss Sulivan goes up to Nikolai Levin and offers to read to him from the Bible. Nikolai's response is to call her a "fool!": "Дура!" But Miss Sulivan assumes he must have said "Yes!" ["Да!" instead of "Дура!"] (20:231). The anecdote is biting because Shcherbatsky mocks her not just for her limited Russian vocabulary, but also for her English-style presumption that others will conform to her program. But Prince Shcherbatsky may not get the last laugh. Miss Sulivan has reported to Kitty that when she read to Nikolai Levin, the message of the gospels got through to him—in spite of her bad French accent. As Flora puts it, "For the power [or action] of the Savior is one and the same in all languages. He became peaceful and was happy." Corroboration of the beneficent effect of this gospel reading is provided by a presumably trusted source: the doctor who tended to him tells of how Nikolai Levin indeed seemed moved by Flora Sulivan's reading (20:229).

Miss Sulivan's declaration that "the power of the Savior is one and the same in all languages" could suggest that her evangelical zeal blinds her to different forms of Christian piety. Tolstoy may be ascribing to Miss Sulivan insensitivity to other points of view and the concomitant expectation that others assimilate, which was a popular Russian stereotype of the English. (In his early "Lucerne," Tolstoy presents the English in this light, explicitly associating their expectation that others do things their way with British imperialism and colonialism.) Yet the idea, obviously dear to the evangelicals who inspired Tolstoy's depiction of Flora Sulivan, that Christ's teaching can be expressed in a variety of different tongues (and even with a bad accent) and still be "one and the same," has a rich Christian pedigree. Meanwhile, in the time in which the novel is set, which was nearly synchronized with Tolstoy's present, Lord Radstock, not knowing any Russian when he first arrived in Petersburg, preached in the salons of high society in French, with what Russian observers noted was a bad accent. Lord Radstock did not let language bar him from spreading the gospel. He was also known for walking the streets of St. Petersburg, distributing the Russian Bibles he carried in his pocket, in confidence that the grace of the Savior would be felt by those who took it and read. According to Nikolai Leskov's report, simple folk, even if they could not read the books he distributed or converse with him, warmed to Radstock, of whom they said, "The Lord hasn't given him our language, but he looks at you so kindly, like, and gives away his books and wants to see and speak to everybody." When he would try to speak, "nothing comes out of it, you see his lips move, but no sense comes out."[58] Thus Radstock, like Tolstoy's Miss Flora Sulivan, believed that the power of Christ's message transcended linguistic and cultural differences. Radstock and Miss Flora may have been fools, but if so, they were fools for Christ's sake. (English ones tote Bibles.) Eventually Tolstoy not only eliminated the positive portrait of the English evangelical Flora Sulivan, but also subverted the idea of Christ's teaching being "one and the same" and accessible across languages and cultures (even though Tolstoy himself would soon be concerned with these very questions—on his own idiosyncratic terms). Tolstoy seems to have taken these steps in order to prepare the ground for Levin to affirm his Christian faith in a patently Russian iteration from a muzhik.

Prince Shcherbatsky on English Charity and How to Save Your [Russian] Soul

In the drafts, after replacing the English Flora Sulivan with the duo of Varenka and Mme. Stahl, Tolstoy continued to use Kitty's father as the voice of (Russian) reason and fatherly concern as he undoes her English-style awakening. He tells his beloved daughter that "their" sect (that of Varenka and Mme. Stahl) would banish Kitty on the grounds that you have to be "old and unattractive" to belong to it. Kitty presses her father to be serious. At this point, Tolstoy sketches out the following exchange between Kitty and her father:

> [KITTY:]—But can it be bad that she helps her neighbor, reads the Gospels, teaches . . .
> [PRINCE SHCHERBATSKY:]—It's excellent. But I know one thing, that if it weren't for the misfortunate, what would they do? In England, they create *poors* [in English in the original] on purpose expressly so that there will be someone to collect alms for. I don't like all this Europe.
> [Kitty:]—But really it's not Europe, it's Christianity.
> [PRINCE SHCHERBATSKY:]—No, it's Europe. In Russia, if you want to save your soul, you go to a monastery, but, here, no, here they take away with one hand, and give with the other.
> [KITTY:]—But Varenka is Russian.
> [SHCHERBATSKY:]—She's dear in what's Russian about her, and she's unpleasant in what she has picked up of the local spirit.
> (20:243–45)

Shcherbatsky clearly does not approve of Russian Orthodox women, not Varenka and certainly not Kitty, following the English Evangelical model of "do[ing] all the good you can, particularly to your poor, sick neighbor," even if he has to admit that loving your neighbor is a good thing and part of the Christian idea.

In Shcherbatsky's view, there is something perverse in how the English go about loving their neighbor. Shcherbatsky's critique of English practice echoes the lines of William Blake: "Pity would be no more, / If we did not make somebody poor, / And mercy no more could be,/ If all were as happy as we." As Gertrude Himmelfarb explains, this need for poor folk on whom to bestow charity was a feature of the "Victorian ethos."[59] Victorians were obsessed with charity even while enforcing policies, ideologies, and programs (associated with capitalism, industrialization, and empire) that had the effect of making the poor poorer.[60] In Tolstoy's drafts for *Anna Karenina*, Prince Shcherbatsky emerges as an astute critic of Victorian culture.[61]

Prince Shcherbatsky informs Kitty that there are alternatives to the English approach to loving God and neighbor: "In Russia, if you want to save your soul, you go to a monastery. . . ." Traditional Russian monasticism had been undergoing what the historian Scott Kenworthy describes as a revival, with a growing number of monks, nuns, and novices. Monasteries had grown increasingly important as centers of Russian religious life in the reign of Nicholas I, as part of a reaction against Western[izing] ways. In this respect, Shcherbatsky is correct when he presents this Russian way of "saving your soul" by going to a monastery as an alternative to how it is done in Europe. (And monasticism was a powerful antidote to Radstockism.) According to Kenworthy, the Russian monasteries helped to "reshape" the Russian Orthodox Church and to infuse a new vitality into Russian Orthodoxy.[62]

Retreat into a nunnery had already figured in Turgenev's *Nest of the Gentry* (1859) as a Russian alternative to sordid love plots: after her aborted love affair with Lavretsky (whose wife, presumed dead, shows up back in Russia), Liza lives out her life as a nun in a convent in a remote reach of the Russian Empire where, by God's grace, she saves her soul.[63] In real life, many illustrious writers and thinkers were part of the "massive upsurge" of pilgrims from all social classes who visited the monasteries. Shortly after finishing *Anna Karenina*, Tolstoy made his first visit to the monastery of Optina Pustyn', a major destination for pilgrims that was known for the spiritual guidance provided by its elders. In the final version of the novel, Tolstoy suppressed Shcherbatsky's reference to the role of the monastery in Russian Orthodox life. He does, however, incorporate a haunting reference to this Russian way of saving your soul in *Anna Karenina*'s other plot: as Anna rides in her carriage to go see Dolly, to beg her for help, she remembers how she made a pilgrimage to the Troitsa Monastery back in her youth, in a period when Holy Russia had not yet been violated by the railroad.[64]

Shcherbatsky's declaration that the Russian way of saving your soul is to go off to a monastery suggests that "self-salvation" may be privileged over neighborly love in Russian religious experience, as he understands it.[65] And in the drafts Shcherbatsky overtly presents this Russian way as preferable to the English emphasis on loving your neighbor, which struck him as being contrived and self-serving. (In *Diary of a Writer* Dostoevsky voices a similar skepticism about English-style love of neighbor, when he tells of how Radstock's Russian followers would "*seek out* [my emphasis, LK] the poor so as to do good deeds for them and almost reach the point of giving away their possessions."[66]) In the final version of *Anna Karenina*, although Tolstoy cut Shcherbatsky's direct attacks on English-style love of neighbor, Shcherbatsky continues to embody the traditional religious culture of his milieu and to defend the Russian way (and the purity of his daughter's soul) with his caustic wit.[67]

Kitty's Evangelical Awakening in Soden: A Religion She Could Love

In the final version of *Anna Karenina*, Kitty falls under the influence of Mme. Stahl and Varenka in Soden. While Varenka inspires Kitty by her example, Mme. Stahl proselytizes. She gives Kitty a copy of the gospels in French to read and once, but only once, she "mentioned that in all human griefs consolation is given by faith and love alone and that no griefs are too negligible for Christ's compassion for us" (2:33, 224). Mme. Stahl practices a form of Christianity that seems unidentifiable: "No one knew what religion she adhered to—Catholic, Orthodox or Protestant—but one thing was certain: she was in friendly relations with the highest persons of all Churches and confessions" (2:32, 220). When Kitty's father returns to Soden (having left his wife and daughter there while he traveled to Karlsbad, Baden, and Kissengen "to visit Russian acquaintances and pick up some Russian spirit" [2:34, 227]), he informs Kitty that Mme. Stahl is a Pietist (2:34, 229). But this identification is unsettling in its own way. Shcherbatsky admits he does not really know what Pietism is, but then provides an ostensive definition: "She thanks God for everything, for every misfortune," including the death of her husband. In *Adam Bede*, Lisbeth Bede, grieving over her husband's death, accuses Methodists of "always making trouble out to be a good thing" (10, 154). Shcherbatsky's similar mode of characterizing Mme. Stahl's piety suggests a standard reaction to evangelical forms, but he adds a twist that renders Mme. Stahl's Pietist piety all the more suspect when he tells Kitty that for Mme. Stahl to thank God for her husband's death is "quite funny because they had a bad life together" (2:34, 229).

Pietism was an offshoot of Lutheranism that had some foothold in Russia in Napoleonic times. Shcherbatsky's identification of Mme. Stahl as a Pietist would likely remind Tolstoy's contemporary reader of Radstockism, the deviation from Orthodoxy that was currently in fashion in Russian high society. Meanwhile, in *Anna Karenina*'s other story, at Countess Lydia Ivanovna's, Anna is absorbed by the "interesting" account of a missionary named Sir John's ministry in India (2:7, 137). This Sir John has been identified as a fictional stand-in for Lord Radstock. (Radstock had been to India to evangelize on several occasions before he started coming to Russia.)[68] In *Schism in High Society*, Leskov encourages readers to lump Pietists and Radstockists together. While describing prominent Radstockists and their works, Leskov reminds his readers of some "well-known Petersburg Pietists" who did good works in prisons, schools, and hospitals and who, "instead of making for a ball or the theater or for a friendly game of cards with a crony," would "spend their time writing letters in support of poor people, or read the Bible and speak to them about the Savior of the world."[69] Leskov's account makes it hard to tell a Pietist from a Radstockist.

The religious awakening Kitty undergoes in Soden clearly has an evangelical, non-Orthodox feel. The life she envisions for herself sounds like that of a do-gooder Pietist or Radstockist: "Wherever she lived she would seek out the unfortunate people, help them as much as possible, distribute the Gospel to the sick, the criminal, the dying. The thought of reading the Gospel to criminals, as Aline [the niece of Mme. Stahl] did, especially attracted Kitty" (2:33, 224–25). Kitty does not want to get herself to a nunnery and save her soul there, following the Russian model in Turgenev's *Nest of the Gentry* of Liza. She wants to be like Varenka and Aline, who, as the drafts reveal, had their antecedents in the English Miss Flora Sulivan.

Tolstoy's narrator reports that the new religion revealed to Kitty in Soden "had nothing in common with the religion Kitty had known since childhood." He then suggests why Kitty's childhood religion had failed to satisfy (or even recognize) her spiritual yearnings: it was "a religion that expressed itself in masses/liturgies and vigils in the Widows' Home where she could meet her acquaintances, and in learning by heart with the priest Slavonic texts" (2:33, 224). In a draft of this passage, Tolstoy also mentioned the catechism as one of the defining elements of the Orthodoxy that left Kitty spiritually hungry (20:230). This description thus emphasizes that Orthodoxy piety was rooted in fixed forms and rote learning.[70] In the draft Tolstoy had concluded the descriptive list with a phrase in English, "*it did not answer*," as if to explain why an English (evangelical) model of religious life might well "answer." (Tolstoy's descriptions of what "did not answer" for Kitty look ahead to Leskov's soon-to-be published explanations of why so many disillusioned Orthodox flocked to Radstock.)[71] Further explaining what drew Kitty to this new religion (and what was lacking in her old one) is that the new one was a religion "not simply that she could believe in because she was told to, but a religion that she could love" (224, 2:33).

In Soden, Kitty goes through a phase when it seems to her that she cannot reconcile her new understanding of Christ's teaching with her old way of life. At stake for Kitty is the question that Tolstoy asked repeatedly in one form or another (until his dying day at Astapovo): did taking Christ's teaching to heart mean that one had to make a radical break with life as most people in his circle lived it?[72] Kitty's mother chides her for carrying her *engouement* too far, telling her: "*il ne faut jamais rien outrer*" [one must do nothing in excess] (2:33, 225). In the drafts, her mother specifically told her that it was all well and good "to be kind and help her neighbor," but that she should not take it too far (20:238). How does Kitty respond? Tolstoy's narrator tells us that she thinks to herself, but does not utter out loud to her mother, that a religion that asks you to turn the other cheek or give your shirt as well as your caftan is founded in a spirit of exaggeration.

Kitty's Awakening in Soden: Reading the Gospels

As her unspoken reply to her mother reveals, Kitty has been reading that French copy of the Gospels given to her by Mme. Stahl. For her mother, the very fact that Kitty is reading the Bible is, along with her lack of interest in her society friends in Soden and her joining Varenka in visiting the sick, a sign that she is under the influence of a new evangelical faith that, if allowed to take root, will change the course of Kitty's life. In the religious culture Kitty grew up in, Bible-reading of this kind was not common practice.[73] In some circles it was regarded as suspect and a symptom of foreign, specifically Protestant, influence. Exposure to the scriptures traditionally came in other forms, such as in passages read in Slavonic during the liturgy or as interpreted by clerics.

The project of translating the Bible into the Russian vernacular, in order to encourage the practice of the faithful reading in a form they could more readily understand, began with help from the "English and Foreign Bible Society" under Alexander I, during his mystical-Pietist phase after the defeat of Napoleon. The New Testament was completed and then distributed in a limited way. Under Nicholas I, however, the process of translating the Old Testament was stopped, as was officially sanctioned distribution of Russian New Testaments.[74] (Foreign missionaries and Bible Societies continued their work in a limited way.) Those responsible for suppressing the Russian Bible believed that it was not in the best interest of the Russian Orthodox Church and State to have the Russian text widely available for private use. A characteristic rationale was Alexander Shishkov's declaration that it would be demeaning to the Holy Scriptures to be in people's houses as part of their daily life: the Gospels, treated with such respect in the liturgy, "would lose their dignity," would be "soiled, tattered" when mixed up with household things so that eventually "they would no longer act on human minds and hearts."[75] When Alexander II came to power, the New Testament, which had already been translated, was published. Work on the translation of the Old Testament began again and the Russian Synodal Bible was finally completed in 1876.

But, even when the Bible was available in Russian, the expectation remained that Orthodox believers should read it in the spirit of the Church and interpret it according to Holy Tradition. Sergii Bulgakov explains this as follows: "We should read the Word of God with faith and veneration in the spirit of the Church. There cannot be, there should not be, any break between Scripture and tradition. No reader of the Word of God can comprehend for himself the inspired character of that which he reads, for to the individual there is not given an organ of such comprehension. Such an organ is available to the reader only when he finds himself in union with all in the Church."[76] In Soden, Kitty's reading of the gospels risks being regarded by tradition-bound Russian Orthodox as a "Protestant" way. (Tolstoy himself would take his own approach to the gospels in the years after he finished *Anna Karenina*.)

When Kitty reads—and interprets—the gospels on her own for the first time, she attempts to apply the message she extracts to her own life and to put into action Christ's teachings. As Kitty sees it, this means living as a sister of mercy, in imitation of Varenka, instead of living the life her mother envisions for her. Indeed, her mother, who found the English custom of allowing girls complete freedom to make their own decisions about marriage to be tantamount to letting five-year-olds play with loaded pistols (1:12, 44–45), might well regard this other English practice—of letting girls read the Bible and make up their own mind about its meaning—to be equally ill-advised and dangerous.

Tolstoy's description of the conflict between Kitty and her mother over Kitty's new Bible-based faith resonates with an exchange in George Eliot's *Adam Bede* in which Dinah Morris's aunt (a kind of surrogate mother to this orphan) tells Dinah that she needs to "settle down like any other woman in her senses, instead o' wearing yourself out, with walking and preaching, and giving away every penny you get." Dinah's aunt is convinced that Dinah's understanding of religion is misguided: "And all because you've got notions i' your head about religion more nor what's i' the Catechism and the Prayer-book." Dinah's immediate response is: "But not more than what's in the Bible, aunt." Her aunt then insists that Dinah has misinterpreted the Bible because the authorities ("them as know best what's in the Bible—the parsons and people as have got nothing to do but learn it") do not tell people to behave the way Dinah does. As George Eliot presents it, the conflict is between the aunt's traditional Anglican piety, which bows to the authority of catechism, prayer-book, and clergy, and her Methodist niece's evangelical faith, according to which she acts on her own inspired interpretation of Christ's teachings. The aunt tells Dinah that "if everybody was to do like you . . . the world must come to a standstill," and everybody would cease "bringing up their families, and laying by against a bad harvest." She therefore concludes that Dinah's "can't be the right religion" (6, 122).

The issues that George Eliot addressed in an English context—whether faith should be grounded in established tradition prescribed by church authorities or in direct personal response to the Scripture, and whether taking Christ's teaching to heart means a radical break with life as conventional believers lived it—were of paramount concern to Tolstoy in *Anna Karenina* and beyond. The scene from *Adam Bede* may well have lingered in his consciousness as he composed a more abbreviated version for Kitty and her mother in their different fictional milieu.[77] For this brief period in Soden, Tolstoy ascribes to Kitty attenuated semblances of qualities, ideas, and plot motifs associated with

Dinah Morris. In *Adam Bede*, Dinah's self-sacrificing love of her neighbors, inspired by her evangelical faith, puts her at Hetty's side in prison as she awaits execution and is instrumental in softening Hetty's heart and leading her to repentance. Tolstoy, to be sure, ends up with another plot for Kitty (though in the drafts he toyed with the idea of having Kitty plan to rehabilitate Anna in society). He shuts down Kitty's evangelical phase rather quickly, keeps neighborly love within bounds, and thus ensures that *Anna Karenina* runs a course very different from *Adam Bede*, even if both novels end in epilogues that celebrate forms of family happiness.

Kitty Returns to Russian Ways:
"What Did I have to Do with Some Stranger?"

In the novel as published, Tolstoy cuts short Kitty's "new life" when her father arrives in Soden and quickly sets her back on course. Kitty's father delights in revealing to Kitty that Mme. Stahl is not an invalid with a cross to bear but a vain woman who has retreated to a wheelchair to hide her ugly legs under a lap rug. When Kitty protests that she "does so much good! Ask anyone you like!," Prince Shcherbatsky replies, "Maybe. But it's better to do good so that, if you ask, nobody knows" (2:34, 232). As Gary Saul Morson points out, Shcherbatsky's devastating response echoes the sentiment expressed by Jesus in Matthew (6:1–6) when he says that you should give alms "so that your left hand doesn't know what your right hand is doing" and pray "in secret." (Perhaps Kitty's father is familiar with this teaching, which, as Morson notes, Kitty and Mme. Stahl "had evidently not taken to heart.")[78] From this point on, the "heavenly image" of Mme. Stahl is forever ruined for Kitty.[79]

Tolstoy's decision to have the nasty and fake Mme. Stahl work in tandem with Varenka, both replacing Miss Flora Sulivan, contaminates Kitty's new piety. Under her father's influence, Kitty concludes that her new life was "all a sham because it was all done on purpose, and not from the heart," that she had wanted "to seem better to people, to God, to herself," and that she tried to "deceive everyone" (2:35, 235). What Kitty concludes is in keeping with the message Tolstoy laces throughout *Anna Karenina*, that there needs to be a personal connection for acts of neighborly love to work well. At least this is the case for Kitty, as it will be for Levin.[80] That she was *imitating* Varenka may seem to be a bad thing in Tolstoy's context. But what form should *imitation* of Christ take? (Imitating Christ is not meant to be doing what comes naturally.) And, according to Matthew 25:31–46, when he separates the sheep from the goats, Christ will want to know what Kitty has done for "the least of [Christ's] brethren," the poor, the prisoners, the hungry, all those she wanted to help in Soden. Should imitation of Christ involve a radical commitment to a life beyond self? The comforting answer would be that "we can all be servants of God wherever our lot is cast" (as Dinah Morris puts it [6, 123]) and that Kitty's way of serving the Lord is different from Varenka's. That said, Kitty reverts to a more comfortable, effortless mode of Christian experience, one that does not demand that she change her way of life. Whereas from Varenka Kitty had learned that "you only have to forget yourself and love others, and you would be calm, happy, and beautiful" (2:33, 224), does Kitty now give up on loving others and go back to loving herself? Perhaps she also stops reading the Bible. When Kitty asks Varenka during their spat, "What did I have to do with some stranger?" [Какое мне дело было до чужого человека?] (2:35, 235), we see that Tolstoy's model of loving your neighbor, at least for Kitty, is not that of the Samaritan of the parable who responds to the misery of a stranger.

Tolstoy presents Kitty's sexual attractiveness as an obstacle to her loving her neighbor in the mode of George Eliot's heroines, of Miss Flora Sulivan, or of Varenka. Initially, when she met Varenka in Soden, Kitty "felt that in [Varenka], in her way of life, she would find a model [образец] for what she now sought so tormentingly: interests in life, meaning in life, outside the social relations of a girl to men, which Kitty found repulsive, picturing them now as a disgraceful exhibition of wares awaiting their buyers" (2:30, 215–16). Although Kitty had hoped to leave all this sordid business behind, the model Varenka offers is shown to be only for "sterile flowers," according to Tolstoy's famous designation. Thus, it turns out that father knew best when he told her, in the drafts, that she would be banished from the sect of Mme. Stahl and Varenka because one had to be "old and unattractive" to belong (20:243). By the time Prince Shcherbatsky arrives, the "charm" of Kitty's "new life" has already been "poisoned" by sexual desire (2:33, 227). In a passage in which the narrator describes Kitty largely from her mother's point of view, we had been informed that Kitty was clearly proud of playing the role and fulfilling "the duties of sister of mercy" in the family of Petrov, a sick painter (2:33, 225). However, her efforts on this front fail because she inspires romantic feelings in Petrov, which on some level she had been guilty of cultivating.[81] In the drafts, Tolstoy elaborated further as he imagined variants of interactions between Kitty and Petrov that could have remained chaste in English novels, but were polluted by sexual feeling when Tolstoy appropriated them.[82] For example, in George Eliot's novels, a woman's good looks do not keep her from serving the Lord because, as Dinah Morris puts it, "when God makes his presence felt through us, we are like the burning bush: Moses never took any heed what sort of bush it was—he only saw the brightness of the Lord" (8, 137). But the turn of events between Kitty and Petrov comes as no surprise in the world of Tolstoy's *Anna Karenina*. At the start of the Soden episode, the narrator had informed us that Varenka lacks what Kitty has in excess: "the restrained fire of life and an awareness of her own attractiveness" (2:30, 215). Varenka succeeds as a sister of mercy, but, in Tolstoy's sex-ridden world, Kitty's sexual appeal bars her from this mode of Christian life (as a sister of mercy). In *Anna Karenina*, sterile flowers are born that way, from their mother's womb. If you are Kitty, there is no point in attempting, according to Christ's suggestion in Matthew 19:12, to make yourself one for the kingdom of heaven's sake.[83] (After *Anna Karenina*, Tolstoy would take a different stand on this.)

On the eve of her departure from Soden, Kitty herself finally rejects, as wrong for her but perfect for Varenka, the role of the sister of mercy. She does, however, salvage her friendship with Varenka. Tolstoy thus incorporates what Sharon Marcus has identified as a topos of the English novel in which feminine amity becomes a stage in the Bildung of a bride in a companionate marriage plot. Marcus argues that through friendship the young woman matures and gains better knowledge of herself in order "to choose a husband more wisely."[84] What prevails from this point on is a modified version of this English scenario as Kitty's marriage plot continues: Kitty has gained important self-knowledge from her relations with Varenka and her experience in Soden (even if it is that she is different from Varenka).

Kitty's Feat of Sisterly Love: Comforting her Brother-in-Law

As she prepares to leave Soden, in (delayed) reaction to "all the weight of that world of grief, sickness, dying people in which she had been living," Kitty declares that she wants to be back in the fresh air of Russia, at Ergushevo, with Dolly and the children (2:35, 236). Before her trip to Soden, Kitty had helped Dolly nurse all six of her children from scarlet fever (2:3, 126). The Tolstoyan message is that Kitty succeeded as a sister of mercy *within the family*, where she belongs.[85] The obvious question is whether Kitty would be permanently content in this role of caring for someone else's children, even her own sister's. As her face reveals to Levin during the dinner party that culminates in their engagement, Kitty feels horror at the thought of ending up an old maid.

Everything that ran amok in Kitty's attempt to nurse the sick and comfort the dying in Soden falls into place in Part 5, when Kitty, now married to Levin (and pregnant), tends to Nikolai Levin at his deathbed as his "sister." (Kitty's remark to Nikolai that he never would have guessed back in Soden that she would one day become his "sister" prompts the reader to connect the two episodes and see the second as the fruition of the first [5:17, 492]). Levin marvels at his wife's skill as a nurse—she notes proudly that in fact she learned a lot in Soden—as well as at her sense of how to behave in the face of death. By contrast, Levin himself does not know what to do and feels inadequate and terrified. He quotes the gospels to himself: "Thou hast hid these things from the wise and prudent, and hast revealed them unto babes" (5:19, 496). Levin concludes that Kitty's faith is what imparts to her a mysterious sense of how to face death. Indeed, at Nikolai's deathbed in the Russian railway hotel, Kitty promotes Russian Orthodox practice when she convinces Nikolai to receive the sacrament of communion and unction, during which he prays fervently and after which he tells Levin that it was a comedy he performed for Kitty's sake. (Unlike the English Protestant Miss Flora Sulivan of the drafts of the Soden scenes, Kitty does not try to read him the gospels.)

At the deathbed of Nikolai Levin, Kitty's success as sister of mercy explains why she failed at Soden. Tolstoy's message is clear: the sisterly care does good because it is not extended to a random stranger and, moreover, in this familial context, it does not run the risk of becoming sexualized, as it had in Soden. What happens at Nikolai's deathbed reinforces what was intimated in Soden; namely, that it may be fine for Miss Flora Sulivant or her replacement, Varenka, to care for strangers, but that Princess Kitty Shcherbatsky, the progenetrix of the continuation of the Levin line, must keep her nursing skills—and neighborly love—strictly within the bounds of family.

The Bachelor Levin at Pokrovskoe:
His Peasant Brothers' Keeper

While Kitty makes her benighted attempt as a sister of mercy in Soden, Levin goes through a parallel stage in his masculine sphere. Back in Russia, he seeks meaning in life on his own, without a wife, by doing good on his ancestral estate. From early in the drafts, Levin has been preoccupied with what Tolstoy calls the "Russian idea," by which is meant that Levin sought to ameliorate the life of the peasants. As Levin returns to his estate after Kitty's refusal and his meeting with his brother Nikolai, we are told that Levin "regarded the reforming of economic conditions" [advocated by Nikolai, who had communist leanings] "as nonsense, but he had always felt the injustice of his abundance as compared with the poverty of the peasants." But what was Levin to do? The only solution he sees at this point is "to work still harder and allow himself still less luxury" (1:26, 93). Levin lacked interest in the kind of philanthropy that occupies his bachelor brother Koznyshev. Justifying his withdrawal from *zemstvo* affairs (3:3, 246), Levin declares that he does not care whether a random peasant Alyoshka has stolen a ham, nor about building *zemstvo* hospitals, nor about anything in which personal interest is not involved, as David Herman has observed.[86] But Levin does care about those near and dear to him. Thus, when his peasant nanny Agafya Mikhailovna sprains her wrist, Levin sees to it that it is treated. In explaining his position to Koznyshev, Levin justifies his lack of interest in peasant schools on the grounds that he will not be sending his children to them (and that the peasants themselves do not want to either), and he declares his passionate interest in military service, "which touches the future of my children, my brothers and myself" (3:3, 246). As these references to his (modal) children suggest, family is paramount to his understanding of how human beings are bound together. Like Kitty, he asks: What has he to do with strangers? What business of his is their well-being? The message for him, as for Kitty, is that he needs the grounding in family for his work for the common weal to make sense or for love of neighbor to kick in.[87]

Levin rejects not only Koznyshev's style of philanthropy, but also the liberal-minded and extravagant measures taken by the landowner Sviyazhsky to improve Russian estate life. (For example, Sviyazhsky procures new-fangled machines from the West [3:27, 332].) In a telling detail, Sviyazhsky is childless and thus in a position to squander his patrimony. Levin comes up with his own mode of working for the common weal as he attempts to organize the labor force according to new principles. Having determined (in an echo of English political theory) that self-interest is what motivates people, Levin develops a scheme for surrendering parts of his farm to peasant collectives. The peasants would work harder and better, he reasons, because they would be motivated by self-interest. As he institutes this new system, he finds that those collectives that are held together by family ties have the most hope of succeeding. He explains to Agafya Mikhailovna that he is doing this for the peasants because it is good for him, by which he means that he stands to gain in a material sense through this venture since the peasants are motivated to work harder and Levin will collect his part. But Agafya Mikhailovna understands him to be saying that he is doing this for the sake of his soul. Levin muses about bringing about "a revolution, a bloodless but great revolution" with its cradle at Pokrovskoe (3:30, 344). Thus, not unlike Kitty in her attempt to love her neighbor in Soden, Levin tries to put an ideal into action.

When he comes to Pokrovskoe to visit, Levin's dying brother Nikolai points out the falsity of his endeavor, much as Kitty's father made her see that she was trying to be someone she was not. Nikolai tells Konstantin that he is playing at communism just to be original but without any conviction, whereas for it to succeed one has to be willing to give up established forms of life, including family and property (3:32, 350). According to Nikolai Levin, then, communism requires a radical upheaval. He makes a brief allusive comparison to early Christianity. (For example, many early Christians took to heart Jesus's warning in Luke 18:22 that it is not sufficient just to keep the commandments: you must also "sell all you have and distribute it to the poor.") At this point, Levin realizes that he is not ready for the "revolution" he had been toying with. Just as Kitty retreats to more conventional forms of Orthodox piety that can be practiced without upsetting the nest of the gentry, so too does Levin stop short of surrendering his patrimony.[88]

As Part 3 ends, Levin is overwhelmed by the thoughts about death that set in when Nikolai visits. After his marriage, Levin is distracted from death, but he continues to feel torn between his realization that all he truly cares about is his family (as he puts it, all he truly cares about is that Kitty, pregnant with his heir, does not stumble) and his guilty feelings about not doing good for his neighbor.[89] He compares himself at this point to Koznyshev, who is about to seal his fate as a bachelor when he fails to propose to Varenka, devoting himself instead to philanthropic and patriotic causes, out of what Levin earlier described to himself as a lack of passion. Clearly, Koznyshev loves his neighbor from his armchair and at his desk. Kitty asks what Levin would say of her father, "Is he bad, too, since he's done nothing for the common good?" Levin responds that Prince Shcherbatsky is fine the way he is because of his "simplicity, clarity, and kindness" (6:3, 560). The message is that Russian Orthodox believers like Shcherbatsky do not torture themselves with the question "but who is my neighbor?" and the related questions about social justice that torment Levin. Perhaps, when Levin finds faith, he will just *know* who is neighbor is. As Tolstoy would note (in his later commentary on the Gospels) in regard to the lawyer's challenge to Jesus, "but who is my neighbor?" (Luke 10:29), this question can become a "trap": "To avoid falling into it, one must not reason, one must act."[90]

Levin's relative wealth vis-à-vis the peasants, which had felt to him like an "injustice" in his bachelor days (1:26, 93), appears to bother him to some degree still, even now that he is a father-to-be. But, as he reveals in conversation with Oblonsky and Veslovsky while hunting, he believes that because of his "responsibilities to the land and to [his] family" he has no right to take radical steps to remedy the inequality between him and the peasants by giving up his estate and privileges (6:11, 588). Levin concludes that the only way he can remedy the situation is "negatively," or as he put it: "in the sense that I'm not going to try to increase the difference of situation that exists between him and me." Veslovsky accuses him of sophistry; Oblonsky tells him that he should "either admit that the present social arrangement is just and then defend your own rights, or admit that you enjoy certain unjust advantages, as I do, and enjoy them with pleasure." Veslovsky and Oblonsky then go off to take pleasure in the company of peasant women, leaving Levin uneasy, especially about his policy of going along with an unjust system and acting justly "only in the negative sense" of not adding to the injustice. Is this enough?

In Part 8, we are told that Levin had given up trying "to do something that would be good for everyone, for mankind, for Russia, for the district, for the whole village" and that he had begun "to limit himself more and more to living for himself." Now that he is married with an heir, Levin feels "he, like a ploughshare, cut deeper and deeper into the earth" (8:10, 790). This is because, as a family man, his sphere of self-interest has expanded to include his wife and son, as well as others who are intimately linked to him through marriage; and it continues to include his brother and sister and the peasants, to whom he has a historical and geographical connection and whose well-being is inter-connected with his family's. Much as Kitty in Soden asked, in an angry rhetorical question, "What did I have to do with some stranger?," Levin does not concern himself with the misery of strangers; he has his hands full with relatives.

Loving Your Sister-in-Law at Pokrovskoe and Declaring War in the Balkans

On the last day of the action of *Anna Karenina*, Kitty and Levin are nestled in their safe haven at Pokrovskoe with their extended family and one non-relative, Katavasov, while others, including Vronsky, Yash-vin, and Veslovsky, have set off by train to suffering and death in the Balkans. As Tolstoy brings Levin, that happy family man left suicidal by his lack of faith, to a final illumination about loving his neighbor, he returns to the question of "who is my neighbor?" But Levin *knows*, now that he has faith—or now that he is a father?—that his neighbors are those at Pokrovskoe in his family circle. (Some readers might object to this definition, as Dostoevsky did.) In making the argument—and providing parable-like demonstration of how this works instead of ra-tionalizing the definition—Tolstoy draws on topical material, the war in the Balkans, to explain how Levin's understanding of loving one's neighbor differs from that of Koznyshev and others. Tolstoy also returns to questions raised by Kitty's ill-fated attempts at loving her neighbors in Soden and, more cursorily, those raised by Levin's attempts at eco-nomic and labor reform on his estate. Tolstoy thus integrates these early episodes to show not only that they were necessary stages in the separate development of bride and groom, but also that they contained the germ of the religious and political message of the multiplot novel as a whole.

On the last day of the action of *Anna Karenina*, before describing Levin's spiritual crisis over the past months and his revelation after a dialogue with a peasant that he has found faith and that he had been living all along "according to those spiritual truths he had sucked in with his milk" (8:12, 797)—amounting to living for God and loving rather than throttling your neighbor—the narrator describes Kitty's meditations on the state of her husband's soul. Kitty has retreated from those gathered at Pokrovskoe so that she can breastfeed baby Mitya. At this point, Agafya Mikhailovna first announces to Kitty the landmark in baby Mitya's development: he has learned to recognize those near and dear to him. As the "experiment" enacted later reveals, this means that he excludes strangers.

Kitty's thoughts move from the immediate tasks of the day to her husband's lack of faith (or unbelief, неверие). Kitty knows that Levin is devastated by this, yet she herself is not concerned, although according to Church doctrine this lack of faith would bar him from heaven. Kitty sees, in anticipation of what Levin himself concludes in the next several chapters, that he has been living by Christian law even without being a believer. But how does Kitty know?

As the ultimate proof, she remembers that Levin had proposed that Kitty give Dolly her portion of property the two sisters owned so that Dolly would not have to sell her portion as a result of her husband's failings.[91] Kitty concludes: "What kind of unbeliever is he? With his heart, with that fear of upsetting anyone, even a child! Everything for others, nothing for himself, Sergei Ivanovich simply thinks it's Kostya's duty to be his steward. His sister, too. Now Dolly and her children are in his care. And there are all these muzhiks who come to him every day as if it were his business to serve them" (8:7, 784–85). Kitty's model of the Christian law of loving your neighbor does not appear to take strangers into account. It is rooted in the family, in being one's brother's keeper rather than a sister of mercy or a good Samaritan. And Kitty concludes by telling Mitya, now finished sucking his milk and fast asleep, "Yes, be just like your father, be just like him."

As Kitty meditates on what she sees as proof of Levin's Christian spirit, despite his ostensible "lack of faith," she explicitly thinks to herself: "Better let him stay that way than be like Mme Stahl, or like I wanted to be that time abroad. No, he's not one to pretend." This reference to her experience in Soden makes explicit the relevance of this episode to the finale of *Anna Karenina*. Kitty determined that she herself had been pretending when she imitated Varenka (or the heroine of an English novel) and dreamed of caring for the sick, comforting prisoners by reading them the gospels, or practicing other forms of neighborly love outside the family circle. It is not surprising that Kitty would prefer the state of her husband's soul to the religiosity of Mme. Stahl, who was revealed to be mean-spirited, hypocritical, and lacking in Christian charity.

But why bring up Mme. Stahl at this critical point? (She has not been mentioned in the narrative at all since Part 2, except once in Part 6 in reference to Varenka's plight.) In the context of Kitty's reflection on the state of Levin's soul—and just as Levin's unpretentious creed of being his brother's keeper triumphs—this mention of Mme. Stahl calls to mind the perversions of Christian love done in the name of religion, as well as deviation from traditional Orthodox practices. In Kitty's experience, Mme. Stahl figures as a prime example of piety to avoid, but the reference to Varenka's guardian will resonate in the reader's mind with cases of religious perversion in other reaches of the novel as well.

Shortly after Kitty remembers Mme. Stahl, the menfolk discuss the war in the Balkans (Dolly listens and at one point even speaks up), and Prince Shcherbatsky names Mme. Stahl out loud as one of the primary warmongers, along with Countess Lydia Ivanovna and Ivan Ivanych Ragozov. (This threesome has, as Shcherbatsky caustically puts it, "declared war on Turkey." [8:15, 805].) Prince Shcherbatsky's yoking together of Mme. Stahl and Countess Lydia is a jarring reminder that the world of the two plots is one and the same even if the narrative keeps the plots to a large degree separate.

Anna Karenina, "Little Sisters," Angry Christians, and Radstockists in Petersburg High Society

Countess Lydia Ivanovna is to Anna's plot what Mme. Stahl is to Kitty's plot: the parallelism between them is part of the hidden structure of *Anna Karenina*. Each woman is beset by and tempts others with perverted and pernicious forms of Christian piety.[92] That they both are alienated from their husbands and lacking a child of their own suggests that they eroticize religious experience to compensate for what they lack. In Part 1, when Anna returns to St. Petersburg from Moscow, hoping to fit comfortably back into her old life, Countess Lydia visits her almost immediately and talks to her about the Little Sisters (1:32, 108). The narrator identifies this as a "philanthropic, religious-patriotic institution," suggesting that the mission of these Little Sisters is imperialist and nationalist and not the practice of sisterly love in the spirit of Christ. In her inner monologue after Lydia leaves, Anna comments that Lydia is "always angry" even though she is a "Christian" and that she always regards people as enemies. Her penetrating comment on the contradiction in Lydia's religious behavior suggests that Anna has an intuitive grasp of what makes a true Christian. (If chapter and verse were to be cited in support of her intuition, it would be 1 John 4:20: "If a man say, I love God, and hateth his brother, he is a liar: for he that loveth not his brother whom he hath seen, how can he love God whom he hath not seen?") As it first appears in context, Anna's new insight into Lydia and her Little Sisters *hating* their brothers and sisters might seem to be, like her observation about Karenin's ears and, more poignantly, the fleeting initial disappointment she feels when she sees Seryozha, a change of perception she has undergone because passion for Vronsky has rocked her to the core. "All this was there before, but why didn't I notice it before?," she says to herself as she comments on Lydia's anger (1:32, 108). But if her observation about Lydia's mean-spirited piety is recalled later and placed in the context of the concern with expressions of Christian teaching that permeates both plots, it stands as an ominous warning.[93] Not only will Anna's instincts prove right in regard to Lydia when she comes to the fore in the action in Part 5, but in Part 2 Kitty makes a parallel observation about Mme. Stahl when she notes that Mme. Stahl's contempt for the Shcherbatsky family is "contrary to Christian kindness" (2:33, 224). That Lydia and Mme. Stahl join forces in Part 8 thus makes perfect sense: Tolstoy has already twinned them.

When Lydia Ivanovna is most active in the novel, as Karenin's comforter—and Anna's antagonist—she has moved from being an "angry Christian" associated with the philanthropic, religious-patriotic "Little Sisters" to being overtly identified with "that new explanation of Christian doctrine that had lately spread in Petersburg" (6:22, 511). She converts Karenin to this doctrine, with dire consequences for Anna. The narrator notes that Karenin "vaguely sensed" that something was wrong with this doctrine, which promised him full salvation because of his new faith, but that he, "despised by everyone," needed "an invented loftiness" "from which he . . . could despise others." And so "he clung to his imaginary salvation as if it were salvation indeed" (5:22, 511).

Given the press and the talk about Radstockists at the time *Anna Karenina* was written and published, it would have been natural for Tolstoy's readers to assume that he wrote in reaction to this movement as he described "the new Christian doctrine that had lately spread in Petersburg." Tolstoy ends the long list of people that Lydia Ivanovna had "been in love with" (in her perverted "Platonic" way) with "one English missionary." The English evangelical origins of Lydia Ivanovna's doctrine of salvation by faith are made overt later when she talks ecstatically about two devotional works with the English titles *Safe and Happy* and *Under the Wing*.[94] Thus, Tolstoy reintroduces English-style evangelical piety (in a different strain from that which tempted Kitty) into the world of *Anna Karenina* and then makes it critical to Anna's plot. Meanwhile, in the other half of the double story, with Kitty back in the fold, content in the faith of her childhood, Tolstoy will bring Levin to spiritual crisis and, ultimately, in the words of Dostoevsky, to "get faith in God from a muzhik."

Tolstoy's interest in Radstock intensified in the wake of a visit he received in February 1876 from the Radstockist Bobrinsky. In March 1876, Tolstoy asked Alexandrine Tolstoy if she knew Radstock and what impression he had made on her.[95] Alexandrine Tolstoy responded: "I've known Radstock very well for three years now and like him very much for his extraordinary integrity and love." She wrote that Radstock had sincere disciples, like Bobrinsky, whose faith impressed her (as it had Tolstoy), but that some of Radstock's followers, through no fault of his own, were "caricatures." Alexandrine Tolstoy also wrote of Radstock that "he does not know human nature at all and does not even pay attention to it because, according to his system, every human being in a moment's time can unfetter himself from all his passions and evil inclinations if only he has the desire to follow the Savior."[96] She reported that Radstock was known for being able to convert someone within an hour. (Leskov refers to Radstock needing only half an hour for some conversions.) In response, Tolstoy wrote that he shared Alexandrine's skepticism about these instantaneous conversions. Tolstoy adds that "[t]he doctrine of grace descending on someone at the English club or at a meeting of stockholders has always seemed to me not only stupid but immoral." Tolstoy contrasted the Radstockist conversion experience to his own crisis. He referred to his own long-term spiritual torment as he sought faith in God, saying that he considered "this effort and suffering the very best thing of all that [he] was doing on earth."[97]

When publication of *Anna Karenina* resumed in December 1876 after a hiatus of several months, the installment opened with the chapter describing Karenin's sorry life after Anna leaves his house (Part 5, Chapter 21 [according to the now standard book format]).[98] In the next chapter, Countess Lydia Ivanovna pays an unannounced call on Karenin; by the end of that chapter, the narrator reports Lydia's satisfaction that "she had almost converted him to Christianity—that is, turned him from an indifferent and lazy believer into an ardent and firm adherent of that new explanation of Christian doctrine that had lately spread in Petersburg" (5:22, 511). Notable is the extent to which Tolstoy depicts "adherents of the new explanation" in a negative way: Lydia Ivanovna is utterly lacking in the milk of human kindness, and she practices an outrageous and self-serving form of the doctrine of salvation by faith. Whereas the form of alien evangelical piety that Kitty falls victim to in Soden encouraged good works and did not preach hatred (even if Mme. Stahl herself was a hater), Countess Lydia Ivanovna's message is presented not only as a deviation from Orthodoxy, but as a perversion of Christian teaching. Lydia Ivanovna behaves cruelly—telling Seryozha "that his father was a saint and his mother was dead" (5:22, 510), denying "in the spirit of Christian love" Anna's request to see her son and thus (as the narrator tells us) "wound[ing] Anna in the depths of her soul," which was "the secret goal that Countess Lydia Ivanovna concealed from herself" (5:25, 520), and, ultimately, blocking the divorce. Lydia Ivanovna uses her doctrine of faith by salvation to justify whatever she wants to do.

Lydia Ivanovna and Karenin Preach a New Doctrine, Stiva Oblonsky Cites the Orthodox Catechism

While Lydia Ivanovna's cruelty is enough to discredit the doctrine she promotes, Tolstoy also stages a debate on theological issues, using Stiva Oblonsky as the opponent of Lydia Ivanovna and Karenin and, by extension, as the voice of traditional Orthodoxy. (Tolstoy's logic seems to be that if even Oblonsky can detect what is faulty in their doctrine, then it really must be anathema.) In Part 7, Oblonsky is on a mission to Petersburg both to secure a post for himself with the United Agency for Mutual Credit Balance of the Southern Railway Lines and to make a final plea for the divorce, which Anna now is willing to accept even if this means formalizing the loss of her son. Oblonsky at first urges Karenin to take pity on Anna and appeals to him as a Christian, remembering the genuine feeling of Christian forgiveness that took hold of Karenin when Anna lay dying after giving birth to her daughter. (The narrator has already made it clear that whatever Karenin felt then was very different from what has taken over now, when he is under the influence of Lydia Ivanovna's "new explanation of Christian doctrine.") Karenin now informs Oblonsky that "Christian law" prohibits divorce, in a possible echo of Radstock's stand against divorce, to which Oblonsky counters that the Orthodox Church in fact allows it. Tolstoy may have learned about Radstock's view on divorce through Leskov's *Schism in High Society*.[99] Karenin tells Oblonsky that he needs "to think it over and look for guidance" (7:18, 725). Oblonsky is soon summoned to Lydia Ivanovna's, where, as Oblonsky's Petersburg acquaintances tell him, his sister's fate will be decided by someone named Landau, a French clairvoyant and would-be healer.

At this meeting, to each of Oblonsky's attempts to make his case about the divorce, Lydia Ivanovna replies with bombastic religious rhetoric stemming from her self-serving interpretation of the doctrine of salvation by faith. When she claims that "there is no sin for believers," Oblonsky counters with a line he remembered from the catechism: "faith without works is dead."[100] At this point, Karenin breaks his silence to identify the source of the line (Epistle of St. James) and to declare, "How much harm the wrong interpretation of that passage has done! Nothing so turns people from faith as this interpretation: 'I have no works, I cannot believe,' when that is said nowhere. What is said is the opposite." In his anxiety about what "faith without works is dead" really means, Karenin shows possible vestiges of conscience and/or of traditional Orthodox views. But Lydia Ivanovna denies that good works have value, scoffs at Orthodox praxis, and demeans Russian monks (whose stature and importance to Russian religious life had in fact been growing): "To labor for God, to save your soul by works, by fasting . . . these are the wild notions of our monks." Her recipe for salvation is "simpler and easier." Karenin chimes in, "We are saved by Christ, who suffered for us. We are saved by faith" (7:21, 735).[101]

To further illustrate her program of salvation by faith, Lydia Ivanovna decides to read aloud from "*Safe and Happy, or Under the Wing*" (whose titles in the original are in English). Before reading, Lydia Ivanovna cites the example of Marie Sanin as proof of this faith's power: "Do you know Marie Sanin? Do you know her misfortune? She lost her only child. She was in despair. Well, and what then? She found this Friend, and now she thanks God for the death of her child. That is the happiness that faith gives!" (7:21, 736). Lydia Ivanovna's illustrative proof—using the example of someone who thanks God for the death of a loved one—suggests that her piety is perverted in much the same way as Mme. Stahl's: when Kitty's father attempted to explain to Kitty what Pietism was, he described how Mme. Stahl "thanked God for everything," including the death of her husband (2:34, 229). (Once again, echoes prompt the reader to connect the plotlines.)

Countess Lydia finally starts reading "*Safe and Happy, or Under the Wing*," but the reader is left to imagine the content. The reading soon puts both Landau and Oblonsky to sleep (actually, the narrator leaves it unclear whether the former "slept, or pretended to sleep"). Landau eventually speaks out to banish Oblonsky. The next day, Oblonsky "received from Alexei Alexandrovich a definitive refusal to divorce Anna and understood that this decision was based on what the Frenchman had said in his real or feigned sleep" (7:32, 738–39). Whereas it had seemed earlier that Karenin may have been operating on principle in denying the divorce (that of "Christian law," as interpreted according to this "new doctrine"), the twist Tolstoy adds, by having Lydia Ivanovna and Karenin listen to Landau, makes Karenin and Lydia Ivanovna seem all the more ridiculous.

As Alexandrine Tolstoy understood when she read these sections of *Anna Karenina* (at the Empress's, no less) and reported back to Tolstoy by post, he had "perfectly and truthfully captured the type of followers and adorers [fem.] of Radstock who, not understanding the heart of this teaching (which is, even so, not fully worked through), pervert both themselves and religion to the extreme."[102] Why did Tolstoy feel compelled to depict Radstockism in such a negative way? As Heier points out, Tolstoy leaves out important features of Radstock's movement that might have added balance to the depiction. Heier asks: "Where are their philanthropic activities and their sincere help to the needy? Where is Lord Radstock himself or Count Bobrinskij, about whose faith even Tolstoy had marvelled?" Tolstoy also omits any reference to the role that Bible-reading played in the piety of the Radstockists. Heier argues that Tolstoy had his personal reasons for being skeptical of Radstockism even though there was some common ground in their approaches to Christian faith. Tolstoy was certainly leery of the doctrine of salvation by faith and shows what can go wrong with it. (That it depends on Christ's divinity also made it problematic to Tolstoy.) Heier suggests that "Tolstoj's deliberate and severe slander of the Radstockist teaching in the novel may have been the result of Tolstoj's temporary return to the church of his forefathers. It was precisely in 1877, the year in which he completed *Anna Karenina*, that he, as never before, had attempted to accept Orthodox teaching [and adhered to rituals of Orthodoxy]."[103] Indeed, Tolstoy's spiritual biography can help explain why Tolstoy presents Radstockists in *Anna Karenina* in such a negative light. Insofar as Tolstoy externalized his own religious crisis in his fiction, the process focuses on Levin but does not remain confined to him. It expands to all reaches of Tolstoy's multiplot novel not only as Tolstoy wrote his (and

Levin's) way back (temporarily and very tenuously) to the Orthodox Church, but also as he devised subplots aimed at confounding English evangelical piety.

Tolstoy's nasty caricature of Radstockists fits neatly into the "hidden architectonics" that Tolstoy uses to convey his anxious message in *Anna Karenina*. Thus, we are reminded of the unity of the world of the novel as we see that both plots suffer different incursions of evangelical Christianity with origins in England. True to Tolstoy's mode of working with *apparent* but possibly false oppositions to create tension, "that new Christian doctrine" of salvation by faith and utter disregard of good works "that had lately spread in Petersburg" counters and complements the evangelical piety and life of "do[ing] all the good you can, particularly to your poor, sick neighbor" that tempts Kitty in Soden as she reads the gospels. Kitty, however, concludes that this expression of Christian teaching was not for her: "What did I have to do with some stranger?" (2:35, 235). And then she returns to the bosom of her Orthodox faith. By contrast, Karenin, even though he "vaguely sensed" the "erroneousness" of this doctrine (5:32, 511), stands firm in his surrender to Lydia Ivanovna and makes use of Radstock-like rationale against divorce. Perhaps, had Karenin listened to Oblonsky and returned to conventional Orthodox views on divorce and what it means to be a Christian, things would have been different for Anna.

The faith Levin finally finds in Part 8 is free of the English-style alternatives to Orthodox ways that threaten of the world of the novel. Levin's faith is rooted in the muzhik Fyodor's folk theology and it is a "gift from God." (It is certainly not that preached by Radstock as he made converts at the English Club.)[104] To arrive at this point, Tolstoy went through a process of discrediting English evangelical Christian teaching, which he had encountered in a pure form in the fiction of George Eliot and which had recently cropped up, in what he considered a mongrel form, in Russian high society. Tolstoy's artistic method was to anatomize his models, reimagine them, and adapt them to his novel. By making the likes of Mme. Stahl and Countess Lydia Ivanovna into the gurus of these non-Orthodox sects, he ensured that the scenario of salvation (in the finale), which culminates in Levin "get[ting] faith in God from a muzhik" and leaves Levin and others "safe and happy" at Pokrovskoe, would (on the level of doctrine, although possibly not on the level of feeling) be a satisfying conclusion to *Anna Karenina* as a whole.

Loving Your Neighbor at Pokrovskoe and
Ignoring Your Slavic Brethren:
Levin Gets Faith in God from a Muzhik

As Tolstoy wrote *Anna Karenina*, the pros and cons of humanitarian
military intervention in the Balkans on behalf of the Serbs were debated
all around Europe, from Parliament in London, where compassion got
mixed up with geopolitics, to Russian estates, like Tolstoy's fictional
Pokrovskoe.[105] When Prince Shcherbatsky notes that war in Serbia has
been declared by "Ivan Ivanych Ragozov and Countess Lydia Ivanovna
with Madame Stahl," this makes the war suspect. The past behavior of
Mme. Stahl and Countess Lydia Ivanovna makes it likely that they are
now simply perverting Christian ideas and abusing Christian rhetoric.
The casual mention in the same sentence of these two bearers of deviant
forms of Christian piety, hitherto functioning in the two separate plots,
provides us with a haunting reminder that the worlds of this novel are
still one—at a critical time as the novel draws to its close in Part 8.

Koznyshev responds by saying: "No one declared war, but people
feel for the suffering of their neighbors and want to help them" (8:15,
804). Similar rhetoric circulated at the send-off of the volunteers in the
Moscow train station earlier in Part 8, despite all the indications that
most were going for reasons that seemed to have little to do with loving
their neighbor.[106] At Pokrovskoe, Levin is against this war: he argues
that killing violates Christian teaching. And he adds that decisions to
go to war—and thus violate the commandment not to kill—can only
be made by rulers. But Levin further claims to feel no special love for
his Slavic brethren. Levin's declaration that he does not feel this love is
not surprising, given his vision of neighbors as existing within very
close range. The "neighbors" Koznyshev speaks of loving are distant in
space—a very long train-ride away.[107] As for Koznyshev, it may be an
open question whether he supports war out of compassion for those
distant others who are victims of atrocities, or out of Slavic jingoism, or
simply in order to latch onto a cause to divert himself from disappointment at the lackluster reception of his recent book. As for Mme. Stahl
and Countess Lydia Ivanovna, the ringleaders, it is suggested that they
are now simply applying on a larger scale their abuse of Christian rhetoric to get their way as they advance nationalist and imperialist goals.
This puts Levin's isolationist, family-centered definition of the neighbor
in a different light. Those familiar with Tolstoy's later life will find in
Levin's stand inklings of Tolstoy's eventual full-scale pacifism, contempt

for nationalism, defiance of empire, and embrace of religious tolerance. But, in the context of *Anna Karenina*, Levin's argument against the war, shared by Prince Shcherbatsky (who in the drafts proudly declares that "here in the country, we feel no compassion," by which he means that "we" feel nothing for our Slavic brethren [20:558]), is a form of Kitty's question in Soden, "What do I have to do with some stranger?"

The ending of *Anna Karenina* appears to endorse this inward-turning view (even if, ultimately, the reader of this multiplot novel is left to question it). It looks ahead to Freud's arguments in *Civilization and Its Discontents* in which, "adopt[ing] a naïve attitude" toward the commandment to love thy neighbor as thyself, he asks how such a thing is even possible. He is especially leery of the idea of a stranger being loved as a neighbor: "Indeed, I should be wrong to do so [extend neighborly love and care to a stranger], for my love is valued by all my own people as a sign of my preferring them, and it is an injustice to them if I put a stranger on a par with them."[108] As Freud sees it, his duty is first and foremost to what he (in James Strachey's translation) calls "my own people."

The justification of loving "[one's] own people," as opposed to strangers, is reinforced by the "experiment" that Kitty and Agafya Mikhailovna stage for Levin to prove that baby Mitya recognizes his own people (8:18, 814).[109] But it is most directly affirmed when Levin "finds faith from the muzhik" Fyodor. In this return to the bosom of Orthodoxy at Pokrovskoe Levin is untouched by the English-style evangelical Christian spirit, which tempted Kitty in Soden and which, in corrupted form, took over Karenin in Petersburg. Rather, he reaffirms "those spiritual truths he had sucked in with his milk as a babe" (8:12, 797). According to Nikolai Leskov's report, Dostoevsky, when challenged by the Radstockist Zasetskaia to tell her why Russians were better Christians than everybody else, failed to formulate an adequate response but told her that the muzhik in the kitchen would know, just ask him.[110] What happens to Levin with his muzhik seems to validate Dostoevsky's retort.

Tolstoy's muzhik in the field captures in folk iteration the essence of Christian teaching—in a form that Levin can embrace. The understanding Fyodor communicates to Levin about how to fulfill the double commandment to love God and to love thy neighbor responds to the doctrinal debates that hover over all of the plots of *Anna Karenina*. Fyodor speaks, somewhat cryptically, of a peasant Platon, who lives for the soul and remembers God, whereas Mityukha Kirillov lives for the belly. Platon, "a wealthy and good muzhik," "won't skin a man," whereas Mityukha "takes no pity on a peasant" and "pushes till he gets his own/what he's after" (8:11, 794).

At the end of Part 7, as Anna meditates on the struggle for survival that she sees going on around her, she remembers that Vronsky's friend Yashvin, a gambler, told her that he felt no pity for his opponent. His only goal was to "leave his opponent without a shirt," just as his opponent struggled to do the same to him (7:29, 761). Thus, the high society gambler and officer Yashvin (now off at war in the Balkans) behaves like the muzhik Mityukha, who tries to skin his neighbor. By using these similar images—skinning someone and leaving someone without a shirt—to describe what the peasant Mityukha and the officer Yashvin, respectively, want to do to their neighbor, Tolstoy signals another link that binds his double story together: human nature is the same all over, among peasants and gentry.

When he is pressed by Levin for an explanation of *how* Platon lives for the soul and remembers God, the muzhik Fyodor sets Levin himself up as another example of someone who lives for the soul: "Everybody knows how—the truth, by God's way. People are different. Now, take you even, you wouldn't offend anybody either . . ." (8:11, 794). With these words, Levin is overwhelmed by joy and feels a blinding light. Fyodor makes no attempt to engage in ratiocination about who counts as a neighbor. What is remarkable about his formulation is that the emblem of loving one's neighbor is formulated in negative terms of *not* skinning him rather than in the more emphatic gospel terms of giving one's shirt and kaftan as well. A bit later, Levin offers what appears to be another "negative" definition of loving one's neighbor: it amounts to "not throttling him" (8:12, 797).[111]

By contrast, when Kitty fell under the spell of evangelical piety in Soden and read the gospels for herself, she took the message of the Sermon on the Mount more literally and wondered whether Christ was calling for radical upheaval of her life. Thus, when her mother told her that loving her neighbor was all well and good but that she should not overdo it ("*Il ne faut jamais rien outrer*"), Kitty stood firm before God. "But her daughter said nothing in reply, she only thought in her heart that one could not speak of excessiveness in matters of Christianity. What excessiveness could there be in following a teaching that tells you to turn the other cheek when you have been struck, and to give away your shirt when your caftan is taken?" (2:33, 225). At this point Kitty assumed that Christ asks for a wholehearted surrender. Similarly, when

Karenin spontaneously forgives Anna on her deathbed—before Countess Lydia converts him to her weird form of evangelical mysticism—he,
too, finds himself ready to follow this commandment: "I want to turn
the other cheek, I want to give my shirt when my caftan is taken" (4:17,
414).[112] Neither Kitty nor Karenin continues in this spirit: Kitty reverts
to a more moderate practice, and Karenin surrenders to the coarse force
around him and eventually to Lydia Ivanovna. Thus, on both sides of
Tolstoy's double story, the message seems to be that the Christian spirit
that would make you give your shirt as well as your caftan is too extreme
to be genuine or lasting.

Loving your neighbor means, at least at Pokrovskoe, that you should
not skin him—nor take *his* shirt. But it also seems to mean that you do
not have to give him *your* shirt.[113] After all, Platon, the example of godliness in Fyodor's parable-like illustration, "was a wealthy . . . muzhik";
he has not divested himself of everything to help the poor. Nor does
Levin want to do so. (As he revealed in his conversation with Oblonsky and Veslovsky, he was tortured by his relative wealth vis-à-vis the
peasants, but he was not about to take radical steps to divest. It was his
responsibility to preserve his patrimony [6:11, 588].) Although Levin is
convinced that the inequality that exists between him and the peasants
is unjust, he feels that the best he can do to remedy the situation is to
"act negatively, in the sense that I'm not going to try to increase the
difference of situation that exists between [the peasant and himself]."
But Levin's conscience nags him: "Can one be just only negatively?"
(6:11, 589). Should Levin, in other words, divest himself of both shirt
and caftan, or is it enough simply not to skin a man? His muzhik in the
field gives him the answer he wants.

The muzhik Fyodor's reassurance late in the novel that Levin follows the "Platonic" model of living for the soul and remembering God
appears to lay to rest these concerns, at least for the immediate present,
as Levin ecstatically thanks God for granting him faith. His life can continue as before with his home-grown Russian variant of "love thy
neighbor"—living for those near and dear to him. If we literalize the
narrator's metaphor that Levin had imbibed these spiritual truths with
his milk and remember that Levin had a peasant for a wet nurse,[114] then
it becomes clear that the strain of Christian truth that Levin took in was
that of the Russian folk. (No influence of English-style evangelicism,
no individual reading of the gospels, no incursions of English social
thought.) This image of Levin imbibing a Russian variant of Christian
teaching recalls Tolstoy's exclamation to Alexandrine Tolstoy after first

reading George Eliot in 1859: "Happy [or Blessed] are those who, like the English imbibe with their milk Christian teaching, and in such a lofty, purified form as evangelical Protestantism."[115] At that point, the faith of his fathers (and wet nurses) had left Tolstoy spiritually hungry so that he even seemed to envy the English, much as he would later envy the Radstockist Bobrinsky for the happiness his faith gave him.[116] But, in the finale of *Anna Karenina*, Tolstoy finally answers George Eliot and the Radstockists. Tolstoy shows Levin happy with the form of Christian teaching that he had originally imbibed with the milk of his wet nurse and that has just been confirmed by the words of his muzhik in the field.

The message Levin gets is that he can be a believer and still continue his way of life, caring for those in his family.[117] It appears that Levin can save his soul without retreat to a monastery and, better yet, without leaving Pokrovskoe. However, as the novel draws to its bitter end, Tolstoy introduces doubt into Levin's joyful religious awakening: he begins to wonder whether God would have revealed his truth exclusively to Christians—what about those of other faiths? In fact, while Levin is asking about the exclusion of others, he is called in to the "experiment" in which Mitya recognizes his own people. As he goes back out, the doubt returns, but Levin ultimately decides to surrender to God's infinite wisdom. Levin thinks to himself: "And I don't have the right or possibility of resolving the question of other beliefs or their attitude to the Deity" (7:19, 816). The message seems to be that it is fine, at least for tonight, for Levin simply to love those near and dear and leave strangers to God's protection. Thus, Tolstoy includes this final mention of those beyond the fold and raises the possibility of them, too, being loved by God.

But where does this leave Anna? The narrow definition of "neighbor" that appears to prevail in Pokrovskoe seems to justify the fact that nobody seems to remember her. She "is allowed to drop out," in the words of Virginia Woolf. That Tolstoy allows Anna to drop out is one of the signs that the world Tolstoy imagines in *Anna Karenina* and his poetics of the multiplot novel differ in profound ways from those of George Eliot, whom Tolstoy admired throughout his career for how she novelized the Christian idea—in its pure English Protestant evangelical form. *Adam Bede*, a novel that Tolstoy praised in *What Is Art?* as one of the few exemplars of the genre that promoted love of God and neighbor, ends differently from *Anna Karenina*. In *Adam Bede*, Hetty dies. George Eliot even seems to allow her to "drop out." But, as J. Hillis Miller has argued, the community is restored in the finale. Those who gather in love have been knit together and changed, with their pain and sorrow turned into "sympathy—the one poor word which includes all our best insight and our best love" (50, 531). Thus, Adam Bede himself has become less harsh in his judgments and Arthur Donnisthorne, who had ruined Hetty Sorrel, has understood that "There's a sort of wrong that can never be made up for." He is welcomed back into the community (Epilogue, 584).[118] And George Eliot indicates that Hetty is lovingly held in the hearts of the family that gathers at the end.[119] As *Anna Karenina* ends, Tolstoy gives a semblance of restoring community as Levin and his loved ones appear to be "safe and happy" under the *pokrov* [protective veil] for this summer night, but the fact that nobody recollects Anna Karenina unsettles this ending in profound ways, making whatever safety and happiness are felt at Pokrovskoe seem all the more precarious.

5

╠═╗║╥╦╝╚╗║╔║║╨╦═╗║╚╦═╣

The Eternal Silence
of Infinite Spaces

Pascal and Tolstoy's Anna Karenina

Reading Pascal at Yasnaya Polyana, Not at Pokrovskoe: Pascal Hidden in *Anna Karenina*

"Without knowing what I am and why I'm here, it is impossible to live" (8:9, 788). Beset by this thought, Levin, although a "happy family man" and a healthy person, has been "several times so close to suicide that he hid the rope lest he hang himself with it, and was afraid to go about with a rifle lest he shoot himself" (8:9, 789). Thus, in Part 8, after Anna Karenina has killed herself, we find Levin suicidal. As Kitty puts it to herself while breastfeeding baby Mitya soon after the action of Part 8 shifts to Pokrovskoe, Levin's crisis is the result of being a "non-believer." He has been searching in vain for answers to his questions in "all sorts of philosophies," (8:7, 784). A bit later, as the narrator reports on Levin's crisis, he specifies that the philosophers Levin read were "Plato, and Spinoza, Kant, Schelling, Hegel, and Schopenhauer" (8:9, 787). In addition, on the recommendation of his brother Koznyshev, Levin read the theological works of the Slavophile Aleksei Khomyakov (8:9, 788). Levin finds Khomyakov's doctrine about the Church ultimately no more satisfying than the constructs of the philosophers (8:9, 788). Where was Levin to turn?

Missing from Levin's reading list is Pascal, whom Tolstoy read with great interest during the spiritual crisis that he lived through as he was finishing *Anna Karenina*.[1] This omission is marked since Tolstoy had incorporated into Levin's crisis other elements of his own experience. For example, Tolstoy imparts to Levin the disillusionment he himself felt after reading Khomyakov in the spring of 1876. (Tolstoy wrote in a letter that he had "expected more."[2]) That same spring, Tolstoy had written to Alexandrine Tolstoy that he was preoccupied with death and was desperate for faith, but, as he sought answers with all the strength of his soul, one thing was clear: he would not find what he needed in philosophy.[3] Neither would Levin. But Tolstoy chose to leave out of his tale of Levin's crisis the *Pensées* of Blaise Pascal.

In the spring of 1876, Tolstoy wrote admiringly of Pascal at the end of a letter in which he confided to Alexandrine Tolstoy about his spiritual unrest. Of the recent visit of the Radstockist Aleksei Bobrinsky to Yasnaya Polyana, Tolstoy wrote: "Nobody ever spoke to me better about faith than Bobrinsky. He is impossible to refute because he does not try to prove anything; he just says that he believes and you feel that he is happier than those who do not have his faith, and the main thing you feel is that the happiness of his faith cannot be gained by means of mental effort, rather it comes only by a miracle."[4] Tolstoy also thanked Alexandrine, an Orthodox believer, for praying for him but expressly warned her *not* to try to convert him because proselytizing would not do any good. He assured her that he was meditating "ceaselessly on questions about the meaning of life and death." At the end of his letter, Tolstoy intimated that Pascal was inspiring him in a way that "philosophers," the evangelicals Bobrinsky and Radstock, and Alexandrine with her Orthodox piety had not.[5] In her response to this letter, after reporting on Radstock (at Tolstoy's request) and setting forth her reservations about his approach to faith, Alexandrine Tolstoy expressed her joy that Tolstoy had finally found Pascal: "It is something else entirely compared to Radstock and company."[6] By this she presumably meant that Pascal, unlike Radstock, understood human nature and that Pascal's model for arriving at faith (through a desperate search for God) would be more kindred to Tolstoy.

Sergei Gessen has argued that, much as Tolstoy had been taken with Rousseau in his early period and with Schopenhauer in the middle period, in his late period he was "under the sign of" Pascal.[7] Indeed,

Tolstoy continued to read, respond to, and spread the word about Pascal in the years to come. But, in fact, Tolstoy was already under this sign as he finished *Anna Karenina*. He mentioned Pascal to Alexandrine Tolstoy not long before publication of *Anna Karenina* came to a halt for several months, during which Tolstoy struggled to make himself carry on with the novel and life. (Publication halted with the April 1876 issue, at the point of Nikolai Levin's death and Kitty's pregnancy; it started up again in December 1876 with the tales of Lydia Ivanovna's conversion of Kare-nin.) In April 1877, as Tolstoy was writing the "epilogue" to *Anna Karenina*, Tolstoy asked Afanasy Fet if he had read Pascal.[8] By the next spring, while Tolstoy, with *Anna Karenina* behind him, occupied himself with his own quest to "save [his] soul,"[9] Pascal was being read, to Tolstoy's great joy, by his fifteen-year-old son Sergei.[10]

What, then, does the omission of Pascal from Levin's reading list signify? After all, Levin *failed* to find answers, much less faith, in the theologian and philosophers he read: Khomyakov, Plato, Kant, Spinoza, Hegel, and even Schopenhauer.[11] Perhaps Tolstoy chose not to include Pascal because unlike the other philosophers, Pascal might actually have *helped* Levin. Instead of referring to Pascal by name in *Anna Karenina*, Tolstoy chose to hide Pascal's presence—to make him, like the God of Pascal's universe, a hidden presence. Even so, Tolstoy left telltale signs in *Anna Karenina* of his engagement with Pascal's *Pensées*.

As *Anna Karenina* draws to a close, Tolstoy novelizes aspects of the experiences of the protagonist(s) from Pascal's fragments.[12] Levin appears as a nineteenth-century Russian version of Pascal's *chercheur* (seeker), who shudders at the eternal silence of infinite spaces; who becomes obsessed with death; who becomes frustrated with language, all but regarding it as a prison house; who occasionally goes through the motions of faith even without yet believing; who makes the wager (where the odds are infinity to nothing) and chooses God; and, above all, who seeks God, truth, and faith in the only mode that Pascal approved, "en gémissant" [moaning (in anguish)].[13] While the influence of Pascal is most directly felt in how Tolstoy shaped and resolved Levin's terror, the spirit of Pascal hovers over all the plots of *Anna Karenina*, especially as the novel nears its end. Key correspondences between Levin's and Anna's desperate attempts to answer life's questions have a common Pascalian aura. "What does Anna have to do with Levin?" becomes a different question if one takes into account the eternal silence of infinite spaces that terrified Pascal. By reading *Anna Karenina* through the prism of Pascal's *Pensées*, we gain perspective on the linkage of *Anna*

Karenina's plots. Like Levin, Anna mistrusts language, resorts to fitful inner conversation, feels the need to divert herself from an abyss that only faith could fill, and is subject to the Pascalian agony—"that anguish and that abandonment in the horror of the night" (L919/S749)—all these similarities remind the reader at the end of the novel of how Anna and Levin connect, even though their plots end differently.

The Obscurity of Language in Tolstoy's Labyrinth of Linkages and Pascal's *Pensées*

The anxiety that surfaces in Tolstoy's works about the limits and obscurities of language from *Childhood* on comes to a head in *Anna Karenina* as Tolstoy shows Levin and Anna each suffering from a mistrust of language but still desirous of spanning the abyss between language and thought, if not in verbal intercourse with their beloveds (which often fails for both), then in the inner monologues—and the prayers— they engage in most poignantly as they face death.[14] In *Anna Karenina*, the narrator often indicates that Levin finds spoken language inadequate to express matters close to his heart. The situation worsens when he is overcome by thoughts of death. And, as the novel ends, Levin chooses to keep silent about his newfound faith in God rather than tell Kitty. Levin assumes she knows without him telling her. Thus they may have reached what the psychologist of language Lev Vygotsky describes as that heightened state of "shared apperception by communicating parties" that makes it unnecessary to bother to articulate messages completely and formally.[15] Or perhaps the emphasis here is not so much on their intimacy—because after all, Levin goes on to recall the "wall" separating the "holy of holies of [his] soul from others, even [his] wife"—as it is on the fact that this faith in God cannot be communicated in fallen human language. As Levin says, it is "a secret that's necessary and important for me alone and inexpressible in words" (8:18, 816–17). Here Tolstoy has Levin voice the Pascalian truth that "the things of God [are] inexpressible" (L272/S303).

Levin's fitful incommunicability connects in Tolstoy's "labyrinth of linkages" to Anna's own troubled verbal state.[16] Anna's problems with language differ from Levin's—for example, Tolstoy at one point shows Anna all but degenerating into a pathological liar after the pattern of Emma Bovary. But she, like Levin, suffers from the apprehension that thought and (external) language are separated by an abyss. Throughout the novel and with mounting intensity just before her suicide, Anna struggles because her words fail to express not only the intensity of her love but also, more poignantly, the misery she feels; she concludes that all spoken words are lies. At one point, desperately seeking solace, Anna keeps repeating, "My God!" but, as the narrator (very articulate as he reads the minds of characters in verbal distress) tells us, "neither the 'my' nor the 'God' had any meaning for her" (3:15, 288).[17] Anna will become, as Justin Weir has put it, increasingly "incommunicada" throughout what remains of her life.[18] In Anna's last hours, after her visit to Dolly fails to bring her comfort, Anna sees passers-by talking on the street and asks herself, "Is it really possible to tell someone else what one feels?" (7:29, 760).

While Anna seems to conclude that language has neither meaning nor use because of what she has done, the fact that Levin experiences a similar despair over language suggests that this may be part of the human condition. Tolstoy thus novelizes an understanding of language close to that of Pascal. Pascal despaired of the flawed state of human language: "Man has fallen from a state of glory and communication with God into a state of sorrow, of penitence, and of estrangement [éloignement] from God" (L281/S313).[19] For Pascal, linguistics and theology intertwine closely so that incommunicability is the result of the Fall. From the Pascalian perspective, we see why both the obviously "fallen" Anna and the relatively upstanding Levin suffer from the same sense of language failing them.

Pascal uses various means to evoke anxiety about language and to question its capacity for expressing the truth.[20] Whereas Descartes and others engaged in positivist projects to achieve clarity in language and make it less arbitrary, Pascal believed that such clarity was impossible this side of heaven. According to Pascal, God is truthful; for him, word and thought (and intention and result) are one.[21] But this is not the case for humankind. Thus, as Nicholas Hammond explains, "the main function of language must be to convince man of his corruption, of his fall from truth, a fall which in turn explains the obscurities of language."[22] Asks Pascal, "What do we conclude from all our obscurities, then, if not our unworthiness?" (L445/S690). Pascal writes that "man is nothing but deception, falsehood and hypocrisy, both in himself and in regard to others. He does not want to be told the truth. He avoids telling it to others; and all these dispositions, so far removed from justice and reason, have their natural root in his heart" (L978/S743). In another fragment, Pascal writes, "Truth is so obscured in our time, and falsehood so well established, that there would be no way of knowing the truth if one did not love it" (L739/S617). But how is man to arrive at this truth?

In the spirit of Pascal, Tolstoy presents the language available to his fictional heroes as inherently flawed. Although at times the characters themselves speak out on the inadequacy of language (as when Anna asks herself whether there is any point in trying to tell someone what one feels), more often it is the narrator who draws attention to the failings of the characters' language. Tolstoy's narrator approaches (but does not reach) the divine not simply because he is so much more "telepathic" than the mortal characters (while not omniscient) but also because he, somewhat like God in Pascal's universe, is able to bridge the abysses between thought and language that threaten to engulf the characters. He does not suffer from their obscurities.

Facing Death in *Anna Karenina*: "We die alone"

In Part 8, we are told that Konstantin Levin's despair about death first set in at the time he understood that his beloved brother was dying (8:8, 785). In Part 3, as Nikolai visits Konstantin at Pokrovskoe, "death, the inevitable end of everything, presented itself to him for the first time with irresistible force" (3:31, 348). The narrator relates the brothers' conversation, only to add that what they said was if not meaningless then inconsequential, for *had* they both been able to speak "from the heart," "they would have looked into each other's eyes, and Konstantin would have said only, 'You're going to die, to die, to die!' and Nikolai would have answered only, 'I know I'm going to die, but I'm afraid, afraid, afraid!' And they would have said nothing else, if they had spoken from the heart" (3:32, 349). What they end up saying feels false and estranges them from each other. In parting, Nikolai says, his voice trembling, "'Anyhow, don't think badly of me, Kostya!'" The narrator interjects: "These were the only sincere words spoken," as if to suggest that in moments of true humility in the face of death, human beings, even flawed and bitter ones like Nikolai, can use language to communicate truth. Levin kisses his brother but "there was nothing he could or knew how to say to him." Levin thereafter "saw either death or the approach of it everywhere" (3:32, 351–52). Now aware of death, Levin, like the Pascalian protagonist, regards language as a prison house and the universe as *cachot*.

As Virginia Woolf identified the distinctive markers of Tolstoy's fiction in "The Russian Point of View," she observed that his heroes are obsessed with death in a way that prompts them to ask, even in moments of apparent happiness, the fundamental question "but why live?" Tolstoy's own life reveals that he, too, was often overwhelmed by fear of death and had a desperate desire to figure out the meaning of life.[23] As he wrote *Anna Karenina*, he went through a protracted period of being tormented by this question, but it was not new: he had experienced the terror of death at Arzamas in 1869 and later described it in "Notes of a Madman" (1884). Donna Orwin has argued that Tolstoy drew on Schopenhauer at the time of Arzamas as a way through this struggle.[24] But, ultimately, Schopenhauer did not answer.

In Pascal, whom Tolstoy read as he wrote *Anna Karenina*, Tolstoy found another approach to the same questions. Pascal uses his *Pensées* to do just what Virginia Woolf suggested Tolstoy did in his fiction: remind us of death with a searing intensity that makes us ask fundamental questions such as "but why live?" In the words of Phillippe Sellier, "Pascal obsessively reminds us of the proximity and inescapability of death." Pascal uses different strategies and images to bring death home to the reader. Sellier detects in the relevant fragments the kernel of the "Platonic scenario [of Socrates] at death's door." Pascal, like Plato's Socrates, calls for his protagonist to "cease losing himself in agitations external to his own soul in order to turn inward and scrutinize the only truly important reality; our ultimate destiny 'where everything is at stake' [où il va de tout]."[25] With these stakes, Pascal argues, it behooves man to focus on ultimate questions (Tolstoy's "but why live?") and to seek to find out whether, come death, he "will fall into nothingness or into the hands of an angry God" (L427/S681). Pascal asserts that he can "approve only of those who search while moaning in anguish" and that he can "have nothing but compassion on those who sincerely moan and lament their doubt" (L405/S24; L427[série III]/S681).

Levin is a hero after Pascal's heart because he suffers from doubt and moans in anguish as he searches for God. Levin is last seen in Part 3 telling Kitty's cousin, "It is time for me to die!" However, when he reappears in Part 4, Levin is once again bent on marrying Kitty Shcherbatsky. What has become of Levin's concern with death? Has he managed to forget? Tolstoy shows Levin succumbing to romantic love, the diversion that is the stuff of novels, but even so Tolstoy suffuses this love plot with Pascalian disquietude. While the natural temptation is to see the love of Levin and Kitty as superior to that of Anna, Vronsky, and Karenin (and that of Dolly and Oblonsky), Tolstoy's multiplot structure complicates this judgment by besetting all these characters with a metaphysical loneliness. Although Levin and Kitty appear to transcend the fallen language of the Oblonsky realm as they engage in "mystic intercourse" with dazzling telepathy in the betrothal scene, the underlying message is that what really matters should not be entrusted to human speech (4:14, 397–98). Were *Anna Karenina* not a novel infused with Pascalian terror, this "mystic intercourse" might signal that theirs was a match made in heaven.

Tolstoy draws attention, in small but disquieting ways, to gaps in understanding between people, even his loving couple. At the height of happiness, Levin misreads Kitty's mind when, unexpectedly moved by the language of the liturgy during their wedding, he assumes that Kitty understands it all as he does. The narrator breaks in to announce that "Levin was mistaken," leaving the reader with no illusions about human communication even in this apparently blissful moment. While this might not mean much in the context of a simpler courtship novel, in which it would just be a sign that we cannot expect perfect understanding of the other even in the best of marriages, in *Anna Karenina* these seemingly inconsequential indications of failed intersubjectivity carry greater weight. Given the Pascalian aura of this novel, Levin's misunderstanding of Kitty signals the cosmic loneliness and terror of the human condition, which in *Anna Karenina*, as in Pascal's realm, can only be relieved by faith. Attempts to cure this condition in the marriage bed will fail.

When Levin marries and fulfills the natural urge to reproduce, Levin's life conforms to the Schopenhauerian paradigm of life and death cancelling each other out. (And Kitty is declared pregnant by the very doctor who pronounces Nikolai Levin dead.[26]) But, ultimately, when Levin's thoughts of death return after the birth of baby Mitya, Levin follows a more Pascalian scenario. Even as a *pater familias* with a legitimate male heir, Levin finds himself obsessed with death and consequently isolated from everyone around him, even his loving wife and his son. Levin's spiritual isolation fits the Pascalian paradigm, which insists that wives, children, doctors, priests, and even friends are of no use in the face of death: "We are foolish to rely on the company of our likes," because "they are wretches, like us, powerless, like us, and they will not help us: we die alone" [on mourra seul]. Pascal counsels us to "act as if we were alone" (L151/S184). Only when we are (as if) alone, according to Pascal, is it possible to "seek the truth without hesitating" (L151/S184).

Pascal's emphasis on being alone in order to seek truth (and God) is hard to reconcile with the Christian commandment to love one another, as Ernest Havet, one of the major nineteenth-century Pascal scholars, observed.[27] Certainly, the action of *Anna Karenina* depends on people loving one another according to the Christian commandment and the faith Levin finds is closely tied to neighborly love. Yet to some degree, Levin remains spiritually aloof even from those near and dear neighbors we see him loving in Part 8. And the novel ends with Levin reinforcing that "wall between the holy of holies of his soul" and others, including his wife. After vividly recalling that Christ was all alone in Gethsemane, to suffer "pain and abandon in the horror of the night," Pascal counsels his seeker to embrace this same loneliness: "One must rip oneself away from one's nearest and dearest in order to imitate him [Christ]" (L919/S749). What we might see as the Pascalian dimension—Levin's spiritual aloofness—changes the tenor of the novel and, ultimately, draws its plots closer together, in a primal way, because Anna herself is so alone as she faces death in her Gethsemane at the railroad station.

Levin's New Convictions:
I Do Not Know Who Put Me in This World

To show how Levin reached the state of despair we find him in at end of *Anna Karenina*, Tolstoy's narrator explains that what Levin called "new convictions" had "imperceptibly, during the period from twenty to thirty-four years of age, come to replace the beliefs of his childhood and youth" (8:8, 785). That Levin's "new convictions" were totally inadequate became clear to him when he faced the death of his brother Nikolai: "From that moment when, at the sight of his beloved brother dying, Levin had looked at the questions of life and death for the first time in the light of the new convictions, as he called them, he had been horrified, not so much at death as at life without the least knowledge of whence it came, wherefore, why, and what it was" (8:8, 785). These "new convictions" take as axiomatic that God (if he ever existed) has withdrawn from active presence in the universe and from intervention in human affairs.

The pseudo-scientific secular mindset that Levin exchanged for his childhood faith appears to be widespread among Levin's educated peers, although Levin's brother Koznyshev, brother-in-law Lvov, and father-in-law Shcherbatsky are all Russian Orthodox believers. Stiva Oblonsky, however, thrives on these new convictions. Oblonsky disregards traditional religious beliefs, and does not remember that he has been created in the likeness of God and, thus, is responsible for his actions; he appeals instead to his ancestor the ape as if to reinforce his basic point that in committing adultery he is just doing what comes naturally, or he ascribes his reprehensible behavior to "reflexes of the brain."[28] Levin, however, takes the ramifications of these new convictions more seriously than Stiva. When Levin walks in on a conversation between Koznyshev and a professor of philosophy about where to draw the line "between psychological and physiological phenomena in human activity," what Levin really wants to know is what happens after death. Is there no further existence after the death of the body? (1:7, 24–25). According to Pascal, the first (and only) priority should be to seek the answer to this very question. As Pascal writes, "the immortality of the soul is something so important to us, something that touches us so profoundly, that we must have lost all feeling to be indifferent to knowing the facts of the matter" (L427[série III]/S681). In his concern with questions that scientists dismiss, Levin shows his Pascalian affinities even before he starts to seek answers "moaning in anguish" [en gémissant].

The conflict Tolstoy stages between traditional faith and new convictions—or between divine revelation and scientific inquiry—appears topical to the nineteenth-century world of *Anna Karenina*, but it is a variation on an old theme. The seventeenth-century version fed into Pascal's *Pensées*: developments in science and secular culture caused Pascal's contemporaries to question the role of God in human life and the universe.[29] René Descartes, often seen as Pascal's antagonist, was wedded to reason as the means of arriving at truth—even religious truth. Descartes militated for a scientific method that seemed not to depend on God, despite his assertions to the contrary.[30] Pascal quipped that Descartes was not able to get rid of God completely: he still needed him for a "chiquenaude" [flick, fillip] to set the universe in motion (L1001).

According to Levin, "the latest belief on which all researches of the human mind in almost all fields were built" and the "reigning conviction" that Levin himself had "involuntarily adopted" (after abandoning the faith of his fathers) could be summed up as follows: "In infinite time, in the infinity of matter, in infinite space, a bubble-organism separates itself, and that bubble holds out for a while and then bursts, and that bubble is—I!" (8:9, 788). Levin's formulation of the prevailing wisdom of his new scientific age echoes Bazarov, the arch-nihilist hero of Turgenev's *Fathers and Sons*, who declaims:

> The tiny space I occupy is so infinitely small in comparison with the rest of space, in which I am not, and which has nothing to do with me; and the period of time in which it is my lot to live is so petty beside the eternity in which I have not been, and shall not be. . . . But in this atom, in this mathematical point, blood circulates, the brain functions, and also desires something. . . . What ridiculousness! Isn't it hideous? What pettiness![31]

In turn, Bazarov's summary of the human condition reflects Turgenev's own engagement with Pascal. At various points in his work, Pascal describes the universe from the point of view of an "I" without faith in God:

> I do not know who put me in the world, nor what the world is, nor what I myself am. I am in terrible ignorance of all things. . . . I see those terrifying spaces of the universe that imprison me and I find myself tied to one corner of this vast expanse, without knowing why I am placed in this place rather than in another, nor why this little amount of time allotted to me to live has been given to me at this point instead of another bit of time in this eternity that has preceded me and that will follow me.
>
> I see nothing but infinities on all sides, that imprison me like an atom and like a shadow that lasts only for an instant and returns no more.
>
> All I know is that I must soon die; but what I am most ignorant of is this death, the very thing that I cannot escape. (L427/S681)

Whereas Pascal intended contemplation of the infinite to inspire metaphysical angst, Bazarov *appears* to deny this dimension and contents himself with his materialist vision of a godless universe.[32] Bazarov thus boasts to Arkady that he only looks up at the sky when he has to sneeze.

Levin, however, is no Bazarov. New materialist convictions do not satisfy him. Following one of the scenarios intimated in Pascal's *Pensées*, Levin presses on to find an answer to the question "who put me here?" [qui m'y a mis?] (L68/S102). Levin declares: "Without knowing what I am and why I'm here, it is impossible for me to live. And I cannot know that, therefore I cannot live" (8:9, 788).

Levin and the Verbal Traps of the Philosophers

In his chronicle of Levin's crisis, the narrator specifies that Levin turned to those philosophers "who gave a non-materialist explanation of life," specifically, Plato, Spinoza, Kant, Schelling, Hegel, and Schopenhauer. This suggests that Levin sought in these philosophical texts an antidote to Bazarov-style materialism. But the philosophers did not provide answers to Levin's questions. This is not surprising because, according to Pascal, people who believe what philosophers have to say "are the most empty and foolish of all" (L143/S176). Levin, too, comes to see philosophy as a solipsistic and pointless enterprise:

> Their thoughts seemed to him fruitful when he read, or was himself devising refutations of their teachings, the materialistic in particular; but as soon as he began reading, or himself devised, solutions to life's problems, the same thing occurred every time. Following long definitions of vague words such as *spirit, will, freedom, substance*, and deliberately entering the verbal trap [ловушка слов] set for him by the philosophers, or by himself, he seemed to begin to understand something. But he had only to forget that artificial line of thought, and to return direct from real life to what had appeared satisfactory so long as he kept to the given line of thought—and suddenly the whole artificial edifice tumbled down like a house of cards, and it was evident that the edifice had been constructed of those same words differently arranged, and without regard for something in life more important than reason. (8:9, 787–88)

Levin's complaint that philosophers rely on nothing more important than reason resonates with Pascal's repeated cautions about reason. For example, Pascal declares reason to be volatile: "Ludicrous reason, blowing with the wind in every direction!" (L44/S78). The best that can be done with reason, according to Pascal, is to use it to understand its own limits and the "infinity of things that go beyond it" (L188/S220).[33] After all, "it is the heart that experiences God, and not reason. This is what faith is. God felt by the heart, not by reason" (L424/S680). As will be seen below, the truth that Levin ultimately finds about loving one's neighbor is not arrived at by reason but rather through revelation or as a truth that had been with him all along (or, as he put it, that he "sucked in with his milk").

Because the philosophers rely on reason alone, Levin views their work as nothing but artificial constructs and meaningless "word traps." That philosophers spend their time attempting to define the words they use reflects the (hopeless?) obscurity of their language.[34] Yet, to Pascal's way of thinking, recognizing the obscurity of language can potentially be a step toward finding faith in God. This Pascalian truth was one that, elsewhere in *Anna Karenina*, the artist Mikhailov instinctively grasped. In his painting of Christ before Pontius Pilate, an important focus in Tolstoy's multiplot novel, Christ's face expresses a "consciousness of the vanity of words" that, along with love and readiness for death, gives him the expression of tender mercy (5:11, 474). The narrator does not explicitly indicate that Anna herself registers this on gazing at the painting when she remarks on the pity Christ shows for Pilate, but she seems to have inklings of this Pascalian truth. If in *Anna Karenina*, as in Pascal's *Pensées*, he or she who seeks God needs to apprehend the obscurity and futility of language in order to transcend it and feel divine love, then Levin's rejection of the philosophers' verbal traps, like his silence in key moments, is a sign that he is inclining his heart (back) to faith. The narrator, in fact, describes Levin's process of acquiring "new convictions" as one of replacing his former "faith" with "words" (8:8, 785). For Levin to escape from his Hamlet-like state of "words, words, words . . ." and of suicidal feelings ("To be, or not to be . . ."), he needs to accept divine revelation: the Word.

Inner Conversation

According to Pascal, divine truth is to be found by man when he is in a state of metaphysical solitude, bordering on terror. Levin experienced this terror in the months before the last day of the action of *Anna Karenina*. During this stage, Levin engaged in the silent "inner conversation"— conversation intérieure—that Pascal sets forth as the way to find truth and approach God. "We must remain in silence as much as possible and converse with ourselves only of God, whom we know to be the truth, and in this way we persuade ourselves of it" (L99/S132). As Nicholas Hammond observes, "interior conversation" can lead to an "interior conversion."[35]

The Pascalian model of conversion differs from Radstock's conversions brought about, person to person, according to Alexandrine Tolstoy's report, "in about an hour of time" [phrase in English in her Russian original]. In her view, Radstock had no understanding of human nature whatsoever: how could he believe that people could simply rid themselves of their passions and bad habits "in a moment of time"? She wrote that Radstock "often relates episodes of this kind: *'I met with a French gentleman. He was a complete unbeliever. I spoke with him in the garden, we prayed together and he went away a Christian'* [italicized words were in English in the Russian original]."[36] Tolstoy wrote back to express his disdain for instant conversions "at the English Club or at a meeting of shareholders," and to say that he believed that conversions took "labor and torments" and that at the very least this experience was a reward in itself even if it did not result in the "comfort of faith."[37]

For Tolstoy's hero Levin, as he seeks faith, spiritual work and torments take the form of a Pascalian "inner conversation." Thus, Tolstoy makes use of a narrative technique that he had been practicing since his debut as a writer. In an early review, Nikolai Chernyshevsky praised him for representing "the dialectics of the soul" and observed that Tolstoy's monologues were essentially dialogical.[38] Thus, Tolstoy's trademark mode of narrating consciousness was well suited to Pascal's "inner conversation." Pascal uses this term rather than "inner monologue," suggesting that his solitary seeker engages in a dialogical process, or one that considers multiple points of view.[39]

Tolstoy, most famously, gives us Anna Karenina's inner monologue (or what, following Pascal, should be seen as an "inner *conversation*") before her death. In Tolstoy's novel, as in Pascal's *Pensées*, inner conversation occurs in consequence of man's state of estrangement from God (and possibly from other people), but it is also a means of transcending ordinary verbal intercourse and *possibly* reaching higher truth. Thus, Pascal warns that it behooves us to control this interior conversation well and keep it in check. (It is "une conversation intérieure, qu'il importe de bien régler.") Absent this control, interior conversation can lead to a psychic hell. This threatens Anna Karenina in her inner conversation (verging on chaotic stream of consciousness) before her death: up until the last minute, she wonders whether human beings were put on this earth simply to hate each other (7:29, 760). In Part 8, Levin's "inner conversation," by contrast, stays focused on God and his truth, according to the Pascalian prescription.

Pokrovskoe as Pascalian *Cachot*

On the final day of the action of *Anna Karenina*, as Levin tends to his responsibilities at Pokrovskoe, he continues to engage in his "inner conversation," in which his lack of faith and his desire to believe torment him. (To Kitty's relief, he has at least given up reading philosophy.) We are told that "he sought in everything a link to his [Pascalian] questions: 'What am I? And where am I? And why am I here?'" (8:11, 792). As he watches peasants working the threshing machine, he muses gloomily, "Why is all this being done?" (8:11, 793).

> "What am I standing here and making them work for? Why are they all bustling about and trying to show me their zeal? Why is this old woman toiling so? (I know her, she's Matryona, I treated her when a beam fell on her during a fire)," he thought, looking at a thin woman who, as she moved the grain with a rake, stepped tensely with her black-tanned bare feet over the hard uneven threshing floor. "That time she recovered; but today or tomorrow or in ten years they'll bury her and nothing will be left of her, nor of that saucy one in the red skirt who is beating the grain from the chaff with such a deft and tender movement. She'll be buried, too, and so will this piebald gelding—very soon," he thought, looking at the heavy-bellied horse, breathing rapidly through flared nostrils, that was treading the slanted wheel as it kept escaping from under him. "He'll be buried, and Fyodor, the feeder, with his curly beard full of chaff and the shirt torn on his white shoulder, will also be buried. And now he's ripping the sheaves open, and giving orders, and yelling at the women, and straightening the belt on the flywheel with a quick movement. And above all, not only they, but I, too, will be buried and nothing will be left. What for?" (8:12, 793)

When Levin imagines everyone around him dying, from Matryona to the piebald gelding, he engages in the Gedankenexperiment proposed by Pascal when he asks us to imagine the universe as a *cachot* [dungeon] in which we are all condemned to death. Pascal writes: "Imagine a number of men in chains, all condemned to death, where some are slaughtered each day in the sight of the others, and those who remain see their own condition in that of their fellows and, looking at each other with grief and without hope, wait for their turn!" (L434/S686). Such, writes Pascal, is the condition of men (without God.) For all its homey comfort, Pokrovskoe, Levin's safe haven, becomes like the rest of the Pascalian universe, nothing but a *cachot*.[40]

But, at this point, Levin appears to find the answers to the questions that have been tormenting him. It happens in response to a seemingly random conversation with the muzhik Fyodor—whom Levin had just been imagining dead along with everyone else. Dissatisfied with how Fyodor had been feeding the threshing machine, Levin takes over the task. When they break for the peasants' dinner, however, they fall into conversation about who might rent a certain field. Fyodor mentions a peasant named Platon who "lives for his soul and remembers God," as opposed to another peasant Mityukha Kirillov who lives selfishly, only for his belly. When Levin questions Fyodor about the meaning of these words, Fyodor expresses the belief that Levin, in fact, may already be "remembering God." Levin then experiences a "new, joyful feeling," as if "blind[ed] by the light" of new thoughts (8:11, 794).

After various inner protests about the apparent senselessness of this message, mysterious and incomprehensible and yet deeply meaningful to him, Levin realizes that what he now has is *faith*. Contemplating the sky, "Levin ceased to think, and only as it were hearkened to mystic voices that spoke joyfully and anxiously about something among themselves. 'Can this really be faith?' he wondered, afraid to believe his happiness. 'My God, I thank Thee!' he said, choking back the rising sobs, and wiping away with both hands the tears that filled his eyes" (8:13, 800). Levin thus surrenders to Pascal's mystic "inner conversation," and acknowledges his faith to be *a gift from God*. (The suggestion is reinforced by the fact that the name of the peasant through whose lips Levin receives this gift from God is Fyodor, the Russian version of Greek Theodoros, meaning "gift from God.") What happens to Levin puts Pascal's thought into novelistic action, for *faith*, according to Pascal, is "a gift from God" (L7/S45).[41] That Levin is "a landowner who gets faith in God from a muzhik," as Dostoevsky would quip later in *Diary of a Writer*, shows Tolstoy being true to Russian roots, but in a way that also accords with the Pascalian wisdom that simple folk have a special capacity for faith.[42] Pascal writes, "Do not be surprised to see simple people believe without reasoning about it: God makes them love him and hate themselves; he inclines their heart to believe. We will never believe with an effective belief based on faith unless God inclines our heart. And we will believe as soon as he inclines it" (L380/S412). Whereas some people (including Tolstoy) might need to read the Scriptures or maybe even the *Pensées* in order to believe, many simple folk, according to Pascal, do not: "Those who believe without having read the Testaments do so because they have an entirely holy inward disposition and what they hear about our religion resonates with it. They feel that a God has created them. They want to love only God" (L380/S 413). Thus, God "inclines the hearts" of these simple folk to faith and they, for their part, feel love for their Maker.

Instead of inclining Levin to faith by having him read Pascal, Tolstoy exposes him to peasant piety. The naïvely faithful peasants, whose company Levin is so fond of, have more to offer him than the philosophers, with their manipulations of reason. Furthermore, Levin is explicit in declaring that loving our neighbor is *not* what *reason* tells us to do: "Reason discovered the struggle for existence and the law which demands that everyone who hinders the satisfaction of my desires should be throttled" (8:12, 797). Levin then reaffirms his membership in the community of believers, which, as he notes, consists of "millions of the most diverse people: sages and God's fools, children and old men—along with everyone, with some peasant, Lvov, Kitty, beggars and kings," all "indubitably understanding one and the same thing" (8:13, 799–800). Tolstoy rather closely echoes Pascal's observation that different people—"princes, subjects, nobles, commoners, old, young, strong, weak, sages, fools; the healthy, the sick; from all lands, of all times, of all ages and of all conditions"—all concluded that the happiness that is the goal of human life was not possible without faith in God (L148/S181).

Levin hails faith as a "gift from God," but what is the connection between Levin's *searching* for God and God's *gift* of faith? Does God simply act in mysterious (arbitrary, from an earthly perspective) ways to incline certain hearts to faith? Or has all the searching Levin has been doing *en gémissant* made him a worthy recipient of the gift of faith? At one point, Pascal has God say to Pascal's protagonist, "Take comfort. You would not seek me if you had not found me" (L919/S751). Thus, Pascal suggests that man is not a purely passive recipient of faith, even though in some of Pascal's fragments faith is a gift and God inclines the heart toward faith. Similarly, in the Russian Orthodox context, Tolstoy's point of reference in *Anna Karenina*, salvation depends on a mysterious synergy between God and man.

For Pascal, faith and the divine light are gifts from God, but human beings make themselves receptive to these gifts through prayer and praxis. Levin shows this receptivity when he lives according to the spiritual truths that he imbibed with his milk, and when he prays to God in moments of crisis, such as at Nikolai's death and at Kitty's labor. "Besides that, while his wife was giving birth an extraordinary thing had happened to him. He, the unbeliever, had begun to pray, and in the moment of praying he had believed. But that moment had passed, and he was unable to give any place in his life to the state of mind he had been in then" (8:8, 787). Thus, despite his "new [secular] convictions," Levin had, in fact, been making himself receptive to God and truth, which according to Pascal, can only be found in God.

Pascal's Sky over *Anna Karenina*

At key moments in *Anna Karenina*, Levin interrogates the sky as if in search of signs from above to tell him how (and even whether) to live his life. In Part 2, while hunting with Oblonsky, Levin watches Venus and the Great Bear in the sky; the stars appear to dictate the question he poses to Oblonsky about Kitty (2:15, 164–65). In Part 3, after spending a night on a haycock musing about marrying a peasant before catching sight of Kitty riding by in a carriage, Levin again seeks signs from the sky above that would tell him what to do (3:12, 278). And, on the last day of *Anna Karenina*, Levin looks to the sky more than once. Levin ponders the blue daytime sky right after his encounter with the peasant Fyodor just before concluding he has been granted faith. Later, as a thunderstorm rages, Levin's attention is once again drawn to the sky. Worried about his son and wife, who have gone to the woods, Levin races to the wood, watching an oak, in whose shade baby Mitya often napped, as it is struck by lightning and bursts into flames: "The whole earth caught fire and the vault of the heavens seemed to crack overhead." If nature can annihilate the sturdy oak, then Kitty and Mitya are certainly at its mercy. Levin attempts to bargain with God: "My God! My God, not on them!" (8:17, 811). Either God is merciful or Levin is lucky, for Mitya and Kitty are safe and sound. Then, as night falls over Pokrovskoe, while inside Kitty nurses Mitya, Levin briefly retreats from his family and goes outside to stare up at the nighttime sky, watching the Milky Way above:

> Instead of going back to the drawing room, where voices could be heard, he stopped on the verandah and, leaning on the rail, began looking at the sky.
>
> It was already quite dark, and in the south, where he was looking, there were no clouds. The clouds stood on the opposite side. From there came flashes of lightning and the roll of distant thunder. Levin listened to the drops monotonously dripping from the lindens in the garden and looked at the familiar triangle of stars and the branching Milky Way passing through it. At each flash of lightning not only the Milky Way but the bright stars also disappeared, but as soon as the lightning died out they reappeared in the same places, as if thrown by some unerring hand. (8:19, 815)

The fact that Levin is staring at the Milky Way in the sky (which evokes cosmic maternal milk), while inside his wife breastfeeds his baby son, hints at some kind of correlation between Levin's earthly existence and the stars. Levin feels that his earthly life at Pokrovskoe is "good."[43] And yet, whatever connection there is between God, stars, and Levin remains appropriately obscure and mysterious—and subject to doubt.

Levin appears in the familiar pose of the Tolstoyan hero who looks to the sky for an affirmation of what is going on in his soul or for an impetus for spiritual change. In *War and Peace*, Tolstoy's heroes often find their moments of epiphany in communion not with other human beings, but in silent contemplation of the sky. In *War and Peace*, indeed, the sky seems very responsive to the spiritual needs of Tolstoy's heroes: comets appear, on cue, when needed to inspire or reinforce an epiphany, and the stars of the Milky Way get "carried away, sporting in the black sky" and "whisper[ing] to one another something joyful and mysterious."[44] But, as Donna Orwin has observed, nature is more inscrutable and God more remote from human affairs in *Anna Karenina* than in *War and Peace*.[45] Tolstoy's own deep engagement with Pascal in part accounts for this feature, but adding to the effect is Tolstoy's familiarity with a corpus of Russian metaphysical nature poetry, much of it about stargazing and some of it even written under the sign of Pascal.[46]

Pascal's God is the *Deus absconditus*, hidden from view in the universe. Whatever signs he has left of his presence in the universe have been obscured and can be read only by those who have divine light. And there can be no rational proof that meaning is there. As Pascal declares, the heavens offer no *proof* of the existence of God:

> But for those in whom this light is extinguished and in whom we are trying to rekindle it, these people destitute of faith and grace, who, seeking with all their light whatever they see in nature that can lead them to this knowledge, find only obscurity and darkness; to tell them that they have only to look at the smallest things surrounding them to see God openly, to give them as the only proof of this great and important matter the course of the moon and planets, and to claim to have completed the proof with such an argument, is to give them ground for believing the proofs of our religion are indeed weak. (L781/S644)

In fact, as David Wetsel writes, for Pascal "proofs of God's existence drawn from 'les ouvrages de la nature' ('the works of nature') are useless in bringing about the conversion" of a seeker.[47]

At Levin's premarital confession, the Russian Orthodox priest attempts to do exactly what Pascal had warned would be of no use. When Levin confesses that his main sin is doubt and that he doubts everything, "sometimes even the existence of God," the priest asks Levin: "What doubt can you have of the Creator when you behold His creation? . . . Who has adorned the vault of Heaven with luminaries?" (5:1, 441) The priest evidently expects the stars to *prove* to Levin that God exists, but Levin is not convinced and continues to doubt. Perhaps Levin even thinks, in the spirit of Pascal, that the proofs the priest offers are "indeed weak."[48]

As *Anna Karenina* draws to its close, Levin's Pascalian "inner conversation" continues as he notices the stars, disappearing and reappearing "as if thrown there by some unerring hand":

> "Well, what is it that disturbs me?" Levin said to himself, feeling beforehand that the resolution of his doubts, though he did not know it yet, was already prepared in his soul.
>
> "Yes, the one evident, indubitable manifestation of the Deity is the laws of goodness disclosed to the world by revelation, and which I feel within myself, and by acknowledging which I do not so much unite myself as I am united, whether I will it or not, with others in one community of believers which is called the Church." (8:19, 815)

In this passage, when Levin goes from contemplation of the stars in the sky (and lightning) to meditation on the moral law, Tolstoy's readers have detected echoes of the concluding part of *Critique of Practical Reason*, especially the famous lines engraved on Kant's tombstone:

> Two things fill the mind with ever new and increasing admira-
> tion and awe, the more often and steadily we reflect upon them: *the*
> *starry heavens above me and the moral law within me*. I do not seek
> or conjecture either of them as if they were veiled obscurities or
> extravagances beyond the horizon of my vision; I see them before
> me and connect them immediately with the consciousness of my
> existence.[49]

Kant's formula about the starry heavens above and the moral law within was to become a favorite of Tolstoy's in later years.[50] Vyacheslav Ivanov maintains that there is something so basic and innate about this connection between the starry sky and the law within that you "do not have to be Kant or with Kant to appreciate this connection."[51]

Levin declares that the moral law or "the laws of goodness" that he feels within was made known to the world through Divine Revelation, and that this law is "the one evident, indubitable manifestation of the Deity." (Here Levin's formulation departs from Kant's.) In his refer-ences to this truth being a manifestation of the Deity and made known through revelation, as in his acknowledgment that he is "united, whether I will or no, with others in one community of believers called the Church," Levin seems to accept Orthodox tradition.[52] This ending, however, is also consonant with Pascal's *Pensées*, where Divine Revela-tion figures as the closest thing to a proof of God's existence that the Pascalian vision provides. As David Wetsel puts it, Pascal's "purpose has been to create a void within the mind of the *chercheur* which only Revelation can fill."[53] Pascal argues that the only incontrovertible proof of God's existence and the only signs from God are the Scriptures, through which God revealed himself and his law.

If Pascal's *Pensées* are thus taken as an argument for faith, Pascal's strategy or objective (if such words can be used in regard to these "frag-ments," which were left in a disordered state) is first and most obviously to underline humankind's utter desperation and isolation in the natural world. Pascal writes: "Men are in darkness and estranged from God. . . . He has hidden himself from their knowledge—this is even the name he is given in the Scriptures, *Deus absconditus* [the Hidden God]" (L427/ S681). This theme is repeated often. Elsewhere he writes: "I look in all directions and see only darkness everywhere. Nature offers me nothing that is not a matter of doubt and anxiety" (L429/S682). Although Pascal argues that there are no overt, incontrovertible signs in the universe of God's presence, so that, as a consequence, nature *cannot be used to prove God's existence*, Pascal still asserts that God has left certain signs of himself, however obscured, that are still discernible to—and decipherable by—the faithful.

Speaking in the voice of Divine Wisdom, Pascal attempts to explain why God has hidden whatever signs he has left of himself in the universe: "If [God] had wanted to overcome the obstinacy of the most hardened, he could have done so by revealing himself so manifestly that they could not doubt the truth of his essence, as he will appear the Last Day, with such bursts of lightning and such convulsions of nature that the dead will be resurrected and the most blind will see him. But this is not how he has wanted to appear in the sweetness of his coming, because, since so many men make themselves unworthy of his mercy, he has wanted to leave in sin those who want to remain there" (L149/S182). Divine Wisdom argues that God, rather than reveal himself (and thereby force people to have faith by proving his existence), "chose to make himself perfectly knowable to those who seek him sincerely with their whole heart and to remain hidden from those who flee him. . . . He thus tempers knowledge of himself by giving signs of himself that are visible to those who seek him, and not to those who do not seek him" (L149/S182). In this manner, "there is enough light for those who seek to see and enough darkness for those of a contrary disposition" (L149/S274). As Sara Melzer explains, Pascal's narrator "argues that although God does speak to us, he does not speak the language of reason which would be revealed through any system of signs." If any order or meaning is to be found in the world, Melzer continues, "it depends less on what one may think to be objectively inscribed in it and more on what they project onto it out of the inner light given by God."[54] This Pascalian stance on how God reveals himself is what Tolstoy arrives at for Levin as *Anna Karenina* draws to a close. Suddenly, the world has meaning for Levin, but this meaning is not necessarily objectively there. Nor is it one that Levin or anybody can prove. Rather, in accordance with Pascal's scenario, it is one that Levin has projected onto the world out of the inner light given to him by God, who has suddenly granted him the gift of faith.[55]

Once the Pascalian seeker has accepted this Revelation, then using God's light, he may be able to decipher God's other signs in the universe. Pascal argues in one fragment that, contrary to popular opinion, in the

Christian faith "the birds and the sky" do *not* "prove [the existence of] God." Rather, "God gives the light to some souls so that this is so, but for most it is not." Faith for Pascal does not guarantee that the universe will cease to be terrifying and cease to seem like a Godforsaken place. Pascal emphasizes that Nature does not provide us with *proof* of God's existence. But it is still possible that God has left signs of his existence, which can be mystically read by some of the faithful.[56] Thus, when Levin looks at the Milky Way, appearing and disappearing in the midst of the lightning, what he sees in the heavens is *possibly* a sign of God. But he stops short of seeing this as "proof" of God's existence, according to the (feeble) argument of the priest during Levin's premarital confession. Levin understands that whatever comfort the stars provide is provisional—his new feeling of faith is what matters, for without this faith the Milky Way means nothing.

At one point, however, doubt starts to creep in and threatens Levin's communion with the stars and hence his illumination about God. Having asserted that the one incontrovertible manifestation of God is charity (he calls it the laws of goodness), given to man through Revelation, Levin starts to wonder: What about the Jews, what about the Muslims, the Confucians, the Buddhists? "Can these hundreds of millions of people be deprived of the highest good, without which life has no meaning?" (8:19, 815). A bit earlier, he had noted that the Buddhists and Mohammedans "also confess and do good" as he asks why—how can it be?—that God would have limited revelation to the Christian Church alone? (8:18, 814). Levin's concern with their fates resonates with the ecumenical spirit that he had voiced earlier that day in the political discussion over the war in Serbia: Levin had asserted that he felt no particular "brotherhood" with his Orthodox co-religionists and that he is not moved to jump to their defense in their war against the Turks. Levin had been wrestling with questions about who was his neighbor and whether his love should extend beyond those who gather at Pokrovskoe or beyond those in the community of the Church that he now feels a part of.

And yet, in the final moments of *Anna Karenina*, Levin, remembering his question about whether God would "deprive hundreds of millions of people" of "the highest good without which life has no meaning," decides to surrender to God's wisdom: "I don't have the right or possibility of resolving the question of other faiths and their attitude to the Deity" (8:19, 816). In one of his final declarations in the novel, Levin accepts what has "been revealed to [him] by Christianity" (8:19, 816).

He seems to conclude that it is not for him to answer the question of whether God cuts off hundreds of millions of people from true happiness. "What am I doing? To me personally, to my heart, unquestionable knowledge is revealed, inconceivable to reason, and I stubbornly want to express this knowledge by means of *reason and words* [my italics, LK]" (8:19, 816). Thus, Levin gives up (at least for this summer's evening) on "resolving the question of other faiths and their attitude to the Deity" because, with his human tools of reason and words, he would not get anywhere. He would then be creating word traps like a philosopher. Levin conforms to Pascal's way of thinking and, accepting that this truth is "inconceivable to reason," leaves the question of the salvation of others in the hands of the Lord.

The Loss of True Happiness and Attempts to Fill the Infinite Abyss with Finite Things

As *Anna Karenina* ends, Levin concludes that his life is no longer meaningless and that he has the power to put good into his life (8:19, 817). Up until this point, he had been struggling to fill a void. According to Pascal, yearnings of the sort that Levin experiences result from the fact that human beings, fallen as they are, still bear within them a trace of a former state of true happiness. Pascal asks, "What then does this craving and this helplessness cry to us, if not that there was once a true happiness in man, of which all that now remains is the mark and empty trace?" (L148/S181). Pascal explains that man "tries in vain to fill it [this void] with everything around him." But it is of no use, "since this infinite abyss [le gouffre infini] can be filled only with an infinite and immutable object—that is, only with God himself" (L148/S181).

The condition of craving happiness, of suffering from loss of the "true good," as described by Pascal, applies not just to Levin but to all in *Anna Karenina*. As Pascal writes, "All men seek to be happy. This is without exception, whatever different means they use. They all strive toward this end" (L148/S181). Each of Tolstoy's unhappy heroes and heroines tries to fill the void of existence as he or she desperately pursues happiness. This includes Oblonsky and Dolly. Oblonsky is usually labeled a hedonist and was called a villain by Dostoevsky. But from the Pascalian point of view Oblonsky is diverting himself from the same fear of death that so overwhelms Levin. In Part 4, when Oblonsky comes to invite Levin to the dinner that brings Kitty and Levin together, he responds to Levin's obsessive talk of death and of the futility of human existence (as when Levin says, "It's true that it's time to die") by saying that this kind of talk is "old as the hills!" [старо как мир!] (4:7, 375). Then, when Levin tells him (in a distinctly Pascalian vein) that "one spends one's life diverting oneself [развлекаясь] with hunting or work, in order not to think about death," Oblonsky listens, smiling "subtly and gently." He then responds: "Here you're coming over to my side. Remember, you attacked me for seeking pleasure in life" (4:7, 375–76). When Levin goes back to talking about death, Oblonsky tells him to come to dinner, as if in echo of the "let us eat and drink; for tomorrow we die," which, according to Paul, is the motto of the nonbelievers (1 Corinthians 15:32). Oblonsky understands Levin's terror in the face of death, but his own answer to those feelings is to seek pleasure (and hurt his family in the process).

Even Dolly, often regarded as Tolstoy's ideal mother figure, is still subject to the craving for happiness that Pascal regards as the condition of all men and women. On the way to Vozdvizhenskoe, Dolly, who "never had time to think," falls into thought: "All the previously repressed thoughts suddenly came crowding into her head, and she thought about the whole of her life as never before, and from all different sides" (6:16, 606). As she ponders what Anna has done, Dolly declares: "[Anna] wants to live. God has put that into our souls" (6:16, 608). This "desire to live" is what Pascal had in mind when he wrote, "What then does this craving and this helplessness cry to us, if not that there was once a true happiness in man, of which all that now remains is the mark and empty trace . . . ?" (L148/S181). At this point, Dolly not only refrains from judging Anna, she even fantasizes about taking a lover herself. Motherhood may not have filled Dolly's *gouffre infini*.

If one reads *Anna Karenina* through the prism of Pascal's *Pensées*, distinctions between the different means by which characters pursue happiness cease to have significance; all human attempts to find happiness in created earthly things are bound to fall short and end in misery. Only God can fill the *gouffre infini* [infinite abyss] and make man truly happy:

> [God] alone is man's true good. And since man has forsaken him,
> it is strange that nothing in nature has been capable of taking
> his place: stars, heavens, earth, elements, plants, cabbages, leeks,
> animals, insects, calves, serpents, fever, pestilence, war, famine,
> vices, adultery, incest. And since man has lost the true good,

everything can seem equally good to him, even his own destruction, though it is so contrary to God, reason, and nature, all at once.

Some seek the good in authority, others in curiosities and in the sciences, and others, in sensual delights. (L148/S181)[57]

Pascal's list of the things that fail to fill the infinite abyss includes items that are relevant to Levin, such as the stars (Levin contemplates them at key points), plants (Levin cares for his crops), calves (Levin takes pleasure in the birth of Pava's calf and in animal husbandry in general), insects (in the midst of his ecstasy over his newfound faith Levin comes to the aid of "a little green bug," whose ascent of a stalk of couch-grass is blocked by a leaf of angelica).

In Part 8 we also learn that Levin has found a new interest in life in the form of beekeeping, which occupies him now as raising calves did earlier. In her inner monologue about Levin's torment over being a non-believer, Kitty muses: "[Kostya] must have gone to the apiary again. Though it's sad that he goes there so often, I'm glad all the same. It diverts him [Это развлекает его]. Now he's begun to be more cheerful and better than in the spring. Then he was so gloomy and tormented himself so that I began to be frightened for him. How strange he is!" (8:7, 784). When Kitty refers to beekeeping as something that "diverts" her husband, she uses a term that, in its French equivalent, has rich Pascalian significance (as Tolstoy would have noticed from his reading of the *Pensées*): "Divertissement" was one of the subject headings Pascal used as he gathered his fragments into related categories; when Pascal referred at various points to diversions and to human beings diverting themselves, he was not simply talking about amusing occupations, but efforts to turn away from painful contemplation of the human condition.[58] Kitty's use of the term is freighted with at least some of the same connotations even if Kitty herself is oblivious of the Pascalian resonance.

Whereas Levin's diversions seem to have some *relative* merit, especially in comparison to those of other husbands in the novel, Pascal maintains that none of these diversions, however innocent, noble, and consuming, can fill the void, give life meaning, or bring true happiness. An infinite abyss cannot be filled with finite things. Pascal's list also includes adultery, which Anna tries to stuff into her "*gouffre infini*," as well as war, which Vronsky ultimately uses to divert himself. Earlier in the fragment that contains this list, Pascal observes that the same desire to find happiness and to fill the abyss motivates "every action of every man, even of those who go hang themselves" (L148/S181). Should Anna's suicide be seen in this light?

The Same Desire, Accompanied by Different Perspectives: We All Want Something Sweet

Pascal's list draws together stars, sky, earth, elements, plants, cabbages, leeks, animals, insects, calves, serpents, fever, plague, war, famine, vices, adultery, and incest to prove that none of these items can take the place of God. (Nor can all of them together.) In his commentary on the *dénombrement* (enumeration) in this fragment, David Wetsel observes that Pascal moves in seemingly logical fashion through a "survey of all the traditional categories of created things" to "phenomena that have invaded nature since the Fall" (plague, war, famine), and, finally, to "man's own vices" (incest, adultery).[59] What, however, are we to make of the inclusion of cabbages and leeks in this list? Pascalian irony is at play, for, as Wetsel explains, "to search for God in any created thing . . . is as foolish as to search for happiness in a cabbage or a snake."[60] By collapsing these diversions, whether the lofty, the mundane, or the depraved, into one list, Pascal wreaks havoc on the value systems that people rely on to give structure and meaning to earthly life, or for that matter to novels.

In *Anna Karenina* Tolstoy sets up what appear to be elaborate structures for distinguishing between various earthly occupations, and he tempts us to draw evaluative judgments. In this vein, we might well conclude that Levin's life is better than Anna's. (Or that Anna's life makes a better plot for a novel or film.) But what happens when, reading with Pascal's *dénombrement* in mind, we stop opposing calf-lovers to adulterers and see what they have in common? And what does the commonality reveal about the human condition? Yes, Anna is a fallen woman, marked by her adultery, in contrast to Levin and Kitty, who raise calves, bees, and children and seem to live a good life. And yet, with Pascal, we might ask to what extent Levin and Kitty, too, like the rest of mortals, are also fallen pleasure-seekers bent on diverting themselves from what really matters. They are fallen not only in the sense that they have inherited the sin of Adam and Eve, but, as Anna puts it, in the sense that "we all want something sweet" so that even Kitty wants her "dirty ice cream" (7:29, 760).

In the same fragment that includes Pascal's list ("the stars, the sky, the earth, the elements, plants, cabbages, leeks, animals, insects, calves, serpents, fever, plague, war, famine, vices, adultery, incest") and the assertion that all human beings are driven by the same desperate desire to be happy, Pascal encourages the reader to deconstruct binary oppositions: "What makes some go to war and others not go is the same desire in both [to be happy], accompanied by different perspectives [accompagné de différentes vues]" (L181/S148). If we again regard *Anna Karenina* in the spirit of Pascal, then the binary opposition set up in Part 8 between those who go to go to war and promote it (Vronsky, Veslovsky, Yashvin, and other "villains" of the novel like Countess Lydia Ivanovna and Mme. Stahl) and those who stay home and conscientiously object to the war (Levin, Prince Shcherbatsky) ceases to signify. To be sure, Tolstoy seems to vilify warmongers and even to set up the camps at Pokrovskoe in a way that encourages the reader to judge them. But if we follow Pascal, then members of both camps are driven by the same desire that God put in all of us. As *Anna Karenina* draws to a close, readers who have been schooled to expect poetic justice might assume that as Vronsky goes off to die at war, he is getting his just deserts or redeeming himself through sacrifice, while Levin is being rewarded at home at Pokrovskoe. And it may even seem, as it does to Vronsky's mother, that Anna got what she deserved (8:4, 778). Others in the novel do not go this far, of course, but those who gather at Pokrovskoe still give no sign of remembering her.

Yet even as Tolstoy riddles *Anna Karenina* with binary (and ternary) oppositions, he undermines these oppositions with an anxiety about such evaluative judgments. Tolstoy, as we know, was prone to defamiliarizing the reality he represented; that process often involves defying automatic judgments based on normative value systems or on the topoi of other novels. Reading Pascal perhaps prompted Tolstoy to take his defamiliarizing to a more metaphysical level, thus threatening to shatter the structures he so painstakingly constructs. In this same vein, while Anna is no Pascal, she still shows flashes of a penetrating insight, possibly due to her estrangement from life, which, for example, allows her to see *through* the obvious differences between Levin and Vronsky to understand just why Kitty fell in love with both of them.

The process of destabilization begins with the opening sentence of the novel, when Tolstoy prompts the reader to think in terms of binary oppositions only to undermine them in what follows, and continues on through the end of the novel. Tolstoy sets up significant distinctions between his characters and encourages readers to separate the sheep from the goats, and yet he also makes *Anna Karenina* mysteriously polysemous—and Pascalian. When Pascal's fragments are brought to bear on *Anna Karenina*, the effect is to draw into question distinctions one might be tempted to make between Levin and Kitty on one side and Anna and Vronsky on the other, with Dolly and Oblonsky in between. Pascal puts earthly pursuits in perspective when he declares in one fragment that "in the face of these infinites, all finites are equal" (L199/S230).

Inspired by Pascal, Tolstoy hints at a more metaphysical point of view, which blurs the distinctions between opposing value systems. Many readers might revert to—or embrace afresh—standard viewpoints, which may be rooted in earthly common sense, the social order, the values of the community, or a desperate need to survive. But at least they will be arrived at through a deeper process of inquiry into the human condition, as seen under the sign of Pascal.

Inclining the Hearts of Levin and Anna: Pascal's Wager in *Anna Karenina*

Levin fills the void with stargazing, calf breeding, and beekeeping; Anna fills it with adultery. But from the Pascalian point of view neither adultery, nor bees, nor words, nor even stars can fill the infinite abyss or satisfy humankind's yearning for true happiness. Faith alone will. When Levin gazes up at the stars and affirms that his life is no longer meaningless, it is not because the stars have told him so. Rather, it is because he himself now has faith, which gives meaning to his life and allows him to even read meaning into the stars. In one of the haunting linkages from Levin's plot to Anna's, Anna turns to God in her final hour. Before plunging to her death under the train, she makes the sign of the cross. Her last words are "Lord, forgive me everything!" (7:30, 768). For this moment, it would seem, Anna, who (like Levin at the end of Part 8) has experienced the terror of the eternal silence of infinite spaces, affirms the presence of God in the universe, recognizes his teaching, and, most significantly, repents of her sin.

Early in her inner conversation, Anna had dismissed gestures of devotion as hypocritical or meaningless: "The bells ring for vespers and this merchant crosses himself so neatly! As if he's afraid of dropping something. Why these churches, this ringing and this lie? Only to hide the fact that we all hate each other" (7:29, 761). While seated on the train, she again reacted to signs of Christian piety: "Finally the third bell rang, the whistle sounded, the engine screeched, the chain jerked and the man [her neighbor in the train compartment] crossed himself. 'It would be interesting to ask him what he means by that,' thought Anna, looking at him spitefully" (7:31, 766). And yet, although Anna had denied God's truth, in the moment before her death she makes the sign of the cross that she had minutes before rejected as meaningless. As she prepares to jump under the train, she is hindered by her red handbag and tries to get rid of it;[61] as she waits for the next carriage, "a feeling seized her, similar to what she experienced when preparing to go into the water for a swim, and she crossed herself. The habitual gesture of making the sign of the cross called up in her soul a whole series of virginal and childhood memories" (7:31, 768). As she makes the sign of the cross, this gesture of worship, seems to become a meaningful act of religion: it resurrects her virginal self, floods her with memories of childhood, returns her to a state of innocence and love, if only for an instant. It seems to free her of her passion. This is reinforced symbolically when she attempted to rid herself of her red handbag. We are told that "suddenly the darkness that covered everything for her broke and life rose up before her momentarily with all its bright past joys" (7:31, 768).

Anna's gesture of piety as she makes the sign of the cross has its analogue in Pascal's *Pensées* when he writes of the value of habit and, specifically, of going through the motions of religious praxis. They help "incline," "direct," or prime the human "machine" toward faith.[62] To the dismay of many critics of Pascal, in the "argument of the wager," Pascal urges the non-believer to follow the example of believers: "Follow the way by which they began: they acted as if they believed, took holy water, had masses said, etc. This will make you believe naturally and make you more like the beasts [vous abêtira]. 'But this is what I am afraid of.' And why? What do you have to lose? But to show you that this is the way, this diminishes the passions, which are your great obstacles, etc." (L421/S680). As Bernard Howells has argued, Pascal's strategy is to focus purposely on "gestures" that a non-believer "will think closest to crass superstition and which indeed frequently are so" because Pascal believed that these instinctive, mechanical gestures help to overcome the "pleasure-seeking, self-seeking will," which is the "real obstacle to belief."[63]

Seen in relation to Pascal's understanding of these gestures, Anna's unthinking, mechanical act of making the sign of the cross becomes potentially significant. Anna has been locked in the hell of her conscience or her own unregulated "inner conversation." But as she makes the sign of the cross, Anna makes a gesture of turning outward and, ultimately, toward God.[64] The sequence of events in Anna's last moments is frantic. Horrified at what she is doing, she asks, "Where am I? What am I doing? Why?" She tries to save herself from the train, but is unable to do so. She can only cry out, "Lord, forgive me for everything!"[65]

The next part of *Anna Karenina*, when Levin considers suicide but then receives faith as a gift from God, invites readers to reconsider the sequence of events before Anna's death. Although Levin's experience is unique to him and true to his character as we know it, Tolstoy puts Levin through some of the same stations of the passion of Anna Karenina. He makes this most explicit and most poignant when the questions Levin asks echo Anna's just before her death. Levin asks: "What am I? And where am I? And why am I here?" (8:11, 792). Anna had asked: "Where am I? What am I doing? Why?" (7:31, 768). Playing on the dramatic irony of the double plot, according to which readers are privy to links between plots that are unknown to the characters, Tolstoy prompts readers to recollect Anna, even as everyone at Pokrovskoe seems to have forgotten her, and to see that she, like Levin, was seeking deliverance from a Pascalian *cachot*.

Anna's inner monologue in her last hours recalls Pascal's notion of the inner conversation: it is a means of arriving at faith, but it must be carefully controlled and kept focused on God and his truth. Anna's "inner conversation" is out of control and ungodly as she projects onto others the hatred she feels. She not only condemns others for their passion for "dirty ice cream" but also assumes the worst about them. But, ultimately, Anna acknowledges God and his truth. She takes responsibility for what she has done, blaming herself, admitting that she was a slave to her passions, that she hurt others. Finally, Anna's inner conversation, when punctuated by the sign of the cross, culminates in her Pascalian questions—"Where am I? What am I doing? Why?"—and leads her to pray, "Lord, forgive me for everything!" Certainly, Anna has not been living by the spiritual truths that Levin sucked in as a babe; nor has she been suppressing her passions, as Pascal prescribes. (When she rids herself of her red handbag she makes a gesture in this direction.) As she herself admits, she was willing to sacrifice even her son for her passion for her lover, as long as it satisfied her (7:30, 764).

Yet Tolstoy plants signs in the novel that Anna, too, at least before her passion for Vronsky, had lived by the spiritual truth of loving her neighbor.[66] When Anna returns to St. Petersburg in Part 5 to visit her son, the porter Kapitonych is loyal to her because in all his years he has seen nothing but kindness from her (5:30, 535). We are also reminded of Anna's past piety in her final hours as she is on her way to Dolly's in a last-ditch plea for compassion. In her stream-of-consciousness associative process, as she responds to street signs, Anna recalls the Mytishchi springs on the road to the Trinity monastery. "And she remembered how long, long ago, when she was just seventeen years old, she had gone with her aunt to the Trinity Monastery." In her imagination, in fragmented form, Anna resurrects her virginal self with her "red hands" and her former hopes and dreams (7:28, 757). That she used to make pilgrimages to monasteries does not in and of itself mean that her faith was deep, but it was a foundation of religious culture and habit for her to revert back to or, better, to reaffirm in a conscious and responsible way at a later time. It suggests that Anna had the habits of religion that might help "incline" the "machine" (to borrow Pascal's terminology) to faith.

As we know from elsewhere in *Anna Karenina* (and in Tolstoy's oeuvre), childhood faith, "sucked in with one's milk as a babe," as Levin put it in his ecstatic epiphany, is the faith that matters. It is there, latent, possibly to be summoned up in a quasi-instinctive, reflexive way, especially in a moment of life or death. But Levin was especially impressionable: we are told that "church services always had an effect on [Levin]" (6:26, 647), even when he simply joined his peers Koznyshev, Oblonsky, Sviazhsky, and Vronsky at the elections in Kashin Province and went to the cathedral to "swear the most terrible oaths to fulfill all the governor's hopes." "When he uttered the words, 'I kiss the cross,' and turned to look at the crowd of young and old people repeating the same thing, he felt himself moved" (6:26, 647). Later in the novel, when Kitty is in labor, Levin, a professed "unbeliever," to his own surprise prays to God "feeling, in spite of so long and seemingly so complete an estrangement, that he was turning to God just as trustfully and simply as in his childhood and early youth" (7:14, 713). He believes in God in that moment, even if it does pass. He even "knows" that in this moment "neither all his doubts, nor the impossibility he knew in himself of believing by means of reason" hindered him from turning to God (7:13, 709). Whether these moments when latent piety and religious nostalgia surface will amount to anything is one of Tolstoy's mysteries. They do not ensure that faith will be granted. Yet Tolstoy punctuates Levin's experience with them as if to suggest that it would be harder for him to find faith without them.[67]

According to the pattern Pascal suggests, this "inclination" of "the machine" that is Konstantin Levin primes him for faith. Perhaps Anna is subject to the same scenario. In these scenes of life and death, both Anna and Levin revert back to—or resurrect—the joyous piety of childhood and youth in one of the powerful situational rhymes of this novel. But one important difference distinguishes Tolstoy's dynamic in Anna and Levin from Pascal's: whereas Pascal advocates that his seeker *consciously* go through the motions (of taking holy water, of having masses said), in the hope that the good habits will lead them to faith, Tolstoy's heroes Levin and Anna hark back to their childhood devotion in times of crisis more spontaneously and less purposefully, without "wagering" and calculating the possible gain.

When we remember that, different as their plots are, Anna and Levin inhabit a single novel, then we may ask whether Anna's prayer to God, prompted by her gesture of making the sign of the cross, suggests that she has rid herself of enmity and passion. Has she, too, been granted faith? Or is she doomed forever in Tolstoy's universe because she, unlike Levin, lost sight of the spiritual truths that are the heart of Christian praxis?

Whether Anna falls into a void, into the arms of an angry God, or into those of a merciful one is left open in *Anna Karenina*. But that is true of Levin, too. It is unclear what will ultimately happen to him. As with Pascal's *Pensées* in which, as Pascal scholars have argued, the reader is given an extreme degree of leeway in making sense of the text (and may well feel overwhelmed by the abyss), interpretation of vital questions in *Anna Karenina* is left open to the reader. What does Anna have to do with Levin? Tolstoy clearly uses the double plot to force the reader to connect and disconnect the two plots. It is tempting to dismiss Anna's cry for mercy as the train car bears down as an empty exclamation or perhaps just another deathbed conversion: convenient, cheap, expedient. By the same token, one may wonder about the faith in God Levin gets from his muzhik. But in Anna's plot, as in Levin's, these prayers to God, unlike so much else that is uttered out loud, might come from the heart. All these questions are left for the reader to ponder. What is clear is that, even as on the surface of the action in Part 8 it appears as though Anna has, as Virginia Woolf observed, been allowed to drop out, beneath the surface of the novel, in the labyrinth of linkages that yokes the two plots, the reader is prompted to reconsider Anna's life and death from the Pascalian perspective that permeates the ending of *Anna Karenina*. The divergences and convergences of plot yield new awareness. The point is not to try to whitewash Anna by highlighting commonalities between her and Levin or even by pointing out that they are embroiled in the same human condition (according to which both are fallen even if Anna's "fall" into adultery makes her situation more acute). Nor is the point to show that Levin himself is not without sin. Rather, by yoking the two plots—and placing a Pascalian sky over all the plots of *Anna Karenina*—Tolstoy challenges, and perhaps changes, our perspectives in a profound way.

Pascal's Poetics in *Anna Karenina*

Tolstoy kept Pascal hidden in the labyrinth of linkages of *Anna Karenina* instead of mentioning him directly. Indirect evidence in *Anna Karenina* supplements the direct evidence elsewhere that Tolstoy felt an affinity for Pascal's understanding of the human condition and his arguments for faith.[68] And, in the arc of their experience in the novel, Levin (more fully) and Anna (more fitfully) imitate the Pascalian seeker who apprehends the terrifying silence of infinite spaces, feels misery without God, yearns for happiness, seeks to fill the infinite abyss (*gouffre infini*) in his soul with earthly diversions, and sees death everywhere, but eventually appeals to God as the only source of happiness.

If *Anna Karenina* novelizes aspects of Pascal's *Pensées*, then perhaps Tolstoy took to heart not only their content but also their form, seeking to reproduce Pascal's special art of persuasion. Pascal's poetics reflects his awareness of the limits of language, his anxiety about apologetics as such, his sense of the futility of imposing rational or mental order ("l'ordre de l'esprit") on material that may be inherently disorderly, his embrace of digression (as natural to the order of charity), his awareness that understanding this side of heaven is subject to a "continual reversal of pro and con" (L93/S127), and his belief that different and even opposed truths need to be taken into account.[69] Even with a corrective for the fact that his work was left unfinished by his death, these features suggest that Pascal embraces an open-ended poetics that thrives on indeterminacy. Lucien Goldmann has argued that the fragment is the only form suited to Pascal's tragic vision. Moreover, the "disorder" of the Pascalian fragment is essential to Pascal's vision of language and his method for engaging his readers. Pascal makes his readers doubt the truth(s) of human reason, rhetoric, and language, in order to urge them to search for a different truth that is, as Sara Melzer has argued, beyond the text.[70]

For many readers, the ending of *Anna Karenina* feels tenuous and provisional, even when Levin finds faith. The impact is unsettling, in the spirit of Pascal.[71] As in Pascal, where, according to Nicholas Hammond, the reader is engaged in an active role "in the persuasive framework" by different means, which include the use of multiple points of view to create "a more flexible and less dogmatic form of argumentation" that gives the reader "greater autonomy," so, too, is the reader of *Anna Karenina* left to make sense on his or her own.[72] As Pascal himself wrote in one of his fragments, "We are ordinarily persuaded better by the reasons we have discovered ourselves than by those that came into the minds of others" (L737/S617). The Pascal-like contingency of earthly understanding shatters any sense of closure achieved at the end of the novel.

Throughout *Anna Karenina*, Tolstoy often suggests binary oppositions that thrive on value judgments.[73] But then Tolstoy, in the spirit of Pascal, reminds us of the need to change perspectives or to acknowledge gaps or silences. Like Pascal, Tolstoy was aware of the need for modes of expression that work their ways into the reader's minds and memories. Whereas in Pascal's *Pensées* the reader contends with the fragmentariness and disorder that frustrate traditional modes of linear understanding, *Anna Karenina*, for all its apparent completeness, makes demands on the reader that are similar. The doubleness (or plurality) of plot cuts both ways: even as it simulates a sense of interconnectedness, it creates discontinuity and fragmentariness. Readers of *Anna Karenina* are forced to read not just "for the plot," but for the multiplot, which, especially in Tolstoy's iteration of this form, adds a sense of disorder and uncertainty to the process of reading the novel. The reader is likely to become unsettled by Tolstoy's undermining of traditional novelistic strategies: the world of *Anna Karenina* transcends the often homey imagined communities and contained worlds brought to life by other novelists, and instead resembles Pascal's *cachot* and eternally silent infinite spaces.

Much as Pascal presents us with an apparent hierarchy as he moves in the *dénombrement* of *divertissements* that humans use to fill the *gouffre infini*, from the stars to incest and adultery, but then leaves us in a state of puzzlement about how the cabbages and leeks figure in—so, too, does Tolstoy go to great lengths to present Levin's Pokrovskoe as the best estate man can achieve this side of Eden, only then to plant reminders of its precariousness. Is Levin just cultivating his own garden? Certainly Levin's affirmation of living for the soul rather than for the belly and of the need to love one's neighbor rings true. But is this supposed to dispel all doubt?[74] Faith may well be the answer, but Tolstoy makes it clear that Levin himself may not remain content with his illumination. Have those questions about whether God would deny salvation to the faithful of other creeds really been laid to rest in Levin's consciousness, which is, in fact, prone to rational order, even if he does yearn for liberation from it? Where does this put Anna Karenina?

Tolstoy leaves these questions open. Perhaps the real glory of *Anna Karenina* lies in how, in the spirit of Pascal, Tolstoy makes *Anna Karenina* into a novel that simulates poetic disorder and religious experience because it draws all forms of certainty into question, fosters doubt, and ultimately leaves leaps of faith or acts of interpretation up to the reader.[75] Tolstoy thus puts the reader of his multiplot *Anna Karenina* in the same position as the reader of Pascal's fragments, left to find a truth beyond the text.

6

Virginia Woolf and Leo Tolstoy
on Double Plot and the Misery
of Our Neighbors

For Whom the Bell Tolls in Mrs. Dalloway
and Anna Karenina

Loving Your Roses and Caring for Your Bees: Feeling Nothing for the Armenians or for the Serbs

"She cared much more for her roses than for the Armenians. Hunted out of existence, maimed, frozen, the victims of cruelty and injustice (she had heard Richard say so over and over again)—no, she could feel nothing for the Albanians, or was it the Armenians?)—but she loved her roses (didn't that help the Armenians?)—the only flowers she could bear to see cut" (120).[1] Thus writes Virginia Woolf of Mrs. Dalloway, as she contemplates the roses that her husband, a Conservative Member of Parliament, has brought her before setting off to the House of Commons to participate in a committee to address the fate of the Armenians. As Trudi Tate explains in "*Mrs. Dalloway* and the Armenian Question," the novel is set in June 1923, just before the British Empire and others signed the Treaty of Lausanne, which did away with the plan for an Armenian homeland and returned many Armenians to Turkish rule. Tate argues that Virginia Woolf was aware that Britain was to some degree responsible for what the Armenians had already suffered under Turkish rule (since, out of self-interest, Britain pushed in 1878 for Turkey to have control over the Armenian people and lands) and that Virginia Woolf understood that the Treaty of Lausanne amounted to further "betrayal" of the Armenians.[2] Following Tate's argument, we can see that Woolf brings to bear on her novel the concerns that occupied her generation in the aftermath of the Great War. Clarissa Dalloway's declaration that she feels nothing for the suffering of the Armenians and her suggestion that loving her roses might help, together with the activities of Richard Dalloway and others of the ruling class, are all evidence of Woolf's engagement with social and political issues, and also of deep concern with the problem of how to respond to the misery of others. As she wrote *Mrs. Dalloway*, which she envisioned as a modern novel, she attempted to compose a novel that in form and content could do justice to these complex issues.

Given that Virginia Woolf—as she put it in a letter to Vita Sackville-West in 1929—had "nearly every scene of *Anna Karenina* branded in [her],"[3] we might also see Clarissa Dalloway's denial of feeling for the Armenians as Woolf's response to Levin's assertion at the end of *Anna Karenina* to the members of his family circle (whom he hosts at the apiary, feeding them cucumbers and honey) that he feels nothing for the suffering of his Slavic brethren, the Serbs (8:15, 806). (Like the Armenians in *Mrs. Dalloway*, the Serbs at the time of the war in the Balkans in the 1870s were regarded as victims, "hunted out of existence, maimed, frozen, the victims of cruelty and injustice.") Much as Clarissa Dalloway tries to carry on by loving her roses, so too does Levin by loving his bees. Neither pretends to feel the pain of distant others: for all their faults—Clarissa's self-absorption and narrow-mindedness and Levin's righteousness and judgmentality—these two at least do not profess compassion they do not feel or that they have no intention of acting on. Both Woolf and Tolstoy thus raise questions about what is to be done: Is the best plan to love locally and trust that this will help globally? Is Koznyshev's response, or Richard Dalloway's, any better? What does the pain of others have to do with me? *Mrs. Dalloway* and *Anna Karenina* are permeated by these unsettling questions. Both novelists used the multiplot form to haunt the reader with them. In some respects, what Woolf writes of Russian fiction is also true of *Mrs. Dalloway*: the questions posed are "left to sound on and on after the story is over in hopeless interrogation that fills us with a deep, and finally it may be with a resentful, despair."[4]

These remarks about the pain of distant others, seemingly unrelated to the action of *Mrs. Dalloway*, reverberate because *Mrs. Dalloway* is deeply concerned with human relatedness, just as *Anna Karenina* is.[5] To address this question, Woolf created her own version of a complex novel with more than one plot. In doing so, she reckoned with an aspect of *Anna Karenina* that disturbed her—namely, a sense that Anna "is allowed to drop out." In the finale of *Anna Karenina*, those who gather at Pokrovskoe to feast on cucumbers and honey forget about Anna Karenina. That Tolstoy allowed this to happen filled Woolf with resentful despair.

Virginia Woolf, the Russian Point of View, and Tolstoy's Question

Virginia Woolf's reading of the Russians, as she was starting to become a novelist herself, had an important impact on her work and, by extension, on the modern novel. Virginia Woolf's engagement with Russian writers (not just Tolstoy, but also Dostoevsky, Turgenev, and Chekhov) was fruitful: as she attests in her essays, diaries, and letters, she saw in their work the *potential* of the novel as a genre capable of apprehending the human condition and conceptualizing consciousness. In her own novels Virginia Woolf then took this to a new level—not imitating it, but responding to it, reacting against it, and recreating the novel in the process. To be sure, many forces other than the Russians conspired to push Woolf to write what she envisioned as "modern" novels. Possibilities include "a revolution of domestic order," post-Impressionist art, Einsteinian time-space, the analytic philosophy of Bertrand Russell, Freudian thought, and other trends, all or some of which Virginia Woolf is thought to have had in mind when she famously declared that "on or about December 1910 human character changed."[6]

Tolstoy's death in November 1910 may have added to the significance in Woolf's mind of that particular season. Woolf (then Virginia Stephen) had just become familiar with Tolstoy's major novels: she read *Anna Karenina* for the *first* time (of three documented readings) in the summer of 1909. She read *War and Peace* in the summer of 1910, when she was convalescing after a break-down at an institution called Burley in

Twickenham. In her diary a year before her death, Woolf would remember that reading *War and Peace* was "a revelation" to her as she read it "in bed, at Twickenham" in that summer of 1910. The revelation is thus associated with that experience of recovery in an asylum.[7] There is, to my knowledge, no recorded response of Virginia Stephen to the death of Tolstoy in November 1910. In a letter written on Christmas Day of 1910 ("on or about" the time when "human character changed") she reported that she received a copy of Tolstoy's "What I Believe" as a present from Jean Thomas, who had cared for her at Twickenham. How did Virginia Stephen respond to her Christmas present? She complained to Vanessa Bell, her sister, that "[Jean Thomas] sent a long serious letter with it, exhorting me to Christianity, which will save me from insanity. How we are persecuted! The self conceit of Christians is really unendurable."[8] There is no further mention of "What I Believe," but she remained consistent in her skepticism about any pious answers Tolstoy might proffer to the question of "Why live?," which, according to Woolf (as she wrote in "The Russian Point of View"), always lurks, "like a scorpion," haunting his fictional heroes, and was the distinctive constant of his fiction. For Woolf, "because the kingdom of God is within you" was not an adequate answer to the question "Why live?"

As she wrote in "The Russian Point of View," what "enthrall[ed]" and "repelled" Woolf about Tolstoy was her sense that the Tolstoyan hero, "some rather lonely figure," goes on seeking throughout life. This is what imparts an air of inconclusiveness to Tolstoy's fiction — his stories "do not shut with a snap like the stories of Maupassant and Mérimée." She writes that "Tolstoy," "we may be sure," "was still asking himself" the riddle of existence "when he died." She assumes that the question that tortures Tolstoy's fictional heroes, even at the height of their happiness, was one that bothered Tolstoy, too, even in his late years when he was writing treatises that seemed to suggest he had the answers.[9]

Tolstoy as "Origin of All Our Discontent": *Mrs. Dalloway* as Her Double-Plot Answer

In 1929, looking back, Virginia Woolf described what reading *Anna Karenina* had meant to her as a novelist: "That is the origin of all our discontent. After that of course we had to break away."[10] In *Mrs. Dalloway* (1925), she had done just that. In *Virginia Woolf and the Russian Point of*

View, Roberta Rubenstein confirms that Tolstoy's "realism" was for Woolf the "catalyst for the literary discontent that prompted the modernist shift."[11] Robert Belknap has suggested that techniques used by Tolstoy and other nineteenth-century Russian novelists were among those appropriated and transformed by Western novelists in their "modernist departures from nineteenth-century rules." Belknap notes Tolstoy's way of using double (and triple) plotting to complicate judgment.[12] Thus, in *Virginia Woolf and the Migrations of Language*, Emily Dalgarno argues that "in *Mrs. Dalloway* Woolf adapted the double plot of *War and Peace* and *Anna Karenina* to create a modernist narrative."[13] Following the leads of these scholars, I explore what Woolf's "modernist" adaptation of the multiplot *Anna Karenina* reveals about Tolstoy's original, and which qualities prompted Woolf to make this "modernist shift."

In both *Anna Karenina* and *Mrs. Dalloway*, the title character ends up sharing the novel with another character, who has a plot of his own, but whom she meets just once (in *Anna Karenina*) or never (in *Mrs. Dalloway*).[14] In regard to Woolf's double story, Julia Briggs writes: "*Mrs. Dalloway* is the story of a day in the lives of a man and woman who never meet—a society hostess who gives a party, and a shell-shocked soldier who commits suicide. What they have in common or why their stories are told in parallel, the reader must decide, for this is a modernist text, an open text, with no neat climax or final explanation, and what happens seems to shift as we read and reread."[15] The same could be said of *Anna Karenina*: how the lives of Anna Karenina and Konstantin Levin connect "seems to shift as we read and reread." And is not *Anna Karenina* also an "open text, with no neat climax or final explanation"?[16] As they breed doubt, both these novels thrive on the particular form of desire that double- or multiplot novels create in their readers. This desire works in different directions (and on more than one axis of thought) as the reader seeks to know not only what happens to this or that character, but also how the plots connect.

The mystery of what Anna Karenina and Konstantin Levin have to do with each other may be what draws readers back to *Anna Karenina*. As discussed earlier in this study, *Anna Karenina* has been dogged by questions about its unity, from those of Tolstoy's contemporary Sergei Rachinsky, whose complaints prompted Tolstoy to make his famous claim about keeping the *connections hidden*, to those of Boris Eikhenbaum, who suggested that the novel is "built on very open and simple parallelism of two lines" connected by a dotted line [пунктир].[17] And, in fact, Virginia Woolf (in private) joined the chorus of those who registered their dismay at Tolstoy's handling of the double story: "What is disturbing is the constant change from place to place—one story to another—The emotional continuity is broken up—Unavoidable, but there seems to be a diversion of power. . . . What seems to me is that the construction is a good deal hindered by the double story. It offends me that the book ends without any allusion to Anna. She's allowed to drop out; never comes into Levin or Kitty's mind again."[18] Woolf wrote these notes in 1926, one year after she published *Mrs. Dalloway*. Had she herself handled the double plot differently so as to avoid this pitfall? On a basic level, Woolf mitigated against "diversion of power" in *Mrs. Dalloway* by constraining its action in time—to one day—and in space—to London. More significantly, as will be argued below, as she wrote a deeply troubling double story of her own, she took measures to maintain "emotional continuity" in her double plot and to keep the dead from "drop[ping] out."

The double- or multiplot form has an English pedigree and thus was not something that Virginia Woolf was first or primarily exposed to in its Russian iterations, even if Tolstoy's loomed large for her. In fact, the Russian practitioners of multiplot were inspired at least to some degree by English models. English dramas and novels thrive on multiplottedness, as exemplified by classics such as *King Lear* and *Middlemarch*.[19] Virginia Woolf describes *Middlemarch* as "the magnificent book which with all its imperfections is one of few English novels written for grown-up people."[20] In *Le Roman russe* (1886), Melchior de Vogüé suggested that tolerance for complexity and contradiction is a common denominator between English and Russian fiction, in contradistinction to the monism of the French novel.[21]

Though she was aware of its English pedigree, Virginia Woolf recognized tolerance of multiplottedness as a feature of the Russian point of view. Thus, Woolf reacted in her notebooks against Percy Lubbock's complaints in *Craft of Fiction* (1921) about Tolstoy's double plot in *War and Peace* and the lack of unity and form in this novel. She writes that "surely you can't see form apart from the emotion wh[ich] makes it."[22] She considered it her mission as both a critic and novelist to defy Lubbock's dictates on the craft of novel-writing. Embracing this aspect of the (nineteenth-century) Russian point of view was essential to her modernist program. As is clear from her defense of the Russians against Lubbock (a disciple of Henry James), Woolf's private criticisms of

Tolstoy's double story in *Anna Karenina* did not mean that she agreed with Henry James's critique of "loose and baggy monsters," and his self-declared "mortal horror of two stories, two pictures, in one."[23] When James wrote his double-plotted *Tragic Muse*, his solution for achieving unity was to hint that a romantic attachment would form between the hero of one plot and the heroine of the other in the ever-after beyond the novel. The emotional unity that Woolf sought was of another order entirely.

In reference to the form of *Mrs. Dalloway*, J. Hillis Miller has written, "The most important themes of a given novel are likely to lie not in anything which is said abstractly, but in significances generated by the way in which the story is told."[24] Bearing this in mind, we should expect to see in Woolf's handling of the double plot and its narration her most sacred ideas and also, possibly, an expression of her discontent with Tolstoy's double plot in *Anna Karenina*.[25]

Readers of *Mrs. Dalloway* marveled at the architectonics of the novel (or questioned its structure), as had been the case with *Anna Karenina*. E. M. Forster suggested that *Mrs. Dalloway* defied the laws of time and space that regulate daily life and normal novels. He contrasts her work to other English novels, which are like galleries hung with an "infinite" number of pictures and windows, "so that every variety of experience seems assured, and yet there is one factor that never varies: namely, the gallery itself." He explains that in traditional novels "the gallery is always the same, and the reader always has the feeling that he is pacing along it, under the conditions of time and space that regulate his daily life. Virginia Woolf would do away with the sense of pacing. The pictures and windows may remain if they can—indeed the portraits must remain—but she wants to destroy the gallery in which they are em-bedded and in its place build—build what? Something rhythmical. *Jacob's Room* suggests a spiral whirling down to a point, *Mrs. Dalloway* a cathedral."[26] Forster's characterization of *Mrs. Dalloway* as a cathedral recalls Tolstoy's own descriptions of the hidden architectonics and inner connections between plots in *Anna Karenina*. Similarly to Tolstoy, Woolf speaks of her "tunnelling process" for "tell[ing] the past by install-ments," and her method of "dig[ging] out beautiful caves behind [her] characters. . . . The idea is that the caves shall connect and each comes to daylight at the present moment."[27] Paul Ricoeur suggests that "the two fates of Septimus and Clarissa essentially communicate through the closeness of the subterranean 'caves' visited by the narrator."[28] Thus, both Tolstoy and Woolf depend on hidden, labyrinthine structures beneath the surface of plot.

Yet Tolstoy's cathedral of *Anna Karenina* differs in one respect from that of Woolf: Anna and Levin, who have been kept apart for most of the novel, meet in Part 7 in an important episode that Joan Grossman has presented as the keystone to Tolstoy's arch. This meeting prompts the reader to grasp deeper connections between Anna and Levin even as Tolstoy denies further contact between them and, after Anna's death, any signs of recollection. By contrast, the "cathedral" that is *Mrs. Dalloway* defies gravity, omitting such a keystone. Clarissa Dalloway and Septimus Warren Smith never meet "on the level of plot or acquaintance." But Woolf's "tunnels" seem to provide a means of drawing them together in the dimension of Clarissa's consciousness for long enough for Woolf to formulate the question that hovers over both this novel and *Anna Karenina*: What does the suffering of others have to do with me?

Translating Brotherly Love into English

In "The Russian Point of View" (1925), published the same year as *Mrs. Dalloway*, Woolf identifies in Russian literature a supreme concern with compassion and brotherhood, but, returning to the point she had made in "The Russian View" (1918), she notes that "brother" as a form of address (between non-siblings) does not work in English. It is untranslatable. She offers "mate" as a native equivalent, but only to indicate that while it may be the closest alternative, it is still off because there is something "sardonic" about it.[29] Her point is that the English have trouble feeling the brotherhood in "common suffering" that she believed was central to the Russian point of view of the human condition. (The Russian experts Woolf had been exposed to, such as Dr. C. Hagberg Wright, whom she cites, disseminated stereotypes about the Russian people being prone to "deep sadness."[30]) Woolf writes that "the cloud that broods above the whole of Russian literature" is "the assumption that in a world bursting with misery the chief call upon us is to understand our fellow-sufferers."[31] Woolf thus reveals her expectation that the Russian novel prompt us to attempt to understand our fellow-sufferers and take their misery to heart. In *Mrs. Dalloway*, written at the height of her engagement with Russian literature,[32] Woolf uses the English language in all its glory to encourage readers to ask if Septimus

Warren Smith and Clarissa Dalloway are brother and sister. And she evokes the English equivalents of the "compassion" and "comprehensiveness" (qualities she associated with the Russian novel)[33] as she issued the call in *Mrs. Dalloway* to take to heart the misery of others.

In "The Russian Point of View," Virginia Woolf drew attention to the pressure English novelists feel to sort people into different classes and categories, whereas, by contrast, as she saw it, the human intercourse the Russians (especially Dostoevsky) described was looser. In *Virginia Woolf and the Real World*, Alex Zwerdling suggests that in *Mrs. Dalloway*, under the influence of the Russian point of view, Woolf "moves . . . from the traditional social satire of the English novelist of manners" to more pointed criticism of the English system.[34] (Woolf declared in her notebooks that she meant in *Mrs. Dalloway* "to criticize the social system, & to show it at work, at its most intense.")[35] To show the social system "at its most intense," Woolf depicts the "governing class" giving its parties, composing its letters to the editor, working on its committees, writing its bills, and in general trying to carry on with the business of the British Empire in the wake of the Great War, while the poor of London go hungry, veterans suffer from shell-shock, war-ravaged Europe suffers, and India starts to revolt. Woolf shows that the sister Goddesses Proportion and Conversion (99–100), "disguised as brotherly love," are used to control *not only* Septimus Warren Smith, the shell-shocked veteran of the Great War who throws himself out of the window rather than submit, but also other individuals, disenfranchised groups, colonized peoples, and possibly, on some level, Mrs. Dalloway herself. When Septimus Warren Smith's death is announced by Dr. Bradshaw and his wife, as an excuse for being late to the Dalloways' party, Richard Dalloway thinks of adding a provision to a bill to address the deferred effects of shell-shock. Similarly, on his way home through London earlier, as he registers the suffering of people he passes ("poor mothers of Westminster"; "children kicking up their legs; sucking milk"; neglected children who cross dangerous traffic at Piccadilly alone; prostitutes; a female vagrant, whose reaction to the roses he is carrying causes a "spark," "not that they would ever speak"), he responds by blaming "our detestable social system" for these people's pain, and tells himself, "happiness is this" (115–17), as he holds a bouquet of roses and thinks of his love for Clarissa. In view of his activities as Member of Parliament, he could be said to be working for the greater good. And his own daughter Elizabeth asks whether "being on committees and giving up hours and hours every day," all to "help . . . the poor," makes him "a Christian" (136). Woolf uses these encounters with the suffering of others and these questions about what makes "a Christian" to add to the anxiety bred by the double plot (or triple plot if Doris Kilmer's story is given franchise within the novel) about what the misery of our neighbors has to do with us.[36]

It is in this larger context that we should see Clarissa Dalloway's responses to distant suffering: "She could feel nothing for the Albanians, or was it the Armenians? But she loved her roses . . . didn't that help the Armenians?" (120). As Trudi Tate observes, this response is "so preposterous that it draws attention to itself."[37] This response is not, however, Mrs. Dalloway's final word on the subject: as she continues to think about her party, feeling "suddenly" (after points of ellipsis in the narrative) "for no reason that she could discover, desperately unhappy," she comes up with rationales, but the reader still wonders whether the suffering of the Armenians might not be starting to affect her, for all her protests (120). Ultimately, Clarissa's response to Armenian suffering is linked, via Woolf's tunnels and caves, to her response to Smith's death, which is remote but at closer range than the suffering of the Armenians. This suicide is also the culmination of *Mrs. Dalloway's* other plot. When Clarissa learns of the death of this stranger, her response at first is to ask, "What business had the Bradshaws to talk of death at her party?" (184).[38]

Clarissa at this point withdraws from her party (into the very room in which "the chairs still kept the impress of the Prime Minister and Lady Bruton," who had retreated there to talk about a political matter) to think about the suicide of this shell-shocked soldier (184–86). Zwerdling notes that "[i]n feeling a sense of kinship with Septimus, Clarissa is crossing class lines in her imagination, for certainly he is beyond the pale of her set."[39] Her thoughts range from imagining the suicide in her own body, to asking why he had done it, to wondering whether his act was in response to the inability to communicate with others, to guessing that Dr. Bradshaw had "forc[ed]" his soul and made "life intolerable" to him, to feeling "very like him—the young man who had killed himself." Whether her response amounts to empathy or whether it merely "appropriates" or "romanticizes" his death has been at the heart of the critical debates on Woolf's novel.[40] A judgment has not been reached, in accordance with the laws of modernist double-plot where meaning is open-ended and the reader is left to ponder.

For Whom the Bell Tolls at Tolstoy's Pokrovskoe and in Woolf's London

If we continue to read *Mrs. Dalloway* as a response to *Anna Karenina*—to imagine that Woolf's cathedral sprang from the ruins of *Anna Karenina*, with Woolf creating beauty out of its weightiness—then perhaps Virginia Woolf is not only "criticizing [her] social system" but also criticizing the separate peace that Tolstoy creates for Levin and his loved ones at Pokrovskoe at the end of *Anna Karenina*. As *Anna Karenina* ends, Levin has reaffirmed his faith in God and has declared love of neighbor to be what guides his life. But who then is Levin's neighbor? At Pokrovskoe, Levin tends his beehives, and his neighborly love extends beyond Kitty and baby Mitya but only as far as to Dolly and her brood and to the peasants whose welfare connects to his. When Kitty tells Mitya to be just like his father, a good Christian because he loves others, she has in mind specifically his charity at close range.

That Levin survived his suicidal crisis is a victory, but the ending of *Anna Karenina* still disturbs. As discussed in chapter 4, Dostoevsky, who was all for military intervention in Serbia, argued that Russians must not stand idly by; they must defend their Slavic brethren. He took Tolstoy to task (holding him personally responsible for Levin's views) for the narrow range of Levin's love for neighbors. Grandstanding in *Diary of a Writer*, Dostoevsky asked at what distance Levin's love for his near one [ближний] kicks in. Surely, Dostoevsky argued, the tender-hearted Levin, who takes joy in his own baby's bath, should feel for those Serbian babes tortured in front of their mothers. Dostoevsky summarizes Levin's response: "Kitty's in fine spirits and had a good appetite today; we've given the boy a bath and he's begun to recognize me: what do I care what goes on over there in another hemisphere? *There is no immediate feeling for the oppression of the Slavs and there cannot be any*, because I don't feel *anything*" (italics in original).[41] Tolstoy presents the Christian love for Slavic brethren as an empty construct; those who promote the war (such as Countess Lydia Ivanovna and Koznyshev) and those who go off to fight in the war (Vronsky, Veslovsky, Yashvin) all do so in response to personal disappointment and emptiness, rather than out of true neighborly love or true desire to alleviate distant suffering. Dostoevsky was not the only novelist to admire *Anna Karenina* but at the same time to feel something was amiss with the ending. Virginia Woolf was another. Like Dostoevsky, but for very different reasons, Woolf was disturbed by the insularity of the family happiness (or unhappiness) at the end of *Anna Karenina*. Woolf was "offend[ed]" by the end of *Anna Karenina*: "she's allowed to drop out" and [she] "never comes into Levin or Kitty's mind again."[42]

Evidently, Virginia Woolf *remembered* Anna as she read Part 8, and the reader, critic, and artist in her expected Levin or Kitty to think about Anna. But it does not happen. Nor does Anna come into Dolly's consciousness at this point. Dolly announces as she feeds her brood cucumbers and honey from Levin's apiary that Vronsky is off to Serbia, but the narrator gives no indication that she grieves for or even remembers Anna. In fact, Dolly seems not to be thinking about Anna (which one might have expected after the mention of Vronsky), but is instead following the conversation about the Balkan War. She even chimes in on the men's conversation. Of all those who gather at Pokrovskoe, Dolly is the one we might most expect to think of Anna. The lapse is especially marked because of the pattern Tolstoy had set up of having Dolly remember Anna and register concern for her in other parts of the novel. In fact, Dolly's consciousness is one zone in which the separate, at times polarized, plots of *Anna Karenina* have come together. Thus, for example, at Kitty's wedding, Tolstoy lets us know that, in addition to thinking back to her own wedding, Dolly recalled other brides who, "just like Kitty, stood with love, hope, and fear in their hearts": "she also remembered her dear Anna. . . . she, too, had stood pure in her orange blossom and veil. And now what? 'Terribly strange,' she murmured" (5:5, 456). But Tolstoy gives no indication in this final scene at Pokrovskoe that Dolly remembers "her dear Anna."

For those who gather at Levin's apiary at Pokrovskoe as the novel ends, it is as if Anna's life were not grievable.[43] Oblonsky may have shed a tear for his sister at the train station earlier that day, but, as Dolly once remarked, his tears are like water. If thinking about Anna at this point had been simply too painful for those at Pokrovskoe, then Tolstoy's narrator might have indicated this.[44] After all, this highly telepathic narrator has often revealed to us what thoughts and feelings the characters have but do not utter out loud. But the narrator in *Anna Karenina* gives no indication that Anna figures in anyone's consciousness at Pokrovskoe. At the train station in the provincial capital earlier in Part 8, the narrator revealed that Anna comes to Vronsky's mind (not surprisingly) as he speaks with Koznyshev; before that, Vronsky's mother had said out loud that Anna "ended as such a woman should have ended," to which Koznyshev responds, "It's not for us to judge, Countess" (8:4, 778).[45] For those who share Countess Vronsky's view or Levin's when he dismissed *all* fallen women as vermin (1:11, 41), then the ending of *Anna Karenina* poses no challenges: good riddance to Anna Karenina. If those who gather at Pokrovskoe share the sentiments of Koznyshev (as seems to be the case), rather than those of the Countess, then they might at least remember her.

In the "epilogue," we learn that Levin has undergone months of anguish during which he "hid a rope lest he hang himself with it, and was afraid to go about with a rifle lest he shoot himself" (8:9, 789). But, as the novel ends, it becomes clear that Levin will go on living because he has found faith and understood that he must "live for God" and continue to "love his neighbor" (8:12, 796; 797). To be sure, Levin's suicidal anguish suggests a kinship between him and Anna, as does the fact that she begs God for mercy before her death. But this connects them "inwardly" rather than on the surface, or "on the level of plot or acquaintance of the characters," as Tolstoy put it.[46] The aftermath of their one meeting and the one intersection of their plots seemed to be that hereafter, despite the compassion Levin felt, Anna would now be beyond his "zone of liability to pain." Levin should hereafter focus his compassion at closer range. As Part 8 continues, it seems that Levin's survival depends on loving only neighbors who are near and dear to him and possibly also on disregarding the misery of others—from the Serbs to Anna Karenina.

Woolf takes into account Levin's religious crisis, but still objects to the treatment of Anna. Immediately after recording her chagrin that Anna "never comes into Levin or Kitty's mind again," Woolf writes: "All the stress finally upon his religious feelings—as if they predominated momentarily, as they wd [would] in real life; but this is unsatisfactory in a work of art where the other feelings have been around for so long."[47] Woolf here admits that this ending is more *life-like* than it would have been had Kitty and/or Levin remembered Anna at this point.[48] Is Woolf suggesting that, in real life, we all get caught up in our own concerns, whether it is saving our souls or giving our parties, instead of ever really taking to heart the misery of others and remembering the dead? Is this what Woolf finds so disturbing in the end of *Anna Karenina*? Did she perhaps expect *Anna Karenina*, as a work of art, to express a truth different from this grim truth about real life?

Insofar as *Mrs. Dalloway* can be read as Woolf's reaction to *Anna Karenina*, then, we should look at how she recreates in Clarissa Dalloway and her set English variations on Levin's exclusion of distant suffering, whether that of the Serbs or, closer to home, Anna Karenina. Whereas Clarissa Dalloway herself may be limited, the thrust of *Mrs. Dalloway* is to challenge Clarissa's position on "loving her roses" and to call for her to open her consciousness to the misery of others, including, first and foremost, that of the suicide Septimus Warren Smith. Before the novel ends—with its indication of the party and life going on—Woolf includes a form of communion, albeit very imperfect and problematic, as Clarissa Dalloway contemplates the life and death of Septimus Warren Smith.

Virginia Woolf conveys a profound sense of loneliness, no less than Tolstoy (whose novel ends with Levin affirming the isolation—"there will be the same wall between my soul's holy of holies and other people, even my wife" [8:19, 817]). As for Clarissa, she had despaired earlier, saying to herself, in regard to the (unintroduced) neighbor she has observed in the house opposite "ever so many years": "here is one room: there another. Did religion solve that, or love?" (127). But when this neighbor again comes briefly into her sight and consciousness as she retreats from the party to think about Septimus Warren Smith, Clarissa feels both connected to and yet still isolated from her neighbor. Whether this feeling represents a fleeting moment of communion is left an open question for the reader. In the course of *Mrs. Dalloway*, Woolf thus shows Clarissa's consciousness ranging from the Armenians (or Albanians) to this neighbor across the way and to Smith, as she tries, in her own way, without appeal to religion, to consider the question that dogs this novel, much as it did *Anna Karenina*: "Who is my neighbor?" Earlier, Elizabeth Dalloway had wanted to know if her father's committee work to help the poor made him a good Christian. Thus, *Mrs. Dalloway* reminds the reader of the range of possible definitions of neighbors. So, too, does *Anna Karenina* as a whole. But in Part 8, when Kitty tells baby Mitya to be just like his father, a good Christian because he loves others, she has in mind specifically his charity at close range to Dolly and the peasants. Whereas Kitty is convinced that Levin does what is right, in *Mrs. Dalloway* neither Elizabeth nor her mother expresses certainty. Thus, Elizabeth responds to her own question about her father, by thinking to herself, "it was difficult to say." Still, the narrow definition of neighbor as those near and dear that is promoted by Kitty and practiced by Levin in Part 8 is subjected to the doubt bred by the poetics of Tolstoy's multiplot novel. The attempt to ask whether Elizabeth's father qualifies as a Christian because of his charity to others—like the attempt to confirm that Mitya's father does—testifies to the anxiety let loose in both *Mrs.*

Dalloway and *Anna Karenina* about what the misery of others has to do with us.

Even as Woolf suggests that Mrs. Dalloway and the rest of the "governing class" fail Septimus Warren Smith, much as they fail the Armenians and the mothers begging in the park, she includes a brief moment in which Clarissa Dalloway thinks about the death of Septimus Warren Smith. Thus, the thrust of the novel is to connect them, even though they never meet. Periodically, even as their physical paths through London do not cross, Clarissa and Septimus Warren Smith both hear Big Ben tolling at the same time. Toward the novel's end, Septimus Warren Smith has thrown himself out the window in his desperate attempt to save himself from Dr. Holmes and Dr. Bradshaw, and news reaches Clarissa Dalloway's party. After her initial question of why people are talking of death at her party, Clarissa Dalloway ponders this death.

Whereas Tolstoy, ending *Anna Karenina* "without any allusion to Anna," had allowed her to "drop out," Woolf does not allow Septimus Warren Smith to "drop out" of *Mrs. Dalloway*. Woolf's act of focusing Clarissa's consciousness on the death of Septimus Warren Smith (and on the life of her neighbor across the way) draws her plots together to avoid the "diversion of power" that, in her view, marred Tolstoy's handling of his "double story."[49] Woolf uses Clarissa's response, flawed as it is, to bring home to her readers the truth about the interrelatedness of human lives at stake in her double story. As Woolf first read Tolstoy and other Russians, she identified as "the cloud that broods above the whole of Russian literature" the need "in a world bursting with misery" to "attempt to understand our fellow-sufferers."[50] While she may have been inspired by "the Russian point of view," Woolf ultimately anchors *Mrs. Dalloway* in her English tradition. The truth that Woolf embodies in her double-plotted *Mrs. Dalloway* is a variation on that of John Donne's "Seventeenth Meditation," in which he writes that "no man is an island," that "any man's death diminishes me," that the "misery of our neighbors" is ours, and in which he counsels, "never send to know for whom the bell tolls; it tolls for thee."[51] Without embracing Donne's theology, Woolf novelizes his insights about the interrelatedness of human lives. Woolf issues a call to her readers, who, like Clarissa Dalloway and others at her party, are left to respond. In *Mrs. Dalloway*, as Big Ben tolls, "its leaden circles dissolv[ing] in the air," it tolls for Clarissa and by extension for us all.

Tolstoy's Labyrinth of Plots in *Anna Karenina*

Virginia Woolf wrote that Tolstoy's fiction leaves its readers with a sense that "if honestly examined life presents question after question which must be left to sound on and on after the story is over."[52] This is especially true of *Anna Karenina*, a multiplot novel that has been criticized for its faulty structure and lack of proper closure. Any answers to the novel's big questions are subject to doubt when examined in Tolstoy's "labyrinth of linkages." If, according to Julia Briggs's definition, a modernist text is "an open text, with no neat climax or final explanation," in which "what happens seems to shift as we read and reread," then *Anna Karenina* might be seen as a *modernist* multiplot novel.

The provisional feel of *Anna Karenina* owes something to the fact that Tolstoy himself was searching for meaning as he wrote. *Anna Karenina* thus reflects his desperation to believe in God, to know who his neighbor is, and to understand what then should be done. Tolstoy tried to answer these questions more directly and deliberately after *Anna Karenina*, in didactic works and attempts to "narrate the self."[53] In regard to Tolstoy's letter to Strakhov in which he introduces the concept of the "labyrinth of linkages" in *Anna Karenina*, Irina Paperno argues that it shows that in April 1876, when he was desperate to finish *Anna Karenina*, Tolstoy was growing frustrated by "art's inherent inability to deliver a clear message" and by his sense of "the author's lack of control over his text." Paperno notes that Tolstoy was annoyed at readers and critics who purported to know what it was that he was saying in *Anna Karenina*: if that were the case, quipped Tolstoy, then "ils en savent plus long que moi" [they know more about it than I do].[54] Tolstoy, in other words, was aware that once loose in his "labyrinth of linkages," readers make their own way.

While the "inability to deliver a clear message" may be a quality of all art, the multiplot novel is an art form that is especially open to interpretation. Peter Garrett explains that "the centripetal impulse that organizes narrative around the development of a protagonist and the impulse that elaborates an inclusive pattern of simultaneous relationships" pull the reader in different directions and create "fundamental tensions" that "prevent [these novels] from resolving into any single stable order or meaning."[55] Tolstoy is a master of creating—and then, after the novel ends, leaving the reader with—that particular desire that comes when reading for the multiplot, the reader's desire to understand how the plots connect.

Various forces come together to create doubt in the reader, perhaps even more intensely than in the Victorian multiplot novels that provide Garrett's point of reference. Tolstoy wrote *Anna Karenina* from within a Russian literary tradition that not only thrived on deviating from Western forms, but also featured protagonists obsessed by the fear lest they die without leaving a trace (or a monument). Fear of death adds a metaphysical anxiety that defamiliarizes and deconstructs. Also contributing to the polysemy of *Anna Karenina* is the fact that Tolstoy, like Hawthorne in *The Scarlet Letter*, internalized the masterplot of the gospel pericope of the woman taken in adultery from the gospel of John, which actually tells the tale of the members of the community being "convicted by their own conscience." When this gospel scenario is externalized in Tolstoy's novel of adultery, the result is a multiplot novel. Tolstoy also shared what has been characterized as an English tolerance for complexity of form, the result of an attempt to depict the whole scope of human experience (including relations with God). Tolstoy, perhaps more than his English counterparts who wrote multiplot novels—not only George Eliot but even Virginia Woolf—leaves up to the reader the task of making connections between the plots. Tolstoy also refrains from restoring community to the novel as a whole. Tolstoy's intense religious searching, in the spirit of Pascal, inflected *Anna Karenina* with a sense of cosmic uncertainty, which leaves the reader to seek his or her own meaning.

In *Anna Karenina* Tolstoy attempted to express nothing short of the meaning of life in the form of a novel. As George Levine argued that *Middlemarch* had done, *Anna Karenina* describes "the quest, at whatever cost, to make one's individual life both internally coherent and coherent with the community in which it moves."[56] As *Anna Karenina* narrates the adultery and death of Anna, chronicles the family life of the Oblonskys, and ends with Levin's illumination about loving God and his neighbor, the novel forces us to consider how it all fits together. Tolstoy engages questions that through the ages have been at the heart of religious, humanitarian, ethical, social, and political thought. *Anna Karenina* asks questions like "Am I my brother's keeper?," "What do I have to do with a stranger?," and "Who is my neighbor?" (And, as Freud wanted to know in regard to the commandment to love one's neighbor, "Can it be possible?") Tolstoy, as ever, wants to know if we can escape "the tragedy of the bedroom." *Anna Karenina* forces us to consider questions like, "Who of us is without sin?" As Virginia Woolf observed, *Anna Karenina* asks questions about the meaning of life, such as "Why live?"

And it asks the Pascalian questions about God and faith: "Who put me here?" In *Anna Karenina and Others*, I have attempted to show how these questions reverberate in Tolstoy's "endless labyrinth of linkages [and plots]" and that Tolstoy's last word to his readers is something like "What sayest thou?"

Notes

Introduction

1. I cite from the English translation of *Anna Karenina* by Richard Pevear and Larissa Volokhonsky (New York: Penguin, 2000) with occasional emendations. In parentheses after references to *Anna Karenina*, I give the part and chapter numbers, followed by the page numbers of the English translation.

2. S. A. Tolstaia, diary entry, March 3, 1877, in *Dnevnik Sofii Tolstoi*, 1:37 (cited in N. N. Gusev, *Letopis' zhizni i tvorchestva L'va Nikolaevicha Tolstogo, 1828–1890* [Moscow: Gosudarvstvennoe izdatel'stvo khudozhestvennoi literatury, 1958], 468).

3. L. N. Tolstoi, *Chetveroevangelie: Soedinenie i perevod chetyrekh Evangelii* (Moscow: ESKMO Press, 2001), 473.

4. Tolstoy joins a host of religious and secular thinkers who have attempted to answer the vexed question of what loving one's neighbor means. In the introduction to their recent inquiry into this question, Slavoj Žižek, Eric L. Santner, and Kenneth Reinhard ("Introduction," *The Neighbor: Three Inquiries in Political Theology* [Chicago, IL: University of Chicago Press, 2013], 5) write of the "radical disagreement" on this subject: "In both Judaism and Christianity, the commandment in Leviticus 19:18 to 'love your neighbor as yourself' functions most canonically as the central law or moral principle par excellence, the ethical essence of true religion, in tandem with the commandment to 'love God.' But the meaning of neither of these injunctions can be taken as self-evident. . . . The intent and extent of the commandment to love the neighbor are obscure and have frequently been points of radical disagreement and sectarian division,

even in mainstream interpretation. . . . Despite its seemingly universal dissemination, despite its appropriation in the name of various moral and political agendas, something in the call to neighbor-love remains opaque and does not give itself up willingly to univocal interpretation. Yet it remains always in the imperative and presses on us with an urgency that seems to go beyond both its religious origins and its modern appropriations as universal reason."

5. L. N. Tolstoi to S. A. Rachinskii, 6 April 1878, #417, *Polnoe sobranie sochinenii*. 90 vols. (Moscow, "Khudozhestvennaia literatura," 1928–58), 62:404. Henceforth all letters and diaries of Tolstoy will be cited from this edition.

6. With two exceptions (*Resurrection* [1896] and *Hadji-Murat* [1896–1904]), Tolstoy did not return to the novel form.

7. Not surprisingly, coming up with a definitive answer to these questions proved to be impossible.

8. Irina Paperno argues that Tolstoy was frustrated with the "lack of control" that he, as author of *Anna Karenina*, had over the meaning of his text; in future philosophical works, he "wanted to find a mode of expression that would . . . convince instantly" (*"Who, What Am I?": Tolstoy Struggles to Narrate the Self* [Ithaca, NY: Cornell University Press, 2014], 43).

9. See Richard Gustafson, *Leo Tolstoy, Resident and Stranger: A Study in Fiction and Theology* (Princeton, NJ: Princeton University Press, 1986), and Inessa Medzhibovskaya, *Tolstoy and the Religious Culture of His Time: A Biography of a Long Conversion, 1845–1887* (Lanham, MD: Lexington Books, 2009).

10. L. N. Tolstoi to A. A. Tolstaia, 3 May 1859, #135, 60:293.

11. L. N. Tolstoi to A. A. Tolstaia, 30 July 1873, #30, 62:44.

12. As Gary Jahn points out, this question is critical to understanding the novel, or at least its *unity*: "the thorny problem of how [Levin's] story connects to Anna's is the crux of any discussion of the book's unity" ("The Crisis in Tolstoy and in *Anna Karenina*," in *Approaches*, ed. Knapp and Mandelker, 71).

13. Multiplotted novels also breed a particular form of dramatic irony: the reader is privy to paradigmatic links between the plots that are unknown to the characters of the different plots.

14. William Empson, *Some Versions of Pastoral* (New York: New Directions, 1974), 27. Robert Belknap discusses Shakespearean double plot in his book *Plots* (New York: Columbia University Press, 2016), based on his 2011 Leonard Hastings Schoff lectures.

15. See Henry James, "*Middlemarch*," in *The Art of Criticism: Henry James on the Theory and the Practice of Fiction*, ed. William Veeder and Susan M. Griffin (Chicago: University of Chicago Press, 1986), 49; "Preface to *The Tragic Muse*," in *The Portable Henry James*, ed. John Auchard (New York: Penguin, 2003), 476. Henry James's own strategy as a novelist for giving the unity necessary to make an artistic whole out of his own double plot, *The Tragic Muse*, was to hint at novel's end that the two heroes of his two separate plots get married in the ever after beyond the novel.

16. L. N. Tolstoi to S. A. Rachinskii, 27 January 1878, #384, 62:377. This letter will be discussed in chapter 3.

17. L. N. Tolstoi to N. N. Strakhov, 23 April 1876, #261, 62:268–70. This letter will be discussed in chapter 1.

18. Boris Eikhenbaum, *Lev Tolstoi: Semidesiatye gody* (Leningrad: Khudozhestvennaia literatura, 1974), 127.

19. Ilya Kliger notes that "Rachinsky's misguided insight should not be too quickly dismissed." According to Kliger, "The unity of *Anna Karenina* is irreconcilably dualistic. It is a unity, in other words, that acquires its distinctiveness precisely as a tension between two narratives that function according to different and even mutually exclusive principles" (*The Narrative Shape of Truth: Veridiction in Modern European Literature* [University Park: Pennsylvania State University Press, 2011], 153).

20. William Faulkner, 1939 interview, cited in Cleanth Brooks, *Toward Yoknapatawpha and Beyond* (New Haven, CT: Yale University Press, 1978), 206. Given Faulkner's repeated declarations that *Anna Karenina* was the greatest novel ever written, it is possible that it was one of the inspirations for *The Wild Palms*.

21. Percy Lubbock, *The Craft of Fiction* (New York: Viking, 1957), 237.

22. Svetlana Evdokimova, in her article on teaching Part 8 of *Anna Karenina*, offers excellent insight into the uneasy relationship between the different plot lines and the different genres novelized in them ("The Wedding Bell, the Death Knell, and Philosophy's Spell: Tolstoy's Sense of an Ending," in *Approaches*, ed. Knapp and Mandelker, 137–43). She proposes that we see the whole of *Anna Karenina* "as a Platonic dialogue on the nature of love, with each character embodying and reenacting a particular view of love" (142). She notes that "Levin's spiritual quest fails to resolve the multiple threads of the novel and cannot be viewed as the novel's teleological end point. But it is the resolution of the novel's Platonic dialogue" (143).

23. Robert Belknap, "Novelistic Technique," in *The Cambridge Companion to the Classic Russian Novel*, ed. Malcolm V. Jones and Robin Feuer Miller (Cambridge, UK: Cambridge University Press, 1998), 246. Robert Belknap suggests that Tolstoy makes *Anna Karenina* into a novel that in fact does what (good) art should do according to Tolstoy in *What Is Art?*: "There he sees art as an instrument not for indoctrinating the reader but for infecting the reader with the highest morality and religion of its time. In this sense, like Dostoevskii in his mature novels, Tolstoi is using the action of this novel to force the reader into active judgment. He did not want self-righteousness but the moral strength that comes from difficult encounters. The critics who make *Anna Karenina* a simple morality text for or against behavior like Anna's risk becoming what Tolstoi disliked most: comfortable" ("Novelistic Technique," 246).

24. Gina Kovarsky, "Mimesis and Moral Education in *Anna Karenina*," *Tolstoy Studies Journal* 8 (1995–96), 61–80; "Rhetoric, Metapoesis, and Moral Instruction in Tolstoy's Fiction: *Childhood, Boyhood, Youth, War and Peace*, and *Anna Karenina*." Ph.D. dissertation, Columbia University, 1998; "The Moral Education of the Reader," in *Approaches*, ed. Knapp and Mandelker, 166–72.

25. On Anna as the victim of her own omens, see Gary Saul Morson, *"Anna Karenina" in Our Time: Seeing More Wisely* (New Haven, CT: Yale University Press, 2007), 118–39; on the "execution of Anna Karenina," see Amy Mandelker, *Framing "Anna Karenina": Tolstoy, the Woman Question, and the Victorian Novel* (Columbus: Ohio State University Press, 1993), 83–100; on Anna's plot as

emplotted and Levin's as open, see Ilya Kliger (*Narrative Shape*, 158–59, note 21 on 227–28).

26. Kovarsky, "Mimesis and Moral Education," 72 and 79 (note 42).

27. On these different understandings of how compassion works, see Robert C. Roberts, "Compassion as an Emotion and Virtue," in *Religious Emotions: Some Philosophical Explorations*, ed. Willem Lemmens and Walter Van Herck, 19 (Newcastle, UK: Cambridge Scholars Publications, 2006), 198–218.

28. J. Hillis Miller, *The Form of Victorian Fiction: Thackeray, Dickens, Trollope, George Eliot, Meredith, and Hardy* (Cleveland, OH: Case Western Reserve Press, 1968), 2.

29. Virginia Woolf, "Reading Notes on *Anna Karenina*," in Roberta Rubenstein, *Virginia Woolf and the Russian Point of View* (New York: Palgrave, 2009), Appendix E, 201.

30. Morson, *"Anna Karenina" in Our Time*, 207, 12.

31. Cain continues: "The mastery with which [Tolstoy's] borrowings from *David Copperfield* have been integrated into *War and Peace* is testified by the fact that they appear to have passed unnoticed." Tom Cain, "Tolstoy's Use of *David Copperfield*," in *Tolstoi and Britain*, ed. W. Gareth Jones (Oxford, UK: Berg, 1995), 76.

32. For example, Morson has detected a whole scene in *Anna Karenina* that closely parallels, but then changes, a scene in Anthony Trollope's *Can You Forgive Her*, which he identifies as the novel that Anna Karenina read on the train in Part 1 (*"Anna Karenina" in Our Time*, 95–96).

Tolstoy had been borrowing scenes like this from *Childhood* on: for example, when Nikolenka enters the room he finds his mother distractedly flooding the tea table with water from the samovar, much as David Copperfield found Aunt Trotwood spilling water from the urn as he entered the room. This parallel is noted in Reginald Frank Christian, *Tolstoy: A Critical Introduction* (Cambridge, UK: Cambridge University Press, 1969), 29.

33. Priscilla Meyer, *How the Russians Read the French: Lermontov, Dostoevsky, Tolstoy* (Madison: University of Wisconsin Press, 2008), 154.

34. Qtd. in Meyer, *How the Russians Read the French*, 154. Sergei Tolstoy, *Tolstoy Remembered by His Son* (trans. Moura Budberg [London: Weidenfeld and Nicolson, 1949]), 57.

35. For insight into Tolstoy's mode of working the ideas of others into the fabric of *Anna Karenina*, see Donna Orwin, "Tolstoy's Antiphilosophical Philosophy in *Anna Karenina*," in *Approaches to Teaching Anna Karenina*, ed. Knapp and Mandelker, 95–103.

36. Eikhenbaum, *Semidesiatye gody*, 185.

37. According to his wife, when Tolstoy read *English* novels, it was a sure sign that he was about to start writing a novel himself: "I know that when Levochka turns to reading English novels he is near to writing" (Sophia Tolstoy, diary entry, 1878, in *Dnevniki*, 1:110, qtd. in C. J. G. Turner, *A Karenina Companion* [Waterloo, Ontario: Wilfrid Laurier University Press, 1993], 109).

Edwina Cruise notes that Tolstoy seems to have turned to English novels when he had "writer's block" ("Tracking the English Novel: Who Wrote the English Novel That Anna Reads," *Anniversary Essays on Tolstoy*, ed. Donna Orwin [Cambridge, UK: Cambridge University Press, 2010], 165).

38. On the English novel as it relates to *Anna Karenina*, Mandelker (*Framing "Anna Karenina"*) and Edwina Cruise ("Tracking the English Novel," in *Anniversary Essays on Tolstoy*, ed. Donna Orwin [Cambridge, UK: Cambridge University Press, 2010], 159–82) are especially helpful, as is the volume edited by W. Gareth Jones, *Tolstoi and Britain* (Oxford, UK: Berg, 1995).

39. Eikhenbaum, *Semidesiatye gody*, 15.

40. Eikhenbaum, *Semidesiatye gody*, 126.

41. Eikhenbaum, *Semidesiatye gody*, 127–28.

42. L. N. Tolstoi, *Chto takoe iskusstvo?*, 30:88; 30:150.

43. L. N. Tolstoi to A. A. Tolstaia, 12 June 1859, #141, 60:300.

44. Woolf, "Reading Notes on *Anna Karenina*," 200–201.

Chapter 1. The Estates of Pokrovskoe and Vozdvizhenskoe

This chapter is a revised version of "The Estates of Pokrovskoe and Vozdvizhenskoe: Tolstoy's Labyrinth of Linkages," *Tolstoy Studies Journal* 8 (1995-96); it also draws from "On a Scavenger Hunt in Tolstoy's Labyrinth of Linkages," in *Approaches to Teaching Tolstoy's "Anna Karenina*," ed. Liza Knapp and Amy Mandelker (New York: Modern Language Association Publications, 2003); and an unpublished paper on Gogol and Tolstoy. My understanding of the working of Tolstoy's labyrinth has been informed by the rich body of work on the structure of *Anna Karenina* and on Tolstoy's linking together of prosaic details into meaningful patterns, including: Moisei Semenovich Al'tman, *Chitaia Tolstogo* (Tula: Priokskoe knizhnoe izdatel'stvo, 1966); Elisabeth Stenbock-Fermor, *The Architecture of "Anna Karenina": A History of Its Writing, Structure, and Message* (Lisse: The Peter de Ridder Press, 1975); Barbara Lonnqvist, "Simvolika zheleza v romane *Anna Karenina*," in *Celebrating Creativity: Essays in Honor of Jostein Bortnes* (Bergen, Norway: University of Bergen, 1977), 97–107, and "'Medvezhii' motiv i simvolika neba v romane *Anna Karenina*," *Scando-Slavica* 41 (1995): 115–30; Sydney Schultze, *The Structure of "Anna Karenina"* (Ann Arbor, MI: Ardis, 1982); Richard F. Gustafson, *Leo Tolstoy, Resident and Stranger: A Study in Fiction and Theology* (Princeton, NJ: Princeton University Press, 1986); Amy Mandelker, *Framing "Anna Karenina": Tolstoy, the Woman Question, and the Victorian Novel* (Columbus: Ohio State University Press, 1993); Donna Orwin, *Tolstoy's Art and Thought, 1847–1880* (Princeton, NJ: Princeton University Press, 1993); Helena Goscilo, "Motif-Mesh as Matrix: Body, Sexuality, Adultery, and the Woman Question," in *Approaches*, ed. Knapp and Mandelker; Vladimir Alexandrov, *Limits to Interpretation: The Meanings of "Anna Karenina"* (Madison: University of Wisconsin Press, 2004); Gary Saul Morson, *"Anna Karenina" in Our Time: Seeing More Wisely* (New Haven, CT: Yale University Press, 2007); Gary L. Browning, *A "Labyrinth of Linkages" in Tolstoy's "Anna Karenina"* (Brighton, MA: Academic Studies Press, 2010).

1. L. N. Tolstoi to N. N. Strakhov, 23 April 1876, #261, 62:268–70. Tolstoy writes: "If I wanted to say in words all that I had in mind to express by my novel, I would have to write the novel just I had written it all over again from the start." He explains why this is so: "In everything, almost everything, that I wrote, I was guided by the need to gather together thoughts linked among themselves in order to express myself, but every thought expressed in words in

isolation loses its meaning and is horribly degraded when it is taken on its own outside of the linkage in which it is found. The linkage itself is brought about not by thought (I think), but by some other means, and to express the basis of that linking directly in words is in no way possible; it can only be done indirectly by using words to describe images, actions, situations." Tolstoy explained that as he composed or corrected segments of his novel, characters would behave or events would unfold in ways he had not consciously foreseen, but that ended up feeling "organically necessary," or true to the (fictional) life that he was creating in *Anna Karenina*. This letter, like the one to Sergei Rachinsky discussed below, is often taken as a key to interpreting *Anna Karenina*. See, esp., Gustafson, *Leo Tolstoy, Resident and Stranger: A Study in Fiction and Theology* (Princeton, NJ: Princeton University Press, 1986), 280–82.

2. L. N. Tolstoi to S. A. Rachinskii, 27 January 1878, #384, 62:376–77. In chapter 3 I will discuss how Tolstoy's *hidden* architectonics affect the form and meaning of his multiplot novel and I will return to Tolstoy's correspondence with Rachinskii.

3. When Henry James dismissed Tolstoy's novels as "large loose baggy monsters" with questionable *artistic* merit or meaning, was it because James failed or refused to appreciate this labyrinth of linkages and the inner continuity it provides? Henry James writes: "But what do such large loose baggy monsters, with their queer elements of the accidental and the arbitrary, artistically *mean?*" (Preface to *The Tragic Muse*, in *The Portable Henry James*, ed. John Auchard [New York: Penguin, 2003], 476); "Tolstoy and D[ostoevsky] are fluid pudding, though not tasteless, because the amount of their own minds and souls in solution in the broth gives it savour and flavour, thanks to the strong, rank quality of their genius and experience" (*Theory of Fiction*, 267, letter to Hugh Walpole, 1912).

4. Roman Jakobson, "On Realism in Art," in *Language in Literature*, ed. Krystyna Pomorska and Stephen Rudy (Cambridge, MA: Harvard University Press, 1987), 25.

5. For discussion of emblematic realism, see Gustafson, *Resident and Stranger*, 202–13.

6. Mandelker, *Framing "Anna Karenina": Tolstoy, the Woman Question, and the Victorian Novel* (Columbus: Ohio State University Press, 1993), 10–11. For a discussion of Tolstoy's complicated relation to realism (in reference to Jakobson, Barthes, and others), see 58–80.

7. Robert Belknap, "Novelistic Technique," in *The Cambridge Companion to the Classic Russian Novel*, ed. Malcolm V. Jones and Robin Feuer Miller (Cambridge, UK: Cambridge University Press, 1998), 245–46.

8. "Now, as if against his will, he cut deeper and deeper into the soil, like a plough, so that he could no longer get out without turning over the furrow" (8:10, 790).

9. See Mandelker for discussion of how this jam-making relates to the courtship plot of Varenka (*Framing "Anna Karenina,"* 73).

10. Tolstoy warned of this in the letter in which he formulated this notion of the labyrinth of linkages. He writes: "but every thought expressed in words in isolation loses its meaning and is horribly degraded when it is taken on its

own outside of the linkage in which it is found. The linkage itself is brought about not by thought (I think), but by some other means, and to express the basis of that linking directly in words is in no way possible; it can only be done indirectly by using words to describe images, actions, situations." (62:268–70).

11. I draw here on Dolly's later explanation to Levin of the difficulties Kitty faced on this fateful day: Dolly tells him that whereas a man proposes "when [his] love has ripened," a maiden lives in "a state of expectation" and "does sometimes feel that she doesn't know who she loves or what to say" (3:10, 270).

12. At various points in the novel, Tolstoy shows Levin in contact with horses, too. Thus, in Part 6, both Levin's and Vronsky's treatment of horses will come into play. Presumably there would have been cows at Vozdvizhenskoe, but the only time that we are told of Vronsky coming into contact with the bovine realm is when he eats beefsteak for breakfast. This is mentioned twice, on the day of the races (which ends in the death of Frou-Frou) and on the eve of Anna's suicide. Even if (or especially if) this was what he usually had for breakfast, it is significant that the two mentions of eating beefsteak are linked to the death of a beloved feminine being. (In later works promoting chastity and/or vegetarianism, Tolstoy often mentions the popular view that eating [too much] beef makes one oversexed.)

13. On the bovine and equine in *Madame Bovary*, see William Nelles, "Myth and Symbol in *Madame Bovary*," in *Approaches to Teaching "Madame Bovary*,*"* ed. Laurence M. Porter and Eugene Gray (New York: MLA Press, 1995), 49–54, and Jonathan Culler, "The Uses of *Madame Bovary*," in *Flaubert and Postmodernism*, ed. Naomi Schor and Henry F. Majewski (Lincoln: University of Nebraska Press, 1980), 1–12.

In *Middlemarch*, Dorothea Brooke wants to give up horseback-riding as part of her ascetic denial of pleasure and as part of her rejection of the ways of the English upper class; Lydgate is distinguished from the men around him by believing that there is something more worthwhile than the "cultus of horse-flesh"; his selfish and headstrong wife Rosamond suffers a miscarriage after she goes against Lydgate's orders and rides (for discussion of this in relation to Anna's horseback riding in Part 6, see below); Fred Vincy's maturation in the course of the novel (much accelerated in its Finale) can be measured by how he controls the passion for horses that defined him as a young man and devotes himself to animal husbandry; in the Finale, we also learn that Fred Vincy has produced "a work on the *Cultivation of Green Crops and the Economy of Cattle-Feeding* which won him high congratulations at agricultural meetings": by novel's end, he "kept his love of horsemanship, but he rarely allowed himself a day's hunting," and "submitted to be laughed at for cowardliness" rather than take risks jumping over fences because he now understood that as a responsible husband and father he should not risk his neck in this way. George Eliot thus uses prosaic details to reveal character, but she does not carry the practice to an absurd degree.

14. Culler, "The Uses of *Madame Bovary*," 7.

15. Tolstoy pegged Levin as a cow lover from the start: in drafts of the novel, the figure eventually christened Levin arrives in Moscow in the opening scene in order to show his cow in an agricultural show (20:52).

16. Levin's relations with Pava and her calf and his fantasy about a wife telling visitors that "Kostya and I tended this calf like a child" are reported in Part 1, Chapters 26 and 27, which in the serial publication was in the installment before the steeplechase.

17. Here again, only retroactively, after other relevant details have accrued, does the reader appreciate the significance Tolstoy ascribes to this act. Dolly's maternal "heroism" only becomes apparent when we see other babes suffer from lack of milk.

18. See chapter 4 for a discussion of how Kitty presents Levin's loving kindness to his extended family as evidence that he is a good Christian. And yet, as Dolly observes to herself in Part 6, as the family of Levin and Kitty grows, they will be less able to afford to help Dolly and her family (6:16, 607).

19. No details are provided beyond this, but patterns at play in Tolstoy's labyrinth might lead to the suspicion that the cook is courting the laundress: just as Oblonsky woos his mistress with a coral necklace (4:7, 373), the cook at Ergushevo woos the laundress with kitchen slops.

20. To prove his point in "A Few Words about War and Peace" about Russian prose works deviating from Western models, Tolstoy cites the examples of Gogol's Dead Souls and Dostoevsky's Notes from the House of the Dead, each of which spawned a school of "deviant" Russian novels, one devoted to the ideal locale of the Russian estate and the other devoted to prison camp. See "A Few Words about War and Peace," in War and Peace, trans. Pevear and Volokhonsky, 1217.

21. See John Bayley (Tolstoy and the Novel [Chicago: University of Chicago Press, 1988], 136–37). On life on the Russian estate, see Priscilla Roosevelt, Life on the Russian Country Estate: A Social and Cultural History (New Haven, CT: Yale University Press, 1995).

22. Country estates figure as settings for the action of Turgenev's novels. And he, too, uses the device of comparing one estate-realm to another within a given novel. (For example, in Fathers and Sons, an implicit comparison is set up between Kirsanov's estate of Mariino and Odintsova's estate.)

23. Eikhenbaum, Lev Tolstoi: Semidesiatye gody (Leningrad: Khudozhestven-naia literatura, 1974), 147–60.

24. Jakobson ("On Realism," 25) writes: "If the hero of an eighteenth-century adventure novel encounters a passer-by, it may be taken for granted that the latter is of importance either to the hero or, at least, to the plot. But it is obligatory in Gogol' or Tolstoj or Dostoevskij that the hero first meet an unimportant and (from the point of view of the story) superfluous passer-by, and that their resulting conversation should have no bearing on the story."

25. In drafts to the novel, Tolstoy lays bare the design of this segment of the novel. He specifically aims for the parallel visits of Veslovsky to Pokrovskoe (where he is discordant) and Dolly to Vozdvizhenskoe (where she is uncomfortable) to reveal contrasts between the two estates. And the corollary is true: Dolly feels at home at Pokrovskoe, just as Veslovsky does at Vozdvizhenskoe. Of Dolly's premature departure from Vozdvizhenskoe, which parallels Veslovsky's hasty expulsion from Pokrovskoe, Tolstoy writes in the draft, "When she left, the hosts and household members at Vozdvizhenskoe felt relief of the sort

that the Levins experienced when Veslovsky left" (20:487). From the final version of the novel, Tolstoy omits this narrative cue, leaving it to the reader to discern this hidden symmetry.

26. Elisabeth Stenbock-Fermor (*The Architecture of "Anna Karenina": A History of Its Writing, Structure, and Message* [Lisse: The Peter de Ridder Press, 1975], 103) sees the contrast of life on the Levin and Vronsky estates as an instance of Tolstoy's predilection for what she terms "diptychs" ("two strongly contrasting situations with a common denominator and a few identical features"). R. P. Blackmur also remarks on the ways in which Tolstoy sets up a comparison between life on the two estates: "Tolstoi gives us hundreds of comparisons and analogies." Blackmur focuses particular attention on the way Veslovsky is received by each of the two households ("The Dialectic of Incarnation: Tolstoi's *Anna Karenina*," in Tolstoy, *Anna Karenina: A Norton Critical Edition*, trans. Aylmer and Louise Maude, ed. George Gibian [New York: W. W. Norton, 1970]), 913.

For an illuminating view of the diptych of Part 6, especially as it presents "sports versus politics" and "politics," see Russell Valentino, *The Woman in the Window: Commerce, Consensual Fantasy, and the Quest for Masculine Virtue in the Russian Novel* (Columbus: Ohio State University Press, 2014), 85–86.

27. *The Craft of Fiction* (New York: Viking, 1957), 237. Other estates are depicted elsewhere in *Anna Karenina*, thus providing for the possibility of a multiple comparison. These are Dolly's Ergushevo and Sviyazhsky's swank estate where he and his wife live their childless life, spending their patrimony on new-fangled machinery and other improvements. But, as Tolstoy sets it up, the descriptions of these two clusters in Part 3 (3:9–10, 266–272; 3:26–28, 326–39) and the contrast between them creates a diptych, with Levin feeling dissatisfied with both, different as they are. One common denominator is that Levin feels that those he visits want him as a groom for their unmarried sister: Dolly upsets Levin by bringing up Kitty (and later writing to ask him to bring over a side-saddle) and Levin is not only convinced his hosts want him to marry Sviazhsky's sister-in-law, but that she has put on "a special dress . . . cut in a special trapezoidal shape on her white bosom" "for his sake." Her bosom "deprived Levin of his freedom of thought" (3:26, 328). In many respects, the contrast between the two estates Levin visits in Part 3 looks forward to that between those Dolly visits in Part 6.

28. In *Dead Souls*, Part 2, Chapter 1, Gogol provides a modal opposite to Nozdryov in Tentetnikov, in whose stables Chichikov's horses are content and find the oats excellent.

29. I cite from Robert Maguire's translation of Nikolai Gogol's *Dead Souls* (New York: Penguin, 2004). Part, chapter, and page numbers are noted in parentheses following the citations.

30. It is even conceivable that Gogol's attempt to provide the interior monologue of Chichikov's horses as he gives their point of view on Nozdryov may have inspired Tolstoy's "Kholstomer" or the segment in *Anna Karenina* that gives us Laska's perspective on the hunt and how her master Levin is handling it.

31. Lesley Chamberlain ("The Right Attitude to Horses: Animals as the Essential Humanizing Influence," *Times Literary Supplement* [March 1, 1996]: 15)

discusses the philosophical and moral importance of having "the right attitude toward horses" (Mayakovsky's phrase) in Western culture, beginning with Plato. Chamberlain mentions the parallel between Nietzsche's embrace of the beaten horse and that of Dostoevsky (in Raskolnikov's dream). Tolstoy's treatment of horses, which Chamberlain does not mention, fits the pattern.

32. In another detail that resonates in Tolstoy's labyrinth, Levin is left to go hungry on the hunt when he discovers that Veslovsky and Oblonsky have eaten all the provisions Kitty had packed for them, including the beef: there are clear intimations that Veslovsky's and Oblonsky's appetites for food, which they indulge without regard for others, correlate to their appetites for sex.

33. Once again, the peasants disapprove of Veslovsky. They find the sight of a man riding sidesaddle ridiculous (6:17, 612).

34. For further discussion of how Tolstoy plays on the meaning of this name, see chapter 5.

35. Mandelker (in Framing "Anna Karenina," 133–35) discusses Anna's desires to emulate the "English happiness" in her reading.

36. It should be noted, in this vein, that Dolly's response here is linked in the labyrinth to the fact that she, in her attempts to bring Kitty and Levin together again in Part 3, asked Levin to bring a sidesaddle so that Kitty would be able to ride. For an unmarried woman, riding horseback would be acceptable and possibly make her seem fetching.

37. Tolstoy, as War and Peace, Anna Karenina, and "The Kreutzer Sonata" attest, earnestly shared Rousseau's views on maternal breastfeeding.

38. Jean-Jacques Rousseau, Émile ou de l'éducation (Paris: Garnier-Flammarion, 1966), 45. In the discussion of Book 1, Milan Markovitch (Jean-Jacques Rousseau et Tolstoï [Paris: Honoré Champion, 1928], 257–76) outlines ways in which Tolstoy was influenced by Rousseau's views on motherhood.

39. For a discussion of these issues, see Mandelker (Framing "Anna Karenina," 28–30).

40. Donna Orwin draws attention to the symbolism of these estate names in Tolstoy's Art and Thought, 1847–1880 (Princeton, NJ: Princeton University Press, 1993), 182. She writes: "[Anna] is condemned to constant motion, which becomes a motif accompanying her until her death. This motion characterizes the world of individualism as a whole as portrayed in the novel, from Safo Shtolc's way of 'rushing forward' (3.18), to Vronsky's estate named 'Vozdvizhenskoe,' suggesting motion, in comparison to Levin's estate 'Pokrovskoe,' suggesting shelter or protection, to the industrial development of Russia, with railroads both facilitating this development and symbolizing it in the novel." In a note to this passage, Orwin comments: "Vozdvizhenskoe is an adjectival form referring either to a Christian holiday, Vozdvizhenie, the Exaltation of the Cross, or to a church named after the holiday. The verbal root, dvig, means 'move.' . . . The name Pokrovskoe has the same relationship to another Christian holiday, Pokrov, the festival of the protection of the Virgin, but in the nineteenth century the word pokrov was also used to mean shelter or protection" (Art and Thought, 245n34).

41. In the liturgy of this feast, the cross is "commemorated in a spirit of triumph, as a 'weapon of peace and unconquerable ensign of victory'" (The

Festal Menaion, trans. Mother Mary and Kallistos Ware, intr. Georges Florovsky [London: Faber and Faber, 1969], 50).

42. I am grateful to Gregory Freidin for informing me of this fact and its relevance to *Anna Karenina*.

43. The phallic associations are present even though the Russian word for erection (of the male member) does not have the etymological root *vozdvig*, which is used in the context of erecting crosses, columns, and monuments.

44. Levin follows the path outlined by Plato (*The Symposium*, trans. Walter Hamilton [Harmondsworth, UK: Penguin, 1980], 90 [208c]): having begotten fleshly progeny, he then (in Part 8) progresses to spiritual progeny, wisdom and virtue.

45. In *War and Peace*, Tolstoy adapts this Gogolian scene, putting the real Napoleon in the place of the Napoleonic Chichikov (who is even rumored to be Napoleon, escaped from exile and back in Russia trying to amass wealth and land): at the battle of Borodino, when Napoleon has a cold, he for the first time, according to Tolstoy, recognizes his own mortality and transfers to himself the sufferings of others that occur on the battlefield; for this brief shining moment, he no longer cares about Napoleonic conquest or any of his others pursuits. Tolstoy also shows Napoleon to be, in the spirit of Chichikov, obsessed with immortalizing himself in his heir, the Roi de Rome.

46. Tolstoy sets forth Levin's attitudes as follows: "It was the world in which his father and mother had lived and died. They had lived a life which for Levin seemed the ideal of all perfection and which he dreamed of renewing with his wife, with his family. . . . Levin barely remembered his mother. His notion of her was a sacred memory, and his future wife would have to be, in his imagination, the repetition of that lovely, sacred ideal of a woman which his mother was for him. He was not only unable to picture to himself the love of a woman without marriage, but he first pictured the family to himself and only then the woman who would give him that family. . . . [F]or Levin [marriage] was the chief concern of life, on which all happiness depended" (1:27, 95).

47. An important difference is that Chichikov has to scheme to get his estate whereas Levin was to the manor/manner born.

48. Suggestions in Part 2 that Chichikov as a child was deprived of fatherly love and that this may explain his shortcomings as a modal husband and family man are the crude Gogolian form of the genetic determinism at play in Tolstoy's fictional families: the Shcherbatsky sisters are faithful wives, the Kuragins are sex fiends, and so forth. Individuals in Tolstoy's world seldom transcend their family identity, with Vera Rostov the one possible exception. (Her parents attribute her distinctive qualities to her having been their first child.)

49. For a discussion of Chichikov's vision of the governor's daughter and Levin's vision of Kitty, both seen through the windows of carriages and functioning analogously in each hero's "quest for masculine virtue," see Valentino, *The Woman in the Window*, 33–36 and 83–84.

50. Had he taken a peasant as a wife (like "Uncle" in *War and Peace*, who makes radical decisions in the face of his own realization of mortality) and sired children by a peasant, he would not have "immortalize[d] the [Levin] family name."

51. For discussion of the tension Gogol sets up between the "ladder of human perfectibility" and the ladder of social success (often incarnated in the table of ranks), see my "Gogol and the Ascent of Jacob's Ladder" (*Christianity and the Eastern Slavs*, ed. Boris Gasparov and others [Berkeley: University of California Press, 1993], 3:2–15).

52. My understanding of this feature of Tolstoy's work draws on Jack Rawlins's discussion of what awareness of death often does within Thackeray's narrative (*Thackeray's Novels: A Fiction That Is True* [Berkeley: University of California Press, 1974], 202–25). Thackeray, one of Tolstoy's inspirations from Sevastopol on, was a master of using the novel form to emphasize the vanity of earthly endeavors. Tolstoy shares his sense that the more you apprehend death as the inevitable end, the more narrative structures collapse.

53. F. I. Tiutchev, *Izbrannye stikhotvoreniia* (New York: Chekhov, 1952), 90, 117.

54. Holy night ascended to the sky / And comforting day, amiable day, / Was rolled up by night like a golden veil, / A veil, thrown over the abyss. / And like a vision the external world has gone . . . / And man, like a homeless orphan, / Now stands, feeble and naked, / Face to face before the dark precipice. // Left completely to himself— / His mind is defunct and his thought orphaned— / In his soul, as in an abyss, he is buried / And from without there is no support, no boundary . . . / And seeming to him now like a distant dream / Is all that is bright, all that is alive. . . / And in the alien, mysterious realm of night / He will come to know his ancestral heritage.

55. For discussion of the importance of Tyutchev to Tolstoy in the period of *Anna Karenina*, see Eikhenbaum (*Semidesiatye gody*, 149–54). Eikhenbaum discusses a meeting that occurred between Tyutchev and Tolstoy on a train in 1871, as well as the common interest of Tolstoy and Tyutchev (and Fet) in Schopenhauer. Tyutchev also shared Tolstoy's affinity for Pascal. (For discussion of the Pascalian dimension of *Anna Karenina*, see chapter 5.)

56. Dmitrii Merezhkovskii, *L. Tolstoi i Dostoevskii: Zhizn' i tvorchestvo* (St. Petersburg: Obshchestvennaia pol'za, 1909), 175.

57. Merezhkovsky (*L. Tolstoi i Dostoevskii*, 175) equates this "bottomless, black, terrifying hole" with "'the bag' into which Ivan Illyich is shoved . . . with his inhuman cry 'I don't want to!'" (This bag may relate to Anna Karenina's red handbag. See below.)

58. Donna Orwin (*Art and Thought*, 160–61, 194) discusses Tyutchev's links to Tolstoy. In connection with Tolstoy's description of his meeting with Tyutchev in a letter to Strakhov, Orwin speculates in a footnote (250n6) about the discussion when they met on the train: "It is possible that this very fact of the spiritual isolation of each human being was a topic of conversation between the two men, and that Tolstoy was influenced in his reflections after their meeting by Tyutchev's belief that 'a word once spoken is a lie.'" François Cornillot ("L'écriture contrapuntique," *Cahiers Léon Tolstoï* 1 [1984]: 27) has suggested that in the final chapter of *Anna Karenina* when Levin looks up at the dark sky and decides to remain silent to Kitty about his spiritual illumination, there is a reference to Tyutchev's "Silentium!"

59. Cornillot, "L'écriture contrapuntique," 40.

60. Tolstoy connects Levin's crisis in Part 8 with his meeting with the dying Nikolai in Part 3, by noting (in Part 8, Chapter 8) that the questions regarding life and death that entered Levin's mind on seeing his dying brother had never left Levin. Rather, events such as his marriage and his wife's pregnancy had only distracted him.

61. For discussion of the problem of "communication" in *Anna Karenina*, see Malcolm Jones, "Problems of Communication in *Anna Karenina*," in *New Essays on Tolstoy*, ed. Malcolm V. Jones and R. F. Christian (Cambridge, UK: Cambridge University Press, 1978), and Justin Weir, *Leo Tolstoy and the Alibi of Narrative* (New Haven, CT: Yale University Press, 2011), 135–46.

62. André Monnier shows how *eros* and *thanatos* are linked in the novel and how *both* couples struggle against these forces, albeit to different degrees ("Eros et thanatos," in *Cahiers Léon Tolstoï* 1 [1984]: 94).

63. In his "Two Aspects of Language and Two Types of Aphasic Disturbance," Jakobson asserts "the primacy of the metaphoric process in the literary schools of romanticism and symbolism" and the corollary (but to his mind "insufficiently" recognized) "predominance of metonymy which underlies and actually predetermines the so-called 'realistic' trend, which belongs to an intermediary stage between the decline of romanticism and the rise of symbolism and is opposed to both." Arguing that the "realistic author" is "fond of synecdochic details," Jakobson notes: "In the scene of Anna Karenina's suicide Tolstoj's artistic attention is focused on the heroine's handbag." In "On Realism in Art," Jakobson again writes of Anna Karenina's handbag, citing it as an instance of the "unessential details" used by realist authors: "Describing Anna's suicide, Tolstoj primarily writes about her handbag" (25). Stenbock-Fermor (*Architecture*, 47–48) discusses Anna's red handbag and refers to Jakobson's treatment of it. Mandelker (*Framing "Anna Karenina*," 67–80) discusses Jakobson and Anna's red handbag within the context of her discussion of various responses toward Tolstoy's (so-called) realism.

64. Osip Mandel'shtam, "Egipetskaia marka," in *Sobranie sochinenii v trekh tomakh*, ed. G. P. Struve and B. A. Filippov, 2nd ed. (New York: Inter-Language Literary Associates, 1971), 2:41.

65. On the interpretation of this dream, see Thomas Barran, "Anna's Dreams," in *Approaches*, ed. Knapp and Mandelker.

66. Gustafson, *Resident and Stranger*, 309; Gustafson (311) notes that the dream combines elements both of Anna's "hallucinatory journey" and the death of the railroad worker earlier.

67. Readers might find that the fate of the mistress of Pokrovskoe is ultimately to follow in the hoofsteps of Pava, Levin's prize milk cow.

68. Sex was not her only sin; as Gustafson (*Resident and Stranger*, 132) argues, "Anna is not punished by Tolstoy for her sexual fulfillment." Tolstoy's view of what happens to Anna follows Rousseau's model for woman's decline into egoism: Rousseau declares that once women deny motherhood, then all moral ties binding human beings together disintegrate ("Chacun ne songe qu'à soi-même"). Thus, Anna's crime is that she does not dedicate her body to motherhood and, as a result, thinks only of herself. There is an additional, Aristotelian association in the image of Anna and her red handbag. Put crudely (in terms

consistent with Tolstoy), Tolstoy's depiction of Anna Karenina carrying around her red handbag illustrates the Aristotelian definition of hysteria, which is said to result from a "wandering" womb, a womb that is not properly weighed down and held in place by a fetus.

69. In Plato's *Symposium* (92 [209e]), recognition of the beauty of the soul comes at a later stage than recognition of the beauty of the body.

70. Anne Hruska ("Infected Families: Belonging and Exclusion in the Works of Leo Tolstoy," Ph.D. dissertation, University of California, Berkeley, 2001) argues that the Tolstoyan family thrives by excluding outsiders. See also Virginia Woolf's brief expression of dissatisfaction at the exclusion of Anna from the minds and hearts of those who gather at Pokrovskoe at the end ("Reading Notes on *Anna Karenina*," Appendix E, in Roberta Rubenstein, *Virginia Woolf and the Russian Point of View* [New York: Palgrave-Macmillan, 2009], 200–201).

Chapter 2. *Anna Karenina* and *The Scarlet Letter*

This chapter has its origins in *"Anna Karenina* and *The Scarlet Letter*: Tolstoy's 'Awful Hieroglyphs' on the Cope of Heaven," a talk given for the Seminar on Slavic Culture of the University Seminars, Columbia University, October 2004.

1. Carol Bensick presents *The Scarlet Letter* as an anomaly and *Anna Karenina* as a more classic case: "But while 'the novel of adultery' is evidently *The Scarlet Letter*'s most appropriate genre, studious comparison of Hawthorne and Tolstoy uncovers a basic anomaly in Hawthorne's relation to their mutual tradition. The classic script, while deploring society's gratuitous tormenting of the adulteress, nevertheless assumes misery to be her unavoidable portion; thus *Anna Karenina*, without otherwise concerning itself with Mosaic law, assumes that somehow 'the Lord . . . will repay' an unfaithful wife" ("His Folly, Her Weakness: Demystified Adultery in *The Scarlet Letter*," in *New Essays on "The Scarlet Letter*," ed. Michael J. Colacurcio [Cambridge, UK: Cambridge University Press, 1985], 37).

2. In references to *The Scarlet Letter* that appear in parentheses, the chapter number is followed by the page numbers in the following edition: Nathaniel Hawthorne, *The Scarlet Letter* (New York: Penguin, 1983).

3. See Sacvan Bercovitch, *The Office of the Scarlet Letter* (Baltimore, MD: Johns Hopkins University Press, 1991), 153. See also Darrel Abel on Hester's "romantic individualism," according to which she denies both God's law and society's claims ("Hester the Heretic," *College English* 13, no. 6 [1952]: 303–9).

4. Donna Orwin (*Tolstoy's Art and Thought, 1847–1880* [Princeton, NJ: Princeton University Press, 1993], 180–82) refers to Anna as a "radical individualist," on the grounds that she places individual happiness above family and moral law.

5. Boris Eikhenbaum, *Lev Tolstoi: Semidesiatye gody* (Leningrad: Khudozhestvennaia literatura, 1974), 119–26.

6. For excellent insight into Tolstoy's response to *Madame Bovary* and the novel of adultery in *Anna Karenina*, see Priscilla Meyer, *How the Russians Read the French: Lermontov, Dostoevsky, Tolstoy* (Madison: University of Wisconsin

Press, 2008), 152–209; Michel Cadot, "La Mort comme évènement social et comme destin personel: Remarques sur *Madame Bovary* et *Anna Karénine*," *Cahiers Léon Tolstoi* 3 (1986). Tolstoy himself failed to mention Flaubert as an influence in the list he drew up later in life and only acknowledged him begrudgingly, claiming to have forgotten him or writing to his wife of *Madame Bovary* that "one can see why the French value it so highly."

7. On October 6, 1856, Tolstoy ended a short letter to Ivan Panaev (#27, 60:92) about the publication of his own *Youth* as follows: "Please forgive me for writing only a couple of words, but the horses are saddled, the weather is glorious, and I'm going out riding in the countryside for the first time after being ill. I really didn't like *The Scarlet Letter*, which you praised, whereas I really liked [what you wrote] about country and city in the August issue." Vladimir Astrov reports that several works by Hawthorne appeared in *The Contemporary* before *The Scarlet Letter*; he also notes that other journals followed with more works by Hawthorne and that several appreciative articles about Hawthorne appeared in Russian journals. See "Hawthorne and Dostoevski as Explorers of the Human Conscience," *New England Quarterly* 15, no. 2 (June 1942): 296–319.

8. Osip Mandelshtam refers to Emma Bovary as "the dark-haired French lover, the little sister of our proud Anna" ("Egipetskaia marka," *Sobranie sochinenii v trekh tomakh*, ed. G. P. Struve and B. A. Filippov, 2nd ed. [New York: Inter-Language Literary Associates, 1971], 2:34). Richard Brodhead numbers *Anna Karenina* among the "far-flung cousins" of *The Scarlet Letter*, along with *Adam Bede*, in *Hawthorne, Melville, and the Novel* (Chicago: University of Chicago Press, 1973), 50.

The influence of *The Scarlet Letter* on *Adam Bede* has been established in George Eliot criticism: scholars have noted that George Eliot took the germ of the plot, even if she omitted adultery per se by having Hetty be a fallen maiden rather than an adulteress like Hester. Scholars have remarked on the facts that the names of the heroines are close (Hetty being a diminutive of Hester), that the fathers of the illegitimate babies born to Hester and Hetty are both named Arthur and have last names beginning in D (Dimmesdale and Donnithorne). In turn, *Adam Bede* is one of the novels recognized as an inspiration and model for *Anna Karenina*. W. Gareth Jones discusses a series of compelling parallels in "George Eliot's *Adam Bede* and Tolstoy's Conception of *Anna Karenina*," in *Tolstoi and Britain*, ed. Jones (Oxford, UK: Berg, 1995).

Thus, *The Scarlet Letter* figured in Tolstoy's literary imagination both directly and via *Adam Bede*. In what follows, my interest is in parallels between *Anna Karenina* and *The Scarlet Letter* as novels of adultery; my particular focus is on the inner rationale of the double plot. At the same time, I acknowledge that George Eliot in her own way opened up the seminal love plot to write a more "inclusive" novel and that her variation on *The Scarlet Letter* is relevant to the questions addressed here.

9. Barbara Hardy discusses the strategy of reading novels "alongside of" each other in *The Novels of George Eliot: A Study in Form* (London: University of London, Athlone Press, 1973). See Carol Bensick on thematic parallels and common plot elements between *The Scarlet Letter* and *Anna Karenina* ("His

Folly"). Bensick does not address the role of the Levin plot in Tolstoy's novel of adultery.

10. Q. D. Leavis, "Hawthorne as Poet," in *Collected Essays*, vol. 2: *The American Novel and Reflections on the European Novel* (Cambridge, UK: Cambridge University Press, 1985), 34.

11. Leavis, "Hawthorne as Poet," 54–55.

12. Peter Garrett, *The Victorian Multiplot Novel: Studies in Dialogical Form* (New Haven, CT: Yale University Press, 1980), 9.

13. The critical importance of this pericope to the European novel of adultery (and to Western art and culture) was established in Tony Tanner's seminal work *Adultery in the Novel: Contract and Transgression* (Baltimore, MD: Johns Hopkins University Press, 1979). David Parker begins his study entitled *Ethics, Theory and the Novel* (Cambridge, UK: Cambridge University Press, 1994) with an examination of this pericope and returns to it at various points in his discussion of *Anna Karenina, Middlemarch,* and other novels. For further discussion of this gospel passage in relation to *Anna Karenina,* see also Dragan Kujundžić, "Pardoning Woman in *Anna Karenina,*" *Tolstoy Studies Journal* 6 (1993): 65–85; Amy Mandelker, *Framing "Anna Karenina": Tolstoy, The Woman Question, and the Victorian Novel* (Columbus: Ohio State University Press, 1993); Mandelker, "Illustrate and Condemn: The Phenomenology of Vision in *Anna Karenina,*" *Tolstoy Studies Journal* 8 (1995–96): 46–60; Gina Kovarsky, "Mimesis and Moral Education in *Anna Karenina,*" *Tolstoy Studies Journal* 8 (1995–96): 61–80; Kovarsky, "Rhetoric, Metapoesis, and Moral Instruction in Tolstoy's Fiction: *Childhood, Boyhood, Youth, War and Peace,* and *Anna Karenina,*" Ph.D. dissertation, Columbia University, 1998; Gina Kovarsky, "The Moral Education of the Reader," in *Approaches,* ed. Knapp and Mandelker, 166–72; Kate Holland, "The Opening of *Anna Karenina,*" in *Approaches,* ed. Knapp and Mandelker, 144–49. For discussion of the relevance of this passage to *The Scarlet Letter,* see Larry Kreitzer's extended commentary in "'Revealing the Affairs of the Heart': Sin, Accusation and Confession in Nathaniel Hawthorne's *The Scarlet Letter,*" in *Ciphers in the Sand: Interpretations of the Woman Taken in Adultery (John 7.53–8.11),* ed. Larry Joseph Kreitzer and Deborah W. Rooke, 138–212 (Sheffield, UK: Sheffield Academic Press, 2000).

14. The phrase "convicted by their own conscience" appears in the King James version, as does a Russian equivalent in the Synodal translation of the Gospel of John. Many translations leave out this phrase, which is thought to have been an interpolation. Tolstoy includes it in his version of the gospels without question. See Tolstoi, *Chetveroevangelie: Soedinenie i perevod chetyrekh Evangelii* (Moscow: ESKMO Press, 2001), 470.

15. In his later gospel commentary, Tolstoy complained about the astounding popularity of this story in art and the popular consciousness, suggesting that people misread it, wanting to focus on the "sensuality" in Christ's interaction with the adulteress and seeing only the message about sexual indiscretions; Tolstoy suggests that what matters in this story is the message about criminal justice: What right do sinful human beings have to punish and execute others? (Tolstoi, *Chetveroevangelie,* 471.)

16. Parker, *Ethics.* Parker argues that the gospel story plays on an introspective process of recognizing similarities with the "other," without "transvaluing"

the differences: "Jesus is implicitly objecting, once again, to an ethic of difference that obliterates any sense of common humanity. It is the element of commonness, the fact that they are sinners too, that the Pharisees, in the grip of their rigid binary code, appear to have forgotten. Jesus' reply forces them to look within." Parker notes that Jesus prompts the Pharisees to "recollect" "those traditions within Judaism itself saying that God alone should judge" (43–52).

17. Tony Tanner (*Adultery*) explains how this gospel story operates and how its dynamics are played out, with variations, in novels of adultery. *Anna Karenina* is not one of the novels he studies at length in his book, but he observes that the tension between compassion and judgment (central to his analysis of the novel of adultery) is at play in—and vital to—Tolstoy's novel (14). Much as the gospel passage itself focuses on revising tradition (John 8:1–11 depicts Jesus responding to previous, authoritative treatments of adulteresses, specifically the Law of Moses), so, too, does each novel of adultery respond to forerunners. The challenge is passed down as each novelist tries his hand at the genre and responds to the implicit challenge of "What sayest *thou*?"

18. Tanner (*Adultery*, 21–22) notes that Jesus "dissolves the group identity" of the scribes and Pharisees and "thrusts" them and the adulteress "back into their own interiority": they are "convicted by their own conscience."

19. References to casting stones and other features of John 8:1–11 in *Anna Karenina* are discussed by the scholars listed in note 13 above.

20. Bercovitch (*Office*, 47) writes that the Puritan community engages in "an act of interpretation" as it applies the law to Hester: "The A embodies the viewpoint of the New England leaders, who have decided not to apply the letter of the law—death for adultery—but instead to define it through the ambiguities of mercy and justice."

21. Abel, "Hester the Heretic," 305.

22. The translation that Tolstoy read in 1856 in *The Contemporary* did not include "The Custom House."

23. Hawthorne writes in "The Custom-House": "I know not whether these ancestors of mine bethought themselves to repent and ask pardon of Heaven for their cruelties; or whether they are now groaning under the heavy consequences of them, in another state of being. At all events, I, the present writer, as their representative, hereby take shame upon myself for their sakes, and pray that any curse incurred by them—as I have heard, and as the dreary and unprosperous condition of the race, for many a long year back, would argue to exist—may be now and henceforth removed" (12–13).

24. Abel ("Heretic," 302). Marshall Van Deusen writes of the "notorious doubleness of judgement which pervades the story of Hester's persecution"; he notes that this "tension" "characterizes" both the narrator and "the societies of which he speaks" ("Narrative Tone in 'The Custom House' and *The Scarlet Letter*," *Nineteenth-Century Fiction* 21 [June 1966]: 67).

25. For a concise discussion of the meanings of the epigraph, see Holland, "Opening." More detailed discussion is found in the work of Morson and Alexandrov, as well as of many of the scholars who have worked on John 8:1–11 in relation to *Anna Karenina*.

26. Tolstoi, *Chetveroevangelie*, 471.

27. Tolstoy is reported to have said: "I chose that epigraph simply, as I have already explained, to express the idea that the evil which a man does has as its consequence all the bitterness that comes not from men but from God and that Anna Karenina experienced in herself. Yes, I remember that it was just that that I wanted to express . . . I meant simply that a punishment for crime follows from above" (M. S. Sukhotin, reminiscences cited in C. J. G. Turner, *A Karenina Companion* [Waterloo, Ontario: Wilfrid Laurier University Press, 1993], 51–52).

28. This trip to the opera is critical to the plot of *Madame Bovary* since it brings Emma, who had been jilted by Rodolphe, back into contact with Léon, who soon thereafter becomes her second lover; Flaubert also shows that Emma's reaction to the opera fires her adulterous yearnings, as did her earlier exposure to literature. Emma is transported by the experience so that "the voice of the heroine seemed to be simply the echo of her own consciousness." And she, manifesting the syndrome that would eventually bear her name, *le bovarysme*, yearns for the same level of tragedy in her own life.

Anna herself had tendencies toward *le bovarysme*. "She so wanted to live herself" that she could not simply read and "follow the reflection of other people's lives"; instead she would transport herself into the fictional world of her English novel and fancied herself an operatic tragedy queen. On this aspect, see Gary Saul Morson, *"Anna Karenina" in Our Time: Seeing More Wisely* (New Haven, CT: Yale University Press, 2007); Morson, "Anna Karenina's Omens," in *Freedom and Responsibility in Russian Literature: Essays in Honor of Robert Louis Jackson*, ed. Elizabeth Cheresh Allen and Gary Saul Morson (Evanston, IL: Northwestern University Press, 1995), 134–52; Julie Buckler, *The Literary Lorgnette: Attending Opera in Imperial Russia* (Stanford, CA: Stanford University Press, 2000); Buckler, "Reading Anna: Opera, Tragedy, Melodrama, Farce," in *Approaches*, ed. Knapp and Mandelker, 131–36.

29. Thus, for example, when Betsy Tverskaya makes an initial show of visiting Anna, she claims to do so knowing that her circle will "cast stones" at her (5:28, 528); as Anna points out, Betsy herself is "the most depraved woman in the world" (6:23, 636). Her Christian charity, like that of Countess Lydia Ivanovna, is a sham.

30. Richard Brodhead uses the term "cross-linking" (*Hawthorne*, 53) to describe Hawthorne's technique of intertwining the characters' psychic worlds and the "real" world of the novel. As in Tolstoy's "labyrinth of linkages," the reading techniques associated with realist novels are rendered inadequate: as we are forced away from reading for the sequential narrative, Tolstoy engages us in his own *procédé poetique*, analogous to that in Hawthorne.

31. See Morson, "Anna's Omens."

32. Although the *pozornyi stolb*, a form of pillory, was used in Russia at the time, this punishment was associated with England and America, where, according to the Brockhaus Efron encyclopedia, it was "extremely widespread." The Brockhaus Efron encyclopedia article on *pozornye nakazaniia* (punishment by shame) also reports that other modes of punishment by shame used in England and America included "bright-colored letters sewn onto clothing" (a detail that Hawthorne's novel may have fixed in the reading public's imagination). The same article notes that up until 1890 convicts in Russia were subject

to "the office of public punishment," which consisted of being brought by cart to a public place, forced to wear a sign designating the crime, and set forth for ten minutes at the pillory, before being sent off to penal servitude. The author of the article observes that that in Russian folk life, punishment by shame played an important role; it cites examples of the form such punishment might take, but there is no mention of the *pozornyi stolb* in the description of Russian folk practice. In *The Idiot*, Dostoevsky uses the notion of standing at the pillory in reference to Ganya's behavior at Nastasya Filippovna's birthday party after she humiliates him by throwing the money into the fire: "Ganechka still had not come to his senses, but felt vaguely yet irresistibly the feverish need to stand at the pillory to the end" (trans. Pevear and Volokhonsky, 1:15, 156).

33. In his dictionary, Vladimir Dal' defines позорный столб as follows: "[a column] to which criminals are set forth for humiliation before the people" (*Tolkovyi slovar' zhivogo velikorusskogo iazyka* [St. Petersburg: M. O. Vol'f, 1912], 3:600). In the translation of *The Scarlet Letter* in *The Contemporary* (*Sovremennik*, Prilozhenie, 1856, no. 9–10), which Tolstoy read (at least enough of to tell Panaev he did not like it), the English word pillory is translated as позорный столб. Instead of providing a direct translation of the title of Chapter 3, "The Recognition," which refers to Hester's and Chillingsworth's mutual recognition of each other when the latter, thought to be lost at sea, suddenly appears to behold his wife on the pillory, the translator rechristened the chapter "Позорный столб" ["The Pillory"], thus making the idea of the pillory more prominent than it was in Hawthorne's original. I am grateful to Robert Davis of Columbia Libraries and Boris Michev of Cornell Libraries for providing me with access to the translation in *Sovremennik*.

34. Later, Hawthorne uses similar terms to describe Arthur Dimmesdale's state of mind as he approaches his final sermon, which is immediately followed by his confession and death: "There was his body, moving onward, and with an unaccustomed force. But where was his mind? Far and deep in its own region, busying itself with preternatural activity, to marshal a procession of stately thoughts that were soon to issue thence" (22, 161).

35. A common source for both Hawthorne and Tolstoy would have been Victor Hugo's *Last Day of a Condemned Man* (1829), which describes his "preternaturally active" man as he rides to the scaffold. For discussion on this subject, see my "*Tue-la! Tue-le!*: Death Sentences, Words, and Inner Monologue in Tolstoy's *Anna Karenina* and *Three More Deaths*," *Tolstoy Studies Journal* 11 (1999): 1–19.

36. As Brodhead observes, Hawthorne constructs the scene so that we are presented with a spectrum "of vantage points by which to frame our initial response to Hester" (*Hawthorne*, 44).

37. As one of the townsmen explains to Chillingsworth, "the penalty thereof is death," but the magistrates "in their great mercy and tenderness of heart" "have doomed Mistress Prynne to stand only a space of three hours on the platform of the pillory, and then and thereafter, for the remainder of her natural life, to wear a mark of shame upon her bosom." The magistrates apply "mercy and tenderness" in order to bring about repentance (and, presumably, salvation) in Hester (3, 58).

38. Tolstoy explained in his later commentary on the gospel passage that the real moral was about vengeance being God's right: the scribes and the Pharisees—unlike Tolstoy's contemporaries—"understood that only he who was without sin could perform an execution and since there were no such people and could not be, then there was nobody to carry it out" (*Chetveroevangelie*, 471).

39. Tolstoy, according to his wife's report, admiring the handiwork on a bathrobe, started to contemplate "a whole world of women's work, fashions, concerns that women live by." Tolstoy then became aware of how his fictional Anna must have suffered from her isolation from all of this. "Anna is deprived of the joys of being occupied with this feminine aspect of life, because she is alone, all the women have rejected her and she has no one with whom to talk about everything that makes up the ordinary, purely feminine round of occupations" (Sophia Tolstoy, diary entry, November 20, 1876, in Turner, *Companion*, 48).

40. As Leavis ("Hawthorne as Poet," 54) makes clear, Tolstoy's concern is hypocrisy: "The chief difference is that the scarlet-lettered young woman has been brought into the centre of the stage and her history used as a measure of the inhumanity of the society she is fixed in. Just as Tolstoy's novel is framed to evoke the response: This is the society that condemned Anna! So Hawthorne makes Hester the critic of the society that similarly rejects and victimizes her."

41. See Liza Knapp, "Style and Theme in Tolstoy's Early Work," in *Cambridge Companion to Tolstoy*, ed. Donna Tussing Orwin (Cambridge, UK: Cambridge University Press, 2002), 161–75, for discussion of the genesis of *ostranenie* [estrangement] in Tolstoy. For the young Tolstoy, the device was a perfect vehicle for his Rousseauean views of civilization.

42. Michael Davitt Bell, "Arts of Deception: Hawthorne, 'Romance,' and *The Scarlet Letter*," in *New Essays on "The Scarlet Letter*," ed. Michael J. Colacurcio (Cambridge, UK: Cambridge University Press, 1985), 47.

43. See Kreitzer, "Revealing the Affairs," 163–72, on Dimmesdale, Hester's "hidden partner," as an analogue to the partner missing from the gospel story.

44. Tony Tanner's reading of the gospel story reveals this (*Adultery in the Novel*).

45. Henry James, *Hawthorne* (New York: Harper & Brothers, 1899), 109.

46. Nina Baym, "The Significance of Plot in Hawthorne's Romances," in *Ruined Eden of the Present: Hawthorne, Melville, Poe*, ed. G. R. Thompson and V. L. Locke (West Lafayette, IN: Purdue University Press, 1980), 51. Given the (past) intimate connection between the female and male protagonists and their link through their child, it might seem fair to suggest that they "share" rather than "divide" the focus; however, Baym's choice of "divide" reflects the fact that Dimmesdale's plot pulls away from Hester's.

47. Although the ostensible main grounds for mystification have to do with the existence and nature of the stigma that Dimmesdale reveals on his chest (is it a supernatural phenomenon, the result of Chillingsworth's weird medicine, a sign from God, or what?), "some" people question what it was that Dimmesdale actually said from the scaffold. The lack of clarity, as with the other multiple choices that Hawthorne is known for in this book, puts the burden

of interpretation on the reader. Tolstoy has his own version of the multiple choice. Thus, in regard to what happens in a critical scene in *Anna Karenina*, the only meeting between Anna and Levin, Tolstoy also seems to give us two versions and leaves it to us to choose: a) the version reported by the narrator, which is presented from Levin's (intoxicated) point of view as we experience the event, and b) the version that Kitty gives after Levin tells her about it. Which is true? Obviously, the reader does not have to choose one to the exclusion of the other. Both of the above or neither may also be allowable answers.

48. Tolstoy's letter to Rachinsky will be discussed in chapter 3.

49. At the end of his life, Tolstoy revealed to his biographer Pavel Biryukov the shame he felt for having fathered a child by Aksinya Bazykina, a married peasant. Tolstoy's confession to Biryukov suggests that he felt a Dimmesdale-like need to finally reveal to the public who revered him "his own red stigmata." (Tolstoy's wife had learned about this from her pre-marital reading of Tolstoy's diary.) Tolstoy chooses to keep non-specific the sexual transgressions that, at certain points in the novel, convict Levin in his conscience to the point of interfering with his tendency to condemn adulteresses and fallen women.

Tolstoy's concern with the hidden sexual guilt of men is further revealed in his work such as *Resurrection*, "The Devil," and "Father Sergius." The heroes of these works are Dimmesdale's Russian cousins. Tolstoy's plots also follow the morphology of *The Scarlet Letter*, with its divided plot that moves from overt judgment of the adulteress or fallen women to the tragic revelation of the hero's own "red stigma."

50. Parker, *Ethics*, 110–12. He writes: "Levin, recollecting 'his own sins and the inner conflict he had lived through' (like the Pharisees in John 8), makes a connection between his experience and Oblonsky's that breaks down the simple judgmental binary pattern of his thinking, whose symbolic emphases have been shaped precisely by those actively forgotten feelings and experiences. And in that, Levin's expanded awareness points to the imaginative fullness of the scene itself: while so carefully defining the two men against each other, it never loses touch with what is common in their experience. For all that may be said about the Levin in Tolstoy, one of the most important strengths of the novel is the almost unfailing resistance it offers to any judgmental tendency in us to read its world as Levin first reads his experience, in terms of simple categorical oppositions. At the same time Levin's momentarily baffled 'But I don't know, I really don't know' goes close to the imaginative heart of *Anna Karenina*, since our own ethical imaginations are constantly being unbalanced and rebalanced by the very twists and turns of the lives in which they are so absorbed" (111). For further analysis of this scene, see Gustafson, *Leo Tolstoy, Resident and Stranger: A Study in Fiction and Theology* (Princeton, NJ: Princeton University Press, 1986); Orwin, *Tolstoy's Art*, 171–78; and Kovarsky, "Mimesis and Moral Education." Mandelker points out the "reversal of Lyovin's initial blanket rejection of all fallen women as 'vermin' which dissolves into compassion as he views Anna's portrait" ("Illustrate and Condemn," 53).

51. Virginia Woolf, "Reading Notes on *Anna Karenina*," in *Virginia Woolf and the Russian Point of View*, ed. Roberta Rubenstein, Appendix E (New York: Palgrave-Macmillan, 2009), 200–201.

52. Hawthorne's fiction thrives on inviting its readers to consider what Franco Moretti calls the polysemy of its hieroglyphics (*Modern Epic: The World-System from Goethe to García Márquez*, trans. Quintin Hoare [London: Verso, 1996], 84–87). But, as John Irwin observes, Hawthorne also reminds his readers of the corollary, a sense of "the shattering of all absolutes because of the loss of objective knowledge" (*American Hieroglyphics: The Symbol of the Egyptian Hieroglyphics in the American Renaissance* [New Haven, CT: Yale University Press, 1980], 241). Hawthorne creates a narrative universe, said to be ruled by "multiple choice" (F. O. Matthiessen, *American Renaissance: Art and Expression in the Age of Emerson and Whitman* [New York: Oxford University Press, 1941], 276), in which Hawthorne seems to encourage "freedom of interpretation." And yet, as Bercovitch (*Office*) argues, this does not mean that all answers are correct (even if there is not just one right answer).

53. Michael Colacurcio, "Footsteps of Ann Hutchinson: Context of *The Scarlet Letter*," *English Literary History* 39 (1972): 459–94.

54. Hawthorne writes: "And, as he drew toward the close, a spirit as of prophecy had come upon him, constraining him to its purpose as mightily as the old prophets of Israel were constrained; only with this difference, that, whereas the Jewish seers had denounced judgments and ruin on their country, it was his mission to foretell a high and glorious destiny for the newly gathered people of the Lord" (23, 215).

55. On the shift from hieroglyphics to Logos, see Gilles DeLeuze, *Proust and Signs*, trans. Richard Howard (New York: G. Braziller, 1972).

56. Thus, for example, in *The Wild Palms* Faulkner gives us a novella of adultery interleaved, chapter by chapter, with another tale: since the plots neither intersect nor even inhabit the same time/space, all the reader can do is look for counterpoint.

Chapter 3. Loving Your Neighbor in *Middlemarch* and *Anna Karenina*

A talk based on this chapter was given in November 2011 at the Convention of the Association for Slavic, East European, and Eurasian Studies in Washington, DC.

1. In his early review of *Anna Karenina*, Matthew Arnold began the tradition of comparing the two novels. See Matthew Arnold, "Count Leo Tolstoi" (1887), in *Leo Tolstoy: A Critical Anthology*, ed. Henry Gifford (Harmondsworth, UK: Penguin, 1971), 60, 69–70. Osip Mandelshtam writes about Anna as Emma Bovary's younger "sister" in "Egipetskaia marka," in *Sobranie sochinenii v trekh tomakh*, ed. G. P. Struve and B. A. Filippov (New York: Inter-Language Literary Associates, 1971), 2:34. Eugène Melchior de Vogüé suggests that the French reader is likely to feel less *"dépaysé"* in *Anna Karenina* than in *War and Peace* because both adultery and suicide are familiar novelistic territory for French readers. De Vogüé also notes that Tolstoy includes the "moralistic and annoying" family thematics associated with "British authors," but that whereas the British authors tend to apply "preconceived rules" in keeping with "the views of the established Church or puritan morals," Tolstoy approaches the material with greater liberty (*Le Roman russe* [Paris: Plon, 1897], 317; 345).

2. Eikhenbaum, *Lev Tolstoi: Semidesiatye gody* (Leningrad: Khudozhestven-naia literatura, 1974), 127–28.

3. Like Flaubert, Eliot sought to depict provincial life and signals by subtitle—Flaubert's is *Moeurs de province*, while Eliot's is *A Study of Provincial Life*. The form appropriate to Flaubert's vision was a single-plot novel of adultery, whereas Eliot's inclusive vision led her to weave together multiple plots. Each novelist has chosen the form that scholars of the novel regard as typical of his or her national tradition. See Barbara Smalley, *George Eliot and Flaubert: Pioneers of the Modern Novel* (Athens: Ohio University Press, 1974).

De Vogüé (*Le Roman russe*, xxxviii) suggests that the English novelists share with the Russians a tolerance for the complexity and contradiction of life, along with a related capacity for seeing many things at once, whereas the French novelists stick to a single plot and single idea. Also typical of the French novel, according to popular thinking, was *Madame Bovary*'s focus on adultery, much as the avoidance of adultery in *Middlemarch* is often considered to be typical of the English novel. For example, Strakhov summed up the popular Russian view, to which Tolstoy to a degree subscribed, when he wrote in his 1870 review of John Stuart Mill that English novels are "the fit reading material for proper women and young girls because England is the classic land of pure family values, just as France is the classic land for amorous adventures" (cited in Eikhenbaum, *Semidesiatye gody*, 115).

The English novel is known in some schools of criticism for *avoiding* adultery as such and exploring related alternatives such as bigamy (for example, in *Jane Eyre*). George Eliot provides the donnée of an adultery novel with the triangle of Casaubon, Dorothea, and Ladislaw; Dorothea resists temptation. But, as Sophia Kovalevskaya observed—to the novelist herself during one of their meetings in London, according to Kovalevskaya's memoir—George Eliot had a way of killing off characters in her novels "precisely at the point when the psychological plot becomes complicated to the degree of extreme tension, when the reader wants to know in what way life will disentangle the consequences of this or that action"; among the cases Kovalevskaya cited to prove her point was that of Casaubon, whose timely death in *Middlemarch* saves Dorothea from being too tempted by an adulterous passion for Ladislaw. (Perhaps Kovalevskaya had in mind what happens when Karenin stays alive in Tolstoy's *Anna Karenina*.) George Eliot's response was to acknowledge that there was some truth to Kovalevskaya's criticism but that in real life death happened in this way. See Raymond Chapman and Eleanora Gottlieb, "A Russian View of George Eliot," *Nineteenth-Century Fiction* 33, no. 3 (Dec. 1978): 348–65.

4. J. Hillis Miller writes that "George Eliot's apparent aim in *Middlemarch* is to present a total picture of provincial society in England in the period just before the first Reform Bill of 1832. She also wants to interpret this picture totally. She wants both to show what is there and to show how it works. The enterprise of totalization, as one might call it, is shared with an important group of other masterworks of Victorian fiction, including Thackeray's *Vanity Fair* (1847–48), Dickens' *Bleak House* (1852–53), *Little Dorrit* (1857–58), and *Our Mutual Friend* (1864–65), and Trollope's *The Way We Live Now* (1874–75). All three novels have many characters and employ multiple analogous plots. They cast a wide net

and aim at inclusiveness, in part by a method of accumulation." Miller goes on to explain that the novelists all devise "strategies of compression, of economy" ("Optic and Semiotic in *Middlemarch*," in *The Worlds of Victorian Fiction*, ed. Jerome H. Buckley [Cambridge, MA: Harvard University Press, 1975], 125).

5.   I refer to the claim Tolstoy made in "A Few Words about *War and Peace*," a discarded introduction to that work. Tolstoy wrote: "What is *War and Peace*? It is not a novel, still less an epic poem, still less a historical chronicle. *War and Peace* is what the author wanted and was able to express, in the form in which it is expressed. Such a declaration of the author's disregard of the conventional forms of artistic prose works might seem presumptuous, if it were premeditated and if it had no previous examples. The history of Russian literature since Pushkin's time not only provides many examples of such departure from European forms, but does not offer even one example to the contrary" (trans. Pevear and Volokhonsky, in *War and Peace*, 1217).

6.   In the list of works that "made an impression on" him that Tolstoy drew up in 1891, under the category of "from 35 to 50 years" (which includes the *Anna Karenina* years from 1873 to 1877), Tolstoy listed three English novelists: Ellen Wood, Anthony Trollope, and George Eliot (letter of 25 October 1891, 66:67–68). For discussion of George Eliot and Tolstoy, see Shoshana Knapp, "Tolstoj's Reading of George Eliot: Visions and Revisions," *Slavic and East European Journal* 27 (1983): 318–26; Edwina Blumberg, "Tolstoy and the English Novel: A Note on *Middlemarch* and *Anna Karenina*," in *Tolstoi and Britain*, ed. W. Gareth Jones (Oxford, UK: Berg, 1995), 93–104; W. Gareth Jones, "George Eliot's *Adam Bede* and Tolstoy's Conception of *Anna Karenina*," in *Tolstoi and Britain*, ed. W. Gareth Jones (Oxford, UK: Berg, 1995), 79–82; Janet Fleetwood, "The Web and the Beehive: George Eliot's *Middlemarch* and Tolstoy's *Anna Karenina*" (Ph.D. dissertation, Indiana University, 1977). *Middlemarch* also figures at various points in Morson, as an exemplar of the prosaic novel as, for example, it seeks to "redefine heroism" (*"Anna Karenina" in Our Time* [New Haven, CT: Yale University Press, 2007], 29).

7.   L. N. Tolstoi to A. A. Tolstaia, 12 June 1859, #141, 60:300–301.

8.   I believe that Tolstoy read *Middlemarch*, although, as far as I know, he did not leave any written comments about this particular George Eliot novel. First published in England in 1871–72, *Middlemarch* appeared in 1872 in Russian translation in *Otechestvennye zapiski*; holdings of the Yasnaya Polyana include a copy in English published in 1872, which shows signs of wear and traces of readers. (The compilers of the volume that lists these holdings suggest that a mark by one of the epigraphs was left by Tolstoy himself, whereas other markings were made by unknown readers.) See *Biblioteka L'va Nikolaevicha Tolstogo v Iasnoi Poliane: Bibliograficheskoe opisanie* (Tula: Muzei-usad'ba/Izdatel'skii Dom "Iasnaia Poliana," 1999), vol. 3, part 1, 329.

9.   This reference to a "home epic" in the "Finale" of *Middlemarch* harks back to the "Prelude," in which we are asked to consider whether "epic life," with "a constant unfolding of far-resonant action," is possible in present times. George Eliot, *Middlemarch*, ed. Rosemary Ashton (Middlesex, UK: Penguin, 1994). Chapter numbers and page numbers in parentheses after citations to *Middlemarch* refer to this edition.

10. According to his wife's diary (3 March 1877), Tolstoy declared, as he was in the late stages of writing *Anna Karenina*: "My idea is now so very clear to me. For a work to be good, one has to love in it the main, fundamental idea. And so, in *Anna Karenina*, I love the family idea [мысль семейная], in *War and Peace*, I loved the idea of the people, in the wake of the war of 1812" (in *Lev Tolstoi ob iskusstve i literature*, ed. K. N. Lomunov [Moscow: Sovetskii pisatel', 1958], 1:411).

11. In the drafts, Tolstoy envisioned at least two further meetings between Anna and Levin beyond the one narrated in Part 7: (a) Anna was to run into Kitty and Levin at a flower show on the day she ended up killing herself (the meeting is replaced in the final version with her visit with Dolly, during which she sees Kitty too); and (b) Levin was to behold the corpse of Anna after her death; this experience was to prompt Levin's own crisis about the meaning of life (in the final version, Levin's horror of death is said to date back to the death of his brother, but there is no apparent trigger for it to overwhelm him when it does). For discussion of these excised meetings, see below.

12. L. N. Tolstoi to S. A. Rachinskii, 27 January 1878, #384, 62:377. Rachinsky was the translator of Charles Darwin and of George Lewes, a contributor to the *Russian Herald*, and a former professor at Moscow University, who had resigned, along with Boris Chicherin and others, in protest of government intervention in academic affairs. He had settled on his estate and devoted much of his time to a school for local peasants. Rachinsky expressed deep gratitude to Tolstoy for Tolstoy's *Azbuka* and *Reader*, which Rachinsky declared to be just as inspired by "the grace of God" as his novels. In their letters back and forth, Tolstoy and Rachinsky would, for example, discuss curriculum and reveal strategies for teaching peasant children long division. Tolstoy clearly took Rachinsky seriously as a correspondent since he eventually revealed to him his concern with "saving [his] soul" and pressed him to explain where he stood on matters of faith. Rachinsky responded that he was finding more and more spiritual satisfaction within Orthodox parameters even if points remained in which his faith was still not fully Orthodox.

On Rachinsky, see Hugh McLean, *In Quest of Tolstoy* (Boston: Academic Studies Press, 2008), 160–62; and the commentary in *Pis'ma Tolstogo i k Tolstomu: Iubileinyi sbornik* (Moscow: Gosudarstvennoe izdatel'stvo, 1928).

13. Joan Grossman, "Tolstoy's Portrait of Anna: Keystone in the Arch," *Criticism: A Quarterly for Literature and the Arts* (Wayne State University Press) 18, no. 1 (Winter 1976): 1. My argument below builds on Grossman's insights into the structure (and meaning) of *Anna Karenina* and into the meeting between Anna and Levin in Part 7.

14. L. N. Tolstoi to N. N. Strakhov, 23 April 1876, #261, 62:269. For discussion, see here chapter 2.

15. Those who write in appreciation of this form often do so in reaction to Henry James's dismissal of loose and baggy monsters on the grounds that they lack artistic meaning or to Percy Lubbock's prescriptions for the "craft" of the novel. Whereas some apologists of the complex novel have affirmed that these novels have coherence *and* meaning after all, others have warned against going too far. Barbara Hardy argues that theory of the multiplot runs the risk of

overemphasizing the *unity* of these novels (*The Appropriate Form: An Essay on the Novel* [London: Athlone Press, 1973], 1–10). As will be seen below, Tolstoy's *Anna Karenina* is in profound respects more off kilter than *Middlemarch*.

16. Gillian Beer, *Darwin's Plots: Evolutionary Narrative in Darwin, George Eliot and Nineteenth-Century Fiction* (Cambridge, UK: Cambridge University Press, 2000), 151–52.

17. As will be argued below, multiplot novels do not always *promote* inclusivity as a value: Tolstoy uses the multiplot form to express wariness about neighborly relations (such as those celebrated in *Middlemarch*) and a retreat into family love.

18. J. Hillis Miller, "Optic and Semiotic," 125.

19. In *The Form of Victorian Fiction: Thackeray, Dickens, Trollope, George Eliot, Meredith, and Hardy* (Cleveland, OH: Case Western Reserve Press, 1968) J. Hillis Miller ties the particular "patterns of intersubjectivity" that dominate in Victorian novels to shifts in religious understanding about the human condition: as God seemed to become more remote, human beings turned to each other: "If Victorian fiction focuses on interhuman relations as the arena of a search for self-fulfillment, this search is governed not only by the apparent absence of God but also by the effacement of any ontological foundation for the self. This lack motivates the longing for other people" (45). The form of the Victorian novels (including many multiplots), as envisioned by Miller, thus emerges in response to—and possibly as a cure for—metaphysical loneliness. Francis O'Gorman notes that J. Hillis Miller is "distinctive in offering a theological explanation for the form" (*Victorian Novel: A Guide to Criticism* [Malden, MA: Blackwell, 2002], 217–18).

20. Beer, *Darwin's Plots*, 137–68. George Levine writes that although Darwin's theories were found to be consonant with the individualist trends of Adam Smith and others, and although Darwin did refer to the "war of nature," Darwin's theory could also be—and was—construed as being "antistruggle and anti-individualist." George Lewes and George Eliot were among those who found in Darwinian "organicism" "a biological justification of the moral predominance of altruism" (Levine, *Darwin and the Novelists: Patterns of Science in Victorian Fiction* [Cambridge, MA: Harvard University Press, 1988], 102).

As Daniel Todes has demonstrated, Peter Kropotkin and other Russian Darwinists saw in Darwin's discoveries the potential for mutual aid; Todes argues that Russian Darwinists tended not to dwell on the Malthusian features of Darwin's thought and not to stress the violent and vicious struggle for survival among humans (*Darwin without Malthus: The Struggle for Existence in Russian Evolutionary Thought* [Oxford, UK: Oxford University Press, 1989]). Hugh Mclean observes that Sergei Rachinsky emphasized "the mutual dependence of organisms" (the phenomenon of mutual aid, later developed by Kropotkin) in "Flowers and Insects," an essay that is, in McLean's estimation, "the best type of *haute vulgarisation*" of Darwin's *Origin of Species*, which Rachinsky was translating at the time. "Flowers and Insects" appeared in *Russkii Vestnik* in January 1863, in the same issue as Tolstoy's "Cossacks" (McLean, "Claws in the Behind," in *In Quest of Tolstoy*, 160–61). After studying Tolstoy's correspondence with Rachinsky, McLean found notable that Tolstoy did not take any interest in

Rachinsky's work and standing as a scientist (162). Rachinsky could have enlightened him about Darwin's work. Instead, Tolstoy assumed that Darwin's discoveries meant simply that nature is red in tooth and claw, and he passed this view along to both Konstantin Levin and Anna Karenina, as will be seen below. One Russian Darwinist, K. A. Timiriazev, complained in print shortly after the publication of the final part of *Anna Karenina* that it was clear that Levin had not read Darwin because "as applied to humans, the struggle for existence signifies not hatred and extermination but, on the contrary, love and protection" (Todes, *Darwin without Malthus* 162).

    21. Levine, *Darwin and the Novelists*, 13, 17–18.

    22. McLean, "Claws in the Behind," 159–80.

    23. Sally Shuttleworth, "Sexuality and Knowledge in *Middlemarch*," *Nineteenth-Century Contexts* 19 (1996): 431.

    24. Franco Moretti, *The Way of the World: The Bildungsroman in European Culture*, trans. Albert Sbragia (London: Verso, 1987), 64.

    25. George Eliot, *Scenes of Clerical Life* (London: Penguin, 1983), 19, 364. In "Janet's Repentance," human relations take all forms, from drunken Dempster's cruel abuse of his drunken wife Janet to the aid that Mrs. Pettifer extends to her: their kiss is described as one of those "earnest sacramental kisses—such kisses as seal a new and closer bond between the helper and the helped" (15, 347). Effusions of this kind are foreign to Tolstoy's world.

    26. As Sally Shuttleworth points out, "at every level, the interdependence of Middlemarch life seems to be based not on harmony, but on conflict." For starters, there is conflict and lack of understanding between classes; the rich have gotten rich by "suck[ing] the life" out of the poor whose labor they need, and so forth (*George Eliot and Nineteenth-Century Science* [London: Cambridge University Press, 1984], 150). While this is true, George Eliot is asking what happens when imperfect humans, such as Dorothea Brooke, Caleb Garth, and others, attempt to love their neighbors as they see fit. There are no illusions that they will make Middlemarch into the New Jerusalem.

    27. Empson, *Some Versions of Pastoral* (New York: New Directions, 1974), 27.

    28. The following works have been especially helpful to my understanding of the multiplot form: Barbara Hardy, *Appropriate Form*; Peter Garrett, *The Victorian Multiplot Novel: Studies in Dialogical Form* (New Haven, CT: Yale University Press, 1980); George Levine, *How to Read the Victorian Novel* (Malden, MA: Blackwell, 2008); J. Hillis Miller, *Reading for Our Time: "Adam Bede" and "Middlemarch" Revisited* (Edinburgh: Edinburgh University Press, 2012); Miller, *The Form of Victorian Fiction*; Miller, "Optic and Semiotic"; O'Gorman, *Victorian Novel*. My observations about how "reading for the multiplot" differs from reading for the (single) plot draw especially on Garrett (see next footnote) and Miller (*Reading for Our Time*, 45–46). Miller writes of *Middlemarch*: "The last page is the goal toward which the whole novel has been moving, inhabited as it has been throughout by 'the sense of an ending.' Usually, for Victorian novels, this is the expected 'happy ending.' The sense of an immanent ending articulates all the parts as the backbone of the narrative. At the same time the image of a progressive revelation of meaning is to be applied to the idea of the 'destinies'

of the characters. Their lives make 'sense' as the gradual revelation of a whole, the 'meaning of their lives.' The end of the novel is the final exposing of the fates of the characters as well as of the formal unity of the text." In *Reading for the Plot: Design and Intention in Narrative*, Peter Brooks discusses the workings of the reader's desire mostly in single-plot novels, although he does observe that subplots, when present, affect the process (Cambridge, MA: Harvard University Press, 1992), 104.

29. Garrett explains that, on the one hand, the reader looks for development in a character or linear progression in a given plotline, but, on the other hand, the presence of the other plots exerts a pull of a different kind and activates other strategies as the reader interprets "the devices of analogical and causal connection, metaphoric and metonymic links between the novel's double [or multiple] plots." According to Garrett, the different principles remain unreconciled; they are "irreducibly different structural principles." But both remain operative and ensure that the search for meaning in these texts is a mysterious and open process (*The Victorian Multiplot Novel*, 8–10). This allows for what Francis O'Gorman calls the multiplot novel's "capacity to mean different things at once" (*Victorian Novel*, 220).

30. Levine, *How to Read the Victorian Novel*, 136, 130.

31. The gender of pronoun to use for the narrator is a vexed question. Back when the identity of George Eliot was still a mystery, Charles Dickens declared it clear—from the narration (of *Scenes of Clerical Life*)—that the author was a woman. By the time she wrote *Middlemarch*, the literary world knew that George Eliot was the pen name of Maryann Evans. The temptation to use the feminine pronoun is strong because one feels in the narrative voice the strong influence of the woman behind the pen. Still, using the masculine gender in this case would signal a distinction between narrator and author. For the most part, I circumlocute to avoid pronouns with the narrator as referent.

32. Jerome Beaty, *"Middlemarch" from Notebook to Novel: A Study of George Eliot's Creative Method* (Urbana: University of Illinois Press, 1960).

33. According to Beaty, George Eliot worried about how readers would respond to the multiplication of plots and division of attention brought about when the novel moved out of "Miss Brooke" (*Notebook to Novel*, 54).

34. When Henry James complains that *Middlemarch* is "an indifferent whole," he reminds us that the "definite subject" cited in the preface was "the central figure," "an ardent young girl" with "the career of an obscure St. Theresa" ("*Middlemarch*," in *The Art of Criticism: Henry James on the Theory and the Practice of Fiction*, ed. William Veeder and Susan M. Griffin [Chicago: University of Chicago Press, 1986], 49). Although James called *Middlemarch* an "indifferent whole," he still recognized the principles of similarity that create tension between the Dorothea and Lydgate plots. Regarding "the balanced contrast between the two histories of Lydgate and Dorothea," he notes that George Eliot's "artistic intentions" "become clear only in the meditative after-taste of perusal" (52). He writes that "each is a tale of matrimonial infelicity, but the conditions of each are so different and the circumstances so broadly opposed that the mind passes from one to the other with that supreme sense of the vastness and variety of human life" (52).

35. For a detailed analysis of how George Eliot joined the two projects "Miss Brooke" and "Middlemarch," see Beaty, *Notebook to Novel*, 3–42; on the "bridge," see 27–28.

36. In the world of Middlemarch portrayed in the novel, neighborly feeling is not the norm. Neighbors are quick to gossip, to shun those who do not conform or appear to have misbehaved; when Brooke is running for Parliament and tries to tell people "I am a close neighbor of yours," they do not recognize him as such (51, 504). Dorothea's acts of neighborly love stand out as quixotic or heroic, depending on one's point of view.

37. Whereas "Miss Brooke" signals the unique status of the first of the eight books of *Middlemarch*, Eliot uses the names of the other books to encourage the reader to seek lateral connections between the plots. For example, the fifth book is entitled "The Dead Hand": it thus invites the reader to find "dead hands" operating in different plots, from Featherstone's attempt to manipulate his relatives through his will, to Casaubon's attempt to manipulate Dorothea into continuing his "Key to All Mythologies" and to prevent her by mortmain from marrying Will Ladislaw.

38. George Eliot's narrator may not in fact always practice what she preaches. With good reason, some readers and critics have felt that too much of the reader's attention still ends up focused on the resolution of the "love-problem" of Dorothea and Will Ladislaw and, in general, on Dorothea's concerns and point of view.

39. What George Eliot wrote in her 1856 essay ("The Natural History of German Life") became her narrator's creed in *Middlemarch*: "Art is the nearest thing to life; it is a mode of amplifying experience and extending our contact with our fellowmen beyond the bounds of our personal lot" (in *Selected Critical Writings* [Oxford, UK: Oxford University Press, 1992], 263–64).

40. Harry E. Shaw, *Narrating Reality: Austen, Scott, Eliot* (Ithaca, NY: Cornell University Press, 1999), 232.

41. Shaw, *Narrating Reality*, 232–33.

42. Like *Middlemarch*, which Henry James dismissed as an "indifferent whole" instead of "an organized, moulded, balanced composition, gratifying the reader with a sense of design and construction" (James, "*Middlemarch*," 48), *Anna Karenina* has also been criticized for formal imperfections. For example, Percy Lubbock, James's disciple, complained about the lack of tension between *Anna Karenina*'s plots (*The Craft of Fiction* [New York: Viking, 1957], 235–50).

43. As Morson observes, whereas *Middlemarch* is aptly named, Tolstoy appears to have purposely "misnamed" the novel (*"Anna Karenina" in Our Time*, 37).

44. John Bayley, *Tolstoy and the Novel* (Chicago: University of Chicago Press, 1988), 188. Kathryn Feuer, "Stiva," in *Russian Literature and American Critics*, ed. Kenneth N. Brostrom (Ann Arbor: University of Michigan Press, 1984). Feuer notes that Stiva "initiates" a number of important linkages in the novel (348).

45. Alison Case and Harry Shaw write that the plots "intersect, but never coalesce" (*Reading the Nineteenth-Century Novel: Austen to Eliot* [Malden, MA: Blackwell, 2008], 187). Beaty suggests that Eliot achieves a full fusion of "Miss Brooke" and "Middlemarch" midway in the novel. But he has in mind the way

the plots take turns (*Notebook to Novel*, 65). This is not to suggest that *all* of the characters interact: for example, George Eliot never brings Mary Garth and Dorothea into proximity with each other; nor do we witness them dwelling in each other's consciousnesses, even though Dorothea and Caleb Garth collaborate closely.

46. J. Hillis Miller notes that different Victorian multiplot novelists use different "means of condensation" as they "cast a wide net and aim at inclusiveness." He contrasts, for example, Dickens's strategy of having the part stand for the whole to Eliot's use of a "sample" of the larger whole (English society) (*Reading For Our Time*, 37-38).

47. Family ties figure in *Middlemarch*, too. Once Dorothea Brooke becomes Mrs. Casaubon, all of the major families in the novel are linked by blood and marriage. Brookes, Casaubons, Dunkirks, Ladislaws, Bulstrodes, Vincys, Lydgate, Featherstones, and Garths connect on a lateral genealogical plan. See "Middlemarch Genealogy," in *Approaches to Teaching Eliot's "Middlemarch,"* ed. Kathleen Blake (New York: Modern Language Association, 1990), Appendix 2, 172-73. George Eliot also makes use of familiar topoi of the English novel as disinherited and neglected heirs return to claim or refuse patrimony. But the concept of neighborhood and neighborliness is what motivates the connections in her novel.

48. Viktor Shklovsky, *Knight's Move*, trans. Richard Sheldon (Champaign, IL: Dalkey Archive Press, 2005), 77.

49. On siblings in *Anna Karenina*, see Anna Berman, *Siblings in Tolstoy and Dostoevsky: The Path of Universal Brotherhood* (Evanston, IL: Northwestern University Press, 2015). On how the Tolstoyan family thrives by excluding others, see Anne Hruska, "Infected Families: Belonging and Exclusion in the Works of Leo Tolstoy" (Ph.D. dissertation, University of California, Berkeley, 2001).

50. In her analysis of the structure of *Anna Karenina*, Elisabeth Stenbock-Fermor (*The Architecture of "Anna Karenina": A History of Its Writing, Structure, and Message* [Lisse: Peter de Ridder, 1975], 100) argues for the central importance of this scene and its status as main keystone.

51. The romantic past of Kitty and Vronsky creates a tension between the two plots. It figures in the consciousnesses of the four main characters (for example, on meeting Levin, Anna understands how Kitty could have loved both Vronsky and Levin, different as they seem) in ways that prod the reader to think about the plots in tandem, but on the surface level of multiplot logistics it has the effect of further polarizing the two main plots—Kitty and Levin actively try to avoid Anna and Vronsky, although they are not entirely successful; thus, for example, Levin is forced into contact with Vronsky as the provincial elections and later at the club in Moscow.

52. At this important juncture of the novel, Tolstoy incorporates motifs or situations that recur across plots and thus prompt the reader to think laterally (to remind us of Anna and Vronsky at this critical moment in the relations of Kitty and Levin). But these same motifs and situations also recur within a given plot and thus work longitudinally. For example, this second proposal harks back to the first one, but it also subliminally summons up, through the mention of "forks" (the silver fork Kitty uses for the mushroom and the pitchfork the

peasant woman used for the hay) and the feminine bodies peeking out from under cloth (Kitty's arm in her lacy sleeve and the peasant woman's "full breasts showing under her white smock"), Levin's alternative to marrying Kitty: marrying a peasant (3:11, 374).

53. In *Darwin's Plots*, Gillian Beer argues that George Eliot uses the web of references to myth and other forms of shared knowledge in *Middlemarch* as one facet of a multifaceted process of "creat[ing] a sense of inclusiveness and extension" in this novel. "Science and mythology create within the work ways beyond the single into a shared, anonymous, and therefore more deeply creative knowledge. Myth, in particular, offers the continuity of collective insight against the anomie of the solitary perceiver." Beer is especially interested in how George Eliot uses "myth as a means of enriching the concept of 'relations'" (*Darwin's Plots*, 161).

Tolstoy uses myth to the same general effect—that is, to bring connections to the surface, to relate the material of his novel to a larger body of knowledge and, in the process, to connect its elements to each other through myth. Whereas Eliot's narrator is prone to more overt mythological references, especially for Dorothea, in *Anna Karenina direct* references to myth or fairy tale do not come from the narrator, but rather from a character (for example, Karenin refers to Helen of Troy and Levin refers to the "Three Bears"). The *indirect* allusions to myth, legend, and literature tend to be activated when a "real" object or situation within one of the plots has mythic or folkloric associations. For instance, when Levin happens to ask Oblonsky about Kitty just at the moment when Venus rises above a birch branch "and the stars of the Great Bear showed clearly," Tolstoy leaves it up to reader to choose: either to dismiss this as the reality effect, or to read into the symbolism, relating it to the other references to bears in the novel (at this point, the reader already knows that Levin used to refer to the Shcherbatsky sisters as the Three Bears of the fairy tale; the bear hunts will come later), as well as to the rich mythic, folkloric, and literary associations with bears, from Tatiana's dream of the bear in *Eugene Onegin* (with its Russian folkloric associations with sex) to Greek mythological explanations of how the Great Bear constellation landed in the sky: the virgin-goddess Artemis, outraged when her companion Callisto bore a child by Zeus, turned her into a bear, which Zeus then made into a constellation (to protect her from the wrath of Hera or Artemis or her son, according to different variants). Bears were associated with mating and marriage; at the festivals at Brauron in the honor of Artemis, soon-to-be-eligible maidens "acted the bear" in her honor in symbolic atonement for the slaying of a bear, her sacred animal, and as part of the ritual preparation for their role as brides. For discussion of the bear motif in *Anna Karenina*, see M. S. Al'tman, "Medvezh'ia svad'ba," in *Chitaia Tolstogo* (Tula: Priokskoe knizhnoe izdatel'stvo, 1966), 141–43; B. Lennkvist, "'Medvezhii' motiv i simvolika neba v romane *Anna Karenina*," *Scando-Slavica* 41 (1995).

54. George Eliot writes of Dorothea's response to the Featherstone funeral: "Scenes which make vital changes in our neighbours' lot are but the background of our own, yet, like a particular aspect of the fields and trees, they become associated for us with the epochs of our own history, and make a part of that unity which lies in the selection of our keenest consciousness" (34, 326).

55. Although Tolstoy's narrator does not prompt the reader explicitly to make connections across plots, Tolstoy's narrator does, at various points, *tell* the reader what to think about a given situation.

56. Tolstoy drafted an early version of this scene in which Karenin and Dolly came closer to Eliot-style cries "soul to soul" for help. The scene was to end with Karenin spending two hours with Dolly's children, who had become fond of him (20:331–35). But Tolstoy ended up with a bleaker version of this scene, one that reinforces the sense that human beings are isolated from each other.

57. When Karenin returns shortly thereafter to (what he thinks will be) Anna's deathbed, he follows Dolly's advice to forgive as he is carried away by Christian love and forgiveness for his wife, her love child, and even her lover. But these feelings (which many readers mistrust because they seem insincere or too good to be true) last only until the "coarse force" associated with society takes over his soul again.

58. Henry James, *"Middlemarch,"* 51.

59. Beaty, *Notebook to Novel,* 9–10.

60. For further discussion on this point, see chapter 5 on Tolstoy and Pascal.

61. This is not to say that fictional Middlemarch is a hotbed of neighborly love. Dorothea's declaration that she believes that "people are almost always better than their neighbours think they are" makes it clear that her Middlemarch neighbors judge each other pretty harshly. But neighborly love is the ideal to strive for. The narrator of *Middlemarch* attempts to plant the seeds of Dorothea-like faith in humankind in readers of *Middlemarch.*

62. Virginia Woolf, *A Room of One's Own* (New York: Harcourt, 1989), 84.

63. See David Trotter, "Space, Movement, and Sexual Feeling in *Middlemarch,*" in *Middlemarch in the 21st Century,* ed. Karen Chase (Oxford, UK: Oxford University Press, 2006), for further commentary on the critical debate about whether "domestic realism is . . . up to the task of representing sexuality" (45). Readers and critics alike have expressed disappointment that a love plot fails to develop between Dorothea and Lydgate, who stand out as the two "heroes" of the novel, similar perhaps in their desire to help humankind, which they have trouble acting on in Middlemarch. Henry James (*"Middlemarch"*), perhaps out of disappointment in Ladislaw (whom many regard as an unfit mate for Dorothea), wished that George Eliot had developed more between Lydgate and Dorothea, presumably of a romantic nature since in the next breath he notes that the disadvantage of this scenario would have been that the novel would then have been without Rosamond Vincy. James writes: "Lydgate is so richly successful a figure that we have regretted strongly at moments, for immediate interests' sake, that the current of his fortunes should not mingle more freely with the occasionally thin-flowing stream of Dorothea's. Toward the close, these two fine characters are brought into momentary contact so effectively, as to suggest a wealth of dramatic possibility between them; but if this train had been followed we should have lost Rosamond Vincy—a rare psychological study" (51). The "mingling" of fortunes James envisions seems to be romantic in nature, although he does praise Eliot for "treat[ing]" Lydgate "so little from what we may roughly (and we trust without offence) call the sexual

point of view" (51). James implies that had George Eliot further developed Lydgate "from the sexual point of view," Lydgate would have developed and acted on sexual feelings for Dorothea. George Levine suggests: "In a conventional realist novel, [Lydgate] would certainly have been Dorothea's lover and ultimate husband. The two stories join just at the point when it is too late for that happy romantic resolution" (*How to Read the Victorian Novel*, 137).

64. Barbara Hardy writes that *Middlemarch* is "only restrictedly truthful in its treatment of sexuality" (*Appropriate Form*, 106; see the discussion on pages 106–31); by contrast, she believes that the quotient of sexual truth in *Anna Karenina* is higher (164–68).

65. Henry James, "*Middlemarch*," 151.

66. Grossman, "Tolstoy's Portrait of Anna," 1.

67. George Eliot writes: "But any one watching keenly the stealthy convergence of human lots, sees a slow preparation of effects from one life on another, which tells like a calculated irony on the indifference or the frozen stare with which we look at our unintroduced neighbour. Destiny stands by sarcastic with our *dramatis personae* folded in her hand" (11, 95).

68. Levin thus reverts back to that judgmental tendency which surfaced, but was tempered, when, dining with Oblonsky in Part 1, he declared all fallen women vermin. (That scene had ended with his being "convicted by his own conscience" and refraining from further moralizing.) In this scene in Part 7, he undergoes a more dramatic "reversal": Amy Mandelker sees here the "reversal of Lyovin's initial blanket rejection of all fallen women as 'vermin' which dissolves into compassion as he views Anna's portrait" ("Illustrate and Condemn: The Phenomenology of Vision in *Anna Karenina*," *Tolstoy Studies Journal* 8 [1995–96]: 53).

69. Grossman, "Tolstoy's Portrait of Anna," 8–9. Grossman also argues that the portrait captured Anna when she was at a happy stage in her life (during the "honeymoon" in Italy), whereas the woman Levin meets is unhappy: the effect, then, is to arouse his pity for her.

70. Tolstoy suggests that under the special circumstances of labor and giving birth, a woman's soul may be revealed (without the mediation of art). For example, we are told that Vronsky himself had only come to know Anna's soul as she lay dying after giving birth, just as we are told that Levin only comes to see "the very core of [Kitty's] soul" when "all the veils are taken away" while she is in labor (7:13, 707–8)—which happens soon after his return home from Anna's, where he beheld the portrait that in its uncanny way revealed Anna's soul.

71. Nicholas Royle, "The Telepathy Effect," in *The Uncanny* (Manchester, UK: Manchester University Press, 2003), 256–76.

72. See David Parker, *Ethics, Theory and the Novel* (Cambridge, UK: Cambridge University Press, 1994), 112–13, on how this passage reveals Karenin's need for "categories," which contrasts to Levin's capacity (at least at certain points) for admitting to being baffled by life, as when he concedes to Oblonsky, "But I don't know, I really don't know" in the restaurant scene after his initial attempt to declare the whole category of fallen women "vermin." As Parker observes, Karenin feels that he "*must* know."

Excellent insights in an unpublished paper by Karen Leibowitz drew this passage about Karenin to my attention (term paper, 2002, University of California, Berkeley, "Dostoevsky, Tolstoy, and the French").

73. Vladimir Alexandrov, *Limits to Interpretation: The Meanings of "Anna Karenina"* (Madison: University of Wisconsin Press, 2004), 165, 113.

74. That Levin does not know what was going on inside Kitty does not necessarily diminish their joy or detract from the intimacy between them. (The narrator notes that Kitty was so moved by what she was feeling that she could not even listen to the words of the liturgy.) However, the need to inform the reader that Levin lacks access to Kitty's interiority and makes the common mistake of assuming that the other's feelings match his own is a move typical of Tolstoy's narrator. It reflects his view of the human condition in general and a more particular desire to add a degree of irony in his description of Levin's introduction to married life. Unlike Karenin, Levin may try to imagine what is going on in the abyss of his wife's soul, but, Tolstoy indicates, he has no way of understanding feminine experience and thus makes judgments based on what he does know, that is, himself.

75. Similarly, as J. Hillis Miller observes, Eliot "did not, the evidence of her novels suggests, have much confidence that people (as opposed to telepathic narrators) have spontaneous insight into what another person is thinking or feeling" (*Reading for Our Time*, 9). While it may be true that Tolstoy and Eliot both show their characters' judgments about others' thoughts and feelings to be faulty, Eliot is more active than Tolstoy in *promoting* the benefits of wondering about the consciousnesses of others and of becoming aware of their "equivalent center of self."

76. Grossman, "Tolstoy's Portrait of Anna," 13.

77. Karenin thinks to himself: "Questions about her feelings, about what has been or might be going on in her soul, are none of my business; they are the business of her conscience and belong to religion" (2:8, 144).

78. As Dorothea asks, "What do we live for, if it is not to make life less difficult to each other?" (72, 733–34).

79. See Grossman, "Tolstoy's Portrait of Anna," on Levin's "kinship" with Anna (11–14).

80. S. A. Rachinskii to L. N. Tolstoi, 6 January 1878, in Tolstoi, *Pis'ma Tolstogo i k Tolstomu*, 223–24.

81. S. A. Rachinskii to L. N. Tolstoi, 5 February 1878, in Tolstoi, *Pis'ma Tolstogo i k Tolstomu*, 224–25. Rachinsky agreed that Tolstoy has achieved "absolute unity" "since two sides of one and the same idea play out." But Rachinsky explained that his earlier criticism was addressed at the *outer* architecture of the novel, which he, admittedly old-fashioned in his aesthetic sense, still felt was important.

82. Stenbock-Fermor, *Architecture*, 13.

83. In the drafts Tolstoy considered having Anna, in her desperation before she ends up committing suicide, go to a flower show where she catches sight of Kitty and Levin (20:525–27). Whereas Kitty refuses to approach Anna out of consideration (as she explains to Levin) for the possible pain such a meeting might cause Anna, husband and wife agree that Levin, who observes how

piteous Anna is, should approach her. Kitty even approves of the compassion that prompts Levin to want to do this: "Kitty saw that spark of tenderness and kindness that she loved above all in her husband" (20:527). When Levin talks to Anna, however, he does so "with that eternal delusion of happy people," and thus he tells her "about his happiness, that their child was now better, that they had been staying in Moscow because of his health, but now were going to the country." Then Levin refers to something Vronsky had told him, which reveals to Anna that Vronsky, unbeknownst to her, had been visiting the Levins. She thinks to herself, jealously, "Yes, à ses premiers amours." In this scene, Tolstoy shows Levin's spark of compassion but ultimately suggests that—because of that "eternal delusion of happy people"—Levin is unable to provide Anna any comfort, for all his good will. In much the same way, Anna's compassion is overshadowed by her jealousy: at that moment she can only think about Vronsky's possible attraction to Kitty. Tolstoy's realism is such that this meeting was bound to be a dead end (with both parties responsible for the failure). Once again, in Tolstoy's world of *Anna Karenina*, human contact fails. In the final version of the novel, Tolstoy "replaces" this encounter with Anna's visit to Dolly's (where she sees Kitty). Thus, Tolstoy still has Anna encounter character(s) from the other plot and be exposed to their happiness, from which she is excluded, before she kills herself.

84. Mandelker acknowledges the action of eros in this scene but sees Levin's ability to feel compassion for Anna, a fallen woman he had hitherto judged so harshly, as a step in his spiritual conversion. She finds the model of John 8 at work here, as Levin learns Christ's lesson to the scribes and Pharisees. Mandelker also argues that Kitty eventually forgives Anna, when they eventually meet again in Part 8 (*Framing "Anna Karenina": Tolstoy, the Woman Question, and the Victorian Novel* [Columbus: Ohio State University Press, 1993], 114–16).

85. Hardy, *Appropriate Form*, 106–31, 164–68.

86. Martha Nussbaum, *Upheavals of Thought* (Cambridge, UK: Cambridge University Press, 2001).

87. In a Christian context, judgment of non-desert does not come into play; for example, the prodigal son brought his suffering on himself, but the father shows compassion anyway. Robert C. Roberts uses this case to illustrate the contrast between gospel-based views of compassion and those, like Nussbaum's, that are rooted in Aristotle's judgment of non-desert ("Compassion as an Emotion and Virtue," in *Religious Emotions: Some Philosophical Explorations*, ed. Willem Lemmens and Walter Van Herck [Cambridge, UK: Cambridge University Press, 2008], 204–5).

88. Grossman, "Tolstoy's Portrait of Anna," 3.

89. In later writings Tolstoy rejects this notion, envisioning a world where brotherly love does not depend on blood, sacrament, or contract. The draw of *Anna Karenina* is the troubled nature of its message: the inner connections encourage the reader to question the "family first" message that sounds on the surface of the novel.

90. See Hruska, "Infected Families."

91. Sharon Marcus, *Between Women: Friendship, Desire, and Marriage in Victorian England* (Princeton, NJ: Princeton University Press, 2007), 77.

92. Marcus observes that what happens between Rosamond and Dorothea (as it contributes to the successful denouement of Dorothea's marriage plot with Will) fits a pattern according to which, contrary to the assumption of many critics and readers, "courtship between men and women proceeds in tandem with declarations of female amity" (*Between Women*, 76).

93. Eliot provides us here with a convergence on the surface of the novel, a link on the level of plot [фабула] and character (acquaintance) of the sort that Tolstoy dismissed in his letter to Rachinsky.

94. Marcus, *Between Women*, 77. In the "bridge" that joins "Miss Brooke" to "Middlemarch" the narrator underscores the opposition between Miss Brooke and the type of woman that Lydgate fancies (which turns out to be Rosamond). Their embrace thus breaks down the oppositions that appear to structure the novel. Tolstoy, similarly, depends on the reader intuiting the paradigmatic connections between the plotlines and characters, but he denies the kind of embrace, on the surface of the plot, that Eliot provides.

95. Marcus, *Between Women*, 78.

96. Marcus, *Between Women*, 78–79.

97. On the dynamics of the double plot in the *Iliad*, see Robert Rabel, *Plot and Point of View in the "Iliad"* (Ann Arbor: University of Michigan Press, 1997).

98. Lewes, as cited in Shuttleworth, "Sexuality and Knowledge," 427.

99. David Trotter makes this point in "Space, Movement," 44–45.

100. I draw in what follows on my discussion of Dolly's failure to comfort Anna and the Darwinian paradigm at play in "*Tue-la! Tue-le!*: Death Sentences, Words, and Inner Monologue in Tolstoy's *Anna Karenina* and *Three More Deaths*," *Tolstoy Studies Journal* 11 (1999).

101. David Herman, "Allowable Passions in *Anna Karenina*," *Tolstoy Studies Journal* 8 (1995–96): 24.

102. For example, Ilya Kliger argues that Anna's plot appears emplotted in a way that Levin's is not. Thus, her death appears to be predetermined (*The Narrative Shape of Truth: Veridiction in Modern European Literature* [University Park: Pennsylvania State University Press, 2011], 155–58 and n. 21, 227–28). Gary Saul Morson, however, has argued that the omens that appear to prefigure Anna's death are figments of her own self-indulgent imagination ("Anna Karenina's Omens," in *Freedom and Responsibility in Russian Literature: Essays in Honor of Robert Louis Jackson*, ed. Elizabeth Cheresh Allen and Gary Saul Morson [Evanston, IL: Northwestern University Press, 1995], 134–52). My concern here is with what Dolly does, or rather fails to do. Assuming that Dolly has some degree of freedom and a concomitant degree of responsibility for her actions, we might ask whether she could have done more to help Anna at this key moment when Anna wrestles with contingent suicidal feeling.

103. Mandelker, *Framing "Anna Karenina,"* 52. Mandelker notes that Dolly "feels it more important to counsel Kitty about breast-feeding than to respond to Anna's obvious distress."

104. The narration sticks close to Anna as she projects nasty feelings onto Kitty and wonders what she ever expected of Dolly; but it does report briefly on the inner struggle Kitty goes through before coming out to greet Anna.

105. The message the reader extracts is likely to be much more complicated, in accordance with Tolstoy's poetics of the multiplot.

106. In the drafts, Tolstoy notes that Levin started to see Dolly through Kitty's eyes as a "heroine" and a "magnificent woman," instead of simply a "simple, kind, somewhat bedraggled, insignificant woman" (20:464). While the passage in the drafts may be there to show that Levin's appreciation of the feminine world expands through marriage, it presents Dolly as heroic, at least in the eyes of Levin (and Kitty).

107. In contrast, there is evidence that Anna had been receptive to Dolly's troubles. When Levin visits Anna (a few months before in the time of the novel, but only 50 pages away), Anna mentions that Dolly had been there the day before and been indignant about Grisha's problems with his Latin teacher at school (7:10, 698).

108. K. A. Timiriazev, "Darvin kak obrazets uchenogo," cited in Todes, *Darwin without Malthus*, 162. In the finale of the novel, Professor Katavasov, on greeting Levin at Pokrovskoe, gets right down to business, asking Levin, "Have you read Spencer?" Levin replies, "No, I didn't finish. However, I don't need him now." When Katavasov expresses surprised interest, Levin announces, "I mean I've finally become convinced that I won't find in him and those like him the solution to the questions that interest me. Now . . ." (8:14, 802–3). Levin has just had his illumination about loving one's neighbor and living for the soul and thus has no further need of Spencer and others. Tolstoy viewed Spencer as an advocate of the most vicious "social Darwinism," as can be seen in "On the Meaning of the Christian Religion" (a draft thought to have been composed in 1875): "Spencer and Darwin demand the killing of the weak and the prohibition of their marriages, because human progress is retarded [by their reproducing themselves]. This is indubitable for people who do not see any aim of human life beyond earthly life. But this is contrary to love, the basic emotion of human nature, and this very fact proves that the aim of life cannot be earthly life alone" (cited and translated by McLean, "Claws in the Behind," 172).

109. For Tolstoy's view of the peasants as an extension of the family, see Anne Hruska, "Love and Slavery: Serfdom, Emancipation, and Family in Tolstoy's Fiction," *Russian Review* 66, no. 4 (October 2007): 627–46.

110. In the Finale of *Middlemarch*, it might seem that, with the scattering from Middlemarch of the Ladislaws, Lydgates, and Bulstrodes, the different strands of the novel separate. The focus seems to be on family life, not neighborly love. Yet, while Dorothea is now known as wife and mother, with her energy apparently sucked into those roles, the narrator also affirms the lasting, if diffusive, effect of her love on those who knew her. This includes not just her family, but neighbors like Rosamond, Lydgate, Caleb Garth, and others. In *Middlemarch*, George Eliot creates a realm where souls cry out to each other "without other consciousness than their moving with kindred natures in the same embroiled medium, the same troublous fitfully-illuminated life"—and her narrator works hard to encourage readers to feel part of that medium. What difference this makes will depend on the reader. But the impulse of *Middlemarch*, with its metaphors of dispersion and diffusion, is to encourage empathetic imagination and neighborly love, in thought, word, and deed. In George Eliot's *Middlemarch*, mutual aid is conceivable beyond the family circle.

Although the *ideals* of community that *Anna Karenina* and *Middlemarch* strive for are much the same—both feature mutual aid and love—Tolstoy puts the thrust on *channeling* them through the family and letting them trickle down (or radiate outward) from the family. In fact, George Lewes envisioned something similar. He argued that sexual instinct is "the first of the sympathetic tendencies, the germ of Altruism" and that once sexual instinct is domesticated, then "the love of wife and children extends to relatives and friends, to the tribe, to the nation, to Humanity" (*Problems of Life and Mind* [London: Trubner, 1874], 1:176, cited in Shuttleworth, "Sexuality and Knowledge," 431). At the end of *Anna Karenina*, Levin provides a model for family happiness achieved by domesticating the sexual instinct; as Lewes envisioned, the love of wife and child extends to others. But this happens for Levin under the aegis of his newly rekindled Christian faith.

111. Levine, *How to Read the Victorian Novel*, 130.

112. Rachinsky translated Lewes's *Physiology of the Common Life* in 1861.

Chapter 4. Loving Your Neighbor, Saving Your Soul

A talk based on this chapter was given in November 2015 at the Convention of the Association for Slavic, East European, and Eurasian Studies in Philadelphia.

1. My understanding of this question is informed by Avishai Margalit's discussion in *The Ethics of Memory* (Cambridge, MA: Harvard University Press, 2002), especially 40–47.

2. Cathy Popkin discusses the importance of "recognizing one's own people" as it relates to questions of empire and selfhood in *Anna Karenina*. She points out that "it is not entirely clear in Tolstoy's novel . . . what the unit of selfhood might be: the individual self? One's family? One's 'circle'? One's class? One's nation? All God's people?" See "Teaching Literature and Empire: The Case for *Anna Karenina*," in *Teaching Nineteenth-Century Russian Literature: Essays in Honor of Robert L. Belknap*, ed. Deborah Martinsen, Cathy Popkin, and Irina Reyfman (Boston: Academic Studies Press, 2014), 233–45.

3. Virginia Woolf, "Reading Notes on *Anna Karenina*," in *Virginia Woolf and the Russian Point of View*, ed. Roberta Rubenstein, Appendix E (New York: Palgrave-Macmillan, 2009), 200–201. For discussion of Woolf's response, see chapter 6.

4. F. M. Dostoevskii, *Polnoe sobranie sochinenii v tridtsati tomakh*, ed. V. G. Bazanov et al. (Leningrad: Nauka, 1972–90), 25:193–206 (hereafter *PSS*). English translation: Fyodor Dostoevsky, *A Writer's Diary*, trans. Kenneth Lantz (Evanston, IL: Northwestern University Press, 1994), 1061–77.

See Gary Saul Morson (*"Anna Karenina" in Our Time: Seeing More Wisely* [New Haven, CT: Yale University Press, 2007], 214–22) on Dostoevsky's response to the end of *Anna Karenina* and Tolstoy's rejection of "moral Newtonianism" in favor of a case-by-case approach to moral decisions. Morson writes: "Distance really does affect responsibility. Moral Newtonians with their universal laws presume that ethics does not respect persons. The moral law treats everyone as of equal value. Tolstoy regards such a view as monstrous. No one is a disembodied agent lacking connections to particular people. . . . For Tolstoy, morality may be described in terms of concentric circles. We owe our greatest responsibility to our family, then to our neighbors, relatives, or co-workers, then to people in our community, and, only several circles later, to people we have never met on the other side of the world, and only beyond that to 'Martians.' When someone bids us to do unto others, ask them *which* others. Because time and energy are limited, demand to know unto which others we will consequently do less. Responsibility never entirely evaporates at any distance, but it does diminish. To be precise, it diminishes not with physical but with what might be called *moral distance*" (217). While I agree that Levin seems to arrive at this ethos in the finale, when it validates his way of life and resolves his crisis, the workings of Tolstoy's multiplot *Anna Karenina* engender doubt about the program outlined above (with its tight focus of neighborly love on kith and kin) and push the reader to keep on questioning.

5. These definitions derive from Margalit, *Ethics of Memory*, 41–42, as he addresses the difficulties of answering the question of how to identify the neighbor that one is instructed to love in Leviticus 19:18 ("Thou shalt love thy neighbor as thyself"). He notes the variety of interpretations of what this means, from a very close definition (the member of one's own sect) to a "universalistic approach," one example of which is Rabbi Ben Azzai, who argues that "the commandment to love (care)" is extended to "all one's fellow human beings." Margalit writes in regard to the Good Samaritan in Luke, "the idea here is that the notion of a neighbor is powerful enough to cross tribal, religious, and ethnic boundaries. The Good Samaritan encountered his fellowman in a face-to-face situation. Witnessing his suffering, 'he had compassion on him.'" Margalit observes that it is "this physical proximity" that explains the use of the word neighbor in this context" (41–42).

In the Russian Orthodox context in which Tolstoy wrote (even if he did not simply adopt conventional views), there was similarly a range. Tolstoy shows, for example, that Koznyshev (in benign form) and the other Pan-Slavists seem to operate with a definition that equates "neighbor" with "co-religionist." However, other Orthodox thinkers took a more universalist approach. Among these was St. Tikhon of Zadonsk (Timofei Savelievich Sokolov), author of *True Christianity* (1776). Tikhon, in the spirit of the parable of the Samaritan, reminds his readers that strangers *are* still your neighbors and that you are obliged to help your neighbors (not just love them in an abstract way). And Tikhon also makes strong arguments for gospel-inspired notions of sharing one's wealth with those in need. Tikhon focuses on the "I/thou" relationship with the neighbor. This feature resonates with Tolstoy's understanding of neighborly love, with its focus on the personal connection—it has to be heartfelt, not forced. See St. Tikhon of Zadonsk, *Istinnoe khristianstvo*, in Tikhon Zadonskii, *Sochineniia preosviashchennago Tikhona, episkopa Voronezhskago i Eletskago* (St. Petersburg: Ivan Glazunov, 1825–26), 10, "O liubvi k blizhnemu" (289–319), and 11, "O milosti k blizhnemu" (320–38).

6. Lev Tolstoi, *Chetveroevangelie: Soedinenie i perevod chetyrekh Evangelii* (Moscow: ESKMO Press, 2001), 473.

7. Tolstoi, *Chetveroevangelie*, 473.

8. Dickens and Eliot were among the novelists to adapt the novel to explore the vexed question "Who is my neighbor," which, over the ages, has also been the subject of theological treatises, philosophical discourses (Kant, Schopenhauer),

and *sui generis* works such as Kierkegaard's *Works of Love*. A later landmark in response was *Civilization and Its Discontents*, in which Freud develops full-blown theories to explain anxieties about loving one's neighbor that are in some respects close to Levin's, especially when Freud points out that family should come first (*Civilization and Its Discontents* [New York: Norton, 1961], 100–101). In their recent inquiry into "love your neighbor," Slavoj Žižek, Eric L. Santner, and Kenneth Reinhard ("Introduction," in *The Neighbor: Three Inquiries in Political Theology* [Chicago, IL: University of Chicago Press, 2013], 5) draw attention to the opacity of this commandment and the variety of (often conflicting) interpretations, from its early iteration in Leviticus 19:18 to the present day.

9. In this letter to Alexandrine Tolstoy, Tolstoy drew a distinction between pity aroused (in him) by those suffering from the famine and the pity aroused (in her) by the former prostitutes for whom Alexandrine did charitable work. He wrote: "Your Magdalens are very piteous, I know, but pity for them, as for all sufferings of the soul, is more in the mind, or in the heart, if you wish, but for people who are simple, good, and healthy (both physically and morally), the pity one feels is from one's whole being—it is shameful and painful to be a human being when one looks at their suffering" (L. N. Tolstoi to A. A. Tolstaia, 30 July 1873, #30, 62:43). Although the distinction he draws is between the suffering of the body (the result of hunger) and the suffering of the soul (the result of the degradation of having been a prostitute), it is possible that Tolstoy is relying on a "judgment of non-desert": Tolstoy's compassion for the victims of famine is greater because he judges them to be innocent victims (and "good" people) who do not in any way deserve their suffering. By contrast, because he seems on some level to judge Alexandrine's "Magdalens," their suffering does not affect him in the same way.

10. L. N. Tolstoi to A. A. Tolstaia, 6 March 1874, #58, 62:173.

When famine struck Samara again in 1891, Nikolai Leskov wrote Tolstoy, asking what could be done to help. This time, Tolstoy responded that simply collecting alms for the hungry did not help the problem; rather, efforts should be made to spread brotherly love and to devote one's whole life to doing good deeds. Tolstoy suggested that only this approach would eliminate famine and suffering (L. N. Tolstoi to N. S. Leskov, 4 July 1891, #1, 66:11–12). Part of this letter was published (without permission) and caused a stir. However, when Tolstoy and family members then went to Samara and witnessed the suffering themselves, Tolstoy swallowed the principles he had just announced and devoted himself to famine relief work. This episode shows Tolstoy himself still in flux about the meaning and praxis of "love your neighbor." He could declare from his haven in Yasnaya Polyana that there was no point in getting involved in Samara, that "love" was the answer, but once in Samara, face to face with the hungry, he acted on the love he felt. His behavior is consistent with his interpretation of "who is my neighbor" in his *Four Gospels*, where he says that the point is not to ratiocinate about who your neighbor is, just have faith and act accordingly.

11. Tolstoy externalizes his own mistrust of charity and "doing good on purpose" in *Anna Karenina*, in which all acts of charity and philanthropy are

subject to scrutiny. As is argued below, by intimating that most such acts were performed for the wrong reasons, often for personal gratification, Tolstoy by process of elimination appears to justify the restrictive mode of loving your neighbor that Levin models and embraces in the finale.

12. L. N. Tolstoi to A. A. Tolstaia, 3 May 1859, #135, 60:294. The "profession de foi" Tolstoy sets forth (and comments on) contains the seeds of Tolstoy's later *Confession* and the description of Levin's path from the naïve faith of his childhood to his struggle to return to the Orthodox Church. In 1859, however, Tolstoy confessed that traditional Orthodoxy and even the gospels did not speak to his soul.

13. Nikolai Leskov, "Velikosvetskii raskol, Grenvil' Val'digrev lord Redstok, ego zhizn', uchenie i propoved'," *Pravoslavnoe obozrenie*, nos. 9-10 (Sept.-Oct. 1876) and no. 2 (Feb. 1877), published in book form in two editions later in 1877, cited here from the translation *Schism in High Society*, trans. James Yeoman Muckle (Nottingham, UK: Bramcote Press, 1995). For analysis, see Hugh McLean, *Nikolai Leskov: The Man and His Art* (Cambridge, MA: Harvard University Press, 1977), 331-37.

14. L. N. Tolstoi to A. A. Tolstaia, 12 June 1859, #141, 60:300-301.

15. In *Schism*, before focusing on Radstock's missionary work in Russia, Leskov describes Radstock's life and activities back in England, where he was deeply involved in charitable activities. The excerpt below is representative of Leskov's account of Radstock's charity work: "Of all the philanthropic institutions founded by Radstock, the one which deserves the most attention is the 'Shelter for young tramps' (Grotto boys), which occupies Lord Radstock intensively and which he himself keeps supplied with new recruits. Whenever he meets a homeless boy, he immediately invites him to the Shelter, gives him food, drink and education and instills in him his own fortifying religion—the 'good news' of complete forgiveness. Sometimes he walks the streets at night seeking out the homeless, and sometimes even rescues from the authorities young thieves who have been sentenced to a reformatory, and teaches them to live honestly and cheerfully" (26). For more on Radstock in Russia, see Edmund Heier, *Religious Schism in the Russian Aristocracy 1860-1900: Radstockism and Pashkovism* (The Hague: Nijhoff, 1970).

16. As McLean explains, Leskov was the self-proclaimed "spiritual janitor" of Russia at the time: Leskov's ulterior motive in writing this exposé of Radstock and his followers was to draw attention to the need that Leskov saw for reform within Orthodoxy itself (*Leskov*, 331-38).

17. Leskov, *Schism*, 101. McLean describes Leskov's strategy as follows: "By thus appearing to analyze the motives for defection from Orthodoxy, Leskov was able to make the *Orthodox Review* print harsh judgments about the national church, which he then affected to refute" (Leskov, *Schism*, 335). Leskov mentions a number of areas of discontent among the Orthodox faithful that may have contributed to Radstock's popularity, such as a yearning for Protestant-style parish life, lack of regard for the Orthodox clergy and administration, the need for prayer to be more meaningful (and comprehensible—i.e., not in Slavonic), an interest in hearing inspiring sermons.

18. Konstantin Pobedonostsev, letter of May 10, 1880, quoted in Heier, *Religious Schism*, 129.

19. Although Tikhon was embraced by the Church and canonized in 1861, Florovsky presents him as something of a Westernizer within the Russian religious culture of his time; he cites his "constant focus on the remembrance and contemplation of the sufferings of Christ" (Georgii Florovskii, *Puti russkogo bogosloviia* [Paris: YMCA Press, 1982], 125).

Heier (*Religious Schism*, 48–49) writes: "Part of the reason for the success of the [Radstock-Pashkov] movement was that it was not entirely new. Long before Lord Radstock's arrival in Russia the devotional and moral application of the humiliation of Christ, the call to meekness, poverty, humility, and obedience had been brought to the attention of the Russian people. This manifested itself primarily in the veneration of saints, and in the monasteries contemplative monasticism reached its acme in the 1860s and 1870s. Both were important factors in the revival of the spiritual life of the country." Heier notes that Tikhon himself, like the later Radstockists, had sought "a revival of the Christian ideal" (49). The Radstockists thus used parts of Tikhon's *True Christianity* as they spread their teaching.

20. Malcolm Jones, "Dostoevskii and Radstockism," in *Dostoevskii and Britain*, ed. W. J. Leatherbarrow (Oxford, UK: Berg, 1995), 164. He notes that Dostoevsky stopped short of direct criticism of Radstock in what he wrote on him in *Diary of a Writer*, although Dostoevsky is reported to have argued bitterly about Radstock with Zasetskaia (the daughter of Denis Davydov, the poet-hussar of the Napoleonic wars).

21. Dostoevsky, *A Writer's Diary*, 421; for the Russian text, see *PSS* 22:98–99.

22. Heier, *Religious Schism*, 60. In 1876, in "Lord Radstock," Dostoevsky reported that he had heard Radstock preach three years before, which would mean early in his ministry in Petersburg. (Radstock arrived during Lent of 1873.) In *The Adolescent* (1875), the pilgrim Makar Dolgorukii counsels, "Go and give all that thou hast to the poor and become the servant of all."

23. This was the catechism used to instruct the Russian Orthodox of Tolstoy's fictional world. As discussed below, Stiva Oblonsky musters what he learned in the catechism when he attempts to argue with Karenin and Countess Lydia Ivanovna about their doctrine of "faith alone."

24. Florovsky mentions the importance of philanthropic works to Radstockists and cites as examples their visits to prisons and their reading the Holy Scriptures to prisoners (Florovskii, *Puti*, 402). In *Schism in High Society*, Leskov also reminds his readers that Russian Orthodoxy did have its own tradition and some models for Christian charity. He notes that interest in charity work had intensified in Russia in the wake of the Crimean War, during the period of reforms, well before Radstock set foot in Russia.

25. Iuliia Zasetskaia was one of the most impressive Radstockist activists and one of the few to break openly with Orthodoxy and identify as a Protestant. Dostoevsky met her when he was invited to visit the homeless shelter that she had worked to establish in Petersburg. Although she and Dostoevsky were to argue bitterly over faith, Dostoevsky retained respect and affection for her. (See Jones, "Dostoevskii and Radstockism," and also see below.)

26. Leskov, *Schism*, 93–94. Muckle notes that it is not clear whether the "camps" Leskov mentions are prison camps or military camps.

27. Florovskii, *Puti*, 402.

28. In February 1875, Tolstoy's wife received a letter from Elizaveta Ivanovna Mengden, an old acquaintance, who wrote on behalf of Maria Grigorievna Peiker [Peucker]. Mengden reported that Peiker had "completely given herself to the influence of English preachers and acts only according to their instructions" (Mengden to S. A. Tolstaia, qtd. in notes to *PSS*, 62:145). Mengden wrote that Peiker was establishing *The Russian Worker: A Spiritual-Ethical Journal*, which was intended for the folk. They wanted to appeal to Tolstoy for advice on how to go about making the journal accessible to the folk. Tolstoy responded in detail, doubting whether "ladies" would be able to produce such a journal. He noted, however, that if it were written in a way that was right for the people, it would not matter what ideas it promoted (sectarian, protestant, or other) because it would be free of falsehood (62:143–44). Tolstoy launched his own project of writing and publishing for the folk the very next month, in March 1875. At this point, he finally received an answer to a letter written in November 1874 to Archmandrite Leonid Kavelin, suggesting an anthology for the people of the lives of saints. Tolstoy's interest in writing "for the folk" predates the query from the Radstockists, but it may have intensified as a result of his exchange with them. (N. N. Gusev, *Lev Nikolaevich Tolstoi: Materialy k biografii s 1870 po 1881 god* [Moscow: Nauka, 1963], 197–200).

29. One of the original Russian disciples of Radstock was the mother of Vladimir Chertkov, Tolstoy's disciple in later years. Before embracing Tolstoy's teaching, Chertkov himself had been under the sway of Radstockism.

30. See Hugh McLean, "Tolstoy and Jesus," in *In Quest of Tolstoy* (Boston: Academic Studies Press, 2008).

31. Bobrinsky fought in the Crimean War, was active in the reforms, served as the Minister of Transportation, and then, inspired by Radstock, joined the Evangelical movement and "devoted his life and wealth between 1874 and his death in 1894" to this cause (Heier, *Religious Schism*, 83). His activities included work in the movement to disseminate Russian Bibles. He was also involved in various forms of social activism and charitable works in Petersburg and around his estate in Tula, where he set up schools and built hospitals. Heier (83) describes Bobrinsky as "the living example of a repentant nobleman."

32. L. N. Tolstoi to A. A. Tolstaia, 20–23 March 1876, #253, 62:261. Tolstoy also mentioned how impressed he was with Bobrinsky's faith in a letter of February 21, 1876, to S. S. Urusov, who was an Orthodox believer. Tolstoy wrote that both men's faith left him envious of their spiritual calm (62:249).

33. It has been argued that various forms of dissent, evangelicalism, or nonstandard piety (such as Dickens's "sentimental radicalism") had a disproportionate impact on the English novel. The Dissent movements are also credited with the inward turn of the English novel. In his reading of English novels, Tolstoy was exposed to an array of treatments of English piety, which included Anthony Trollope's more garden-variety Church of England attitudes, Charlotte Yonge's Oxford neo-Catholic leanings, and, of course, a variety of portraits of evangelicals, often within the same novel. (For example, the gamut in *Jane Eyre*

runs from Brocklehurst to Helen Burns.) he was, however, especially taken with evangelical Protestantism as depicted by George Eliot. In response to her "Janet's Repentance" from *Scenes of Clerical Life*, Tolstoy wrote to Alexandrine Tolstoy, "Happy [or Blessed] are those who, like the English imbibe with their milk Christian teaching, and in such a lofty, purified form as evangelical Protestantism" (12 June 1859, #141, 60:300–301). In "Janet's Repentance," the focus is on an evangelical minister, beloved by his followers and resented by others in the community. It is not surprising that the evangelical strain in English piety captured Tolstoy's imagination. Among the features commonly associated with this strain are a focus on a personal reading of the Bible, emotional spirituality, devotion to good works, and decreased importance of liturgy and church hierarchy (both of which were important to traditional Russian Orthodoxy). In her later work, George Eliot novelizes various religious experiences, but she often favors evangelicals, such as the Methodists Dinah Morris and Seth Bede or the Anglican Dorothea Brooke. The latter shows, especially in her maidenhood, evangelical tendencies. (The very tendencies that make her an interesting novelistic heroine are considered suspect by many Middlemarchers, and her marriage to the distinctly non-evangelical Anglican Casaubon, thought to be bishop material, does not rid her of non-conformist tendencies; her marriage to Will Ladislaw, with his Polish [Catholic and/or Jewish] heritage shows her continued sympathy for dissent.) Valentine Cunningham (*Everywhere Spoken Against: Dissent in the Victorian Novel* [Oxford, UK: Clarendon, 1975]), discussing how English novelists reacted to dissent, argues that George Eliot was more tolerant than many of her contemporaries.

34. Morson discusses parallels between the lesson Kitty learns in Soden and the one that Levin learns back at Pokrovskoe during the same period (*"Anna Karenina" in Our Time*, 168–75).

35. Whereas the chapters set in Soden (2:30–35) are the finale of Part 2 in the book version of *Anna Karenina*, in initial serial publication these chapters were the start of the third installment, which ended with Levin catching sight of Kitty in the carriage as she travels to Ergushevo on her return from Soden. Thus, the whole third installment of the serial publication is devoted to Kitty in Soden and Levin back home; it ends with their paths crossing again. (Anna and Vronsky do not appear.) In the canonical eight-part book, where Part 2 ends with Varenka's promise that she will visit Kitty when the latter gets married, the structural divisions do not punctuate the courtship plot in as obvious a way. (Kitty's future marriage is still presented as inevitable, but this courtship plot is submerged.) See William Mills Todd III, "Anna on the Installment Plan: Teaching *Anna Karenina* through the History of Its Serial Publication," in *Approaches*, ed. Knapp and Mandelker, for discussion of the different emphases in the serial publication and the book form.

36. Andrew Durkin ("Laclos's *Les liaisons dangereuses* and Tolstoj's *Anna Karenina*: Some Comparisons," *Russian Language Journal* 37 [1983]: 128) and Helena Goscilo ("Tolstoy, Laclos, and the Libertine," *Modern Language Review* 81, no. 2 [1986]) have noted that this episode has a precedent in *Liaisons dangereuses*, in an episode where an act of charity becomes a cynical seductive ploy.

37. And yet, as she subsequently relates to Kitty, from whom she hides Vronsky's charity at the train station, Anna had heard from Vronsky's mother during their train ride together that Vronsky was prone to generous chivalric acts: as a youth he rescued a drowning woman and more recently he had given up part of his inheritance to his brother, who, we learn later, had married the dowerless daughter of a Decembrist. There seem to be no particular grounds for suspecting that Vronsky had ulterior motives for all these good deeds. And yet, because of the implicit contrast Tolstoy establishes early on between earnest Levin and cavalier Vronsky, the latter's acts—which, had they been done in another spirit or more clearly grounded in an ethos of neighborly love, might have been feats of Christian charity—become suspect.

38. By Part 3, Levin himself contemplates abandoning patriarchal tradition and putting into effect the "new life" of toil about which he has been musing. This would involve selling his family estate, buying land, and marrying a peasant. He then sees Kitty go by in her carriage on her way to Ergushevo and abandons his plan for a "new life."

39. Sharon Marcus (*Between Women: Friendship, Desire, and Marriage in Victorian England* [Princeton, NJ: Princeton University Press, 2007], 23–108) argues that feminine friendship figures in English courtship plots as part of the bride's preparation. Here Tolstoy, under the likely influence of English novels, borrows and modifies the topos, in the association of Varenka and Kitty.

40. As F. K. Prochaska argues in *Women and Philanthropy in Nineteenth-Century England* (Oxford: Clarendon, 1980), acts of charity to the poor, the sick, and others were central to women's piety, as well as an outlet for self-expression and action beyond the confines of family. He also notes that these acts of charity went hand in hand with reading the Bible: the women were moved to put their interpretation of Christ's teaching into action.

41. Tolstoy uses both Sulivan and Sulivant in the drafts.

42. See Liza Knapp, "The Names," in *Approaches*, ed. Knapp and Mandelker, 16, 25n3.

Tolstoy also may have associated the name Flora with Flora May from Charlotte Yonge's *Daisy Chain*, in which, in a moment of crisis, Flora has an outburst about what she comes to see as her former false piety. Although the circumstances are more extreme (Flora has lost her child), there is some similarity between her realization and Kitty's about *trying* to do right. Flora May declares to her father: "I have never set my heart right. I am not like you nor my sisters. I have seemed to myself, and to you, to be trying to do right, but it was all hollow, for the sake of praise and credit." The narrator elaborates: "The simplicity and hearty piety which, with all Dr. May's faults, had always been part of his character, and had borne him, in faith and trust, through all his trials, had never belonged to her. Where he had been sincere, erring only from impulsiveness, she had been double-minded and calculating, and, now that her delusion had been broken down, she had nothing to rest upon. Her whole religious life had been mechanical, deceiving herself more than even others, and all seemed now swept away, except the sense of hypocrisy, and of having cut herself off, for ever, from her innocent child" (*The Daisy Chain or Aspirations: A Family Chronicle* [Leipzig: Tauchnitz, 1856], 2:297).

43. Amy Mandelker, *Framing "Anna Karenina": Tolstoy, the Woman Question, and the Victorian Novel* (Columbus: Ohio State University Press, 1993), 56. Mandelker observes that Varenka is a precursor of Tolstoy's post-crisis feminine ideal. Thus, while Tolstoy suggests in *Anna Karenina* that imitation of Varenka is not right for his Russian Kitty, in later life he would advocate this mode of being for all women.

44. Frances Power Cobbe, "Female Charity—Lay and Monastic," *Fraser's Magazine* (Dec. 1862): 774–88.

45. This argument was made by Lytton Strachey, who features Florence Nightingale as one of his "eminent Victorians" in the book by this title published in 1918.

46. In "Sevastopol in May," as these sisters of mercy comfort the sick and dying, they show an "active, practical engagement," which Tolstoy's narrator contrasts to "empty, feminine, morbidly weepy compassion" (4:37–38). In the final Sevastopol tale, one sister of mercy protests against the violence of war, saying, "My God, when will it all end!" (4:84).

47. In *The Scarlet Letter* (written in 1849, before the Crimean War), Nathaniel Hawthorne wrote of what eventually became of his adulteress, Hester Prynne: "She was self-ordained a Sister of Mercy, or, we may rather say, the world's heavy hand had so ordained her, when neither the world nor she looked forward to this result" (13, 141). Hawthorne's example suggests that this role of sister of mercy is one not for faithful wives or hopeful brides, but for those who deviate from the norm of marriage and patriarchal family structures.

In a key moment in *Madame Bovary* (1856), written during the Crimean War when Florence Nightingale and other heroines of Sevastopol had captured the popular imagination (in fact, French sisters of mercy were the first to arrive on the scene in Sevastopol), Emma Bovary shows her true mettle when she is asked to hold a basin into which the blood of one of Charles Bovary's patients flows. (Justin, the medical assistant, has fainted.) This scene is significant not only because Emma meets Rodolphe, her future lover, in this moment of bloody crisis, but also because it suggests that Emma is fit to be a nurse. That Hester and Emma had the potential for success as sisters of mercy reinforces the implicit message in *Anna Karenina*, that the role of sister of mercy—or of someone who performs acts of love for neighbors outside of the family sphere—is not right for faithful brides and good mothers.

Dostoevsky, in *Demons*, also contributes to the myth of the heroines of Sevastopol: Sophia Matveevna, the itinerant Bible-seller who comforts Stepan Trofimovich in his last days and brings about his apparent deathbed conversion, had been a nurse at Sevastopol, caring first for her husband and then devoting herself to others. She thus combines two of the strains of feminine behavior (nursing and Bible-based piety) that Tolstoy would seek to contain in *Anna Karenina*.

48. When the narrator notes that this English woman does not act on instinct, in contrast to Kitty, Tolstoy emphasizes that faith is not just a matter of doing what comes naturally: for Flora, her faith means that she acts according to a law, not one thought up by people, but a law given and revealed by God (20:230). Later, in the novel itself, when Levin marvels at Kitty's behavior at

Nikolai's deathbed, the narrator, writing as if from Levin's point of view, asserts that Kitty's actions were not "instinctive, animal, unreasoning," but motivated by faith and thus coming from the soul (6:19, 497).

49. Edwina Cruise ("Tracking the English Novel: Who Wrote the English Novel That Anna Reads," in *Anniversary Essays on Tolstoy*, ed. Donna Orwin, 159–82 [Cambridge, UK: Cambridge University Press, 2010]) and Gary Saul Morson (*"Anna Karenina" in Our Time*, 96) point to Trollope.

50. I am grateful to Sharon Marcus and Nicholas Dames for reading and responding to this passage. Marcus observed that the depiction of Flora Sulivan has Dickensian antecedents. Flora Sulivan has an aura that recalls Florence Dombey (*Dombey and Son*), Amy Dorritt (*Little Dorritt*), and Esther Summerson (*Bleak House*). As he read *Bleak House* in 1854 the young Tolstoy had been taken in by Esther's apparent devotion to loving and serving her neighbor. (He refers to her "childish prayer" to God, consisting of her vow to be industrious, clean hearted, and contented, inspiring the love of all around her [19, 486].) The young Tolstoy was clearly drawn to what he took as earnest expressions of piety that he found in English novels. Tolstoy seemed to find inspiration in them, as he tried to give voice to his own religious yearning. He records in his diary his approval of her prayer to God (12 July 1854, 47:11–12), then the next day recorded his own, in which he includes pleas to God that he may live in love for others and for the good of his neighbor.

Dames found in the back story of Miss Flora Sulivan evidence that Tolstoy had as one of his inspirations Lilly Dale of Trollope's *The Small House at Allendale*. The topos of a marriage delayed—indefinitely—while the groom amasses capital appears in this novel, and the sums even coincide: both grooms set 800 pounds as what they would need to marry. Lily Dale is marked by the fact that she does not marry.

Other heroines of English novels end up devoting themselves to husband and family, after spending periods of maidenhood or widowhood loving their neighbors. George Eliot's Dinah Morris is the most telling case, since she goes from being a charismatic Methodist preacher, giving rousing sermons to the poor in the fields and visiting Hetty Sorrel on death row (where she changes Hetty's heart), to eventually marrying and settling into family life among the Bedes. Through all of this she still maintains her luminous faith.

Tolstoy's Flora Sulivan also recalls Mary Garth and Dorothea Brooke of *Middlemarch*. Mary Garth provided a model of "pledging her troth" to a childhood sweetheart, then waiting for him to be ready for marriage. Whereas George Eliot brings this marriage plot to a happy end, Flora Sulivan's groom seems to have abandoned her.

On the first day of the action of *Middlemarch* Dorothea comes home exhausted from the infant school she has established, then busies herself with her plans for cottages (1, 11). Though she feels a strong need to love and care for her neighbors, Dorothea expresses uncertainty about how to go about it. "I don't feel sure about doing good in any way now: everything seems like going on a mission to people whose language I don't know" (3, 29). In fact, one of her reasons for marrying Casaubon is her desire to improve the housing around the parish of Lowick (3, 33). She is aware that her uncle is in his own way serving the public, advocating for a sheep-stealer condemned to death and also running for Parliament and participating in the movement for reform. But, as she tells him, she takes the call to love her neighbor very seriously and objects to the kind of philanthropist who doesn't "mind how hard the truth is for the neighbours outside our walls." She declares: "I think we have no right to come forward and urge wider changes for good, until we have tried to alter the evils which lie under our own hands" (39, 389).

51. George Eliot, *Adam Bede* (Middlesex, UK: Penguin, 1980). Chapter numbers and page numbers in parentheses after citations refer to this edition.

52. The narrator suggests that Dinah had a manner that would be "discouraging to a lover" (3, 77). Seth Bede despaired that Dinah would never love him, nor any man, "as a husband," but this eventually changes (11, 167).

53. We learn in the epilogue that Dinah preaches no more. This is, however, because the Wesleyans had decided to forbid women from preaching. Dinah submits rather than do as Seth had hoped, join another group that "put no bonds on Christian liberty" (Epilogue, 583).

54. Princess Maria Bolkonsky in *War and Peace* may be regarded as Tolstoy's Napoleonic-era Russian Orthodox version of the Victorian Protestant heroine whose commitment to loving her neighbor could interfere with marriage and family life. Princess Maria is torn between earthly and family love (for her father and her nephew at first and later for her husband and children), on the one hand, and love of God, on the other. She still feels this tension in the epilogue: she feels guilty that she is not able to love others, starting with her nephew, as she loves her own children. She thus feels that she is not living up to Christ's commandment to love everyone. At one point, before marriage, Maria muses about devoting herself totally to God. But her fantasy is not to be an English-style sister of mercy, but rather a homeless pilgrim, like the God's folk that she welcomes. Tolstoy thus provides a distinctively Russian Orthodox scenario.

55. George Eliot, to be sure, was aware of the wide variety of expressions of evangelical piety. Her fiction also includes negative depictions of Evangelicals, such as Bulstrode in *Middlemarch*, who justifies his base actions on the grounds that all he does is for the glory of God. But Eliot's narrator notes that evangelicals are not the only ones prone to this mode of using a grand end to justify cruel means: "There is no general doctrine which is not capable of eating out our morality if unchecked by the deep-seated habit of direct fellow-feeling with individual fellow-men" (61, 619).

56. *The Works of the Rev. John Wesley* (London, 1872), 7:123, qtd. in Prochaska, *Women and Philanthropy*, 9.

57. In the final version of the Soden episode, Nikolai Levin and Masha are still present and tended to by Varenka, but they play a lesser role.

58. Leskov, *Schism*, 38.

59. See Gertrude Himmelfarb, *The De-Moralization of Society: From Victorian Virtues to Modern Values* (New York: Vintage, 1996), 143–69, for discussion of this paradox. Himmelfarb (143) reports that John Wesley, known for his ministry

to the poor, still promoted the policy of "Gain all you can . . . Save all you can . . . Give all you can."

60. Daniel Siegel writes: "The struggle to let go gripped Eliot's own society, in which charity-minded liberals and conservatives alike endeavored to prove that they could give as good as they could get. Parting with one's money, setting aside one's airs of respectability, even befriending the 'wrong' kind of people— these were all the philanthropic achievements of an enlightened and prosperous middle class, exactly the crowd who, in their regular lives, knew how to *make* money and meet all the *right* people. In other words, the competitive spirits that drove professional enterprise also drove the charity business" ("Losing for Profit," in *Middlemarch in the Twenty-First Century*, ed. Karen Chase [New York: Oxford University Press, 2006], 158). Prince Shcherbatsky's comments about the English and their "poors" address this same paradox.

61. In Tolstoy's early "Lucerne" (1857), written not long after he served in the Siege of Sevastopol, Tolstoy's narrator asks why a people so invested in institutional charity show no compassion for a beggar in front of them. Tolstoy suggests that the English are incapable of real fellow feeling, in other words, that they are only capable of what Dickens called "telescopic charity" (in *Bleak House*, a novel Tolstoy had read). George Eliot's "Janet's Repentance," which Tolstoy read in 1859, provided him with a more positive example of English charity: he wrote approvingly to Alexandrine Tolstoy about the pure expression of the Christian idea through acts of charity and neighborly love depicted in this work.

62. Scott M. Kenworthy, *The Heart of Russia: Trinity-Sergius, Monasticism, and Society after 1825* (New York: Oxford University Press, 2010), 1–9.

63. Like Kitty, Turgenev's Liza in *Nest of the Gentry* has been disappointed and compromised by a man and seeks meaning in life "outside of the relation of girls to men" (as Tolstoy's narrator, speaking for Kitty, puts it). Turgenev's heroine had given her heart to Lavretsky (and possibly gone too far with him in the garden), only to find that he was not a widower after all but a still married man. Turgenev's heroine's response to romantic humiliation was to get herself to a nunnery, where she (by the grace of God) saved her soul by living in strict obedience to Christian law. Shcherbatsky's wry reference to going to a monastery suggests that if Kitty does not end up married (to Levin), then saving her soul in a nunnery would be preferable—and more Russian—than life as a sister of mercy in Soden.

64. Stephen Baehr notes that when the construction of a railroad line from Moscow to Trinity-Sergius Monastery was proposed, the Metropolitan of Moscow objected, arguing that "pilgrims would come to the monastery in railroad cars, on which all sorts of tales can be heard and often dirty stories, whereas now they come on foot, and each step is a feat pleasing to God." See Baehr, "The Troika and the Train: Dialogues between Tradition and Technology in Nineteenth-Century Russian Literature," in *Issues in Russian Literature Before 1917*, ed. J. Douglas Clayton (Columbus, OH: Slavica, 1989), 88.

65. See Mother Maria Skobtsova, "The Second Gospel Commandment," in *Essential Writings* (Maryknoll, NY: Orbis, 2003), for discussion of how this second

gospel commandment (love your neighbor) "captivated and interested Russian religious thought" even if "Orthodoxy, owing to historical circumstances, occasionally adopted . . . a somewhat excessive emphasis on the path of self-salvation more characteristic of the religions of the East" (58).

66. Dostoevsky, "Lord Radstock," *A Writer's Diary*, 419; *PSS* 22:98.

67. In the final version of the novel, in one of Levin's two enumerations of the Orthodox faithful whose faith inspires him to want to re-embrace the faith of his fathers, Prince Shcherbatsky figures, along with Kitty, L'vov, and 99 percent of the folk. Shcherbatsky's views are not *vox populi*, but in Levin's mind he figures as a mainstream Orthodox believer.

68. Heier argues that Tolstoy created "Sir John" with Radstock in mind (*Religious Schism*, 86). C. J. G. Turner notes that "the title is reminiscent of Lord Radstock" but also suggests that another inspiration for Sir John could have been an English missionary to India named Mr. Long, whom Tolstoy had met in the early 1870s (*A Karenina Companion* [Waterloo, Ontario: Wilfrid Laurier University Press, 1993], 141).

69. Leskov, *Schism*, 98. Leskov's *Schism* appeared serially *after* this particular section of *Anna Karenina* was published.

70. In the characterization of the religion of Kitty's childhood, the references to fixed forms and received knowledge recall the centrality to Orthodox faith of "Holy Tradition," which Sergii Bulgakov describes as "the living memory of the Church, containing the true doctrine that manifests itself in its history" (*The Orthodox Church*, trans. Elizabeth S. Cram, ed. Donald A. Lowrie [London: Centenary Press, 1935], 19–20). As John Anthony McGuckin explains, this tradition is "the gateway to the theology of revelation" and is ideally understood to be "the essence of the life-saving Gospel of Christ brought to the world through the church by the power of the Holy Spirit of God" (*The Orthodox Church: An Introduction to Its History, Doctrine, and Spiritual Culture* [Malden, MA: Blackwell, 2008], 90).

71. Tolstoy's descriptions of what "did not answer" for Kitty look ahead to Leskov's more detailed explanations in *Schism in High Society* of why so many Orthodox flocked to Radstock and his evangelical religion. For example, Leskov allows that it is no wonder that many are drawn to Radstock's more emotional prayers and want to pray in that way "instead of rattling off with indifference the words of others, which they may not even fully understand." Leskov also notes that not only do "our ladies" not understand Slavonic, but neither do many of the men who have studied it (*Schism*, 34–35).

72. V. A. Zhdanov (*Tvorcheskaia istoriia "Anny Kareninoi": Materialy i nabliudeniia* [Moscow: Sovetskii pisatel', 1957]) finds that the drafts about the effect of Miss Flora Sulivan on Kitty lack "artistic truth" because Tolstoy ascribed to Kitty his current spiritual concerns without motivating them or making them seem natural to Kitty (166–67). Zhdanov suggests that in the next draft Tolstoy transferred to Varenka traits of Miss Sulivan in too "mechanistic" a manner (168), but that the solution of splitting Miss Sulivan into Varenka and Mme. Stahl, and revealing the latter as false, is an improvement. Zhdanov's analysis confirms that the issues at play in Kitty's "spiritual upheaval" were ones that Tolstoy himself reckoned with. In this respect, Tolstoy's novelization of his

own ongoing crisis extends to all reaches of the novel and is not limited to the obvious fictional alter ego Levin.

Zhdanov's complaint about the lack of motivation relates to the fact that Tolstoy does not show Kitty *resolving* the important questions she raises during her awakening, such as the issue of how one can reconcile the demand for complete commitment in Christ's teaching with normal patterns of life. All these questions dissolve when Kitty simply reverts back to her former life and former faith. They would return to haunt Tolstoy himself.

73. Tolstoy would turn to exhaustive Bible study—and revision of the gospels—in the period after *Anna Karenina*. However, Tolstoy documented reading the gospels during stays in Switzerland in 1857 and 1860, at times when he was preoccupied with his desire for faith and the fact of death, the same issues that tormented him later as he wrote *Anna Karenina*. In an unsent letter to Turgenev (written in late March/early April 1857 from Switzerland shortly after Tolstoy fled Paris, where he had spent time with Turgenev and witnessed a beheading), Tolstoy reported that he "sat the whole evening by himself in his hotel room, looked at the moonlit night and the lake, then mechanically opened a book, but that book was the gospels, which the Société Biblique places in all hotel rooms" (47:441). Then twice over the next couple of days in his journal he mentioned taking up and reading the gospels (47:123). Two weeks later, after talking with a certain Petrov, an "ascetic," Tolstoy wrote, "I ask God to grant me this faith" (47:127). During this stay in Switzerland, Tolstoy came into contact with a number of English people, including "preacher's daughters with azure-colored eyes," who may have inspired his later portrait of Miss Flora Sulivan, the preacher's daughter (47:141). In 1860, when Tolstoy was again in Switzerland at the time of his brother's death, he wrote to Alexandrine Tolstoy, "I will fulfill your wish that I read the gospels. I do not have a copy now, but your very good friend Olga Dundukova has promised to give me one" (6 December 1860, #187, 60:362). These references to gospel-reading suggest that both the act of reading the gospels and the fact of having access to a copy registered as events. These two personal experiences of reading the gospels abroad, during a period of longing for faith (1857) and at the time of his brother's death (1860), were thematically close to events involving Kitty in *Anna Karenina*. They provide insight into how Tolstoy worked the residue of his own past experience into his novel, imparting some of it to Kitty. She, too, read the gospels abroad, and Nikolai Levin (a kind of stand-in for Tolstoy's dead brother[s]) was also present: in the drafts, Flora Sulivan reads him the gospels.

74. Florovsky documents and analyzes the various phases in the struggle over the Russian Bible (*Puti*, 147ff.). Florovsky points out that not all Church officials under Nicholas were against the translation. An important champion of making the Bible available in Russian was Filaret Drozdov, Metropolitan of Moscow and author of the Orthodox catechism.

75. A. S. Shishkov, cited in Florovskii, *Puti*, 163.

76. Bulgakov, *Orthodox Church*, 22–23. Bulgakov continues: "The idea that one can himself discern at his own risk and peril, the Word of God, that one may become interlocutor of God is illusory: this Divine Gift is received only from the Church. This gift is received immediately, in its fullness, in union with

the Church, in the temple, where the reading of the Word of God is preceded and followed by a special prayer. We there ask God to aid us in hearing His Word and in opening our hearts to his Spirit" (23).

77. W. Gareth Jones, "George Eliot's *Adam Bede* and Tolstoy's Conception of *Anna Karenina*," in *Tolstoi and Britain*, ed. W. Gareth Jones (Oxford, UK: Berg, 1995), 79–92. Jones argued that *Adam Bede* was seminal to *Anna Karenina*, with Hetty Sorrel as an important prototype for Anna Karenina. He notes a series of other parallels, in the depiction of Arthur Donnithorne and Vronsky, as well as in other thematic elements, such as the use of horses, dogs, and children.

78. Morson, *"Anna Karenina" in Our Time*, 174–75. Morson adds: "It would be hard to find a Gospel passage more in the spirit of this novel." Morson offers Dolly as the character who best embodies this Tolstoyan spirit of "proper charity."

79. Kitty had in fact earlier registered signs that something was awry: in regard to Kitty's own family, Mme. Stahl showed contempt that struck Kitty as being "contrary to Christian kindness" (2:33, 224). At that point, however, Kitty had been so taken with Varenka and the "serious spiritual upheaval" (2:33, 225) that she suppressed these indications that Mme. Stahl was not a true Christian.

80. For discussion, see David Herman, "Allowable Passions in *Anna Karenina*," *Tolstoy Studies Journal* 8 (1995–96).

81. Petrov's wife, Anna Pavlovna, begins to snub Kitty, who then regrets an earlier, innocent period when she and Anna Pavlovna had engaged in "secret confabulations about the invalid" and when the youngest Petrov boy called her "my Kitty" and refused to go to bed without her there. Kitty is forced to examine her recent interactions with Petrov—she focuses guiltily on his tender and too profuse thanks when she handed him a lap rug and, perhaps more significantly, on a portrait that he painted of her. She then admits to her horror that Petrov's wife's anger results from jealousy (2:33, 226–27).

82. In one passage, which Tolstoy crossed out of the drafts, Kitty muses— guiltily—about how Petrov told her that it was only since knowing her that he had come to understand a painting of the Madonna (20:242). The effect here is to taint the image of the Madonna with misplaced erotic feelings. In contrast, in Eliot's world of *Middlemarch*, Dorothea inspires admiration in men without sex rearing its ugly head to spoil her good works. Lydgate is inspired to compare her to the Madonna in the presence of his wife: "This young creature has a heart large enough for the Virgin Mary. . . . She seems to have what I never saw in any woman before—a fountain of friendship towards men—a man can make a friend of her" (76, 768–69). Even though Rosamond shows annoyance at her husband's admiration, which she takes as criticism of herself, the sexual threat is contained.

83. An 1844 English treatise on governesses ("Hints on the Modern Governess System," *Fraser's Magazine for Town and Country* 30, no. 179 [November 1844]: 574) describes governesses in a way that is close to that of Tolstoy's "sterile flower": "They spring up suddenly in premature development, like plants in a hot-house,—old in heart, aged in appearance, before the bloom, of youth is brushed from their years, drawn upwards by the insufferable light, from which, in their glasshouses, there is no shelter. It is no exaggeration to

say that hundreds snap yearly from the stalk, or prolong a withered, sickly life, till they, too, sink, and are carried out to die miserably in the by-ways of the world." For discussion, see Mary Poovey, *Uneven Developments: The Ideological Work of Gender in Mid-Victorian England* (Chicago: University of Chicago Press, 1988), 130.

For discussion of Tolstoy's treatment of the sterile flower [пустосвет], the term used for Sonya in *War and Peace* as well as for Varenka, see Svetlana Grenier, *Representing the Marginal Woman in Nineteenth-Century Russian Literature: Personalism, Feminism, and Polyphony* (Westport, CT: Greenwood Press, 2001).

84. Marcus, *Between Women*, 85.

85. As the two sisters nursed the Oblonsky children, Turovtsyn, a family friend, visited, took pity on Dolly, and pitched in to help, staying for three weeks (this fact is reported by Kitty to Levin after the fact, 4:11, 390). But, in a predictable Tolstoyan twist (that reinforces the "moral" Tolstoy sets up in Soden as sex pollutes Kitty's attempt at being a sister of mercy outside her family), when Dolly fantasizes on her way to Anna's in Part 6 about having an affair of her own, Turovtsyn figures as her modal lover (6:16, 608). This scenario suggests that Dolly was moved by his kindness as he helped nurse the children, but also implies that their intimate, if innocent, contact could be a breeding ground for sexual feeling. Again we see Tolstoy's presumption that sexual feelings take over whenever any man and woman come into contact with each other, whether over sickbed or chamber music.

86. For discussion of the importance of self-interest—and passion—in *Anna Karenina*, see Herman, "Allowable Passions," who notes the many different spheres in which self-interest proves to be a motivating force, from Levin's plan for labor reform, to Kitty's failure in Soden, to Anna's rationale for why she is not interested in peasant schools.

87. In the drafts of the novel, Levin (in the vein of Nekhliudov in "Landowner's Morning"), as he mused about his future married life, imagined that his wife would do (English-style) charity work in the village, work in the school, help the poor, and concern herself with a maternity ward—only to find that his wife did not like "philanthropy." "When she found herself with the people and her heart spoke to her directly, then she helped and was concerned" (20:610). In the final novel Levin does not envision Kitty's involvement in philanthropic activities. In Levin's meeting with Anna Karenina in Part 7, Anna herself speaks up about needing her heart to speak to her directly in order to get involved in charity work. As she explains, she cares for Hannah, the daughter of the English groom, because she feels a connection to her, but she cannot feel that for a whole classroom of pupils and so did not, as Vronsky urged her, get involved in peasant schools (7:10, 699–700).

88. Tolstoy makes it clear in Part 8 that Levin believes that it is his duty to preserve for his son the patrimony that he inherited; thus, any faith he finds will have to allow him to feel justified in keeping Pokrovskoe intact and making it profitable, albeit without *increasing* the economic disparity on which it is predicated. Whereas Levin justifies preserving his patrimony, in Tikhon of Zadonsk's *True Christianity* (1776), a text often cited as an expression of the Orthodox commitment to the second gospel commandment, Tikhon addresses

directly the question of whether it is necessary to preserve patrimony for one's children and concludes that saving one's soul is more important than providing for one's children; thus, in some cases, according to Tikhon, parents should give what they have to the poor rather than hoard it for their children.

Even when he wrote *Anna Karenina*, Tolstoy had inklings of the vision he sets forth in "How Much Land Does a Man Need." When *Anna Karenina* is read with knowledge of what was to come in Tolstoy's life and works, questions arise about the extent to which Tolstoy at the time of composition saw through the comforting solution that his fictional hero Levin finds. Even in the novel as it is written and without appeal to Tolstoy's later biography, Levin's solutions feel tenuous due to the anxious questioning that navigating the double plot requires of the reader.

89. "In my heart I wish for nothing except that you shouldn't stumble now. [Kitty is pregnant with their child.] But when I compare myself with others, especially with my brother [Koznyshev], I feel that I'm bad" (6:3, 560).

90. Tolstoi, *Chetveroevangelie*, 473.

91. In one of the echoes across plotlines, Vronsky made an analogous sacrifice for a sibling: when his brother married, Vronsky had let him keep some of his share of the income from their joint inheritance from their father. Tolstoy thus challenges the reader to make sense of the discrepancies. How is Levin's act different from Vronsky's?

92. At some points in the early drafts, when Anna first appears in the novel, she is reported to be under the influence of Lydia Ivanovna's sanctimonious piety. In the published novel, Tolstoy eliminated signs of this with the exception of Dolly thinking to herself, right as Anna arrives, "As long as she doesn't try to console me! . . . All these consolations and exhortations and Christian forgivenesses—I've already thought of it all a thousand times, and it's no good" (1:19, 66). Anna's query at the train station about whether anything can be done for the widow and children of the man who has just died might have had a different valence if Anna had retained the qualities first ascribed to her in drafts. In one draft of the scene at the train station, when Oblonsky starts to praise his sister, the narrator reveals that Vronsky especially disliked Anna's circle, which is described as having been "a very powerful circle, led by Karenin" and that Vronsky "for fun" called "warped in a refined-Khomyakovesque-Orthodox-feminine-court-Slavophile philanthropic manner" (20:143). Although Tolstoy is describing the social milieu—high society—where Radstock would have an impact, at this stage in the drafts the religious perversion described is not yet Radstockist. The Slavophile and Orthodox Khomyakov, however, had imagined a rapprochement between Orthodoxy and Anglicanism (which would have then been in league against Roman Catholicism).

93. In a draft of the inner monologue on the day of her death, a desperate Anna asks herself why she is not able to heed her maid Annushka's advice to pray to God for help. Anna recalls that whereas she used to pray to God "like a child," Karenin and Lydia Ivanovna "had destroyed her childlike relation to prayer." At the time, she had "tried to enter into their spirit, but could not." Next Anna recalls that the process of losing her faith, which began under the influence of Karenin and Lydia Ivanovna, became more complete as she read and

discussed Renan with Vronsky and Oblonsky, which caused her to reject religion as deception (20:546–47). Thus, Tolstoy shows that Anna suffered from her exposure to different currents, each of which threatened the traditional Orthodox faith that had sustained her before. Presumably, Anna refers here to the piety of Countess Lydia and Karenin in its earlier "refined-Khomyakovesque-Orthodox-feminine-court-Slavophile philanthropic" iteration, before they fell under the spell of Radstock or Landau. But Tolstoy was wary of both, as he was of Ernest Renan's scholarly and historical approach in his popular *Life of Jesus* (1863). As Hugh McLean explains in his study "Tolstoy and Jesus" (*In Quest of Tolstoy*, 118–29), Tolstoy was interested *neither* in the historical Jesus, *nor* in the divinity of Jesus and his role as savior, but rather in enacting what Jesus preached in the Sermon on the Mount. McLean cites the following lines spoken by Tolstoy (recorded in the memoirs of a tutor in the Tolstoy household): "What interest is there in knowing that Christ went out to relieve himself? What do I care that he was resurrected? So he was resurrected—so what! Good for him. For me the important question is what am I to do, how am I to live?" (cited in McLean, 123).

94. Turner (*Karenina Companion*, 179) observes that these titles, which Tolstoy probably made up, suggest that salvation is assured.

95. L. N. Tolstoi to A. A. Tolstaia, 20–23 March 1876, #253, 62:260–62. In this same letter, Tolstoy writes about his visit from Aleksei Pavlovich Bobrinsky: he "struck me very much with the sincerity and ardor of his faith. And nobody has ever spoken to me about faith better than Bobrinsky. He is irrefutable because he does not try to prove, but says only that he believes and you feel that he is happier than others who do not have his faith and you feel, above all, that the happiness of this faith cannot be obtained through mental effort, but has to be received as a miracle."

96. A. A. Tolstaia to L. N. Tolstoi, 28 March 1876, #94, in Lev Tolstoi, *Perepiska L. N. Tolstogo s gr. A. A. Tolstoi: 1857–1903* (St. Petersburg: Obshchestvo Tolstovskogo Muzeia, 1911), 266–69.

97. L. N. Tolstoi to A. A. Tolstaia, 15–17 April 1876, #259, 62:266.

98. As he wrote about the "new Christian doctrine that had lately spread in Petersburg," Tolstoy could have been using, in addition to what he learned from Bobrinsky and from Alexandrine Tolstoy, information about Radstock from other acquaintances and written sources, such as Dostoevsky's *Diary of a Writer* piece of March 1876 and Leskov's *Schism in High Society*, which was published serially in *Pravoslavnoe obozrenie* in September 1876, October 1876, and February 1877. Even if Tolstoy did not actually read these works himself, he could have heard about them from visitors such as Nikolai Strakhov. Countess Lydia Ivanovna's "conversion" of Karenin appeared in December 1876; Oblonsky's encounters and debates with Karenin and Lydia Ivanovna (in Part 7) appeared in April 1877.

99. Turner (*Karenina Companion*, 178) notes that there is a possible reference in Karenin's line "But I may have promised what I had no right to promise" to Radstock's stand against divorce. At this point, Oblonsky has been reminding Karenin that he had earlier promised a divorce and is now going back on his word (which Karenin gave before he was exposed to Radstock). Oblonsky

appeals to Christian feeling, to the spirit of forgiveness Karenin had felt earlier, and to the fact that "in Christian societies, and even in ours as far as I know, divorce is permitted. . . . Divorce is also permitted by our Church" (7:18, 725). But Karenin hesitates. He is under the influence of his new piety. In *Schism in High Society*, Leskov explains that Radstock did not believe in divorce. Leskov (69) even notes that whereas divorce is sometimes granted "on account of adultery," Radstock held that "freedom in Christian love cannot allow a man of Christian convictions to expose a woman in shameful sin."

100. Leskov chides Radstock for taking his doctrine of "salvation by faith" too far and he reports that some people wondered whether Radstock "has lost from his copy of the Bible the second chapter of the Epistle of James" (*Schism*, 56). However, while Radstock may have preached a doctrine of salvation by faith, he himself and his followers were known for their works of Christian charity.

101. As Heier (*Religious Schism*, 91–92) points out, "the *sola fide* teaching of Radstock had no place in [Tolstoy's] religious system."

102. A. A. Tolstaia to L. N. Tolstoi, 22 May 1877, #105, in Tolstoi, *Perepiska*, 284.

103. Heier, *Religious Schism*, 90–91.

104. In the drafts of the episode in Soden, Tolstoy used Prince Shcherbatsky as the voice of Orthodoxy to remind Kitty that the neighborly love she practiced was not the essence of Christianity and that "у нас" [in our Russian realm], at home in Russia, other things—like going to monasteries—were done to save our souls. In the episodes showing "adherents of that new interpretation of Christian doctrine that had lately spread in Petersburg" to its elite, Tolstoy shows Lydia Ivanovna denigrating the Russian way when she dismisses as "wild notions of our monks" the idea that you should "labor for God" or "save your soul by works, by fasting." In drafts, Tolstoy made more explicit what was wrong with this doctrine by identifying what it deviated from—namely, the piety of the Russian folk. What did the Russian folk believe? That you gain salvation through "imitation of Christ" and "by acts of love and of selflessness" (20:432). As Levin's conversation with the muzhik at the end of Part 8 suggests, living out the Christian idea that Tolstoy associates with the Russian folk differs from the English motto that inspired Miss Flora Sulivan and her successor Varenka: "do all the good you can, particularly to your poor, sick neighbor."

105. See Barbara Lönnqvist ("The Role of the Serbian War in *Anna Karenina*," *Tolstoy Studies Journal* 17 [2005]: 35–42) on how the politics of this war play into Tolstoy's concerns. Lönnqvist reports that after M. N. Katkov refused to publish the last part in *The Russian Herald*, the journal in which the novel appeared serially, because of Tolstoy's (or Levin's) stand on the war, Tolstoy reworked the text to make his critique even more pointed.

106. A disproportionate number of the supporters and fighters in the war effort have no families and/or aberrant sex lives: Koznyshev, Vronsky, Yashvin, Mme. Stahl, and Countess Lydia fit this category; that the recently married Veslovsky is off to war is the exception that proves the rule. (He had no business getting married in the first place.)

107. These Slavs are still not, however, simply random strangers in the spirit of the parable of the loving Samaritan (in which Jesus pointedly shows a Samaritan feeling compassion for a Jew, with whom he has no ethnic kinship). Tolstoy offers many indications that he found appeals to Slavic brotherhood to be empty rhetoric. When Koznyshev suggests that compassion for neighbors is what drives these men to war, he operates with an answer to the question "who is my neighbor?" that is very different from that of Levin, for whom neighbor is all but synonymous with family.

108. Freud, *Civilization and Its Discontents*, 100–101.

109. In her illuminating analysis of Mitya recognizing his own people in the bath scene, Kovarsky ("Moral Education of the Reader," 170–71) writes that "Tolstoy has just been representing the deepening understanding in Levin of the way love binds him to other human beings, and in this context the child's recognition of family members carries special meaning. On a metaphoric plane, to recognize one's own people means of course to perceive oneself as connected to the human family. . . . At the same time, the vignette offers a somewhat disturbing commentary on the perils of constructing a community based on facile notions of identity. After all, society excludes Anna from its midst in part because she fails to conform to its norms." For discussion of how the Tolstoyan family defines itself by excluding others, see Anne Hruska, "Infected Families: Belonging and Exclusion in the Works of Leo Tolstoy" (Ph.D. dissertation, University of California, Berkeley, 2001).

110. Leskov wrote about this exchange in 1886 in "O kufel'nom muzhike i proch. Zametki po povodu nekotorykh otzyvov o L. Tolstom," *Sobranie sochinenii v odinnadtsati tomakh*, ed. V. G. Bazanov et al., vol. 11 (Moscow: Khudozhestvennaia literatura, 1958), 134–56. According to Leskov's reports on Dostoevsky's arguments with the Radstockist Zasetskaia, Dostoevsky was never able to answer when she challenged him to say why Russians' faith was better than anyone else's. At one point, Dostoevsky reportedly told her just to go ask the muzhik in the kitchen. This exchange about the "muzhik in the kitchen" dates to the winter of 1875–76. According to Leskov, Dostoevsky's remark about "the muzhik in the kitchen" was a topic of debate in society circles and was known to many. (For discussion, see Malcolm Jones, "Dostoevskii and Radstockism.")

At the end of *Anna Karenina*, Levin finds his equivalent of Dostoevsky's "muzhik in the kitchen" in the form of the muzhik Fyodor who tells him the truth about living for the soul and living for the belly. This is not to say that Tolstoy necessarily had Dostoevsky's "muzhik in the kitchen" in mind, although it is conceivable that Dostoevsky's response to Zasetskaia was familiar to him since Leskov claims that it was the talk of the town that season. It shows, at the least, that both writers were (each in his own way) attempting to arrive at a muzhik-inspired iteration of Russian piety and that on a subliminal level this was a response to Radstockism and all it represented. Dostoevsky later takes Tolstoy to task, in *Diary of a Writer*, for setting it up so that Levin "gets faith from a muzhik." Dostoevsky did not find Tolstoy's apotheosis of the faith of the Russian folk adequate. According to Leskov in "O kufel'nom muzhike i proch.," Tolstoy later answered the question about what the elite has to learn from the "peasant in the kitchen" in "The Death of Ivan Ilych," where the peasant Gerasim shows how to behave in the face of death.

111. Levin opposes love of neighbor to Darwinian struggle for survival. For this discussion, see chapter 3.

112. For discussion of this scene, see Caryl Emerson, "Tolstoy versus Dostoevsky and Bakhtin's Ethics of the Classroom," in *Approaches*, ed. Knapp and Mandelker, 114–15.

113. Fyodor's parable-like illustration of the essence of godliness (and neighborly love) differs from what Tikhon Zadonskii presents in his *True Christianity* (1776). Tikhon, in the spirit of the parable of the Samaritan, reminds his readers that strangers *are* still your neighbors. And he refers to gospel-inspired notions of sharing one's wealth with those in need.

114. "Imbibed with his milk" [всосал с молоком] (8:12, 797) is a figure of speech, and yet it may be significant that the physical milk Levin imbibed as a babe came from the breast of a peasant wet nurse and not from his mother. (Tolstoy specifically tells us that Levin's sentiments for the peasants, which are like a blood-tie, were "probably as he [Levin] said, sucked in with the milk of his peasant nurse" [3:1, 237].)

115. L. N. Tolstoi to A. A. Tolstaia, 12 June 1859, #26, 60:300.

116. In letters written in the spring of 1859 Tolstoy had described to Alexandrine Tolstoy his failed attempts to renew his faith. He turned to the gospels but "found little" there at that point (L. N. Tolstoi to A. A. Tolstaia, 3 May 1859, #135, 60:293).

117. In later autobiographical and programmatic works, such as his *Confession*, Tolstoy holds that commitment to Christianity (as he understood it) required renouncing the "life of [his] class." At one point he would even criticize Radstockists for clinging too much to their privileged way of life.

118. J. Hillis Miller, *Reading for Our Time: "Adam Bede" and "Middlemarch" Revisited* (Edinburgh: Edinburgh University Press, 2012), 32–33.

119. And, in what would have been her last hours—had her sentence not been commuted to "transport o'er the seas" to Australia, thanks to the intercession of Donnisthorne (48, 509)—Dinah was, as she herself put it, Hetty's "sister to the last" (45, 493). By contrast, Tolstoy's Dolly fails to be Anna's "sister to the last."

Chapter 5. The Eternal Silence of Infinite Spaces

This discussion of Pascal and Tolstoy has its origins in my article *"Tue-la! Tue-le!:* Death Sentences, Words, and Inner Monologue in Tolstoy's *Anna Karenina* and *Three More Deaths,"* *Tolstoy Studies Journal* 11 (1999), and a lecture, "The Eternal Silence of Infinite Space in *Anna Karenina;* Tolstoy and Pascal," Yale University, May 2000.

1. B. N. Tarasov reports that Tolstoy's library contained two editions of Pascal's *Pensées*, the 1850 Didot edition and the 1858 Louandre edition. Tarasov believes that Tolstoy's marginalia in the Didot edition (reproduced in *Biblioteka L'va Nikolaevicha Tolstogo v Iasnoi Poliane* [vol. 3, pt. 2, 154–62]) are from Tolstoy's later reading(s). Judging from the marginalia in the Louandre edition in the

Tolstoy museum in Moscow, Tarasov considers this to be the one Tolstoy read "at the beginning or in the height of his religious searchings," in other words, at the time he was writing *Anna Karenina*. See B. N. Tarasov, *"Mysliashchii trostnik": Zhizn' i tvorchestvo Paskalia v vospriatii russkikh filosofov i pisatelei*, 2nd ed. (Moscow: Iazyki Slavianskikh Kul'tur, 2009), 559–60.

That Tolstoy specifically offered to send P. N. Svistunov the Louandre edition in his letter of 19 May 1878 (62:421) further supports Tarasov's view that Tolstoy would have been reading the Louandre edition as he was finishing *Anna Karenina*.

2. L. N. Tolstoi to F. A. Zakhar'in, 1–20 April 1877, #25, 62:321; the commentary on this letter suggests that what Tolstoy read was a collection of Khomyakov's poetry, but N. N. Gusev reports that it was a volume of theological works (*Letopis' zhizni i tvorchestva L'va Nikolaevicha Tolstogo, 1828–1890* [Moscow: Khudozhestvennaia literatura, 1958], 472). C. J. G. Turner points out Tolstoy does seem to have read Khomyakov's "Essay in Catechetic Exposition of the Doctrine of the Church: the Church Is One" (*A Karenina Companion* [Waterloo, Ontario: Wilfrid Laurier University Press, 1993], 188–89).

In the drafts, Levin's reasons for being dissatisfied with Khomyakov are made more explicit: "the polemic and the exclusivity" of the Church "alienated him" to the point where he was unable to believe (20:563). In the final version of the novel, Levin's disappointment in Khomyakov set in after he read church histories by a Catholic writer and by an Orthodox writer and objected to their respective claims to absolute truth and rejection of other truths. This concern with the claims set forth by Orthodoxy (and other creeds) to a monopoly on salvation will continue to eat away at Levin until the bitter end of *Anna Karenina*, when he is disturbed at the idea that God would deny happiness and salvation to the non-Orthodox faithful.

3. L. N. Tolstoi to A. A. Tolstaia, 20–23 March 1876, #253, 62:261. In letters to Alexandrine during this period, after a gap in their correspondence, Tolstoy communicated family news—namely, the deaths of three of Tolstoy's children and his aunt—but, falling back into a pattern set in the late 1850s, he also confided about matters of faith. In fact, his recommendation of Pascal in the letter of 1876 is reminiscent of his recommendation of George Eliot's *Scenes of Clerical Life* in 1859. Tolstoy praised the "evangelical Protestantism" that she depicts in "Janet's Repentance" as a pure expression of the Christian idea. He acknowledged that it was not necessarily for him, personally, but reveals his own longing for faith on his own terms, not to mention his interest in how to work this kind of material into a novel.

4. L. N. Tolstoi to A. A. Tolstaia, 20–23 March 1876, #253, 62:262. Tolstoy's response to this visit and to Radstockism is discussed in chapter 4.

5. The doubting Tolstoy fits T. S. Eliot's profile of Pascal's ideal reader: in Eliot's view, there is "no Christian writer . . . more to be commended than Pascal to those who doubt, but who have the mind to conceive, and the sensibility to feel, the disorder, the futility, the meaninglessness, the mystery of life and suffering, and who can only find peace through a satisfaction of the whole being" (T. S. Eliot, "Introduction," *Pascal's Pensées* [New York: E. P. Dutton, 1958], xix).

6. A. A. Tolstaia to L. N. Tolstoi, 28 March 1876, #94, in Lev Tolstoi, *Perepiska L. N. Tolstogo s gr. A. A. Tolstoi: 1857–1903* (St. Petersburg: Obshchestvo Tolstovskogo Muzeia, 1911), 267–68.

7. Sergei Gessen ("L. N. Tolstoi kak myslitel'," repr. in *Izbrannye sochineniia* [Moscow: Rosspen, 1999]) argues that, ultimately, Tolstoy found Pascal's faith incompatible: Tolstoy could not embrace the God of Abraham and Isaac and perhaps felt *more* comfortable with the God of the philosophers (famously rejected by Pascal in preference for the former). Tolstoy's Jesus was also very different from that of Pascal.

Galina Strel'tsova (*Paskal' i evropeiskaia kul'tura* [Moscow: Respublika, 1994]) and B. N. Tarasov ("*Mysliashchii trostnik*") focus largely on Tolstoy's responses to Pascal after *Anna Karenina*. Both note that Pascal figures prominently in the works that Tolstoy compiled and published. Further, Strel'tsova discusses in some detail Pascal's influence on the post-*Anna Karenina* Tolstoy, especially the *Confession*. Tarasov discusses the Pascalian echoes in "Death of Ivan Ilych."

On the relevance of Pascal to *Anna Karenina*, see also Donna Orwin (*Tolstoy's Art and Thought, 1847–1880* [Princeton, NJ: Princeton University Press, 1993]), C. J. G. Turner (*Karenina Companion*, 118; 183), and Gina Kovarsky ("Rhetoric, Metapoesis, and Moral Instruction in Tolstoy's Fiction: *Childhood, Boyhood, Youth, War and Peace*, and *Anna Karenina*" [Ph.D. dissertation, Columbia University, 1998]; "Signs of Life: Moral and Aesthetic Education in Tolstoy's Fiction" [Ph.D. dissertation draft, Columbia University, 1998]).

8. L. N. Tolstoi to A. A. Fet, 13–14 April 1877, #324, 62:320. N. N. Gusev reports that Tolstoy's wife announced in a letter of 15 April 1877 to her sister that Tolstoy was writing the epilogue (*Letopis' zhizni i tvorchestva*, 472). Turgenev had already proselytized about Pascal to Fet back in 1864 (Strel'tsova, *Paskal'*, 327).

9. L. N. Tolstoi to S. A. Rachinskii, 6 April 1878, #417, 62:404.

10. L. N. Tolstoi to P. N. Svistunov, 19 May 1878, #431, 62:420–21. Svistunov, a Decembrist, had asked Tolstoy to read P. S. Bobrishchev-Pushkin's translation of Pascal. Tolstoy advised against publication on the grounds that the translation itself was wanting and that it was not based on the more complete Louandre edition. Tolstoy told Svistunov that he would gladly lend him the Louandre edition of Pascal but that at present he could not bear to take the book away from his son.

11. This is not to say that these philosophers did not have an impact on *Anna Karenina*. For comprehensive discussion, see Boris M. Eikhenbaum (*Lev Tolstoi: Semidesiatye gody* [Leningrad: Khudozhestvennaia literatura, 1974]), Richard Gustafson (*Leo Tolstoy, Resident and Stranger: A Study in Fiction and Theology* [Princeton, NJ: Princeton University Press, 1986]), Donna Tussing Orwin (*Tolstoy's Art and Thought*), and Inessa Medzhibovskaya (*Tolstoy and the Religious Culture of His Time: A Biography of a Long Conversion, 1845–1887* [Lanham, MD: Lexington Books, 2009]). On Schopenhauer, see Sigrid McLaughlin, "Some Aspects of Tolstoy's Intellectual Development: Tolstoy and Schopenhauer," *California Slavic Studies* 5 (1970); on Kant, see Gary R. Jahn, "Tolstoj and Kant," *New Perspectives on Nineteenth-Century Russian Prose*, ed. George J. Gutsche and Lauren G. Leighton (Columbus, OH: Slavica, 1982), 60–70. Also absent from

Levin's reading list is Rousseau, who was a very important influence on Tolstoy, especially in his youth.

12.   When Pascal died, he left behind what are known as his *Pensées*, notes for a work on the Christian religion, some of which he started to order. Pascal's readers have been left to envision how the fragments would have been shaped into a narrative. Ben Rogers noted that while it is often said that Pascal was preparing an "apology" for the Christian religion, Pascal did not use this word, which "can have misleading implications if it encourages the view that he was aiming to 'prove' the truth in Christianity; Pascal believed that where religion was concerned, you had to believe it, to see it" ("Pascal's Life and Times," in *The Cambridge Companion to Pascal*, ed. Nicholas Hammond [Cambridge, UK: Cambridge University Press, 2003]), 19. There is a range of opinion among Pascal scholars about the shape and form that Pascal's work would have taken (how much of a structured "apology" it would have been) and the degree to which it would have retained the poetics associated with the fragment.

13.   Pascal writes: "Je ne peux approuver que ceux qui cherchent en gémissant" (L405/S24). After citations from Pascal, I give the fragment numbers from the Lafuma (L) and Sellier (S) editions in parentheses. For the modern French version, I used the online edition: http://www.penseesdepascal.fr/index.php. English translations (unless otherwise indicated) are those of Roger Ariew, with modifications, as published in Blaise Pascal, *Pensées* (Indianapolis, IN: Hackett, 2004).

14.   I draw on the discussion of death and language in Tolstoy's works set forth in my articles "Language and Death in Tolstoy's Childhood and Boyhood: Rousseau and the Holy Fool," *Tolstoy Studies Journal* 10 (1998) and *"Tue-la! Tue-le!"*

15.   Vygotsky uses the verbal intercourse between Kitty and Levin, especially their second proposal scene, to illustrate the condensation and abbreviation of external speech that goes with familiarity and heightened understanding. See Lev Vygotsky, *Thought and Language*, trans. and ed. Alex Kozulin (Cambridge, MA: MIT Press, 1997), 237–39. While this may true, it seems that Tolstoy suggests that *even* between two people who share this kind of discourse and familiarity, there are abysses that words cannot span.

16.   On language in *Anna Karenina*, see Justin Weir, "Anna Incommunicada," in his *Leo Tolstoy and the Alibi of Narrative* (New Haven, CT: Yale University Press, 2011), 135–146; Gina Kovarsky, "Mimesis and Moral Education in *Anna Karenina*," *Tolstoy Studies Journal* 8 (1995–96); Malcolm Jones, "Problems of Communication in *Anna Karenina*," in *Essays on Tolstoy*, ed. Malcolm V. Jones and R. F. Christian (Cambridge, UK: Cambridge University Press, 1978).

17.   Tolstoy here draws attention to how Anna's actions have radically altered her relation to self, to other, to religion, to God, and to language. The first-person possessive pronoun fails to signify because her identity has been shaken and likewise the word "God" no longer appears to have a clear reference. Tolstoy here extends the Rousseauean view of language as a social contract, where the meaning of words depends on the conventions of the community of bearers of this language. Anna, having spiritually distanced herself from this community, finds that she can no longer depend on *its* language. However, according

to Pascal (as will be seen below), all fallen human beings have lost the means of direct, transcendent communication with God: Anna's status as fallen woman may simply make more acute this feature of the human condition.

18. Weir, *Leo Tolstoy and the Alibi of Narrative*, 135–46.

19. "L'homme est déchu d'un état de gloire et de communication avec Dieu en un état de tristesse, de pénitence et d'éloignement de Dieu" (L281/S313).

20. Vlad Alexandrescu attributes to Pascal a "mistrust in regard to the capacity of language for expressing truth" (*Le paradoxe chez Blaise Pascal* [Berne: Peter Lang, 1996], 229), and François Paré explains that in Pascal's view "the distance separating thought and truth" is "incommensurable" ("Temps et digression dans les *Pensées* de Pascal," *Études françaises* 37, no. 1 [2001]: 70).

21. Pascal writes, in the translation of Nicholas Hammond ("Pascal's *Pensées* and the Art of Persuasion," in *Cambridge Companion to Pascal*, ed. Hammond, 251): "In God word and intention do not differ, for He is truthful, nor do word and effect, for he is mighty, nor do means and effect, for he is wise." [En Dieu la parole ne diffère pas de l'intention car il est véritable, ni la parole de l'effet car il est puissant, ni les moyens de l'effet car il est sage] (L968/S416).

22. Nicholas Hammond, *Playing with Truth: Language and the Human Condition in Pascal's "Pensées"* (Oxford, UK: Clarendon Press, 1994), 33.

23. Virginia Woolf, "The Russian Point of View" (1923–25), in *The Common Reader, First Series*, ed. Andrew McNeillie (San Diego: Harcourt Brace Jovanovich, 1984), 182.

24. Orwin, *Tolstoy's Art and Thought, 1847–1880* (Princeton, NJ: Princeton University Press, 1993), 156–60.

25. Phillipe Sellier, "L'ouverture de l'apologie pascalienne," translated and quoted in David Wetsel, *Pascal and Disbelief: Catechesis and Conversion in the "Pensées"* (Washington, DC: Catholic University of America Press, 1994), 26–27.

26. See McLaughlin, "Tolstoy and Schopenhauer," on the "eternal cycle of life and death" in *Anna Karenina*.

27. See Blaise Pascal, *Pensées de Pascal: Publiées dans leur texte authentique avec une introduction, des notes et des remarques par Ernest Havet*, vol. 1 (Paris: Librairie Ch. Delagrave, 1866), 202. Havet's comment was prompted by Pascal's fragment about dying alone and the need to act as if we are alone because only then is it possible to "seek the truth without hesitating" (L151/S184).

28. "He could not now be repentant that he, a thirty-four-year-old, handsome, amorous man, did not feel amorous with his wife, the mother of five living and two dead children, who was only a year younger than he" (1:2, 3). Oblonsky's appeal to these "reflexes of the brain" has been taken as a reference to the work of the Russian I. S. Sechenov: "'Reflexes of the brain,' thought Stepan Arkadyich, who liked physiology" (1:1, 3). "At the same time, Stepan Arkadyich, who liked a merry joke, sometimes took pleasure in startling some simple soul by saying that if you want to pride yourself on your lineage, why stop at Rurik and renounce your first progenitor—the ape? And so the liberal tendency became a habit with Stepan Arkadyich" (1:3, 7).

29. Much as Pascal addresses the question of whether the body is a "machine" (a topic of interest to Descartes, who rabidly declared animals to be

nothing more than machines), Tolstoy refers to the discourse by his contemporary Sechenov and others on "reflexes of the brain."

30. As Henry Phillips explains, what Pascal found absurd in Descartes was the latter's claims that "philosophers are better at demonstrating matters of God and the soul than theologians" ("The Inheritance of Montaigne and Descartes," in *The Cambridge Companion to Pascal*, ed. Hammond, 34).

31. Turner (*Karenina Companion*, 183) notes that Levin's lines echo both Bazarov and Pascal. Another common source for this (universal) concern with dying without leaving a trace could be Gogol's *Dead Souls*: when Chichikov escapes from Nozdryov's (opening of chapter 5), he expresses his anxieties about the precariousness of life as follows: "It might well have been my fate to look on God's world no longer. I would have disappeared like a bubble on the water, with no trace at all, leaving no descendants, bequeathing neither property nor an honest name to my future children!" (*Dead Souls*, trans. Robert Maguire [New York: Penguin, 2004]). Levin's immediate solution to his own fear of "disappearing like a bubble" from the eternal silence of infinite spaces that so terrifies him is more like Chichikov's than Bazarov's: Levin, too, focuses on acquiring descendants and property as a form of achieving a sensation of immortality. Ultimately, however, Levin is not satisfied with this material form of immortality. For discussion of Levin as Chichikov and *Anna Karenina* as haunted by *Dead Souls*, see chapter 1 of this study.

32. For discussion of Pascal's influence on the passage of *Fathers and Sons*, see Strel'tsova (*Paskal'*) and Tarasov ("*Mysliashchii trostnik*"), who differ somewhat in their views of how much metaphysical angst Bazarov experiences. Does he remain a nihilist materialist to the bitter end, or does he, perhaps, succumb to Pascalian terror even if he clearly stops short of embracing the faith of his parents that the narrator refers to at the very end? In her commentary on Bazarov's apparent echo of Pascal, Strel'tsova suggests that the nihilist Bazarov draws very un-Pascalian conclusions from this sense of man being caught between two infinities. Strel'tsova observes that Turgenev rejected a number of features of Pascal's thought, starting with his view of nature, and she suggests that Turgenev has Bazarov draw "unpascalian" conclusions from this echo of his fragment. Tarasov also notes that Turgenev was selective and critical as he engaged with Pascal. However, he takes into account the possible ambiguities in Bazarov's response. In regard to Bazarov, given how hard it is to determine the point of view of Pascal's fragments (when, for example, the "I" voices doubt, is it Pascal speaking or is he writing from the point of view of sinner or non-believer?), we might want simply to see Bazarov as a modern Russian variant of Pascal's protagonists. Although some of Pascal's fragments read individually could be used to confirm a strict materialist view of human life, when read in the context of other fragments about the horror at infinite spaces, they could put the "I" in a state of doubt and cosmic despair that primes him for a leap of faith or a wager. While Bazarov clings to his nihilism and scientism, one could perhaps detect in him yearning that his rational self and scientific views deny. Maybe, in fact, he, too, is subject to the terror Pascal describes, even if he is not yet ready to embrace the faith of his parents. For some readers, Bazarov's death suggests that life without love or without God is impossible.

33. See Sara Melzer, *Discourses of the Fall: A Study of Pascal's "Pensées"* (Berkeley: University of California Press, 1986), 57. "Reason's last step is to recognize that there are an infinite number of things that go beyond it. It is feeble only if it does not go so far as to realize this fact" (L188/S220; Melzer's translation). Pascal writes in another fragment: "There is nothing so consistent with reason as this denial of reason" (L182/S213).

34. Levin's comment on the philosophers' use of the "same words differently arranged" [те же перестановленные слова] recalls a comment made by Pascal that "Les mots diversement rangés font un divers sens. Et les sens diversement rangés font différents effets" [Words, differently arranged, have different meanings. And meanings different arranged have different effects] (L784/S645). See Lucien Goldmann, *Le Dieu caché; étude sur la vision tragique dans les Pensées de Pascal et dans le théâtre de Racine* (Paris: Gallimard, 1955 [1956]), 19.

35. Hammond, *Playing*, 228.

36. A. A. Tolstaia to L. N. Tolstoi, 28 March 1876, #94, in Tolstoi, *Perepiska*, 267–68.

37. L. N. Tolstoi to A. A. Tolstaia, 15–17 April 1876, #259, 62:266. As was discussed in the previous chapter, Tolstoy was leery of the reports that Radstock converted people in less than an hour. He wrote to Alexandrine Tolstoy of his own hard spiritual "work" as he attempted to find faith. In this respect, Pascal's model was much more kindred to Tolstoy himself. And it is what his Levin follows, even if there is the sudden illumination at the end.

38. Nikolai Chernyshevskii, "Detstvo i otrochestvo. Sochinenie grafa L. N. Tolstogo, SPb. 1856," in *Polnoe sobranie sochinenii* (Moscow: Ogiz, 1947), 3:425.

39. William Wood, *Blaise Pascal on Duplicity, Sin, and the Fall: The Secret Instinct* (Oxford, UK: Oxford University Press, 2013), 189.

40. Pascal refers to the whole universe as a *cachot* (dungeon; cell) in the following long fragment, which anticipates Levin's agonized search for meaning:

> Let man then contemplate the whole of nature in its lofty and full majesty, and let him avert his view from the lowly objects around him. Let him behold that brilliant light set like an eternal lamp to illuminate the universe. Let the earth seem to him like a point in comparison with the vast orbit described by that star. And let him be amazed that this vast orbit is itself but a very small point in comparison with the one described by the stars rolling around the firmament. But if our gaze stops here, let our imagination pass beyond. It will sooner tire of conceiving things than nature of producing them. This whole visible world is only the imperceptible trace in the amplitude of nature. No idea approaches it. However much we may inflate our conceptions beyond these imaginable spaces, we give birth only to atoms with respect to the reality of things. It is an infinite sphere whose center is everywhere and circumference nowhere. In the end, the greatest perceptible sign of God's omnipotence is that our imagination loses itself in this thought.

> Let man, returning to himself, consider what he is with respect to what exists. Let him regard himself as lost in this remote corner of nature, and from the little cell [cachot] in which he finds himself lodged, I mean the universe, let him learn to estimate the just value of the earth, kingdoms, cities, and himself.
> What is a man in the infinite? (L199/S230)

41. As Michael Moriarty ("Grace and Religious Belief in Pascal," in *Cambridge Companion to Pascal*, ed. Hammond, 144) observes, Pascal's assertions that faith is a "gift of God" and not "the result of a process of reasoning" raise questions about why one would need an apology for the Christian religion like the one that Pascal presents. But, Moriarty notes, Pascal anticipates and responds to these objections in the course of his work. In simple terms, Pascal's work can be part of the conditioning that will ready an unbeliever for what, ultimately, will be a gift of God.

42. Dostoevsky, *A Writer's Diary*, 1072; *PSS* 25:202.

43. And yet myths about the origins of the Milky Way remind the reader that family happiness is indeed precarious: the constellation was formed when Hera wrested the baby Hercules from her breast as he was sucking milk; she had been tricked into feeding her husband's love child. Thus, a reference to the Milky Way, which seems peaceful enough, has associations with various forms of family unhappiness in *Anna Karenina*, from the Oblonsky children who go without milk as the novel opens, to little Anna Karenina suffering until Karenin learns that her wet nurse does not have enough milk, to Kitty's consultation with her sister on how to breastfeed baby Mitya that Anna, desperate for Dolly's comfort, inadvertently interrupts.

44. Gustafson discusses these scenes in *War and Peace* (*Resident and Stranger*, 64–67, 76–81, 282). The excerpts from *War and Peace* are quoted in his translation (282).

45. Orwin, "From Nature to Culture in the 1870s," in *Tolstoy's Art*, 143–70 and esp. 161–63 on Pascal.

46. Eikhenbaum discusses Tolstoy's engagement in the poetry of Tyutchev and Fet as he wrote *Anna Karenina*. See *Lev Tolstoi: Semidesiatye gody*, 174–85. Pascal was a major influence on Tyutchev. See Tarasov, "*Mysliashchii trostnik*," 474–526.

47. Wetsel, *Pascal and Disbelief*, 336.

48. Again, as will be explained below, Pascal believed that those with "live faith in their hearts" will see signs of God's presence in nature; his point about "weak proofs" is that nature itself cannot be used to convince the seeker that God exists or to make him have faith.

49. Emmanuel Kant, *Critique of Practical Reason*, as quoted in Paul Guyer, "Introduction: The Starry Heavens and the Moral Law," in *Cambridge Companion to Kant*, ed. Paul Guyer (Cambridge, UK: Cambridge University Press, 1992), 1.

50. On Kant and Tolstoy, see E. N. Kupreianova, *Èstetika Tolstogo* (Moscow: Nauka, 1966), 106; Jahn, "Tolstoj and Kant"; and Orwin, *Tolstoy's Art and Thought*. There are different views on whether Tolstoy had read Kant at this time (since he claimed in 1887 *not* to have), but Orwin makes a convincing case for exposure in the 1870s (248).

51. Viacheslav Ivanov, "Sporady," in *Po zvezdam* (1909), 368; cited in Omry Ronen, *An Approach to Mandel'stam* (Jerusalem: Magnes Press, Hebrew University, 1983), 64.

52. Levin, however, makes no mention of Jesus's role in Christian Revelation. On the subject of Jesus Christ, Tolstoy's views diverge not only from those of Russian Orthodoxy, but also those of Pascal. Pascal writes that, according to the Scriptures, man after the Fall was left with no means of communicating with God (who was hidden) or of finding him other than through Jesus Christ (L781/S644).

53. Wetsel, *Pascal and Disbelief*, 380.

54. Melzer, *Discourses*, 113.

55. Orwin (*Tolstoy's Art and Thought*, 207) comments on the subjectivity of Levin's epiphany: "The stars reappear 'as if thrown by some accurate hand.' Thus, in a moment of heightened subjectivity, does God make a brief appearance in *Anna Karenina*, and thus, this time strictly confining himself to subjective intuition ('as if'), does Tolstoy again join real and ideal, reaffirming the existence of universal moral law, and the synthesis that alone gives meaning to human life. This synthesis does not contradict the dramatic nature of *Anna Karenina*. On the contrary, as I have argued, without it, and without moral law, there could be no inner drama of good and evil." See also her discussion of Tolstoy's "greater subjectivism" in the 1870s, although she is careful to point out the limits of this (208).

56. See Wetsel, *Pascal and Disbelief*, 279: "Christianity does teach, Pascal explains, that God has established 'des marques sensibles' ('visible signs') in Holy Revelation for the benefit of those who seek him. However, these signs have been veiled so that only those who seek God with all their hearts will find him."

57. The Louandre edition of Pascal, which Tolstoy read as he was writing *Anna Karenina*, reproduces this list in full, whereas the Didot edition (in the Yasnaya Polyana Library) has a truncated and edited version that omits the cabbages, leeks, calves, and serpents and includes the more general "crimes" instead of specifically naming adultery and incest.

58. The commentary on "divertissement" by Pascal scholars describes the rich associations of this word and its cognates for Pascal. See http://www.penseesdepascal.fr/Divertissement/Divertissement4-appro139.php.

59. David Wetsel, *L'Ecriture et le Reste: The "Pensées" of Pascal in the Exegetical Tradition of Port-Royal* (Columbus: Ohio State University Press, 1981), 118.

60. Wetsel, *L'Ecriture et le Reste*, 119.

61. As was discussed in chapter 1 of this study, the red handbag is the symbol of her pleasure-seeking.

62. Pascal writes (ironically, according to Pascal scholars) of man as machine, as when he notes that "we are as much automata as minds"; custom "inclines the automaton, which drags the mind unconsciously with it" (L821/S661). At another point, he writes of the need to "direct the machine" (ployer la machine) (L25/S59).

63. "To this effect the apologist advocates going through the external gestures of devotion, not in the hope that belief will come by a process of autosuggestion

but because the ritualistic gestures of worship are designed to express and there-fore to encourage an attitude to spiritual extraversion which is the opposite of amour-propre." Bernard Howells, "The Interpretation of Pascal's 'Pari,'" *Modern Language Review* 79, no. 1 (1984): 58.

64. Howells, "Interpretation," explains Pascal's view that this state of "spiri-tual extraversion" is necessary in order to turn to God.

65. Anna addresses the very God she had addressed earlier, only to have the narrator inform us that neither "my" nor "God" meant anything to her. The reader is left to decide whether her appeal to God just before death is another one of her meaningless statements or part of her tissue of lies, or whether Anna finally speaks from the heart and gets a message across, in direct language, to an addressee. (For discussion, see my *"Tue-la! Tue-le!,"* 8–9.)

66. As was discussed in chapter 4, Tolstoy indicates more directly in the drafts that Anna's innocent girlhood faith had possibly been compromised by her exposure to "angry" Christians like Countess Lydia and then, eventually, to reading Renan.

67. In the lore about Lord Radstock that circulated (see Leskov or the letter Tolstoy received from A. A. Tolstaia, 28 March 1876), he was said to be able to make a Christian out of someone in a half hour, with no apparent need to prepare the convert along the lines of "inclining the automat/machine." Alexandrine reported to Tolstoy that Radstock "often related incidents of this sort: '*I met with a French gentleman. He was a complete unbeliever. I spoke with him in the garden, we prayed together and he went away a Christian*'" (italicized text is in English in original).

68. This is not to say that Tolstoy embraces Pascal's God or Jesus; and Tol-stoy had a very different response to the Scriptures: whereas Pascal embraced the *apparent* contradictions in the Scriptures, suggesting that what the rational mind took as "digression" was in fact part of divine design, Tolstoy would set about reconciling the gospels and ridding them of contradiction. As C. J. G. Turner points out, Tolstoy did not share Pascal's understanding of miracles (*Karenina Companion*, 118).

69. In the *Pensées*, Pascal writes of the need to take contrary points of view into account: "Two contrary reasons. We must begin with that; otherwise we understand nothing and everything is heretical. And we must even add at the end of each truth that we are remembering the opposite truth" (L576/S479).

70. Sara Melzer argues that Pascal creates in the reader a desire for truth (and faith) that can only be found beyond text (see *Discourses*, esp. 8, 64–68, 142–45). She writes of Pascal's wariness about order and attempts to "impose order on inherently disorderly subject matter" and notes that Pascal "creates the desire for a transcendent order" by drawing attention to the limits of attempts to order what is inherently disorderly (66).

71. Nicholas Hammond has stressed the way Pascal thus engages his reader in an active role "in the persuasive framework": "Just as the existence of different speakers in the text achieves a more flexible and less dogmatic form of argumentation, so too does each individual reader seem to have greater autonomy in making sense of the text for him or herself. However carefully

crafted each argument may be, the coexistence of different viewpoints allows the reader to come to his or her own conclusions" ("Pascal's *Pensées* and the Art of Persuasion," 240).

72. As Caryl Emerson has argued, Tolstoy is not the "monologic" writer that Bakhtin once called him ("The Tolstoy Connection in Bakhtin," in Gary Saul Morson and Caryl Emerson, *Rethinking Bakhtin: Extensions and Challenges* [Evanston, IL: Northwestern University Press, 1989], 147–72).

73. David Parker (*Ethics, Theory and the Novel* [Cambridge, UK: Cambridge University Press, 1994], 107–25) argues that *Anna Karenina* acts on "our own ethical imaginations" in part through a process of overthrowing patterns of judgment and thought that depend on binary oppositions. Parker writes, "Levin, recollecting 'his own sins and the inner conflict he had lived through' (like the Pharisees in John 8), makes a connection between his experience and Oblonsky's that breaks down the simple judgmental binary pattern of his thinking, whose symbolic emphases have been shaped precisely by those actively forgotten feelings and experiences. And in that, Levin's expanded awareness points to the imaginative fullness of the scene itself: while so carefully defining the two men against each other, it never loses touch with what is common in their experience. For all that may be said about the Levin in Tolstoy, one of the most important strengths of the novel is the almost unfailing resistance it offers to any judgmental tendency in us to read its world as Levin first reads his experience, in terms of simple categorical oppositions. At the same time Levin's momentarily baffled 'But I don't know, I really don't know' goes close to the imaginative heart of *Anna Karenina*, since our own ethical imaginations are constantly being unbalanced and rebalanced by the very twists and turns of the lives in which they are so absorbed" (111). The "unbalancing" and "rebalancing" that Parker describes becomes especially critical when the action—and, above all, the reader's imagination—moves back and forth between the plots.

74. As some critics have noted, a reader familiar with Tolstoy's own spiritual and moral travails after *Anna Karenina* (and one who confuses the author's biography with the novel at hand) may read the ending of the novel more warily. While this is true, I have attempted to show that the novel itself—in large part because of its multiplot form—is unsettled and unsettling.

75. In this respect, Tolstoy engages us in a process like that of Jacque Derrida, as described by Mark Taylor: "Like Kant, Kierkegaard and Nietzsche, Mr. Derrida does argue that transparent truth and absolute values elude our grasp. This does not mean, however, that we must forsake the cognitive categories and moral principles without which we cannot live: equality and justice, generosity and friendship. Rather, it is necessary to recognize the unavoidable limitations and inherent contradictions in the ideas and norms that guide our actions, and do so in a way that keeps them open to constant questioning and continual revision. There can be no ethical action without critical reflection. . . . Mr. Derrida reminded us that religion does not always give clear meaning, purpose and certainty by providing secure foundations. To the contrary, the great religious traditions are profoundly disturbing because they all call certainty and security into question. Belief not tempered by doubt poses a mortal danger" ("What Derrida Really Meant," *New York Times*, October 14, 2004).

Chapter 6. Virginia Woolf and Leo Tolstoy on Double Plot and
the Misery of Our Neighbors

This chapter draws on "Virginia Woolf and the Russian Point of View," a lecture at Columbia College, Dean's Day, March 2007. A talk based on this chapter was given in November 2013 at the Convention of the Association for Slavic, East European, and Eurasian Studies in Boston.

1. Virginia Woolf, *Mrs. Dalloway* (New York: Harcourt, 1925). Page numbers in parentheses after citations refer to this edition.

2. Trudi Tate, "Mrs. Dalloway and the Armenian Question," in *Modernism, History, and the First World War* (Manchester, UK: Manchester University Press, 1998), 155–59.

3. Woolf, *The Letters of Virginia Woolf*, ed. Nigel Nicholson and Joanne Trautmann, 6 vols. (New York: Harcourt Brace Jovanovich, 1975–80), 8 January 1929, #1980, 4:4.

4. Woolf, "Modern Novels" (1919), in *The Essays of Virginia Woolf*, ed. Andrew McNeillie, 3 vols. (San Diego; New York; London: Harcourt Brace Jovanovich, 1989–91), 3:36.

5. Another important "model" that Woolf reacted to in *Mrs. Dalloway* was James Joyce's *Ulysses*, a city-specific, one-day, double-plot novel. On Woolf's reading of *Ulysses*, see Julia Briggs, *Virginia Woolf: An Inner Life* (New York: Harcourt, 2005), 72–73.

6. Woolf's famous remark that "character changed" appeared in "Character in Fiction" (1924; in *Essays*, 3:421). Woolf was aware that her pronouncement was going to baffle. Woolf's claim has set scholars speculating on what she had in mind, with one monograph after another, each offering a compelling interpretation of what happened on or about December 1910. A few examples are worth citing. In *Virginia Woolf and the Real World* (Berkeley: University of California Press, 1986), Alex Zwerdling explains that this date marks the advent of "a revolution of domestic order" with profound change to family structures, the social system, sexual mores, and human relationships for Virginia Stephen and her set. Holly Henry in *Virginia Woolf and the Discourse of Science: The Aesthetics of Astronomy* (Cambridge, UK: Cambridge University Press, 2003) argues that the discoveries of Einstein and others had a profound impact on Virginia Woolf's imagination and account for her claim that human character changed on or about December 1910: "new physics and new astronomical vistas of space" challenged old modes of perceptions and encouraged her to rethink the position of man in the universe and create a new kind of narrative with a new aesthetic. Ann Banfield in *The Phantom Table: Woolf, Frye, Russell, and the Epistemology of Modernism* (Cambridge, UK: Cambridge University Press, 2000) suggests that the change Virginia Woolf noted in human character dates from her introduction to the philosophy of Bertrand Russell and its "epistemology of Modernism." Peter Stansky in *On or About December 1910: Early Bloomsbury and Its Intimate World* (Cambridge, MA: Harvard University Press, 1996) recreates the period (in or around December) in Virginia Woolf's life to single out the particular impact of the first post-Impressionist exhibit organized by Roger Fry in November 1910. Finally, Roberta Rubenstein (*Virginia Woolf and the Russian Point of View* [New

York: Palgrave, 2009]) and Emily Dalgarno ("Tolstoy, Dostoevsky, and the Russian Soul," in *Virginia Woolf and the Migrations of Language* [Cambridge, UK: Cambridge University Press, 2012], 69–96) suggest that Woolf's discovery of the Russians brought about the "change" that occurred "on or about December 1910."

7. Woolf, *The Diary of Virginia Woolf* (New York: Harcourt Brace Jovanovich, 1977–84), ed. Anne Olivier Bell, 5:273, entry for Thursday, March 21, 1940.

8. Woolf, Letters, 25 December 1910, #546, 1:442.

9. Woolf writes about this question in both "The Russian Point of View" (1923–25; in *The Common Reader, First Series*, ed. Andrew McNeillie [San Diego: Harcourt Brace Jovanovich, 1984], 181–82), and in an earlier review entitled "Tolstoy's *The Cossacks*" (1917; in *Essays*, 2:76–79). In the latter she makes the suggestion that the question "Why live?" bothered Tolstoy himself until his dying day (78–79). Woolf writes: "Here, as everywhere, Tolstoy seems able to read the minds of different people as certainly as we count the buttons on their coats; but this feat never satisfies him; the knowledge is always passed through the brain of some Olenin or Pierre or Levin, who attempts to guess a further and more difficult riddle—the riddle which Tolstoy was still asking himself, we may be sure, when he died. And the fact that Tolstoy is thus seeking, that there is always in the centre of his stories some rather lonely figure to whom the surrounding world is never quite satisfactory, makes even his short stories unlike other short stories."

10. Woolf, *Letters*, 8 January 1929, #1980, 4:4. In her letter to Vita Sackville-West, Woolf writes (exaggerating the number of years gone by since she last read the novel; a set of reading notes on *Anna Karenina* is from 1926): "Practically every scene of *Anna Karenina* is branded in me, though I've not read it for 15 years. *That* is the origin of all our discontent. After that of course we had to break away. It wasn't Wells, or Galsworthy or any of our mediocre wishy washy realists: it was Tolstoy. How could we go on with sex and realism after that? How could they go on with poetic plays after Shakespeare? It is one brain, after all, literature; and it wants change and relief."

11. Rubenstein, *Virginia Woolf*, 97.

12. Dalgarno ("Tolstoy," 76) cites Robert Belknap's observation about the impact of nineteenth-century Russian novelists on modernist novelists in support of her point about Woolf's modernist adaptation of Tolstoy's double plot. For Belknap's comments, see his "Novelistic Technique," in *The Cambridge Companion to the Classic Russian Novel*, ed. Malcolm V. Jones and Robin Feuer Miller, 233–50 (Cambridge, UK: Cambridge University Press, 1998), 246.

13. Dalgarno, "Tolstoy," 75. Dalgarno also observes in regard to *Mrs. Dalloway* as it relates to *Anna Karenina* (76): "What might have been a novel about the domestic life of Clarissa Dalloway becomes by the addition of a second narrative a novel that problematizes the aftermath of World War I in the civilian population. The double plot averts moralizing by assigning the power of judgment not to the narrator but implicitly to the reader."

14. In the preface to the U.S. edition of *Mrs. Dalloway*, Woolf offered insight into the genesis of her double plot: "In the first version Septimus, who later is

intended to be her double, had no existence" ("An Introduction to Mrs. Dalloway," in The Mrs. Dalloway Reader, ed. Francine Prose [New York: Harcourt, 2003], 11).

But, back in 1902, Virginia Woolf had envisioned writing a (double-plot) play that contains the kernel of Mrs. Dalloway. Woolf wrote: "I'm going to have a man and a woman—show them growing up—never meeting—not knowing each other—but all the time you'll feel them come nearer and nearer. This will be the real exciting part" (Letters, October/November 1902, #57, 1:60, as reported by Briggs, Virginia Woolf, 130).

15. Briggs observes: "Relating events through the consciousness of individuals [as Woolf does in Mrs. Dalloway] provides fewer opportunities for the traditional voice of the narrator to pass judgement, and gives the reader greater freedom to judge, as in a play" (Virginia Woolf, 134). Briggs's comments on how Woolf's narrative techniques place the burden of interpretation on the reader recall those that circulate about Anna Karenina.

16. That Anna Karenina fits this characterization supports the suggestion made by Robert Belknap (and quoted by Emily Dalgarno) that nineteenth-century Russian novels inspired their modernist successors. But, as Belknap also notes, the techniques used by Dostoevsky and Tolstoy were often their appropriations (and transformations) of techniques used by earlier English and Western European novelists ("Novelistic Technique," 246).

17. Boris Eikhenbaum, Lev Tolstoi: Semidesiatye gody (Leningrad: Khudozhe-stvennaia literatura, 1974), 127.

18. Virginia Woolf, "Reading Notes on Anna Karenina," in Virginia Woolf and the Russian Point of View, ed. Roberta Rubenstein, Appendix E (New York: Palgrave-Macmillan, 2009), 197, 200–201.

19. For double plot in English drama, see William Empson, "Double Plots," in Some Versions of Pastoral (New York: New Directions, 1974). In his discussion of "organic unity" (as understood by Leslie Stephen, Virginia Woolf's father), James Stang quotes Van Meter Ames's argument (in Aesthetics of the Novel [Chicago: University of Chicago Press, 1928], 178) that the English tolerance of double plots stems from a belief that "life does not present itself as a simple unity (in accord with the British philosophy of pluralism and empiricism)." Stang notes that Stephen, citing Fielding as a master of the form, wrote that his great novels "have a true organic unity as well as a consecutive story." See James Stang, The Theory of the Novel in England, 1850–1870 (New York: Columbia University Press, 1959), 134–35.

20. Woolf, Common Reader, 168.

21. De Vogüé argues that English and Russian (as opposed to French) authors believe that "representations of the world should be as complex and contradictory as this world itself," with the result showing up in drama and in novels (Le Roman russe [Paris: Plon, 1897], xxxvii–xxxix). Obviously, Victor Hugo is an all-important exception to de Vogüé's rule.

22. From Woolf's archive, cited in Dalgarno, "Tolstoy," 73. For discussion of Woolf's reaction to Lubbock, see Dalgarno, 72–73.

23. Henry James, "Preface to The Tragic Muse," in The Portable Henry James, ed. John Auchard (New York: Penguin, 2003), 476.

24. J. Hillis Miller, "Mrs. Dalloway: Repetition as the Raising of the Dead," in *Fiction and Repetition: Seven English Novels* (Cambridge, MA: Harvard University Press, 1982), 176.

25. My concern here is with the poetics of her novelistic form as a response to Tolstoy. There are other important ways in which Woolf answers Tolstoy in her fiction. Woolf took exception to Tolstoy's attitudes to sexuality and women, which she had gleaned not only from reading his fiction but from the translated memoirs (by Gorky, Goldenweiser, and Tolstoy's wife) about Tolstoy that the Hogarth Press published; in some cases she or Leonard Woolf collaborated with the Russian translator. See Rubenstein, *Virginia Woolf*, 125–29.

26. E. M. Forster, "The Early Novels of Virginia Woolf" (1925), in *The Mrs. Dalloway Reader*, ed. Francine Prose (New York: Harcourt, 2003), 117–18.

27. Virginia Woolf, *A Writer's Diary*, ed. Leonard Woolf (New York: Harcourt Brace, 1954), 60 (on tunneling) and 233–34 (on caves), as quoted in Paul Ricoeur, *Time and Narrative*, trans. Kathleen McLaughlin and David Pellauer (Chicago: University of Chicago Press, 1985), 2:187.

28. Paul Ricoeur, *Time and Narrative*, 2:187–88.

29. Woolf, "Russian Point of View," 175.

30. Woolf, "Russian Point of View," 175. McNeillie notes that Wright was a local expert on Russian literature. Similar stereotypes of Russians as compassionate, large-souled, etc. appear in Maurice Baring's *Landmarks in Russian Literature*, another source known by Woolf and her group. Woolf referred to "the conclusions of the Russian mind" as "compassionate" and "comprehensive" in her 1919 "Modern Novels." This essay was an early version of "Modern Fiction."

31. Woolf, "Russian Point of View," 174.

32. The notebooks for *Mrs. Dalloway* contain traces of Woolf's study of Russian: an exercise and some words in Cyrillic, as well as a note about "The Russian Frame of Mind" in the holograph draft of *The Hours/Mrs. Dalloway*. See Rubenstein, *Virginia Woolf*, 232n16.

33. Woolf writes as follows in "The Russian Point of View": "Moreover, it is not the samovar but the teapot that rules in England; time is limited; space crowded; the influence of other points of view, of other books, even of other ages, makes itself felt. Society is sorted out into lower, middle, and upper classes, each with its own traditions, its own manners, and, to some extent, its own language. Whether he wishes it or not, there is a constant pressure upon an English novelist to recognize these barriers, and, in consequence, order is imposed on him and some kind of form; he is inclined to satire rather than compassion, to scrutiny of society rather than understanding of individuals themselves" (180).

34. Zwerdling, *Virginia Woolf and the Real World*, 141.

35. Woolf, *Diaries*, 2:248.

36. Elizabeth Dalloway contrasts her father's way of being a Christian to that of Doris Kilmer, who "is always talking about her own sufferings" (136). Doris Kilmer is an angry evangelical who has lost her job and is in disrepute because of her refusal to agree with the prevailing opinion that *all* Germans are evil; in a magnanimous gesture Richard Dalloway has hired her to give lessons to Elizabeth; Clarissa worries that she has too much power over Elizabeth.

37. Tate, "*Mrs. Dalloway* and the Armenian Question," 154.

38. Trudi Tate writes: "Clarissa's refusal to think about the Armenian problem is a crucial moment in the novel, and provides us with ways into thinking about the structural relationship between Clarissa and Septimus, the war-neurotic soldier. Who is the victim, who the victimizer; who is responsible for the suffering of others?" ("*Mrs. Dalloway* and the Armenian Question," 159).

39. Zwerdling, *Virginia Woolf and the Real World*, 141.

40. Some (including Miller) affirm the intimate communion of the spirit that Clarissa herself experiences in regard to Septimus, whereas others (Tate, Briggs) regard Clarissa Dalloway's response as more problematic. But, at the least, all agree that Woolf prompts the reader to reckon with Clarissa's response and, by extension, with the question of how the two lives connect. Virginia Woolf's declaration in the preface to the American edition of *Mrs. Dalloway* that she intended that Clarissa kill herself or die at the end of the party has encouraged readers to twin the two heroes and possibly give Clarissa more credit for empathy for Septimus Warren Smith (after her initial displeasure at "death at my party"). Woolf writes: "In the first version Septimus, who later is intended to be her double, had no existence." She also informs the reader that "Mrs. Dalloway was originally to kill herself, or perhaps merely to die at the end of the party" ("An Introduction to *Mrs. Dalloway*," 11).

41. Dostoevsky, *Writer's Diary*, 1099; *PSS* 25:223.

42. Woolf, "Reading Notes on *Anna Karenina*," 200–201.

43. I borrow the term from Judith Butler, *Frames of War: When Is Life Grievable?* (New York: Verso, 2006).

44. In *War and Peace*, for example, the narrator explains that although Pierre understood that the dying Platon Karataev, soon to be shot by the French, was beseeching Pierre with his eyes to come over so he could say farewell, Pierre refused because he was afraid that he would not be able to bear it: he was acting to protect himself from an experience that would have been too painful for him. Here, however, the narrator does not make this kind of excuse for Levin and Kitty.

45. David Parker writes of *Anna Karenina* that "one of the most important strengths of the novel is the almost unfailing resistance it offers to any judgmental tendency in us to read its world as Levin first reads his experience [in the scene when he rejects fallen women as 'vermin'], in terms of simple categorical oppositions" (*Ethics*, 111).

46. Like Tolstoy, Woolf "twins" the hero and heroine of her two plots. E. M. Forster writes that when he first read the novel he assumed that Clarissa killed herself too. And he suggests that "the societified lady and the obscure maniac are in a sense the same person. This foot had slipped through the gay surface on which she still stands—that is all the difference between them" ("The Early Novels," 113).

47. Woolf, "Reading Notes on *Anna Karenina*," 201.

48. Had Anna been remembered, the effect might have been more like what George Eliot creates at the end of *Adam Bede*, when those gathered recall the sinful Hetty with compassion, and community is restored. (See the discussion in chapter 4.) A Russian parallel would be the end of Turgenev's *Fathers and*

Sons, when the dead Bazarov is called to mind (*sotto voce*) as the Kirsanov clan gathers, before the action moves to his graveside where his parents pray. Tolstoy does not provide this kind of closure.

49. Woolf, "Reading Notes," 197, 200–201.

50. Woolf, "Russian Point of View," 174.

51. John Donne, *Devotions upon Emergent Occasions* (Montreal and London: McGill-Queen's University Press, 1975), 86–87.

52. Woolf, "Modern Novels" (1919; in *Essays*, 3:36).

53. Irina Paperno describes the desperate restlessness of Tolstoy's attempts to narrate the self (*"Who, What Am I?": Tolstoy Struggles to Narrate the Self* [Ithaca, NY: Cornell University Press, 2014]). As Richard Gustafson's analysis of Tolstoy's religious life reveals, Tolstoy wrote until the end of his life as a motherless child yearning for providence (*Leo Tolstoy, Resident and Stranger: A Study in Fiction and Theology* [Princeton, NJ: Princeton University Press, 1986], see esp. 14–15).

54. Paperno, *"Who, What Am I?,"* 44–45. For Tolstoy's letter to Strakhov, see 23 and 26 April 1876, #261, 62:268–270. For discussion of this letter, see chapter 1.

55. Peter Garrett, *The Victorian Multiplot Novel: Studies in Dialogical Form* (New Haven, CT: Yale University Press, 1980), 8–10.

56. George Levine, *How to Read the Victorian Novel* (Malden, MA: Blackwell, 2008), 130.

Bibliography

Abel, Darrel. "Hester the Heretic." *College English* 13, no. 6 (1952): 303–9.

Al'tman, Moisei Semenovich. "Medvezh'ia svad'ba." In *Chitaia Tolstogo*. Tula: Priokskoe knizhnoe izdatel'stvo, 1966.

Alexandrescu, Vlad. *Le paradoxe chez Blaise Pascal*. Berne: Peter Lang, 1996.

Alexandrov, Vladimir. *Limits to Interpretation: The Meanings of "Anna Karenina."* Madison: University of Wisconsin Press, 2004.

Arnold, Matthew. "Count Leo Tolstoi." In *Leo Tolstoy: A Critical Anthology*, ed. Henry Gifford, 60–80. Harmondsworth, UK: Penguin, 1971.

Astrov, Vladimir. "Hawthorne and Dostoevski as Explorers of the Human Conscience." *New England Quarterly* 15, no. 2 (June 1942): 296–319.

Baehr, Stephen. "The Troika and the Train: Dialogues between Tradition and Technology in Nineteenth-Century Russian Literature." In *Issues in Russian Literature before 1917*, ed. J. Douglas Clayton, 85–106. Columbus, OH: Slavica, 1989.

Banfield, Ann. *The Phantom Table: Woolf, Frye, Russell, and the Epistemology of Modernism*. Cambridge, UK: Cambridge University Press, 2000.

Barran, Thomas. "Anna's Dreams." In *Approaches to Teaching Tolstoy's "Anna Karenina,"* ed. Liza Knapp and Amy Mandelker, 161–65. New York: Modern Language Association Publications, 2003.

Barthes, Roland. "L'Effet de réel." *Communications* 11 (1968): 84–89.

Bayley, John. *Tolstoy and the Novel*. Chicago: University of Chicago Press, 1988.

Baym, Nina. "The Significance of Plot in Hawthorne's Romances." In *Ruined Eden of the Present: Hawthorne, Melville, Poe*, ed. G. R. Thompson and V. L. Locke, 549–70. West Lafayette, IN: Purdue University Press, 1980.

Beaty, Jerome. *"Middlemarch" from Notebook to Novel: A Study of George Eliot's Creative Method*. Illinois Studies in Language and Literature, 47. Urbana: University of Illinois Press, 1960.

Beer, Gillian. *Darwin's Plots: Evolutionary Narrative in Darwin, George Eliot and Nineteenth-Century Fiction*. Cambridge, UK: Cambridge University Press, 2000.

Belknap, Robert. "Novelistic Technique." In *The Cambridge Companion to the Classic Russian Novel*, ed. Malcolm V. Jones and Robin Feuer Miller, 233–50. Cambridge, UK: Cambridge University Press, 1998.

Belknap, Robert. *Plots*. Leonard Hastings Schoff Memorial Lectures. New York: Columbia University Press, 2016.

Bell, Michael Davitt. "Arts of Deception: Hawthorne, 'Romance,' and *The Scarlet Letter*." In *New Essays on "The Scarlet Letter*," ed. Michael J. Colacurcio, 29–56. Cambridge, UK: Cambridge University Press, 1985.

Bell, Millicent. "The Obliquity of Signs: *The Scarlet Letter*." *Massachusetts Review* 23, no. 1 (Spring 1982): 9–26.

Bensick, Carol. "His Folly, Her Weakness: Demystified Adultery in *The Scarlet Letter*." In *New Essays on "The Scarlet Letter*," ed. Michael J. Colacurcio, 137–59. Cambridge, UK: Cambridge University Press, 1985.

Bercovitch, Sacvan. *The Office of the Scarlet Letter*. Baltimore, MD: Johns Hopkins University Press, 1991.

Berman, Anna A. *Siblings in Tolstoy and Dostoevsky: The Path of Universal Brotherhood*. Evanston, IL: Northwestern University Press, 2015.

Biblioteka L'va Nikolaevicha Tolstogo v Iasnoi Poliane: Bibliograficheskoe opisanie. Tula: Muzei-usad'ba/Izdatel'skii Dom "Iasnaia Poliana," 1999.

Blackmur, R. P. "The Dialectic of Incarnation: Tolstoi's *Anna Karenina*." In Leo Tolstoy, *Anna Karenina: A Norton Critical Edition*, ed. George Gibian, 899–917. New York: W. W. Norton, 1970.

Blake, Kathleen, ed. *Approaches to Teaching Eliot's "Middlemarch*." New York: Modern Language Association, 1990.

Blumberg, Edwina. "Tolstoy and the English Novel: A Note on *Middlemarch* and *Anna Karenina*." In *Tolstoi and Britain*, ed. W. Gareth Jones, 93–104. Oxford, UK: Berg, 1995.

Briggs, Julia. *Virginia Woolf: An Inner Life*. New York: Harcourt, 2005.

Brodhead, Richard H. *Hawthorne, Melville, and the Novel*. Chicago: University of Chicago Press, 1973.

Brooks, Cleanth. *William Faulkner: Toward Yoknapatawpha and Beyond*. New Haven, CT: Yale University Press, 1978.

Brooks, Peter. *Reading for the Plot: Design and Intention in Narrative*. Cambridge, MA: Harvard University Press, 1992.

Browning, Gary L. *A "Labyrinth of Linkages" in Tolstoy's "Anna Karenina*." Brighton, MA: Academic Studies Press, 2010.

Buckler, Julie. *The Literary Lorgnette: Attending Opera in Imperial Russia*. Stanford, CA: Stanford University Press, 2000.

Buckler, Julie. "Reading Anna: Opera, Tragedy, Melodrama, Farce." In *Approaches to Teaching Tolstoy's "Anna Karenina*," ed. Liza Knapp and Amy Mandelker, 131–36. New York: Modern Language Association Publications, 2003.

Bulgakov, Sergii [Sergius]. *The Orthodox Church*. Trans. Elizabeth S. Cram, ed. Donald A. Lowrie. London: Centenary Press 1935.

Butler, Judith. *Frames of War: When Is Life Grievable?* New York: Verso, 2006.

Cadot, Michel. "La Mort comme évènement social et comme destin personel: Remarques sur *Madame Bovary* et *Anna Karénine*." *Cahiers Léon Tolstoi* 3 (1986): 31–40.

Cain, Tom. "Tolstoy's Use of *David Copperfield*." In *Tolstoi and Britain*, ed. W. Gareth Jones, 67–77. Oxford, UK: Berg, 1995.

Case, Alison, and Harry E. Shaw. *Reading the Nineteenth-Century Novel: Austen to Eliot*. Malden, MA: Blackwell, 2008.

Chamberlain, Lesley. "The Right Attitude to Horses: Animals as the Essential Humanizing Influence." *Times Literary Supplement* (March 1, 1996): 15.

Chapman, Raymond, and Eleanora Gottlieb. "A Russian View of George Eliot." *Nineteenth-Century Fiction* 33, no. 3 (December 1978): 348–65.

Chernyshevskii, Nikolai. "Detstvo i otrochestvo. Sochinenie grafa L. N. Tolstogo, SPb. 1856." In *Polnoe sobranie sochinenii*, 3:421–23. Moscow: Ogiz, 1947.

Christian, Reginald Frank. *Tolstoy: A Critical Introduction*. Cambridge, UK: Cambridge University Press, 1969.

Cobbe, Frances Power. "Female Charity—Lay and Monastic." *Fraser's Magazine* (December 1862): 774–88.

Colacurcio, Michael. "Footsteps of Ann Hutchinson: Context of *The Scarlet Letter*." *English Literary History* 39 (1972): 459–94.

Cornillot, François. "L'écriture contrapuntique." *Cahiers Léon Tolstoï* 1 (1984): 25–32.

Cruise, Edwina. "Tracking the English Novel: Who Wrote the English Novel That Anna Reads." In *Anniversary Essays on Tolstoy*, ed. Donna Orwin, 159–82. Cambridge, UK: Cambridge University Press, 2010.

Culler, Jonathan. "The Uses of *Madame Bovary*." In *Flaubert and Postmodernism*, ed. Naomi Schor and Henry F. Majewski, 1–12. Lincoln: University of Nebraska Press, 1980.

Cunningham, Valentine. *Everywhere Spoken Against: Dissent in the Victorian Novel*. Oxford, UK: Clarendon Press, 1975.

Dal', Vladimir. *Tolkovyi slovar' zhivogo velikorusskogo iazyka*. St. Petersburg: M. O. Vol'f, 1912.

Dalgarno, Emily. "Tolstoy, Dostoevsky, and the Russian Soul." In *Virginia Woolf and the Migrations of Language*, 69–96. Cambridge, UK: Cambridge University Press, 2012.

DeLeuze, Gilles. *Proust and Signs*. Trans. Richard Howard. New York: G. Braziller, 1972.

Derrida, Jacques. *Acts of Religion*. Ed. Gil Anidjar. New York: Routledge, 2002.

Donne, John. "Seventeenth Meditation." In *Devotions upon Emergent Occasions*, ed. Anthony Raspa, 86–87. Montreal and London: McGill-Queen's University Press, 1975.

Dostoevskii, Fedor Mikhailovich. *Polnoe sobranie sochinenii v tridtsati tomakh*. Ed. V. G. Bazanov et al. Leningrad: Nauka, 1972–90.

Dostoevsky, Fyodor. *A Writer's Diary*. Trans. Kenneth Lantz. Evanston, IL: Northwestern University Press, 1994.

Durkin, Andrew. "Laclos's *Les liaisons dangereuses* and Tolstoj's *Anna Karenina*: Some Comparisons." *Russian Language Journal* 37, no. 128 (1983): 95–102.

Eikhenbaum, Boris M. *Lev Tolstoi: Semidesiatye gody*. Leningrad: Khudozhestvennaia literatura, 1974.

Eliot, George. "The Natural History of German Life." 1856. In *Selected Critical Writings*, 260–95. Oxford, UK: Oxford University Press, 1992.

Eliot, George. *Adam Bede*. Middlesex, UK: Penguin, 1980.

Eliot, George. *Middlemarch*. Ed. Rosemary Ashton. Middlesex, UK: Penguin, 1944.

Eliot, George. *Scenes of Clerical Life*. London: Penguin, 1983.

Eliot, T. S. Introduction to *Pascal's Pensées*, by Pascal. New York: Dutton, 1958.

Emerson, Caryl. "The Tolstoy Connection in Bakhtin." In *Rethinking Bakhtin: Extensions and Challenges*, ed. Gary Saul Morson and Caryl Emerson, 147–72. Evanston IL: Northwestern University Press, 1989.

Emerson, Caryl. "Tolstoy versus Dostoevsky and Bakhtin's Ethics of the Classroom." In *Approaches to Teaching Tolstoy's "Anna Karenina,"* ed. Liza Knapp and Amy Mandelker, 104–16. New York: Modern Language Association Publications, 2003.

Empson, William. *Some Versions of Pastoral*. New York: New Directions, 1974.

Evdokimova, Svetlana. "The Wedding Bell, the Death Knell, and Philosophy's Spell: Tolstoy's Sense of an Ending." In *Approaches to Teaching Tolstoy's "Anna Karenina,"* ed. Liza Knapp and Amy Mandelker, 137–43. New York: Modern Language Association Publications, 2003.

The Festal Menaion. Trans. Mother Mary and Kallistos Ware. Introduction by Georges Florovsky. London: Faber and Faber, 1969.

Feuer, Kathryn. "Stiva." In *Russian Literature and American Critics*, ed. Kenneth N. Brostrom, 347–56. Ann Arbor: University of Michigan Press, 1984.

Fleetwood, Janet. "The Web and the Beehive: George Eliot's *Middlemarch* and Tolstoy's *Anna Karenina*." Ph.D. dissertation, Indiana University, 1977.

Florovskii, Georgii. *Puti russkogo bogosloviia*. Paris: YMCA Press, 1982.

Forster, E. M. "The Early Novels of Virginia Woolf." 1925. In *The Mrs. Dalloway Reader*, ed. Francine Prose, 108–18. New York: Harcourt, 2003.

Freud, Sigmund. *Civilization and Its Discontents*. Ed. and trans. James Strachey. New York: Norton, 1961.

Garrett, Peter K. *The Victorian Multiplot Novel: Studies in Dialogical Form*. New Haven, CT: Yale University Press, 1980.

Gessen, Sergei Iosifovich. "L. N. Tolstoi kak myslitel'." Reprinted in *Izbrannye sochineniia*. Moscow: Rosspen, 1999.

Goldmann, Lucien. *Le Dieu caché; étude sur la vision tragique dans les Pensées de Pascal et dans le théâtre de Racine*. Paris: Gallimard, 1955 [1956].

Goscilo, Helena. "Motif-Mesh as Matrix: Body, Sexuality, Adultery, and the Woman Question." In *Approaches to Teaching Tolstoy's "Anna Karenina,"* ed. Liza Knapp and Amy Mandelker, 83–89. New York: Modern Language Association Publications, 2003.

Goscilo, Helena. "Tolstoy, Laclos, and the Libertine." *Modern Language Review* 81, no. 2 (1986): 398–414.

Goubert, Denis. "Did Tolstoy Read *East Lynne?" Slavonic and East European Review* 58 (1980): 22–39.

Grenier, Svetlana. *Representing the Marginal Woman in Nineteenth-Century Russian Literature: Personalism, Feminism, and Polyphony.* Westport, CT: Greenwood Press, 2001.

Gromeka, M. S. *O L. N. Tolstom: Kriticheskii etiud po povodu romana "Anna Karenina."* Moscow: I. D. Sytina, 1893.

Grossman, Joan. "Tolstoy's Portrait of Anna: Keystone in the Arch." *Criticism: A Quarterly for Literature and the Arts* 18, no. 1 (Winter 1976): 1–14.

Gusev, N. N. *Letopis' zhizni i tvorchestva L'va Nikolaevicha Tolstogo, 1828–1890.* Moscow: Khudozhestvennaia literatura, 1958.

Gusev, N. N. *Lev Nikolaevich Tolstoi: Materialy k biografii s 1870 po 1881 god.* Moscow: Nauka, 1963.

Gustafson, Richard F. *Leo Tolstoy, Resident and Stranger: A Study in Fiction and Theology.* Princeton, NJ: Princeton University Press, 1986.

Guyer, Paul. "Introduction: The Starry Heavens and the Moral Law." In *Cambridge Companion to Kant,* ed. Paul Guyer, 1–25. Cambridge, UK: Cambridge University Press, 1992.

Hammond, Nicholas, ed. *Cambridge Companion to Pascal.* Cambridge, UK: Cambridge University Press, 2003.

Hammond, Nicholas. "Pascal's *Pensées* and the Art of Persuasion." In *Cambridge Companion to Pascal,* ed. Nicholas Hammond, 235–63. Cambridge, UK: Cambridge University Press, 2003.

Hammond, Nicholas. *Playing with Truth: Language and the Human Condition in Pascal's "Pensées."* Oxford: Clarendon Press, 1994.

Hardy, Barbara. *The Appropriate Form: An Essay on the Novel.* London: Athlone Press, 1964.

Hardy, Barbara. *The Novels of George Eliot: A Study in Form.* London: University of London, Athlone Press, 1973.

Hawthorne, Nathaniel. *The Scarlet Letter.* New York: Penguin, 1983.

Heier, Edmund. *Religious Schism in the Russian Aristocracy 1860–1900: Radstockism and Pashkovism.* The Hague: Nijhoff, 1970.

Henry, Holly. *Virginia Woolf and the Discourse of Science: The Aesthetics of Astronomy.* Cambridge, UK: Cambridge University Press, 2003.

Herman, David. "Allowable Passions in *Anna Karenina." Tolstoy Studies Journal* 8 (1995–96): 5–32.

Himmelfarb, Gertrude. *The De-Moralization of Society: From Victorian Virtues to Modern Values.* New York: Vintage, 1996.

"Hints on the Modern Governess System." *Fraser's Magazine for Town and Country* 30, no. 179 (November 1844): 571–83.

Holland, Kate. "The Opening of *Anna Karenina."* In *Approaches to Teaching Tolstoy's "Anna Karenina,"* ed. Liza Knapp and Amy Mandelker, 144–49. New York: Modern Language Association Publications, 2003.

Howells, Bernard. "The Interpretation of Pascal's 'Pari.'" *Modern Language Review* 79, no. 1 (1984): 45–63.

Hruska, Anne. "Infected Families: Belonging and Exclusion in the Works of Leo Tolstoy." Ph.D. dissertation, University of California, Berkeley, 2001.

Hruska, Anne. "Love and Slavery: Serfdom, Emancipation, and Family in Tolstoy's Fiction." *Russian Review* 66, no. 4 (October 2007): 627–46.

Irwin, John T. *American Hieroglyphics: The Symbol of the Egyptian Hieroglyphics in the American Renaissance.* New Haven, CT: Yale University Press, 1980.

Jahn, Gary R. "The Crisis in Tolstoy and in *Anna Karenina.*" In *Approaches to Teaching Tolstoy's "Anna Karenina,"* ed. Liza Knapp and Amy Mandelker, 67–73. New York: Modern Language Association Publications, 2003.

Jahn, Gary R. "Tolstoj and Kant." In *New Perspectives on Nineteenth-Century Russian Prose,* ed. George J. Gutsche and Lauren G. Leighton, 60–70. Columbus, OH: Slavica, 1982.

Jakobson, Roman. "On Realism in Art." In *Language in Literature,* ed. Krystyna Pomorska and Stephen Rudy, 19–27. Cambridge, MA: Harvard University Press, 1987.

Jakobson, Roman. "Two Aspects of Language and Two Types of Aphasic Disturbances." In Roman Jakobson and Morris Halle, *Fundamentals of Language,* 53–87. The Hague: Mouton, 1956.

James, Henry. *Hawthorne.* New York: Harper & Brothers, 1899.

James, Henry. "*Middlemarch.*" In *The Art of Criticism: Henry James on the Theory and the Practice of Fiction,* ed. William Veeder and Susan M. Griffin, 48–58. Chicago: University of Chicago Press, 1986.

James, Henry. Preface to *The Tragic Muse.* In *The Portable Henry James,* ed. John Auchard, 476–78. New York: Penguin, 2003.

James, Henry. *Theory of Fiction.* Ed. James E. Miller. Lincoln: University of Nebraska Press, 1971.

Jones, Malcolm. "Dostoevskii and Radstockism." In *Dostoevskii and Britain,* ed. W. J. Leatherbarrow, 159–76. Oxford, UK: Berg, 1995.

Jones, Malcolm. "Problems of Communication in *Anna Karenina.*" In *New Essays on Tolstoy,* ed. Malcolm V. Jones and R. F. Christian, 85–108. Cambridge, UK: Cambridge University Press, 1978.

Jones, W. Gareth, ed. *Tolstoi and Britain.* Oxford, UK: Berg, 1995.

Kenworthy, Scott M. *The Heart of Russia: Trinity-Sergius, Monasticism, and Society after 1825.* New York: Oxford University Press, 2010.

Kliger, Ilya. *The Narrative Shape of Truth: Veridiction in Modern European Literature.* University Park: Pennsylvania State University Press, 2011.

Knapp, Liza. "The Estates of Pokrovskoe and Vozdvizhenskoe: Tolstoy's Labyrinth of Linkages." *Tolstoy Studies Journal* 8 (1995–96): 81–98.

Knapp, Liza. "Gogol and the Ascent of Jacob's Ladder: Realization of a Biblical Metaphor." In *Christianity and the East Slavs,* vol. 3:3–15, *Russian Literature in Modern Times,* ed. B. Gasparov, Robert P. Hughes, I. Paperno, and Olga Raevsky-Hughes. California Slavic Studies, 18. Berkeley and Los Angeles: University of California Press, 1995.

Knapp, Liza. "Language and Death in Tolstoy's *Childhood* and *Boyhood*: Rousseau and the Holy Fool." *Tolstoy Studies Journal* 10 (1998): 50–62.

Knapp, Liza. "The Names." In *Approaches to Teaching Tolstoy's "Anna Karenina,"* ed. Liza Knapp and Amy Mandelker, 8–23. New York: Modern Language Association Publications, 2003.

Knapp, Liza. "On a Scavenger Hunt in Tolstoy's Labyrinth of Linkages." In *Approaches to Teaching Tolstoy's "Anna Karenina,"* ed. Liza Knapp and Amy

Mandelker, 198–205. New York: Modern Language Association Publications, 2003.

Knapp, Liza. "Style and Theme in Tolstoy's Early Work." In *Cambridge Companion to Tolstoy*, ed. Donna Tussing Orwin, 121–75. Cambridge, UK: Cambridge University Press, 2002.

Knapp, Liza. *"Tue-la! Tue-le!*: Death Sentences, Words, and Inner Monologue in Tolstoy's *Anna Karenina* and *Three More Deaths*." *Tolstoy Studies Journal* 11 (1999): 1–19.

Knapp, Liza, and Amy Mandelker, eds. *Approaches to Teaching Tolstoy's "Anna Karenina*." New York: Modern Language Association Publications, 2003.

Knapp, Shoshana. "Tolstoj's Reading of George Eliot: Visions and Revisions." *Slavic and East European Journal* 27 (1983): 318–26.

Kovarsky, Gina. "Mimesis and Moral Education in *Anna Karenina*." *Tolstoy Studies Journal* 8 (1995–96): 61–80.

Kovarsky, Gina. "The Moral Education of the Reader." In *Approaches to Teaching Tolstoy's "Anna Karenina*," ed. Liza Knapp and Amy Mandelker, 166–72. New York: Modern Language Association Publications, 2003.

Kovarsky, Gina. "Rhetoric, Metapoesis, and Moral Instruction in Tolstoy's Fiction: *Childhood, Boyhood, Youth, War and Peace,* and *Anna Karenina*." Ph.D. dissertation, Columbia University, 1998.

Kovarsky, Gina. "Signs of Life: Moral and Aesthetic Education in Tolstoy's Fiction." Draft of Ph.D. dissertation, Columbia University, 1998.

Kreitzer, Larry Joseph. "'Revealing the Affairs of the Heart': Sin, Accusation and Confession in Nathaniel Hawthorne's *The Scarlet Letter*." In *Ciphers in the Sand: Interpretations of the Woman Taken in Adultery (John 7.53–8.11)*, ed. Larry Joseph Kreitzer and Deborah W. Rooke, 138–212. Sheffield, UK: Sheffield Academic Press, 2000.

Kujundžić, Dragan. "Pardoning Woman in *Anna Karenina*." *Tolstoy Studies Journal* 6 (1993): 65–85.

Kupreianova, E. N. *Èstetika Tolstogo*. Moscow: Nauka, 1966.

Leavis, Q. D. "Hawthorne as Poet." In *Collected Essays*, vol. 2, *The American Novel and Reflections on the European Novel*, 30–76. Cambridge, UK: Cambridge University Press, 1985.

Leskov, N[ikolai] S. "O kufel'nom muzhike i proch. Zametki po povodu nekotorykh otzyvov o L. Tolstom." 1886. In *Sobranie sochinenii v odinnadtsati tomakh*, ed. V. G. Bazanov et al., 11:134–56. Moscow: Khudozhestvennaia literatura, 1958.

Leskov, Nikolai. *Schism in High Society*. Trans. James Yeoman Muckle. Nottingham, UK: Bramcote Press, 1995.

Leskov, Nikolai. "Velikosvetskii rakol; Grenvil' Val'digrev lord Redstok, ego zhizn', uchenie i propoved'" [Schism in High Society]. *Pravoslavnoe obozrenie*, nos. 9–10 (September–October 1876): 138–78, 300–326; and no. 2 (February 1877): 294–334.

Levine, George. *Darwin and the Novelists: Patterns of Science in Victorian Fiction*. Cambridge, MA: Harvard University Press, 1988.

Levine, George. *How to Read the Victorian Novel*. Malden, MA: Blackwell, 2008.

Lewes, George. *Problems of Life and Mind*. London: Trubner, 1874.

Lomunov, K. N., ed. *Lev Tolstoi ob iskusstve i literature*. Moscow: Sovetskii pisatel', 1958.

Lönnqvist [Lennkvist], B. "'Medvezhii' motiv i simvolika neba v romane *Anna Karenina.*" *Scando-Slavica* 41 (1995): 115–30.

Lönnqvist, Barbara. "The Role of the Serbian War in *Anna Karenina.*" *Tolstoy Studies Journal* 17 (2005): 35–42.

Lönnqvist, Barbara. "Simvolika zheleza v romane *Anna Karenina.*" In *Celebrating Creativity: Essays in Honor of Jostein Bortnes*, ed. Knut Andreas and Ingunn Lunde, 97–107. Bergen, Norway: University of Bergen, 1977.

Lubbock, Percy. *The Craft of Fiction*. New York: Viking, 1957.

Mandelker, Amy. *Framing "Anna Karenina": Tolstoy, the Woman Question, and the Victorian Novel*. Columbus: Ohio State University Press, 1993.

Mandelker, Amy. "Illustrate and Condemn: The Phenomenology of Vision in *Anna Karenina.*" *Tolstoy Studies Journal* 8 (1995–96): 46–60.

Mandel'shtam, Osip. "Egipetskaia marka." In *Sobranie sochinenii v trekh tomakh*, ed. G. P. Struve and B. A. Filippov, 2:3–42. 2nd ed. New York: Inter-Language Literary Associates, 1971.

Marcus, Sharon. *Between Women: Friendship, Desire, and Marriage in Victorian England*. Princeton, NJ: Princeton University Press, 2007.

Margalit, Avishai. *The Ethics of Memory*. Cambridge, MA: Harvard University Press, 2002.

Markovitch, Milan L. *Jean-Jacques Rousseau et Tolstoï*. Paris: Honoré Champion, 1928.

Matthiessen, F. O. *American Renaissance: Art and Expression in the Age of Emerson and Whitman*. New York: Oxford University Press, 1941.

McGuckin, John Anthony. *The Orthodox Church: An Introduction to Its History, Doctrine, and Spiritual Culture*. Malden, MA: Blackwell, 2008.

McLaughlin, Sigrid. "Some Aspects of Tolstoy's Intellectual Development: Tolstoy and Schopenhauer." *California Slavic Studies* 5 (1970): 187–245.

McLean, Hugh. *Nikolai Leskov: The Man and His Art*. Cambridge, MA: Harvard University Press, 1977.

Medzhibovskaya, Inessa. *Tolstoy and the Religious Culture of His Time: A Biography of a Long Conversion, 1845–1887*. Lanham, MD: Lexington Books, 2009.

Melzer, Sara. *Discourses of the Fall: A Study of Pascal's "Pensées."* Berkeley, CA: University of California Press, 1986.

Merezhkovskii, Dmitrii. *L. Tolstoi i Dostoevskii: Zhizn' i tvorchestvo*. St. Petersburg: Obshchestvennaia pol'za, 1909.

Meyer, Priscilla. *How the Russians Read the French: Lermontov, Dostoevsky, Tolstoy*. Madison: University of Wisconsin Press, 2008.

Miller, J. Hillis. *The Form of Victorian Fiction: Thackeray, Dickens, Trollope, George Eliot, Meredith, and Hardy*. Cleveland, OH: Case Western Reserve Press, 1968.

Miller, J. Hillis. "Mrs. Dalloway: Repetition as the Raising of the Dead." In *Fiction and Repetition: Seven English Novels*, 176–202. Cambridge, MA: Harvard University Press, 1982.

Miller, J. Hillis. "Optic and Semiotic in *Middlemarch.*" In *The Worlds of Victorian Fiction*, ed. Jerome H. Buckley. Cambridge, MA: Harvard University Press, 1975.

Miller, J. Hillis. *Reading for Our Time: "Adam Bede" and "Middlemarch" Revisited.* Edinburgh: Edinburgh University Press, 2012.

Monnier, André. "Eros et thanatos." *Cahiers Léon Tolstoï* 1 (1984): 89–96.

Moretti, Franco. *Modern Epic: The World-System from Goethe to García Márquez.* Trans. Quintin Hoare. London: Verso, 1996.

Moretti, Franco. *Way of the World: The Bildungsroman in European Culture.* Trans. Albert Sbragia. London: Verso, 1987.

Moriarty, Michael. "Grace and Religious Belief in Pascal." In *Cambridge Companion to Pascal,* ed. Nicholas Hammond, 144–61. Cambridge, UK: Cambridge University Press, 2003.

Morson, Gary Saul. *"Anna Karenina" in Our Time: Seeing More Wisely.* New Haven, CT: Yale University Press, 2007.

Morson, Gary Saul. "Anna Karenina's Omens." In *Freedom and Responsibility in Russian Literature: Essays in Honor of Robert Louis Jackson,* ed. Elizabeth Cheresh Allen and Gary Saul Morson, 134–52. Evanston, IL: Northwestern University Press, 1995.

Nelles, William. "Myth and Symbol in *Madame Bovary.*" In *Approaches to Teaching "Madame Bovary,"* ed. Laurence M. Porter and Eugene Gray, 49–54. New York: MLA Press, 1995.

Nussbaum, Martha. *Upheavals of Thought.* Cambridge, UK: Cambridge University Press, 2001.

O'Gorman, Francis, ed. *Victorian Novel: A Guide to Criticism.* Malden, MA: Blackwell, 2002.

Orwin, Donna Tussing. "Tolstoy's Antiphilosophical Philosophy in *Anna Karenina.*" In *Approaches to Teaching Tolstoy's "Anna Karenina,"* ed. Liza Knapp and Amy Mandelker, 95–103. New York: Modern Language Association Publications, 2003.

Orwin, Donna Tussing. *Tolstoy's Art and Thought, 1847–1880.* Princeton, NJ: Princeton University Press, 1993.

Paperno, Irina. *"Who, What Am I?": Tolstoy Struggles to Narrate the Self.* Ithaca, NY: Cornell University Press, 2014.

Paré, François. "Temps et digression dans les Pensées de Pascal." *Études françaises* 37, no. 1 (2001): 67–81.

Parker, David. *Ethics, Theory and the Novel.* Cambridge, UK: Cambridge University Press, 1994.

Pascal, Blaise. *Pensées.* Lafuma and Sellier editions. http://www.penseesdepascal.fr/index.php.

Pascal, Blaise. *Pensées.* Trans. Roger Ariew. Indianapolis, IN: Hackett, 2004.

Pascal, Blaise. *Pensées de Pascal: Publiées dans leur texte authentique avec une introduction, des notes et des remarques par Ernest Havet.* Paris: Librairie Ch. Delagrave, 1866.

Phillips, Henry. "The Inheritance of Montaigne and Descartes." In *Cambridge Companion to Pascal,* ed. Nicholas Hammond, 20–39. Cambridge, UK: Cambridge University Press, 2003.

Plato. *The Symposium.* Trans. Walter Hamilton. Harmondsworth, UK: Penguin, 1980.

Poovey, Mary. *Uneven Developments: The Ideological Work of Gender in Mid-Victorian England.* Chicago: University of Chicago Press, 1988.

Popkin, Cathy. "Teaching Literature and Empire: The Case for *Anna Karenina*." In *Teaching Nineteenth-Century Russian Literature: Essays in Honor of Robert L. Belknap*, ed. Deborah Martinsen, Cathy Popkin, and Irina Reyfman, 233–45. Boston: Academic Studies Press, 2014.

Prochaska, F. K. *Women and Philanthropy in Nineteenth-Century England*. Oxford, UK: Clarendon Press, 1980.

Rabel, Robert. *Plot and Point of View in the "Iliad."* Ann Arbor: University of Michigan Press, 1997.

Rawlins, Jack P. *Thackeray's Novels: A Fiction That Is True*. Berkeley: University of California Press, 1974.

Ricoeur, Paul. *Time and Narrative*. Trans. Kathleen McLaughlin and David Pellauer. Chicago: University of Chicago Press, 1985.

Roberts, Robert C. "Compassion as an Emotion and Virtue." In *Religious Emotions: Some Philosophical Explorations*, ed. Willem Lemmens and Walter Van Herck, 198–218. Cambridge, UK: Cambridge University Press, 2008.

Rogers, Ben. "Pascal's Life and Times." In *Cambridge Companion to Pascal*, ed. Nicholas Hammond, 4–19. Cambridge, UK: Cambridge University Press, 2003.

Ronen, Omry. *An Approach to Mandel'stam*. Bibliotheca Slavica Hierosolymitana. Jerusalem: Magnes Press, Hebrew University, 1983.

Roosevelt, Priscilla. *Life on the Russian Country Estate: A Social and Cultural History*. New Haven, CT: Yale University Press, 1995.

Rousseau, Jean-Jacques. *Émile ou de l'éducation*. Paris: Garnier-Flammarion, 1966.

Royle, Nicholas. "The Telepathy Effect." In *The Uncanny*, 256–76. Manchester, UK: Manchester University Press, 2003.

Rubenstein, Roberta. *Virginia Woolf and the Russian Point of View*. New York: Palgrave, 2009.

Schultze, Sydney. *The Structure of "Anna Karenina."* Ann Arbor, MI: Ardis, 1982.

Shaw, Harry E. *Narrating Reality: Austen, Scott, Eliot*. Ithaca, NY: Cornell University Press, 1999.

Shklovsky, Viktor. *Knight's Move*. Trans. Richard Sheldon. Champaign, IL: Dalkey Archive Press, 2005.

Shuttleworth, Sally. *George Eliot and Nineteenth-Century Science*. London: Cambridge University Press, 1984.

Shuttleworth, Sally. "Sexuality and Knowledge in *Middlemarch*." *Nineteenth-Century Contexts* 19 (1996): 425–41.

Siegel, Daniel. "Losing for Profit." In *Middlemarch in the Twenty-First Century*, ed. Karen Chase, 157–75. New York: Oxford University Press, 2006.

Skobtsova, Mother Maria. "The Second Gospel Commandment." In *Essential Writings*. Maryknoll, NY: Orbis, 2003.

Smalley, Barbara. *George Eliot and Flaubert: Pioneers of the Modern Novel*. Athens: Ohio University Press, 1974.

Stang, James. *The Theory of the Novel in England, 1850–1870*. New York: Columbia University Press, 1959.

Stansky, Peter. *On or About December 1910: Early Bloomsbury and Its Intimate World*. Cambridge, MA: Harvard University Press, 1996.

Stenbock-Fermor, Elisabeth. *The Architecture of "Anna Karenina": A History of Its Writing, Structure, and Message*. Lisse: The Peter de Ridder Press, 1975.

Strel'tsova, Galina Ia. *Paskal' i evropeiskaia kul'tura*. Moscow: Respublika, 1994.

Tanner, Tony. *Adultery in the Novel: Contract and Transgression*. Baltimore, MD: Johns Hopkins University Press, 1979.

Tarasov, B. N. *"Mysliashchii trostnik": Zhizn' i tvorchestvo Paskalia v vospriatii russkikh filosofov i pisatelei*. 2nd ed. Moscow: Iazyki Slavianskikh Kul'tur, 2009.

Tate, Trudi. *"Mrs Dalloway* and the Armenian Question." In *Modernism, History, and the First World War*, 147–70. Manchester, UK: Manchester University Press, 1998.

Taylor, Mark. "What Derrida Really Meant." *New York Times* (October 14, 2004).

Tikhon Zadonskii [Timofei Savelievich Sokolov]. *Istinnoe khristianstvo*. 1776. In *Sochineniia preosviashchennago Tikhona, episkopa Voronezhskago i Eletskago*. St. Petersburg: Ivan Glazunov, 1825–26.

Tiutchev, F. I. *Izbrannye stikhotvoreniia*. New York: Chekhov, 1952.

Todd, William Mills III. "Anna on the Installment Plan: Teaching *Anna Karenina* through the History of Its Serial Publication." In *Approaches to Teaching Tolstoy's "Anna Karenina,"* ed. Liza Knapp and Amy Mandelker, 53–59. New York: Modern Language Association Publications, 2003.

Todes, Daniel. *Darwin without Malthus: The Struggle for Existence in Russian Evolutionary Thought*. Oxford, UK: Oxford University Press, 1989.

Tolstoi, Lev. *Chetveroevangelie: Soedinenie i perevod chetyrekh Evangelii*. Moscow: ESKMO Press, 2001.

Tolstoi, Lev. *Perepiska L. N. Tolstogo s gr. A. A. Tolstoi: 1857–1903*. St. Petersburg: Obshchestvo Tolstovskogo Muzeia, 1911.

Tolstoi, Lev. *Pis'ma Tolstogo i k Tolstomu: Iubileinyi sbornik*. Moscow: Gosudarstvennoe izdatel'stvo, 1928.

Tolstoi, Lev. *Polnoe sobranie sochinenii*. Ed. V. G. Chertkov et al. 90 vols. Moscow: Khudozhestvennaia literatura, 1928–58.

Tolstoy, Leo. *Anna Karenina*. Trans. Richard Pevear and Larissa Volokhonsky. New York: Penguin, 2000.

Trotter, David. "Space, Movement, and Sexual Feeling in *Middlemarch*." In *Middlemarch in the 21st Century*, ed. Karen Chase, 37–63. Oxford, UK: Oxford University Press, 2006.

Turner, C. J. G. *A Karenina Companion*. Waterloo, Ontario: Wilfrid Laurier University Press, 1993.

Valentino, Russell. *The Woman in the Window: Commerce, Consensual Fantasy, and the Quest for Masculine Virtue in the Russian Novel*. Columbus: Ohio State University Press, 2014.

Van Deusen, Marshall. "Narrative Tone in 'The Custom House' and *The Scarlet Letter*." *Nineteenth-Century Fiction* 21, no. 1 (June 1966): 61–71.

Vogüé, Eugène Melchior de. *Le Roman russe*. Paris: Plon, 1897.

Vygotsky, Lev. *Thought and Language*. Trans. and ed. Alex Kozulin. Cambridge, MA: MIT Press, 1997.

Weir, Justin. *Leo Tolstoy and the Alibi of Narrative*. New Haven, CT: Yale University Press, 2011.

Wetsel, David. *L'Écriture et le Reste: The "Pensées" of Pascal in the Exegetical Tradition of Port-Royal.* Columbus: Ohio State University Press, 1981.

Wetsel, David. *Pascal and Disbelief: Catechesis and Conversion in the "Pensées."* Washington, DC: Catholic University of America Press, 1994.

Wood, William. *Blaise Pascal on Duplicity, Sin, and the Fall: The Secret Instinct.* Oxford: Oxford University Press, 2013.

Woolf, Virginia. *The Common Reader, First Series.* 1925. Ed. Andrew McNeillie. San Diego: Harcourt Brace Jovanovich, 1984.

Woolf, Virginia. *The Diary of Virginia Woolf.* Ed. Anne Olivier Bell. 5 vols. New York: Harcourt Brace Jovanovich, 1977–84.

Woolf, Virginia. *The Essays of Virginia Woolf.* Ed. Andrew McNeillie. 3 vols. San Diego; New York; London: Harcourt Brace Jovanovich, 1989–91.

Woolf, Virginia. "An Introduction to *Mrs. Dalloway.*" In *The Mrs. Dalloway Reader,* ed. Francine Prose, 10–12. New York: Harcourt, 2003.

Woolf, Virginia. *The Letters of Virginia Woolf.* Ed. Nigel Nicholson and Joanne Trautmann. 6 vols. New York: Harcourt Brace Jovanovich, 1975–80.

Woolf, Virginia. *Mrs. Dalloway.* New York: Harcourt, 1925.

Woolf, Virginia. "Reading Notes on *Anna Karenina.*" In *Virginia Woolf and the Russian Point of View,* ed. Roberta Rubenstein, Appendix E, 195–20. New York: Palgrave, 2009.

Woolf, Virginia. *A Room of One's Own.* New York: Harcourt, 1989.

Yonge, Charlotte. *The Daisy Chain or Aspirations: A Family Chronicle.* Leipzig: Tauchnitz, 1856.

Zhdanov, V. A. *Tvorcheskaia istoriia "Anny Kareninoi": Materialy i nabliudeniia.* Moscow: Sovetskii pisatel', 1957.

Žižek, Slavoj, Eric L. Santner, and Kenneth Reinhard. *The Neighbor: Three Inquiries in Political Theology.* Chicago, IL: University of Chicago Press, 2013.

Zwerdling, Alex. *Virginia Woolf and the Real World.* Berkeley: University of California Press, 1986.

Index